"Kurson breathes life into *Shadow Divers* with consummate skill. . . . But it is far more than mere adventure; this is also a haunting, painful story of obsession and its attendant costs. . . . This is a memorable story, beautifully told."

—*The Sunday Times* (London)

"Mesmerizing." —*Entertainment Weekly*

"Heart-pounding adventure." —*Reader's Digest* (Critic's Choice)

"Kurson's descriptions of some of these forays inside the sub were so harrowing that I frequently caught myself holding my breath. . . . A great book." —*Chicago Tribune*

"Thrilling . . . An amazing story which Kurson tells in a dynamic and agile journalistic style. *Shadow Divers* is a must-read and a genuine page-turner." —*Associated Press*

"Riveting . . . moving." —*USA Today*

"The adventure book of the year." —*Publishers Weekly*

"Riveting reading, full of suspense . . . tightly plotted and remarkably assured." —*Outside* magazine

"Your interest in aquatic matters can start with a glass of water and end with a shower and you will still recognize this true story as one of the most engaging tales you'll read this year."

—New York *Daily News*

"*Shadow Divers* surely ranks with Sebastian Junger's *The Perfect Storm* and Jon Krakauer's *Into Thin Air* in the realm of nonfiction adventure."
—*Chicago Sun-Times*

"A crackling, tension-ripped narrative."
—*The Kansas City Star*

"Kurson marvelously weaves this tale of men who come to the same place in life from opposite sides of the playing field."
—*Orlando Sentinel*

"The phrase 'page-turner' is bandied about too cheaply, but *Shadow Divers* is the real thing."
—*The Dallas Morning News*

"A great beach read . . . *Shadow Divers* is a riveting adventure about the dangers of underwater exploration [that] becomes an intellectual quest."
—*San Jose Mercury News*

"The layperson need not even have an interest in deep-sea diving to appreciate *Shadow Divers*—an interest in history will do; or, short of that, an interest in human beings, in courage and obstinacy, glory and folly."
—*The Columbus Dispatch*

"This is a great sea adventure indeed."
—*New Orleans Times-Picayune*

"Undersea thrills, a gripping mystery, incredible discoveries . . . written with great you-are-there intensity and dynamic verve."
—*The New York Times*

"Superb . . . Once you dive into Kurson's estimable book, you will not surface again till the end."
—*Pittsburgh Post-Gazette*

"Suspenseful, dramatic, and filled with shocking turns."
—*The Atlanta Journal-Constitution*

"Absorbing . . . fantastic."
—*Newsweek*

SHADOW DIVERS

RANDOM HOUSE TRADE PAPERBACKS / NEW YORK

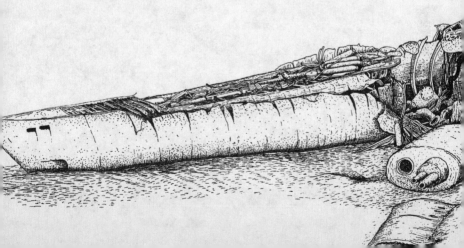

ROBERT KURSON

SHADOW DIVERS

The True
Adventure
of Two
Americans
Who Risked
Everything to
Solve One of the
Last Mysteries
of World War II

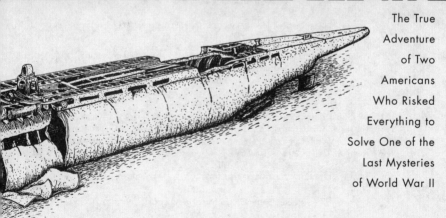

2005 Random House Trade Paperback Edition

Published in the United States by Random House Trade Paperbacks, an imprint of The
Random House Publishing Group, a division of Random House, Inc., New York.

RANDOM HOUSE TRADE PAPERBACKS and colophon are
trademarks of Random House, Inc.

Originally published in hardcover in the United States by Random House, an imprint of
The Random House Publishing Group, a division of Random House, Inc., in 2004.

Title-page art: Dan Crowell

Illustration on page xii © David Lindroth, Inc.

This book contains an excerpt from the forthcoming book *Rocket Men* by Robert Kurson.
This excerpt has been set for this edition only and may not reflect the final content of
the forthcoming edition.

LIBRARY OF CONGRESS CATALOGING-IN-PUBLICATION DATA
Kurson, Robert.
Shadow divers: the true adventure of two Americans who risked everything
to solve one of the last mysteries of World War II / by Robert Kurson
p.   cm.
Includes bibliographical references and index.
ISBN 0-375-76098-9
1. U-869 (Submarine). 2. Excavations (Archaeology)—New Jersey. 3. Nagle, Bill,
1952–1993. 4. Chatterton, John. 5. World War, 1939–1945—Naval operations—
Submarine. 6. World War, 1939–1945—Naval operations, German. 7. Shipwrecks—
New Jersey. 8. Underwater archaeology—New Jersey. 9. Deep diving—New Jersey.
I. Title.
VA515.U158K87 2004   940.54'51—dc22   2003060362

Printed in the United States of America

www.atrandom.com

23rd Printing

For Amy,

the answer to my life's search

For Nate,

already a seeker

Life's splendor forever lies in wait about each one of us in all its fullness, but veiled from view, deep down, invisible, far off. It is there, though, not hostile, not reluctant, not deaf. If you summon it by the right word, by its right name, it will come.

—Franz Kafka, *Diaries*

A few years ago, a friend told me a remarkable story. Two recreational scuba divers had recently discovered a World War II German U-boat off the New Jersey coast. The fifty-six-man crew was still aboard. No government, expert, historian, or navy had a clue as to which submarine it was, who the sailors were, or why it was in New Jersey.

My first reaction was that the story sounded too amazing to be true. Still, it awakened childhood memories in me. For years, my grade school classes had taken field trips to Chicago's Museum of Science and Industry to see its two centerpiece exhibits: a working coal mine and *U-505,* a German U-boat captured in 1944. Most kids preferred the coal mine, which featured moving cars and live explosions. I was drawn to the submarine. This eel-shaped fighting machine, with its furious interior of pipes and wire and gauges and weapons, seemed more terrifying than any bomber plane or Sherman tank. Seeing it resting there, just yards from the banks of Lake Michigan, I imagined this invisible hunter stalking the shoreline where I swam. This U-boat, I thought, could have come to within a mile or two of my house.

I called John Chatterton and Richie Kohler, the two New Jersey divers, and asked if I might fly out to hear their story. We met at Chatterton's house, where he had parked his vintage Royal Enfield motorcycle next to Kohler's late-model Harley. Chatterton was a commercial diver who did underwater construction jobs around Manhattan. Kohler owned a glass-repair business. They dove for shipwrecks on weekends. Each seemed, in every respect, a regular guy.

I promised not to take much of their time. Fourteen hours later, I was still listening. They told of discovering not just a U-boat but mystery, adventure, high-seas rivalries and bitter feuds, and membership in an obsessed culture of immensely brave men. They also told me of an intellectual odyssey, one in which they had made themselves into expert researchers, pored over original documents, learned bits of German, hunted clues abroad, constructed original theories, challenged professional historians, and ultimately rewritten a page of history long presumed to be gospel.

"Sounds like a novel, huh?" Kohler said to me in his thick Brooklyn accent as he fired up his Harley. Driving to the airport that night, I could scarcely believe my luck. In Chatterton and Kohler, I had found two ordinary men who had confronted an extraordinarily dangerous world and solved a historical mystery that even governments had not been able to budge. Any one of the elements of their story raised intriguing possibilities. Taken together, they made for a once-in-a-lifetime writing opportunity. I could no more turn my back on a chance to write the divers' story than they could have turned their backs on the chance to identify the mystery U-boat. In that sense, Chatterton, Kohler, and I already had something in common.

So this is their story. All of it is true and accurate. Nothing is imagined or interpreted, and no literary liberties have been taken. The book is rooted in hundreds of hours of interviews with Chatterton and Kohler, plus countless more hours with divers, historians, experts, relatives, and other witnesses to the events described herein. Dialogue—even that from World War II—is taken directly from interviews I conducted with people who were there and witnessed the events. Everything was checked against multiple sources whenever possible.

While researching the dangers of deep-shipwreck diving, I was struck by a remark the divers made about depth. The mystery U-boat, they said, lay in such deep, dark waters that occasionally they could do little more than dive at shadows. It occurred to me then that there were shadows cast throughout the story—by the fallen crewmen, by World War II, by the seeming infallibility of written history, by questions the divers came to ask about themselves as men. For six years, Chatterton and Kohler were shadow divers. For six years, they went on a remarkable journey. I wrote this book to take you there with them.

TYPE IXC U-BOAT

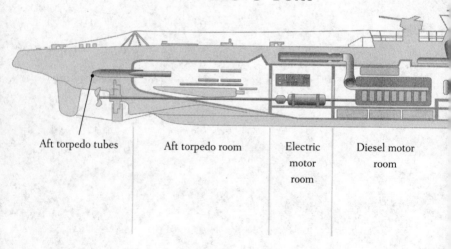

Aft torpedo tubes

Aft torpedo room

Electric
motor
room

Diesel motor
room

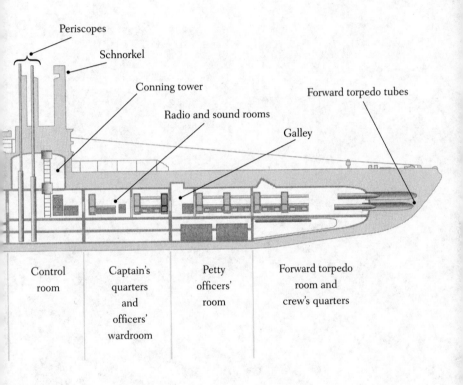

Periscopes

Schnorkel

Conning tower

Radio and sound rooms

Galley

Forward torpedo tubes

Control room

Captain's quarters and officers' wardroom

Petty officers' room

Forward torpedo room and crew's quarters

SHADOW DIVERS

CHAPTER ONE

THE BOOK OF NUMBERS

Brielle, New Jersey, September 1991

BILL NAGLE'S LIFE CHANGED the day a fisherman sat beside him in a ramshackle bar and told him about a mystery he had found lying at the bottom of the Atlantic Ocean. Against his better judgment, that fisherman promised to tell Nagle how to find it. The men agreed to meet the next day on the rickety wooden pier that led to Nagle's boat, the *Seeker*, a vessel Nagle had built to chase possibility. But when the appointed time came, the fisherman was not there. Nagle paced back and forth, careful not to plunge through the pier where its wooden planks had rotted away. He had lived much of his life on the Atlantic, and he knew when worlds were about to shift. Usually, that happened before a storm or when a man's boat broke. Today, however, he knew it was going to happen when the fisherman handed him a scrap of paper, a hand-scrawled set of numbers that would lead to the sunken mystery. Nagle looked into the distance for the fisherman. He saw no one. The salt air blew against the small seashore town of Brielle, tilting the dockside boats and spraying the Atlantic into Nagle's eyes. When the mist died down he looked again. This time, he saw the fisherman approaching, a small square of paper crumpled in his hands. The fisherman looked worried. Like Nagle, he had lived on the ocean, and he also knew when a man's life was about to change.

* * *

In the whispers of approaching autumn, Brielle's rouge is blown away and what remains is the real Brielle, the locals' Brielle. This small seashore town on the central New Jersey coast is the place where the boat captains and fishermen live, where convenience store owners stay open to serve neighbors, where fifth graders can repair scallop dredges. This is where the hangers-on and wannabes and also-rans and once-greats keep believing in the sea. In Brielle, when the customers leave, the town's lines show, and they are the kind grooved by the thin difference between making a living on the water and washing out.

The *Seeker* towers above the other boats tied to this Brielle dock, and it's not just the vessel's sixty-five-foot length that grabs one's attention, it's the feeling—from her battered wooden hull and nicked propellers—that she's been places. Conceived in Nagle's imagination, the *Seeker* was built for a single purpose: to take scuba divers to the most dangerous shipwrecks in the Atlantic Ocean.

Nagle was forty years old then, a thin, deeply tanned former Snap-On Tools Salesman of the Year. To see him here, waiting for this fisherman in his tattered T-shirt and thrift-shop sandals, the Jim Beam he kept as best friend slurring his motions, no one would guess that he had been an artist, that in his day Nagle had been great.

In his twenties, Nagle was already legend in shipwreck diving, a boy wonder in a sport that regularly kills its young. In those days, deep-wreck diving was still the province of the adventurer. Countless shipwrecks, even famous ones, lay undiscovered at the bottom of the Atlantic, and the hunt for those wrecks—with their bent metal and arrested history—was the motion that primed Nagle's imagination.

Treasure never figured into the equation for Atlantic shipwreck divers in the Northeast. Spanish galleons overflowing with gold doubloons and silver pieces of eight did not sink in this part of the ocean, and even if they had, Nagle wouldn't have been interested. His neighborhood was the New York and New Jersey shipping lanes, waters that conducted freighters, ocean liners, passenger vessels, and warships about the business and survival of America. These wrecks occasionally surrendered a rare piece of china or jewelry, but

Nagle and his kind were looking for something different. They saw stories in the Modiglianied faces of broken ships, frozen moments in a nation's hopes or a captain's dying instinct or a child's potential, and they experienced these scenes unbuffered by curators or commentators or historians, shoulder to shoulder with life as it existed at the moment it had most mattered.

And they did it to explore. Many of the deep wrecks hadn't been seen since their victims last looked at them, and would remain lost while nature pawed at them until they simply didn't exist anymore. In a world where even the moon had been traveled, the floor of the Atlantic remained uncharted wilderness, its shipwrecks beacons for men compelled to look.

You had to have steel balls to do what Nagle did in his heyday. In the 1970s and 1980s, scuba equipment was still rudimentary, not much advanced past 1943, when Jacques Cousteau helped invent the system of tanks and regulators that allowed men to breathe underwater. Even at 130 feet, the recreational limit suggested by most scuba training organizations, a minor equipment failure could kill the most skilled practitioner. In searching for the most interesting wrecks, Nagle and the sport's other kings might descend to 200 feet or deeper, virtually begging the forces of nature to flick them into the afterlife, practically demanding their biology to abandon them. Men died—often—diving the shipwrecks that called to Nagle.

Even if Nagle's equipment and body could survive the deep Atlantic, he faced a smorgasbord of other perils, each capable of killing him à la carte. For starters, the sport was still new; there was no ancient wisdom to be passed from father to son, the kind of collective experience that routinely keeps today's divers alive. The sport's cautionary tales, those lifelines learned over beers with buddies and by reading magazines and attending classes, were beaten into Nagle underwater at antihuman depths. If Nagle found himself in some crazy, terrible circumstance—and there were countless of them on these deep wrecks—odds were that he would be the one who would tell the first tale. When he and his ilk survived, the magazines wrote articles about them.

Nagle pushed deeper. Diving below 200 feet, he began doing things scientists didn't fully understand, going places recreational divers had never been. When he penetrated a shipwreck at these depths, he was often among the first to see the vessel since it had gone down, the first to open the purser's safe since it had been closed, the first to look at these men since they had been lost at sea. But this also meant that Nagle was on his own. He had no maps drawn by earlier divers. Had someone visited these wrecks before, he might have told Nagle, "Don't brush against that outboard beam in the galley—the thing moved when I swam by, and the whole room might cave in and bury you if you do." Nagle had to discover all this by himself. It is one thing, wreck divers will tell you, to slither in near-total darkness through a shipwreck's twisted, broken mazes, each room a potential trap of swirling silt and collapsing structure. It is another to do so without knowing that someone did it before you and lived.

The Atlantic floor was still a wilderness in Nagle's prime, and it demanded of its explorers the same grit that the American West did of its pioneers. A single bad experience on a shipwreck could reroute all but the hardiest souls to more sensible pursuits. Early divers like Nagle had bad experiences every day. The sport eagerly shook out its dabblers and sightseers; those who remained seemed of a different species. They were physical in their world orientation and sudden in their appetites. They thought nothing of whipping out a sledgehammer and beating a porthole from the side of a ship, even as their heavy breath hastened nitrogen narcosis, the potentially deadly buildup of that otherwise benign gas in their brains. Underwater, rules of possession bent with the light; some divers cut prizes from the mesh goody bags of other divers, following the motto "He who floats it owns it." Fistfights—aboard boats and even underwater—often settled disputes. Artifacts recovered from wrecks were guarded like firstborn children, occasionally at knifepoint. In this way, early deep-wreck divers had a measure of pirate in their blood.

But not Nagle. In the sport's brawniest era, he was a man of the mind. He devoured academic texts, reference works, novels, blueprints, any material he could uncover on historical ships, until he could have stood in the dockyards of a dozen eras and built the boats alongside the workers. He was a connoisseur of the parts, and he reveled in the life force a boat took on from the interlocking of its pieces. This insight gave Nagle two-way vision; as much as he understood the birth of a ship, he also understood its death. Ordinary divers would come upon a shipwreck and see the mélange of bent steel and broken wood, the shock of pipe and wire as a cacophony of crap, an impediment that might be hiding a compass or some other prize. They would plant their noses in a random spot and dig like puppies, hoping to find a morsel. Viewing the same scene, Nagle repaired the broken parts in his mind and saw the ship in its glory. One of his greatest finds was a four-foot-tall brass whistle from the paddle wheeler *Champion,* a proud voice that had been mounted on the ship's mast and powered by a steam line. The whistle was majestic, but the most beautiful part of the discovery was that underwater it looked like a worthless pipe. Floating amid the wreckage, Nagle used his mind's eye to watch the ship break and sink. He knew the ship's anatomy, and as he imagined it coming apart he could see the whistle settle, right where that seemingly worthless piece of pipe lay. After Nagle recovered two helms from the British tanker *Coimbra* in a single day (finding one helm once in a career was rare enough), his photograph was hung—alongside that of Lloyd Bridges—in the wheelhouse of the *Sea Hunter,* a leading dive charter boat of the time. He was twenty-five.

To Nagle, the value in artifacts like the brass steam whistle lay not in their aesthetics or their monetary worth but in their symbolism. It is an odd sight to see grown men covet teacups and saucers, and build noble display cases to these dainty relics. But to divers like Nagle these trinkets represented exploration, going off the charts. A telegraph on display in a diver's living room, therefore, is much more than a shiny object; it is an announcement. It says, *If someone had been to this ship's wheelhouse before me, he would not have left this telegraph behind.*

It was only time before Nagle's instinct delivered him to the *Andrea Doria,* the Mount Everest of shipwrecks. The grand Italian passenger liner had collided with the *Stockholm,* a Swedish liner, in dense fog off Nantucket Island in 1956. Fifty-one people died; 1,659 were rescued before the liner sank and settled on her side at a depth of 250 feet. The *Doria* was not a typical target for Nagle.

Her location was widely known, and she had been explored by divers since the day after her sinking. But the *Doria* made siren calls to great wreck divers. She was brimming with artifacts even after all these years: serving sets made of fine Italian china and painted with the ship's legendary Italia logo, silver utensils, luggage, ceramic tiles by famed artists, pewter sherbet dishes, jewelry, signs. In Nagle's day, and even today, a diver could explore the *Doria* and worry only about having enough stamina to lug home the prizes he recovered.

Had the *Doria* only her riches to offer, she could not have romanced Nagle so hopelessly. The ship's real challenge lay in exploration. The wreck rested on its side, making navigation dangerous and deceptive. A diver had to conceive the world sideways to make sense of doors on the floor and ceilings to the right. And she was deep—180 feet at her shallowest and 250 feet where she crushed the ocean floor. Men sometimes got disoriented or ran out of air or lost their minds from narcosis and died on the *Doria*. The wreck was so deep, dark, and dangerous that decades after her sinking, entire decks remained unexplored. Those decks were Nagle's destinations.

Over time, Nagle penetrated the wreck in places long relegated to the impossible. His mantel at home became a miniature *Doria* museum. Soon, he set his sights on the bell. A ship's bell is her crown, her voice. For a diver, there is no greater prize, and many of the greats go a career without coming close to recovering one. Nagle decided to own the *Doria*'s bell. People thought he was nuts— scores of divers had searched for thirty years for the *Doria*'s bell. No one believed it was there.

Nagle went to work. He studied deck plans, books of photographs, crew diaries. Then he did what few other divers did: he formulated a plan. He would need days, maybe even a week to pull it off. No charter boat, however, was going to take a diver to the *Doria* for a week. So Nagle, who had saved a good bit of money from his Snap-On Tools days, decided to buy a dive boat himself, a vessel constructed from his imagination for a single purpose: to salvage the *Doria*'s bell.

That boat was the original *Seeker*, a thirty-five-foot Maine Coaster built in New Jersey by Henrique. In 1985, Nagle recruited five top divers, men who shared his passion for exploration, and he made this arrangement: He would take the group to the *Doria* at his expense. The trip would be a dedicated one, meaning the divers went with just one objective—to recover the bell.

For the first few days on the wreck, the divers stuck to Nagle's plan. They found nothing. The bell just wasn't there. At that point, even the hardiest divers would have turned back. A single day on the open Atlantic in a sixty-five-foot boat will turn intestines inside out; Nagle and his cohorts had been out for four days in a thirty-five-foot glorified bathtub. But a man is not so inclined to give up when he sees in panoramas. Nagle abandoned the bow of the *Doria*, where he and his team had been searching, and rerouted to the stern. They would now be flying by the seat of their pants, an improvisation on the deadliest wreck in the Atlantic. No one had ever been to the stern. Yet by conceiving the *Doria* as a single, breathing organism rather than as detached, twenty-foot chunks of wood and steel, Nagle and the others allowed themselves to look in unlikely places.

On the fifth day they hit pay dirt—there was the *Andrea Doria*'s bell. The men rigged it, beat out the bell's pin with a sledgehammer, and sent up the prize on a heavy-duty lift bag. Shock waves rippled through the diving community. According to their agreement, Nagle owned half the bell, and the other five men owned half; the last man living among them would own it outright. Nagle placed the 150-pound bell into the back of his wife's station wagon and asked her to drive it home. When she arrived, the bell wasn't there anymore. She called Nagle, saying, "I don't know what happened to the bell!" Nagle nearly suffered a heart attack. He called the highway patrol and asked, "Did anyone find a giant bell anywhere?" Someone had, in fact, made a report, telling the police something like "I found something and I don't know what it is, but it looks like a big bell and it says *Andrea Doria*." Nagle almost had another attack. He retrieved the bell and insured it for $100,000. He was among the immortals.

Soon an idea began percolating in Nagle's imagination. What if he could run the *Seeker* full-time as a charter boat for divers? That would allow him to earn a living doing what he loved most. "I want to be the guy that turns this into a career," he told friends. He could make a half dozen trips to the *Doria* every year, then use his free time to search for the *Carolina, Texel, Norness,* and *Pan Pennsylvania*—

great ships still missing decades after sinking. His wife and two children lived in Pennsylvania, but he resided in Brielle now; he dated other women and kept a bachelor pad, yet his wife held out hope that he would return someday, and she raised his kids to admire him, so that he could do this now, he could make this business happen. He commissioned a second *Seeker,* this one nearly double the length of the first. It would be outfitted to transport divers to the great wrecks, the ones that required a pioneer's heart.

Almost immediately, Nagle struggled with the business. It wasn't that he lacked for customers. It was that he couldn't abide the customers. This was the wrong problem to have in the charter-boat business. On a dive trip, the captain's real job is to schmooze his patrons; at the end of the day, what the weekend, bread-and-butter customer really wants is to bond with a man of the sea. Nagle had envisioned his business as an endless series of trips to deep and dangerous wrecks like the *Doria* or the *Choapa.* But his patrons desired only the easy, nearby sites, wrecks like the *Stolt Dagali,* SS *Mohawk,* and the *Tolten.* To Nagle, these people weren't divers, they were tourists. He watched them climb onto the *Seeker* with their brand-new lime green fins—lime green!—and listened to their giddy plans to take pictures of lobsters or touch the side of a "real" shipwreck, and he could not hide his contempt for them. He had established a business in order to explore, and now he was beholden to customers who were thrilled precisely because they didn't have to.

And Nagle was drinking. Jim Beam didn't like the *Seeker*'s customers any more than Nagle did. Before long, Nagle became surly with his clients. Often, he stood outside the wheelhouse atop his boat and rained down commentary on stunned customers. He'd shout, "This isn't what diving's about!" or "Look at you greenhorns— go to the Caribbean with those green fins!" or "You dive shop guys got balls selling that garbage equipment to these innocents—you're crooks!" At the end of a trip, after he'd been drinking for hours, he might say, "Get these fucking cattle off my boat!" Friends and crew pleaded with Nagle: "Bill, for Christ's sake, you can't talk that way to paying customers. This is a business!" Nagle didn't care. This wasn't what diving was about.

His drinking worsened. During one charter, Nagle unilaterally decided to reroute to a more challenging wreck, a site that had captured his imagination and begged to be explored. The 150-foot depth of the new wreck was beyond the abilities of the divers on board. The man who had chartered the boat was incensed. "What the hell are you doing, Bill? We're supposed to go to a hundred-foot wreck. My guys can't handle this kind of depth." Nagle growled, "You gotta teach these guys to do decompression diving!" then stormed into the wheelhouse. And that was it. Nagle went where he wanted—he was no goddamn taxi driver, he was no sellout, he would not betray the spirit of diving. But as the 1980s gave way to a new decade, Nagle's drinking began to bleach the greatness of his skills. His shoulder blades became spires on his emaciated frame, his jaundiced skin and stringy hair a goulash of self-abandon. He still swam beautifully, somehow, in the way retired baseball greats still throw gracefully at old-timers' games. But experienced divers noticed that his *Doria* dives had become less strenuous, that he wasn't quite going anymore where no man had been. "Ah, I just gotta get in shape," he'd grumble to his few close friends, which they took as code for "I gotta stop drinking." By 1990, Nagle had made his last *Doria* dive—you couldn't challenge a wreck like that without every ounce of your faculties tuned high, and there had been recent corpses aboard the *Doria* to prove it. Nagle continued to lose customers. Every day, he told the few remaining people he respected about how right things had been in the old days, in the days when diving was great.

This was Nagle's life and business in the late summer of 1991, as Brielle shut down for the season and returned to the rhythms of its regulars. Nagle had spent much of this August day washing the *Seeker* and contemplating his life. Now, with the sun setting, he took a short walk across the dock, through the cratered dirt parking lot, and into an establishment seemingly placed there for him by God. The Harbor Inn was open late year-round. It served Jim Beam. Nagle was thirsty.

No one quite recalls when they started calling it the Horrible Inn, but everyone can tell you why. Hard-core smokers choked on the mushroom cloud of cigarette smoke that hovered over the bar. Bathroom smells wafted with impunity into the small grill area. Skin stuck to everything. Drunken fishermen painted the names of sweethearts onto greasy walls. Once, the owner decided to waterblast off years of built-up nicotine. A fully rigged crew showed up. They turned on the hoses. The water blew holes through the wall.

And there was the clientele. The Horrible Inn didn't serve many, but its faithful were hard-core and local. Bikers, fishermen, street toughs, boat mechanics, deep-wreck divers—this was the constant, unshaven dance card at the Horrible Inn. These men—you didn't dare bring a lady here—weren't interested in pinball machines or pool tables, and they didn't question management's policy to refill peanut dishes with leftovers from other peanut dishes. Customers drank beer and booze from plastic cups, then extinguished their cigarettes in same. Fights erupted. Nagle never budged from the Horrible Inn. Once, word spread through Brielle that a bartender had thrown Nagle out of the Horrible Inn for indecent behavior. No one believed it. It wasn't the idea of Nagle misbehaving that seemed impossible to the town; it was the idea that anyone could do anything indecent enough to warrant expulsion from such a place.

This evening, Nagle took his usual place at the bar and ordered a Jim Beam. And then another. A half hour later, a thirty-eight-year-old fishing boat captain with a dirty shirt ambled into the Horrible Inn to pay his fuel bill. Everyone knew the man as Skeets. Skeets had been around the dock for years and tied up his boat just a few slips from the *Seeker*. His business was small—he took out only four or five fishermen at a time—but he ran it well, which in the charter fishing trade meant two things: he knew where the fish were; and he knew how to keep his mouth shut.

Finding fish, of course, was critical. Customers who chartered fishing boats didn't come back if a captain took them to the desert. Guys like Skeets had to be able to sniff the air, look at the sky, and say, "Gentlemen, today I smell tuna." And then the captain had to take them there, to little sites recorded in tattered notebooks stashed in wheelhouse bottom drawers. Sometimes, this meant a location along the beach; other times, it meant a long journey offshore to one of the canyons. Most often, it meant a trip to the shipwrecks.

To fishermen, shipwrecks mean life. A mass of steel and wood that might have buried human souls becomes a rapid city of marine biology along the ocean floor. Shipwrecks are where the food chain poses for a snapshot. Tiny creatures attach themselves to solid objects. Those creatures attract predators, which in turn attract their own predators, and so on. Soon the wreck has become its own ecosystem. The pelagics—open-water traveling fish like tuna, codfish, and pollack—visit and get fat. Fishing boat captains get fatter.

Keeping your mouth shut was essential. Every fishing charter captain kept a book of public wrecks, the ones everyone knew and cleaned out regularly. But it was the secret wrecks that mattered, and the secret wrecks made the captain. Over the course of his career, a good fishing charter captain like Skeets might build a repertoire of a dozen shipwrecks known just to himself and a handful of others. He might discover some by scanning his bottom finder for sudden humps while out at sea. He might be gifted a prime location by a retiring fisherman to whom he had been kind. He might even trade sites with another captain he trusted. The more wrecks he knew, the more money he made. The more secret wrecks he knew, the more customers coveted his boat.

Fishing charter captains protected their secret sites. Customers were forbidden to bring aboard navigation equipment or even to enter the wheelhouse, lest they stumble upon a site's coordinates. If a captain spotted another boat while fishing, he would pull up his anchor, move off the site, and wait until the potential spy had passed. If another boat shadowed him out of port, he might zigzag into the middle of nowhere, then fish for nothing until the spy slipped away. All the time, he had to stay sharp or he risked his livelihood. They still talk about a captain from the Viking Fleet in Montauk. The man charged a fortune to take two brothers fishing. When he fell asleep, the brothers tiptoed inside the wheelhouse and videotaped his book of numbers. A year later, that captain's golden sites were Grand Central Station.

For the last few years, Skeets had been fishing a once-in-a-lifetime spot, a site about sixty miles off the Brielle coast. He had come upon the place one foggy day while trolling for tuna, a technique whereby a fishing boat drags monofilament line and lures through the water to mimic the movement of squid and other bait. Because the fishing boat is moving while trolling, the captain must keep alert for other boats in the vicinity. In the fog, he does this by scanning his radar. Skeets scanned his radar. Soon he spotted another boat on the screen. But its green blip never moved, meaning that this boat was anchored. To Skeets, that meant one thing—the boat on his radar was fishing a shipwreck.

Skeets turned his boat hard to port, then set course for the anchored boat. Before that boat could respond, Skeets had "jumped it" and had the numbers. The boat turned out to belong to a friend. The friend radioed to Skeets: "Don't tell a soul about this site, Skeets. Don't ever tell a soul about any of this. This one is special."

A few days later, Skeets returned to the site, and the place was glorious—fishermen needed only cast their hooks before schools of fat tuna, sea bass, and cod leaped onto their lines. The best part was that only Skeets and his friend knew about it, which meant he could visit anytime without worry that other captains had wiped out the prize.

But a curious thing happened to Skeets whenever he visited this site. Even as he basked in its largesse, he could not stop himself from wondering about the object at the soul of this underwater bounty. It was big—that much he could see by the crude green blob the mass painted on his bottom finder's screen. It was deep—at least 190 feet. And it was made of steel; he could tell that by inspecting the rust flakes that sometimes stuck to his fishing lures. Beyond that he could divine nothing. He was curious. Something about this site pulled on his instincts. Over a lifetime at sea, a fisherman develops a feel for what matters and what does not. To Skeets, this site mattered.

For years, when Nagle had seen Skeets in the parking lot or washing his boat or paying his fuel bill at the Horrible Inn, he had asked this question: "Say, Skeets, you come across any wrecks out there that haven't been hit by divers?" For years, Skeets had given this answer: "Sorry, Billy, nothing." Today, however, Skeets looked over to Nagle and said something different.

"Billy, I've been fishing this site. You can't believe it. Tuna. Pollack. Big fish."

Nagle raised an eyebrow from the bottom of his bourbon. "Oh yeah?"

"Yeah, Bill. About sixty miles offshore. And deep, your kind of deep, maybe two hundred foot of water. Something's down there. Something big. You should check this thing out. I'm thinking something really big is down there."

Even after several Jim Beams, Nagle knew the difference between dockside chest-puffing and a man's heart. He considered Skeets an excellent captain and a man who knew his ocean. He didn't doubt that Skeets's instinct was pinging properly. Still, Nagle could not and would not request the numbers. Captains had only their reputations, and it would be the reddest violation of professional territory to ask.

Skeets made an offer. "Billy, I'm looking for a little inshore black-fish wreck I know you dive every so often. Give me those numbers, and I'll give you my numbers. But you gotta keep them to yourself. You can't tell anyone."

Nagle nodded.

The two men agreed to exchange the numbers the next day on Nagle's boat. That night, Nagle could not sleep in anticipation of the appointment. The next day, he arrived an hour early and paced the rotted wooden pier that led to the *Seeker*. His instincts throbbed through his body. This meeting was about more than just an object at the bottom of the ocean. This meeting was about the tides turning.

When Skeets finally arrived, Nagle invited him into the *Seeker*'s wheelhouse. The men stood in the tiny compartment, surrounded by hanging navigation equipment, a half-empty bottle of Jim Beam, and the crumpled cowboys-and-Indians sleeping bag Nagle had used since boyhood. They looked each other in the eye.

"Bill, I gotta tell you something," Skeets said. "This site I found is a bad place. This part of the ocean is a bad place, it's a dangerous place. It's in a little depression, there's an edge there, with a huge current coming up over the continental shelf, lots of moving water—"

"Ah, don't worry, Skeets—"

"Really, Billy, it's a bad place. Your guys gotta be top-shelf divers.

You can have dead-calm air and still water, and still the boat could be drifting at three knots. You know what that means, how dangerous the currents are underneath. And it's deep. I'm thinking two hundred feet. I don't know anything about diving, but you better watch your guys."

"Yeah, Skeets, I know, I know. Don't worry. Let's swap the numbers."

Neither man could find a clean piece of paper. Nagle reached into his pocket and pulled out two cocktail napkins from the Horrible Inn. He wrote down his numbers for Skeets—a little blackfish snag south of Seaside lump, just a pile of rocks that made for good fishing. Then Skeets began to copy his Loran-C time differentials across a streak of peanut grease left by Nagle's hand. Captains are not supposed to reveal prize sites. But Nagle could tell Skeets what was down there; Nagle was the one guy Skeets knew who was capable of diving to 200 feet. And Nagle seemed a decent guy, not the kind to blab or sell the numbers to a rival fishing charter.

Skeets handed over the napkin.

"Keep it to yourself," he reminded Nagle. "And for God's sake, be careful."

Skeets let himself out of the wheelhouse, climbed down the steep white wooden stairs, and returned to the dock and his boat. Nagle followed a short time later, pen in one hand, cocktail napkin death-gripped in the other. He walked to the Horrible Inn and ordered a Jim Beam, then began transcribing Skeets's numbers into code on a different napkin. Nagle kept a book of numbers on the *Seeker*, but those were public numbers—go steal them if you want, you son of a bitch. His wallet, however, was reserved for promise. You could kill Nagle and steal his wallet, but those numbers would mean nothing without the code, and Nagle never told anyone the code. He folded the new napkin and tucked it into his wallet, the safe house for his dreams. Then he called John Chatterton.

If Nagle saw himself in any other diver, that diver was John Chatterton, a ruggedly tall and handsome forty-year-old commercial diver whose booming, Long Island–speckled voice had become sound track to the most important wreck dives of the era. By day, Chatterton worked underwater construction jobs around Manhattan, the kind that required a brass helmet and a ten-thousand-degree Broco torch. By weekend, he masterminded some of the most inventive and daring shipwreck dives ever executed on the eastern seaboard. When Nagle looked in Chatterton's eyes, he saw his own best days staring back at him.

They had met in 1984 aboard the *Seeker*. Chatterton had no particular interest in the destination that day; he had signed up simply to observe Nagle, the legend. Soon after, Chatterton took a *Seeker* charter to the *Texas Tower,* an old air force radar installation about sixty miles offshore. The tower had collapsed in a 1961 storm, killing its crew. Its bottom lay jackknifed in sand at 200 feet, making it too dangerous for all but the most accomplished divers. But its top could be easily explored at 85 feet, appropriate for every diver on this trip.

One man got cocky. He already had a reputation as a hotshot, so he surprised no one by concocting a plan to dive the bottom. Soon enough, one of wreck diving's oldest songs sounded from beneath the waves. The man became obsessed with removing a brass window. His air was short but he tried to finish anyway. He drowned. That's how fast it happens at those depths.

Now there was a corpse on the bottom of a very dangerous wreck. Someone had to go get him. That was Nagle's job; ordinarily, he or one of his assistants—his mates—would make the recovery dive. But they had just completed their own dives and could not return to the water until their bodies had off-gassed built-up nitrogen, a process that would take hours.

Chatterton volunteered. A diver unfamiliar with the bottom could easily get lost and never find his way back to the *Seeker,* so Nagle asked if Chatterton knew the mangled topography of the wreck. "Not really, but I'll go anyway," Chatterton said. That answer spoke to Nagle.

Chatterton reached the bottom of the *Texas Tower* and began his reconnaissance. Soon enough, he found the diver—"Doesn't look too bad for a dead guy," Chatterton thought. He tied the man's tanks to a two-hundred-pound lift bag and inflated the bag with air until the body began its ascent to the surface. For good measure, he tied a spool of line from the corpse to the shipwreck; that way, if anything went wrong, there would still be a trail to the body.

Something went wrong. During ascent, the rapidly decreasing water pressure caused the air in the diver's dry suit to expand, turning him into a deceased version of the Michelin Man. As the body surfaced, a giant wave collapsed the lift bag, and the man sank back to the bottom. With nightfall approaching, it would be unsafe for anyone to dive again.

Chatterton volunteered to retrieve the body in the morning. That really spoke to Nagle. The *Seeker* stayed overnight; everyone ate Doritos for breakfast. Chatterton found the body again. This time, the poor guy didn't look so good. His eyelids had been eaten away and his teeth showed; he'd become what divers call a "creature feature." Nagle reeled in the body when it surfaced. "You did a good job," he told Chatterton. "You are a good diver." After that, Nagle and Chatterton were friends.

Before long, Chatterton was crewing on the *Seeker*. In 1987, he made his first trip to the *Doria*. He swam around but did nothing more. The wreck was so dangerous, so terrifying, that he vowed never to return. On the same trip, Nagle recovered a two-hundred-pound wooden sign that read KEEP CLEAR OF PROPELLERS, the most beautiful sign Chatterton had ever seen. He shook Nagle's hand, thanked him for the opportunity, and said, "Bill, I've made my trip to the mountaintop. Once is enough." Nagle, however, knew better.

Chatterton couldn't forget the wreck. In contemplating the *Doria*'s tilted grandeur, he could glimpse shadows of the secrets great shipwrecks offer those who see with their minds. He returned. The *Doria*'s hugeness overwhelmed him; a diver could spend a decade of twenty-five-minute dives on this wreck and never see it all. Again he returned, and marveled at the feeling of being inside places that didn't used to be places, of becoming present in this vast repository of tiny things that had meant something to people. Soon, the *Doria* ran through his bloodstream full-time. Raking leaves or watching a Giants football game or walking the grocery's dairy aisle, Chatterton stitched together his experiences on the *Doria,* and gradually his eyes adjusted, until the quilt of his separate experiences aboard that shipwreck formed a single picture in his mind. "This is why I dive," he told Nagle. "This is what I want diving to be."

Soon Chatterton was going places and finding things on the *Doria* no one had before, not even Nagle and his cohorts in the glory days. His reputation wafted across the bows of dive boats along the eastern seaboard. And he continued to absorb Nagle. He marveled at Nagle's instinct to see the big picture, to envision a ship as it had been in its proudest moment, to study deck plans and captain's logs, to put himself into the mind of the ship's navigator, to construct a dive plan that envisioned the whole ship when only a tiny portion of it was currently knowable. He was astounded to bring up meaningless rusty artifacts from hidden corners on the *Doria* only to have Nagle examine them and divine exactly where he'd been.

Most of all, he and Nagle shared a philosophy. To them, diving was about exploration, about aiming for the everywhere of the unknown. There were a lot of impossible places to go when the world was as big as Chatterton and Nagle saw it, but for God's sake you had to try. You were *required* to try. What were you doing alive, these men thought, if you didn't go and try?

The day after Skeets revealed his secret, Nagle asked Chatterton to meet him at the *Seeker*. The men walked upstairs to the boat's wheelhouse, where Nagle locked the door and related Skeets's story to his friend. What could be at the bottom of that site? The men dealt out the possibilities like solitaire cards. Could it be a warship or a war-era merchant vessel? Almost impossible—military records indicated little action in the area during either world war. Could it be the *Corvallis,* a ship reputedly sunk by Hollywood for a 1930s disaster flick? Faintly possible: it was thought that the filmmakers had bothered to note only the most general location for their shoot, an area that included Skeets's fishing site but also several hundred other square miles of ocean. How about a subway car? Also vaguely possible—New Jersey sunk them purposely to promote marine life, but those locations had been reliably recorded.

Less romantic scenarios seemed more probable. It might be a pile of rocks. It might be a worthless pipe barge. Most likely it was an old garbage barge; in years past, municipalities had stuffed geriatric schooners with trash, cut their masts, and sunk them at no place in particular. Nagle and Chatterton had been to plenty of those.

But maybe, just maybe, it was something big.

Nagle proposed a plan. He and Chatterton would organize a trip to the site. Each would recruit six top divers, guys who could survive a 200-foot plunge into the unknown. It would not be an easy journey—six hours each way in the chill September air. Each diver would pay one hundred dollars to cover fuel and expenses. There would be no promises. Other diving captains offered hush-hush trips to "virgin" sites, but these were always scams; you'd get down there and find a recent diver's orange crowbar on some junky fishing boat, and the captain would actually look you in the eye and say, "Gee, fellas, I had no idea." Not Nagle and Chatterton. They would pitch their trip the way they felt it: It's probably nothing, men, but we have to try.

The trip was booked for Labor Day 1991. Nagle and Chatterton called every good diver they knew. Nearly all of them refused the invitation. Even some of the greats, guys who were supposed to be excited by maybes, turned down the trip. "I'd rather spend my money on a sure thing instead of some wacky pie in the sky" was the standard regret. One diver, Brian Skerry, told Chatterton, "You know what, man? I was born too late. All the really cool wrecks have been found. The age of exploration for shipwrecks is over." That's how it was in 1991. Guys wanted guarantees. Nagle and Chatterton kept calling.

Finally, their lists exhausted, they found their twelfth diver. Chatterton was incensed. "Nobody wants to find anything new! What the hell's going on, Bill?" Nagle, normally bombastic in the face of caution, looked down at the red X's on his list of divers and said to Chatterton, almost in whisper, "These guys don't have the heart for wreck diving, John. These guys just don't get it."

Just after midnight on September 2, 1991, while the rest of Brielle slept, Nagle, Chatterton, and the twelve divers who had signed up for the exploratory trip stuffed the *Seeker* with tanks, masks, regulators, knives, flashlights, and bundles of other gear. They faced a six-hour ride to Skeets's numbers. Some grabbed a bunk and went to sleep. Others hung around the changing table, catching up on one another's lives and laughing about the folly of paying to chase a pile of rocks. At one A.M., Nagle checked the sign-in sheet against the passengers on board. "Get all gear secured," he called to those still awake, then walked up the stairs and into the wheelhouse. Chatterton gave the signal to switch from shore power to generator. The lights in the boat's salon flickered, then gave way to powerful quartzes that bathed the back deck in white. One of the divers pulled the power leads and water feed from the dock and disconnected the shore-based phone line. Nagle lit the twin diesel engines, which danced to protest—*cough-grumble-POP-chum* . . . *cough-grumble-POP-POP-POP-rrmmm*—the disruption of their slumber.

Chatterton pulled in lines. "Bow line off! Stern line hold . . . hold . . . hold . . . okay!" he called to Nagle, then slung the heavy ropes onto the dock. Now the *Seeker* was ready. Nagle switched his wheelhouse lights to dim red, checked his VHF radio, single side-band radio, Loran-C, and radar, and engaged the engines one at a time, the choice method for coaxing a lady from her dock. A few minutes later, the *Seeker* was past the railroad drawbridge and nose up into the Atlantic. Most likely these men were chasing a garbage barge. Most likely the age of shipwreck exploration had passed. But as the Brielle dock faded behind them, Chatterton and Nagle saw possibilities on the horizon, and for that moment the world was perfect and right.

CHAPTER TWO

ZERO VIZ

DEEP-SHIPWRECK DIVING is among the world's most dangerous sports. Few other endeavors exist in which nature, biology, equipment, instinct, and object conspire—without warning and from all directions—to so completely attack a man's mind and disassemble his spirit. Many dead divers have been found inside shipwrecks with more than enough air remaining to have made it to the surface. It is not that they chose to die, but rather that they could no longer figure out how to live.

The sport bears only passing resemblance to its cousin, the resort-area, single-tank scuba familiar to the general public. Safety statistics are difficult to divine. Deep-wreck divers make up a minuscule percentage of the world's twenty million or so certified scuba divers. Their accidents barely blip on the excellent safety record of a sport in which nearly all the participants stay in shallow tropical waters, depend on partners for safety, and desire little more than lovely scenery. In the United States, of the ten million certified scuba divers, it is likely that only a few hundred dive deep for shipwrecks. To those few, it is not a matter of if they will taste death, only of whether they'll swallow. If a deep-wreck diver stays in the sport long enough, he will likely either come close to dying, watch another diver die, or die himself. There are times in this sport when it is difficult to say which of the three outcomes is worst.

Deep-shipwreck diving is unusual in another respect. Because it confronts man's most primordial instincts—to breathe; to see; to flee from danger—the layperson need not strap on the equipment in order to appreciate the peril. He need only contemplate the sport's dangers. They are his dangers, too, and in learning about them he will begin to comprehend the deep-wreck diver and feel his stories. He will understand why capable men give up underwater. He will know why most people in the world would never consider chasing a fisherman's numbers sixty miles out and 200 feet down into the middle of nowhere.

A deep-shipwreck diver breathing air confronts two primary dangers. First, at depths greater than about 66 feet, his judgment and motor skills can become impaired, a condition known as nitrogen narcosis. As he descends farther, the effects of narcosis become more pronounced. Beyond 100 feet, where some of the best shipwrecks lie, he can be significantly handicapped, yet he must perform feats and make decisions upon which his life depends.

Second, should something go wrong, he cannot simply swim to the surface. A diver who has spent time in deep water must ascend gradually, stopping at predetermined intervals to allow his body to readjust to decreasing pressures. He must do this even if he believes himself to be suffocating or choking or dying. Panicked divers who bolt for "sunshine and seagulls" risk a case of decompression sickness, or the "bends." Severe bends can permanently handicap, paralyze, or kill a person. Divers who have witnessed the writhing, screaming agony of a bad bends hit swear that they would rather suffocate and drown on the bottom than surface after a long, deep dive without decompressing.

Nearly all the myriad other dangers lying in wait for the deep-wreck diver involve narcosis or decompression sickness. Both narcosis and decompression sickness are conditions born of pressure. At sea level, atmospheric pressure is roughly equal to the pressure inside the human body. Throwing Frisbees on the beach or riding a bus, we are said to be at one atmosphere of pressure, or 14.7 pounds per square inch. Life feels normal at one atmosphere. The air we breathe at sea level, which is composed of 21 percent oxygen and 79 percent nitrogen, also enters our lungs at a pressure of one atmosphere. The oxygen nourishes our blood and tissue. The nitrogen is inert and doesn't do much of anything.

Things change in water. Every 33 feet below the surface, the pressure increases by one atmosphere. A scuba diver chasing seahorses at 33 feet, therefore, is said to be at two atmospheres, or twice the pressure he experienced at the surface. He barely feels it. But something is going on in the air he breathes from his tanks. While that air is still made up of oxygen and nitrogen molecules in that 21:79 ratio, there are now twice as many of each of those molecules in every lungful of air he breathes. At three atmospheres, there are three times as many oxygen and nitrogen molecules in his lungful of air, and so on.

As the diver breathes underwater, the extra nitrogen molecules being taken into his lungs don't just sit around as they do in a person on land. Instead, they dissolve into the bloodstream and travel into his tissues—his flesh, joints, brain, spine, everywhere. The longer and deeper a diver stays underwater, the more nitrogen accumulates in those tissues.

At a depth of around three atmospheres, or 66 feet, that accumulated nitrogen begins to have a narcotizing effect on most divers. That is nitrogen narcosis. Some compare the effects of narcosis to alcohol intoxication, others to the twilight of a waking anesthetic, still others to the fog of ether or laughing gas. Symptoms are relatively mild at shallower depths—judgment skews, motor skills dull, manual dexterity suffers, peripheral vision narrows, emotions heighten. As a diver descends farther, the effects intensify. At 130 feet, or about five atmospheres, most divers will be impaired. Some become all thumbs and struggle to complete simple tasks, such as tying a knot; others turn "dumb with the depth" and must talk themselves into believing what they already know. As a diver descends even deeper, say to 170 or 180 feet, he might start to hallucinate, until lobsters begin beckoning him by name or offering him unsound advice. Sometimes divers realize that they are "narced" by the sounds they hear. Many experience the "jungle drums," the deafening sound of one's pulse in one's own ears; or they might simply hear a hum, like a buzzing alarm clock lost under a pillow. Below 200 feet, narcosis can supercharge the normal processing of fear, joy, sorrow, excitement, and disappointment. Tiny problems—a missing knife, a bit of silt—can be perceived as unfolding catastrophes and snowball into panic. Serious problems—a depleting air tank or the loss of the anchor line—can appear as niggling annoyances. In an environment as unforgiving as a deep shipwreck, the short-circuiting of judgment, emotion, and motor skills complicates everything.

The nitrogen in the diver's breathing gas poses another problem. It accumulates in his tissues with both depth and time. This is generally not a problem on shallow dives of short duration. On deeper, longer dives, during the ascent the accumulated nitrogen is released from his tissues back into his bloodstream. The rate at which this happens determines whether a diver will suffer from the bends, or even if he'll die.

If the diver ascends slowly, atmospheric pressure decreases gradually and the accumulated nitrogen passes out of his body tissues in the form of microscopic bubbles. The same effect can be observed by slowly opening a soda bottle; if you gradually reduce the pressure inside the bottle, the bubbles stay small. The size of the bubbles is key. Only when nitrogen bubbles are microscopically small inside a diver can they travel efficiently through his bloodstream and back to his lungs, where they can be discharged through normal respiration. This is what a diver wants.

When a diver ascends quickly, however, the surrounding atmospheric pressure drops rapidly. That causes the accumulated nitrogen in his tissues to form massive quantities of large bubbles, just as when you rapidly unscrew the soda bottle's cap. Large nitrogen bubbles are the mortal enemy of the deep diver. When large bubbles form outside the bloodstream, they can press on tissues, blocking circulation. If this happens in the joints or near the nerves, the result will be agonizing pain that might last weeks or even a lifetime. If it happens in the spinal cord or the brain, the blockage can cause paralysis or a fatal stroke. If too many large bubbles make their way back to the lungs, the lungs will shut down, a condition called the "chokes," which can stop a diver's breathing. If too many large bubbles find their way into the arterial system, the diver can suffer a pulmonary barotrauma, or gas embolism, a condition that can cause a stroke, blindness, unconsciousness, or death.

To guarantee that he ascends slowly, keeping the nitrogen bubbles microscopically small, the deep diver deliberately pauses at predetermined depths to allow these bubbles to work their way out of his system. These pauses are known as "decompression stops" and have been optimally calculated by scientists. A diver breathing air who spends twenty-five minutes at a depth of 200 feet might spend an hour working his way back to the surface, stopping first at a depth of 40 feet and waiting for five minutes, then ascending slowly and stopping again for ten minutes at 30 feet, fourteen minutes at 20 feet, and for twenty-five minutes at 10 feet. The amount of time he spends decompressing is a function of depth and time—longer dives and deeper depths mean more decompression. That is one reason why shipwreck divers don't spend hours working underwater; the decompression time for a two-hour dive might be as long as nine hours.

Narcosis and decompression sickness are the patriarchs on the family tree of deep-wreck diving dangers. A diver does not dare board a charter boat bound for a deep wreck unless he honors these perils.

Atlantic divers in the Northeast reach shipwrecks by charter boats. Though some divers own their own recreational boats, such smaller craft cannot withstand the forces of the open Atlantic. Charter boats, most of which are longer than thirty-five feet, are built for the rigors of the sea. Customers often make two dives in a day, but they must wait several hours between turns to fully discharge any nitrogen that remains in their bodies. Dive charters, therefore, often become all-day or overnight affairs.

An excellent diver boards the boat with a plan. For days, maybe weeks before the trip, he contemplates the wreck, studies its deck plans, memorizes its contours, decides on a work area, sets reasonable goals, then constructs a strategy to accomplish those goals. He believes that navigation is the key to safety and success aboard a wreck, and he is unwilling to dig willy-nilly, as do so many wreck divers, in blind hope of finding a prize. He has seen guys who do that, and some of those guys never came up. A well-conceived plan is his religion. Days in advance, he knows what he is supposed to do and where he is supposed to go, and for that reason he will adapt to contingencies; and in the deep Atlantic everything is contingency.

Equipment is the deep-wreck diver's soul mate. It grants him passage into an off-limits world, then stands between him and nature. There are hints of love in the way the diver clips, wraps, fastens, and jury-rigs his 175 pounds of gear until he is part modern art sculpture, part 1950s movie alien. Fully suited, he can only lumber, but the rig feels like life to him. Should any of his equipment fail, he will find trouble. He carries several thousand dollars' worth of gear: strobe lights, headlight, flashlights, up lines, hammer, crowbar or sledgehammer, knives, mask, fins, fin keepers, buoyancy wings, regulators, manifold, compass, mesh goody bag for artifacts, lift bags to float those artifacts to the surface, marker buoy (or "safety sausage") to shoot to the surface in case of emergency, clips, gauges, dials, tools, writing slate, waterproof marker, laminated decompression tables, neoprene gloves, hood, stopwatch, weight belt, ankle weights, jon lines. Then he packs backups for some of this gear. He shuns the casual diver's wet suit for the warmer, more expensive dry suit, which he wears over two pairs of expedition-weight polypropylene underwear. He carries two air tanks, not one. He needs every bit of this stuff.

As the charter boat nears its destination, the captain uses his navigation equipment to put the vessel "on the numbers," or as close to the wreck as possible. His mates—usually two or three divers who work aboard the boat—find footing on the slippery front deck and grab hold of the anchor and its line. A dive boat's anchor is a steel grapple with four or five long teeth, more like the tool Batman uses to scale buildings than the traditional two-fluke instrument tattooed on sailors' biceps. It is attached first to about fifteen feet of chain, then to hundreds of feet of three-quarter-inch nylon line. When the captain gives the order, the mates will drop this grapple, hoping that it lands on and snags the shipwreck.

This precise dropping of the anchor line is critical business. The anchor line does not simply keep the boat stationary. It is the diver's umbilical cord, the means by which he makes his way to the shipwreck and, more important, finds his way back. A diver cannot simply jump off the boat, drop through the water, and expect to land on the wreck. By the time he splashes, his boat likely will have drifted several hundred feet with the current, so that it is no longer over the wreck. Even if the boat remained directly over the wreck, a diver who jumped off and descended without using the anchor line as a guide would find himself a toy in the ocean currents that swirl in different directions at various depths. Those currents might blow him hundreds of feet from the wreck. In the dark waters of the deep Atlantic, where visibility might be as poor as ten inches, a diver who lands even a few feet away from the wreck could wander the bottom for years without finding anything. Even in those rare cases when bottom visibility is pristine, say forty feet, a free-descending diver who lands forty-five feet away from the wreck still won't ever see it. At that point, he must guess at a direction in which to search, and if he guesses wrong, he will become nomad and soon be lost. Only by descending along the anchor line can the diver find his wreck.

The trip back up the anchor line is even more critical. If a diver cannot locate the anchor line, he will be forced to ascend and decompress from wherever he happens to find himself. Such a free ascent is haunted with bad possibilities. He still must decompress—a process requiring an hour or more, depending on his bottom time and depth—but without an anchor line in hand to keep him steady, he will find it more difficult to maintain the precise depths necessary for proper decompression. This invites the bends. The bends is only his first problem. Without an anchor line to clutch, he will also be blown about by currents. Even if he somehow manages to begin his ascent from directly beneath the dive boat, a free-floating diver who decompresses for an hour in a current of just two knots—about two miles per hour—will surface more than two miles from the boat. At that distance, he will likely never see the boat, and the boat will likely never see him. Even if he spotted the boat, he could not hope to swim to it; he is already down-current and carrying hundreds of pounds of equipment, and even a desperate diver cannot swim against those handicaps. He will not drown immediately, because his gear is buoyant and because his suit and buoyancy wings likely contain air. But panic is not far off. He knows that hypothermia in the cold Atlantic is a few hours away. He remembers in fine detail the stories he's heard about sharks attacking divers adrift. He knows that even if he is alive in twenty-four hours, the skin around the cuffs on his dry suit will begin to soften in the salt water, allowing air to leak out and cold water to seep in. Now hypothermia is upon him. He knows that no one back at the boat will realize that he has surfaced; they might presume him lost on the wreck or eaten by a shark, but they will never know for sure because the odds are that if no one sees him between the white swells on the Atlantic's surface, no one will ever find him alive, and to the diver lost at sea, that seems the most terrible result of all.

Because the anchor line is lifeline, it is too risky to simply leave the grapple snagged on the wreck. Currents shift underwater, and grapples can move with that motion and come undone. The grapple, therefore, must be secured. This is the work of the mates, who dive down to the wreck and "tie in." Once the tie-in is complete, the mates release several white foam drinking cups, which rise to the surface and act as signal to the captain and divers that the anchor line is secure. White cups mean go time on Atlantic wreck charters.

When word of the cup sighting reaches the divers, they unpack their rigs and begin to put on their equipment. Once dressed, the diver inspects his equipment, a poking, pulling, coaxing, and stroking similar to that performed by a private pilot on his aircraft. Underwater, he will have no such luxury. If he has questions about his gear, if he has the vaguest inkling that anything is askew, he must act now.

A good diver reveals himself in the way he gears up. He is at one with his equipment. He knows where every piece goes; every strap is the perfect length, every tool expertly placed, and everything fits. He moves instinctively, his hands and stuff in a swoop-tug-and-click ballet until he is transformed into sea creature. He rarely needs help. If another diver moves to assist him, he will usually decline, saying, "No, thank you" or, more likely, "Don't touch my shit." He favors ten-dollar knives over the hundred-dollar versions because when he loses the cheaper ones, he does not feel obligated, under the pressure of narcosis, to risk his life searching the bottom to rescue them. He cares nothing for the prettiness of his gear, and often tattoos it with patches, stickers, and graffiti that testify to past dive exploits. Neon colors do not exist for him; greenhorns who choose those hues don't have to wait long before hearing the boat's opinion on such loudness. When he is fully geared up, a good wreck diver looks like a German car engine; more ordinary divers resemble the interior of a child's toy chest.

When he is standing, the geared-up diver's 350-pound footsteps and hunched posture make him a neoprene Sasquatch. In fins, he takes several seconds to thwack-thud across a slippery deck, and will tumble should a sudden wave strike the boat. Breathing air from his twin tanks, or "doubles," he will have about twenty-five minutes on a 200-foot wreck before he must begin a sixty-minute decompression ascent.

Once in the water, the diver's tanks no longer feel heavy on his body and instead seem to float away from him. He grabs a "granny" line, a yellow rope rigged from the stern to the anchor line under the boat. He taps valves on his dry suit and wings to bleed a bit of air from each, making himself slightly negatively buoyant, so that his body fades just below the surface before stopping, spiritlike, at a depth of just a few feet. He pulls himself along the granny line until he reaches the anchor line. He vents a little more air. Now he slowly begins to sink.

He is on his way to the shipwreck. Most likely, he is going there alone. For all a deep-wreck diver brings along underwater, the most striking part he leaves behind is a "buddy." In recreational scuba, the buddy system is gospel. Divers stay in pairs, poised to help each other. In clear, shallow water, buddies are sound policy. They can share air in the event of equipment failure. They can lead a distressed partner to the surface or unsnag him from a fishing line. They provide comfort and reassurance just by being there. On the bottom of the Atlantic, however, a well-meaning diver can kill himself and his partner. A diver who pretzels himself into a shipwreck's crooked compartment to help another diver might himself become trapped, or he might foul the visibility so badly that neither man can find his way out. A diver attempting to share his air, or "buddy-breathe," with a panicked diver—a basic duty in recreational scuba—also risks his life. A suffocating diver at 200 feet sees a healthy colleague as a magic carpet, and will kill if he must to jump aboard that man's air supply. Panicked divers have slashed with knives at would-be rescuers, torn regulators from their mouths, and dragged them to the surface without decompressing in a mad dash to reach the surface.

Even the act of observing another diver in distress can be dangerous while deep in the ocean. A diver's emotions at 200 feet are already in hyperdrive from narcosis. Should he come face-to-face with a diver who believes he is dying, that diver's eyes will leap across the water and become his own eyes, and he will see, through that man's panic, the spectrum of terrible possibilities that lie just around the corner for himself. He will then either panic himself or, more likely, try to save the distressed diver. Either way, his life has transitioned in an instant from secure to moment-by-moment. This is not to say that divers cannot or do not work together on a wreck—they often do. The good ones, however, never rely on each other for safety. Their philosophy is one of coldly resolved independence and self-rescue.

The diver's descent down the anchor line is little more than feint fall. Typically, it will take him between two and four minutes to reach a wreck lying at a depth of 200 feet. He is virtually weightless as he drops, an astronaut beneath the sea. During the first few feet of descent, the diver's world is blue and clear. Overhead, he can see the sun rubbing yellow polka dots onto the glassine ocean surface. The diver does not see much marine life at shallow depths, though an occasional tuna or dolphin might swim along to investigate his odd shape and noisy, flat-bottomed bubbles. The diver himself hears two primary sounds: the hiss of his regulator on his inhalation and the booming gurgles of his bubbles on his exhalation; together they are the metronome of his adventure. As he descends farther, the scenery evolves in fast-forward; currents, visibility, ambient light, and marine life shift with depth, none predictably. In this way, even the simple descent down the anchor line is adventure.

The diver sinks to 190 feet. Now he stands face-to-face with the shipwreck, crooked and cracked and broken in the way Hollywood never captures violent endings, the way that rises from ordinary objects when they are bent backward against nature. Pipes, conduits, and wires splay from open wounds. Plumbing shows. Fish riding water columns move in and out of the broken vessel. Covered in plant life, only a ship's most basic shapes make sense—a propeller; a rudder; a porthole. Much of the rest must be absorbed and contemplated before the ship reassembles in the diver's mind. Only rarely, when visibility is pristine, can a diver hope to view the entirety of the wreck at one time. Otherwise he sees only cross sections. The tunnel vision of narcosis causes him to perceive even less.

The diver has perhaps twenty-five minutes to work the wreck before he must begin his ascent to the surface. If he has splashed with a plan, he heads straight for the area on the wreck that interests him. Most divers stay exclusively outside the wreck. They come to touch the ship or search for loose artifacts or snap photographs. Their work is steady and conservative. The spirit of the ship, however, lies inside. That is where the stories have settled, where one uncovers the freeze-frames of final human experience. Inside is where the bridge equipment lies—the telegraph, helm, and binnacles that gave the ship direction. It is where portholes rest, where gauges marked by maritime and national stampings lie buried, where pocket watches and suitcases and celebratory champagne bottles rest under blankets of silt. Only inside the wreck will a diver find a ship's brass clock, engraved with its manufacturer's mark and, sometimes, the time of the ship's sinking frozen on its face.

Shipwreck interiors can be terrifying places, collections of spaces in which order has fractured and linearity bent until human beings no longer fit. Hallways dead-end in the middle. Fallen ceilings block stairways. Nine-foot doorways become two-foot doorways. Rooms in which ladies played bridge or captains charted courses are now upside down or sideways or do not exist at all. There might be a bathtub on the wall. If the ocean is perilous outside the wreck, at least it is consistent and extends in all directions. Inside the wreck, where chaos is architect, dangers come camouflaged in every crevice. Bad happens suddenly. For many, the inside of a shipwreck is the most dangerous place they will ever go.

A diver who enters a wreck, especially if he intends to penetrate deeply, must conceive of space differently than he does on land. He must think in three dimensions, digesting navigational concepts—*turn left, drop down, then rise diagonally and follow the seam to the right*—that are nonsensical outside water. He must remember everything—every twist, turn, rise, and fall—and he must do so in an environment of few obvious landmarks and where most everything is sweatered in sea anemones. Should his command of navigation slip, should his memory falter, even for a moment, he will begin to ask questions: *Did I swim through three rooms to reach the captain's quarters or only two? Did I go left-right-right or right-left-right before ascending to this gun turret? Have I changed deck levels without realizing it? Is that the pipe I saw next to the wreck's exit, or is it one of six other pipes I saw while swimming through here?* These questions are trouble. They mean, in all likelihood, that the diver is lost.

A diver lost inside a wreck is in grave danger. He has a finite air supply. If he cannot find his way out, he will drown. If he finds his way out but breathes down his tanks in the process, he will not have enough air left for proper decompression. Narcosis, already humming in the background of his brain, crescendos in the lost diver like a broken record, shouting down reason as it reminds him, *You're lost you're lost you're lost you're lost you're lost . . .* He will be tempted to guess at a way out, but if he does so he will become a child in a funhouse, his blind movements virtually certain to deliver him into the ship's myriad dead ends and false pathways, each of which will only disorient him further. His air drops lower. His time grows shorter. This is how lost divers become corpses.

Even if a diver manages his navigation, he must still contend with issues of visibility. At 200 feet, the ocean bottom is dark. Inside the wreck, it's darker, sometimes pitch-black. If visibility were simply a matter of illumination, a diver's headlight and flashlight would suffice. But a shipwreck is filled with silt and debris. The diver's slightest movement—a reach for a dish, a kick with the fin, a turn to memorize a landmark—can stir the silt and disturb visibility. At times of such stark darkness, the deep-wreck diver is more a shadow diver, aiming at the shapes of a shipwreck as much as at the shipwrecks themselves.

The diver's bubbles do not help. Exhaust from his respiration rises and unsettles overhead silt and rust. Simply by breathing, he has invoked a rainstorm of rust flakes, some as large as peas, many as small as sugar crystals. The bubbles also disturb oil that has invariably leaked from tanks and equipment and spread everywhere in the wreck, and they disperse that oil into a haze and onto the diver's mask and into his mouth. Visibility is now even worse. There is no longer any such thing as right and left. Over there doesn't exist anymore. In a fog of silt and rust and oil, rudimentary navigation seems impossible.

To keep from raising silt clouds, divers learn to travel with a minimum of locomotion. Some move like crabs, using only their fingers to pull themselves along, their fins floating motionless in the water behind them. They do not kick to rise or fall, but rather inflate or deflate their wings, an air bladder between the diver and his tanks used for buoyancy control. When they arrive at an interesting area, they might draw in their knees and arms, adjust their buoyancy, and work while kneeling, their shins only brushing the shipwreck floor.

These measures are stopgap. A diver who spends time inside a wreck will screw the "viz"; it's just a matter of how soon and how badly. Once the silt billows and the rust flakes fall and the oil spreads, visibility in the wreck might stay fouled for several minutes, sometimes longer. Even if a diver has a perfect handle on navigation, he cannot see enough to work his way back now, and if he moves much at all the silt swells further. In zero viz, a diver might be five feet from the exit and never find his way out. This is the kind of realization that doesn't play well with narcosis, where small problems grow larger under jungle drums, and zero viz can seem the largest problem of them all. In an overpowering darkness, the blinded diver is a prime candidate to go lost.

Navigation and visibility issues make for a full mental plate. But the diver must contend with another danger inside a wreck, this one perhaps nastier than any other. In the violence of the ship's sinking, her ceilings and walls and floors likely vomited their guts. Once-civilized spaces are now spaghettied with electric cables, wires, bent metal rods, bedsprings, couch springs, sharpened pieces of broken equipment, chair legs, tablecloths, conduit pipes, and other now-threatening items that once conducted the ship's unseen business. All of it dangles nakedly in the diver's space. All of it stands ready to snag his hose or manifold or any of dozens of other bulky parts that make up the life-support components of his gear. Once tangled, the diver becomes a marionette. If he struggles, he can mummy himself in the stuff. In bad visibility, it is nearly impossible to avoid these nests; there is not an experienced wreck diver who has not become entangled—often.

A diver lost or tangled inside a shipwreck has come face-to-face with his maker. Corpses have been recovered inside wrecks—eyes and mouths agape in terror, the poor diver still lost, still blinded, still snagged, still pinned. Yet a curious truth pertains to these perils: rarely does the problem itself kill the diver. Rather, the diver's response to the problem—his panic—likely determines whether he lives or dies.

Here is what happens to a panicked diver in trouble inside a shipwreck:

His heart and respiratory rates jump. At 200 feet, when every lungful of air requires seven times the volume as that on the surface, a panicked diver can breathe down his tanks so quickly that the needles on his gauges begin to drop into the red before his eyes. That sight further quickens his heart and breath, which in turn further reduces the time he has to solve his problems. Heavier respiration also means heavier narcosis. Narcosis amplifies panic. A vicious cycle has begun.

He responds to panic as evolution designed him to, immediately and forcefully. But in a shipwreck, where every danger is first cousin to every other, a diver's desperation makes an open house of his bad situation. A lost diver who panics, for example, will thrash about in search of an exit. That movement will billow silt and foul the visibility, so that now he cannot see. Blinded, he searches more desperately for a way out; in that struggle, he might become entangled or collapse a heavy object dangling overhead. He breathes harder. He sees his gauges dropping further.

The diver might call for help. Sound travels well underwater, but it is directionless, so even if someone hears his cries it is doubtful they could trace them. When a man is trapped alone in a shipwreck, his brain starts to think in declaratives, not ideas. *I'm gonna die! Get out! Get out!* The diver tries harder. The needles dip. It is dark. It is likely the end.

In 1988, a skilled Connecticut diver named Joe Drozd signed up for an *Andrea Doria* trip aboard the *Seeker*. It would be his first journey to the great wreck, a dream come true. To ensure a safe dive, he added a third air tank—a small emergency, or "pony," bottle—to his normal set of doubles. "Just in case," he reasoned. Drozd and two partners penetrated the wreck through Gimbel's Hole, a foreboding rectangle opened into the ship's first-class section in 1981 by Peter Gimbel, heir to the Gimbel's department store fortune. The opening is black against the dark green ocean and drops 90 feet straight down, a sight that chills the blood of even the most experienced divers.

Shortly after entering the wreck, at a depth of about 200 feet, one of the valve-regulator assemblies on Drozd's back became tangled in a ninety-foot yellow polypropylene line left as a landmark by another diver. Under perfect conditions, a diver would ask his partners to untangle him. At 200 feet, narcosis humming, conditions are never perfect. Drozd reached for his knife; he would simply cut himself free. But instead of using his right hand, as was his custom, he grabbed the knife with his left hand, likely because the entanglement was behind him on that side. The awkward reach to cut the tangled line put pressure against the exhaust valve on his dry suit, a result he likely never expected. As Drozd cut at the snagged line, the air in his suit began to vent, making him negatively buoyant. He began to sink. Depth brings harder narcosis. His narcosis began to pound.

Dropping, Drozd hurtled toward his mental meniscus. Every time he reached to cut the tangled line, he vented more air from his suit and got heavier. His narcosis built, the kind that blocks good ideas, such as changing knife hands. His breathing quickened. His narcosis gained. In the growing urgency of his situation, Drozd breathed dry the first of his two double tanks before switching, mistakenly, to his pony bottle instead of his second full-sized tank.

A few minutes later, Drozd freed himself from the tangled line. At around this time, his two partners realized he was in trouble and swam toward him to help. With narcosis raging, his dry suit constricting tighter, his body sinking farther, he breathed dry what he believed to be his second primary tank.

His two partners reached him. One grabbed Drozd and tried to swim him up and out of the *Doria,* but Drozd was leaden from losing the air in his dry suit. The divers would have to do something to keep Drozd from sinking farther. One filled his own suit with extra air, increasing his buoyancy so that he might grab Drozd and more easily ascend with him out of the wreck. But by now, starved for breath and believing both his primary tanks to be empty, Drozd spiraled into full terror. He flailed against his helpers until the diver who had grabbed him lost his grip. That diver, now overly buoyant and without the heavy Drozd as counterbalance, rocketed out of the wreck and toward the surface of the ocean, unable in the violence of the ascent to vent his suit, which expanded, making him more buoyant with every foot he ascended into shallower, lower-pressure waters. Soon, that diver was at 100 feet and still shooting to sunshine. If he broke the surface without decompressing, he would either suffer serious central nervous system damage or die. He could do nothing to vent his suit in this explosive ascent. The anchor line was nowhere in sight. He kept rising.

Back down at the *Doria,* Drozd spat his regulator from his mouth, a physiological reaction in blind panic. Icy salt water choked his lungs. His gag reflexes fired. His tunnel vision narrowed to blackness. His remaining partner offered Drozd his backup regulator, but Drozd, knife still in hand, slashed wildly at the man, his mind spraying in a million directions, his narcosis pummeling. And then Drozd turned and swam down the wreck, a full tank of air on his back, no regulator in his mouth, still slashing, still cutting the ocean to shreds, and he kept swimming until he disappeared into the blackness of the wreck, and he never came out.

His second partner, also ravaged by narcosis and the terribleness of the moment, was now in danger of panicking himself. He believed both Drozd and his other partner to be dead. He checked his gauges and confirmed what he feared most: he was over his time limit and should have already started his own decompression. He began his ascent believing himself the only one of the three to survive the event.

In fact, the first diver had caught a miracle. At about 60 feet, he finally managed to vent the gas from his suit and slow his ascent. At the same time, he glimpsed the anchor line, a stripe in the ocean from God, and swam over and clutched it as if it were life itself. He survived without injury. The other diver completed his decompression and also survived, terrified but unscathed. Drozd died with a full tank of air on his back.

Not all divers succumb to panic as Drozd did. A great diver learns to stand down his emotions. At the moment he becomes lost or blinded or tangled or trapped, that instant when millions of years of evolution demand fight or flight and narcosis carves order from his brain, he dials down his fear and contracts into the moment until his breathing slows and his narcosis lightens and his reason returns. In this way he overcomes his humanness and becomes something else. In this way, liberated from instincts, he becomes a freak of nature.

To arrive at such a state, the diver must know the creases and folds of dread, so that when it leaps on him inside a wreck he is dealing with an old friend. The process can take years. It often requires study, discussion, practice, mentoring, contemplation, and hard experience. At work, he nods when the boss reveals the latest sales figures, but he is thinking, "Whatever else is wrong inside a shipwreck, if you are breathing you are okay." Paying bills or setting the VCR at home, he tells himself, "If you find trouble inside a wreck, slow down. Fall back. Talk yourself through it." As he gains more experience, he will meditate upon what every great diver advises him: "Fix the first problem fully and calmly before you even think about the second problem."

An ordinary diver will sometimes rush to extricate himself from trouble so that no other diver will witness his predicament. A disciplined diver is willing to risk such embarrassment in exchange for his life. The disciplined diver also is less susceptible to greed. He knows that divers busy grabbing are no longer focused on navigation and survival. He remembers, even under narcosis, that perhaps three-quarters of all divers who have perished on the *Andrea Doria* died with a bag full of prizes. He knows that it is narcosis talking when, after recovering six dishes, he sees a seventh and thinks, "I can't live with myself if someone else gets that dish." He pays attention when a charter captain like Danny Crowell passes around a bucketful of broken dishes and bent silverware and tells his customers, "I want you people to see this stuff. This is what a guy died for. We found it in his bag. Look real hard. Touch it. Are these pieces of shit worth your life?"

Once a diver has exited the shipwreck, he begins the journey back to the dive boat. If all has gone well, he feels exhilarated and triumphant; if he is heavily narced, he might be downright giddy. He cannot relax now. The trip to the surface is rife with its own perils, each of them capable of striking down even the best man.

Once the diver finds the anchor line, he begins his ascent. He cannot, however, simply float balloon-style up the line. If he should lose his focus during such an ascent—perhaps from seeing a shark or by daydreaming—he would find himself rising past the critical stops required for proper decompression. A good diver instead seeks a neutral buoyancy for his ascent up the anchor line. In that near-weightless state, he can propel himself upward with the gentlest pull or kick, but will never find himself free-floating past the crucial stops should he become distracted. As he ascends, he will gradually vent air from his suit and wings to retain his neutrality and prevent any sudden ascent.

Presuming that the water is calm, the ascending, decompressing diver will find himself with an hour or more of idle time at his various deco stops. At around 60 feet, the depth of his first hang, the sun likely will have reappeared and the ocean will have warmed around him. The water might be clear or murky, vacant or thick with jellyfish and other small animals. Most often it will look blue-green. In this weightless transition through worlds, free from narcosis and the storm of dangers at depth, the diver may finally allow himself to become a sightseer on his own adventure.

At the surface and now near the dive boat's bow, the diver swims alongside or under the boat to reach a metal ladder unfolded into the water at the stern. He need only climb aboard to end his dive. In calm seas, the process is routine. In rough seas, a steel ladder becomes a wild animal.

In 2000, a diver named George Place, freshly surfaced from exploring an offshore wreck, reached for the ladder on the dive boat *Eagle's Nest*. Seas raged and fog charcoaled the horizon. In the boat's upward heave, a rung from the ladder uppercut Place's jaw. Stunned and nearly unconscious, he lost his grip. He was cast into the current, disoriented and drifting behind the boat. Dive boats trail a "tag line" from their sterns—attached to a buoy—so that a drifting diver might grab hold and pull himself back. Place couldn't manage to reach the line. A diver who gets behind the tag line runs a serious risk of going lost. Place got behind the line in a hurry.

A witness on board ran to alert the captain, Howard Klein. But by the time Klein reached the back of the boat, Place was out of sight; he just wasn't there anymore. The captain could not simply cut the anchor line and give chase with the *Eagle's Nest*; he still had other divers decompressing on that line. Instead, he grabbed a two-way radio, rushed into his small Zodiac chase boat, and set out to search for the lost diver. Within seconds, in the increasing violence of the seas, Klein disappeared from view, too. A minute later he radioed to *Eagle's Nest* that the outboard motor on his Zodiac had failed. He was also adrift and, in the pitching waves, could see the dive boat only when the ocean's waves crested. By that time, Place's wife, who was a mate aboard *Eagle's Nest*, issued a mayday by radio. She reached only a single fishing boat, but it was an hour away. That boat promised to try to raise a closer vessel. After that, no one could do anything but pray that Place was still conscious in the big Atlantic.

After thirty minutes, Klein coaxed the Zodiac's motor back to life. But he had drifted too far by that time to have any hope of finding Place. He found his way back to the dive boat. A short time later, a radio call came in to *Eagle's Nest*. A closer fishing boat had sighted Place—five miles from the dive boat and alive. He had been adrift for more than two hours. Klein, who now had all his divers back on his boat, retrieved Place, sobbing but healthy. After that, divers aboard the *Eagle's Nest* came to believe in miracles.

Place had been ten seconds from completing a ninety-minute dive and had ended up cheek-to-cheek with death. It was another example of the truth that defines the sport of deep-wreck diving and shapes the lives of those who love it.

On a deep-wreck dive, no one is ever truly safe until he is back on the deck of the dive boat.

CHAPTER THREE

A SHAPE OF POWER

THE SEEKER had twenty minutes behind her when the last embers of Jersey Shore nightlife snuffed out under the gray-black horizon. The boat's external running lights, configured white on the mast, red on the port side, green on the starboard to indicate a "motor vessel under way," now stood as the only evidence of fourteen men who had decided to take a chance.

Nagle and Chatterton set the autopilot in the wheelhouse. It would be six hours until the *Seeker* hit the numbers. In the salon below, the paying customers worked themselves out of their clothes and onto the wooden, infirmary-style bunks that lined the outer edges of the compartment. Most had no trouble securing their lucky spot. Each man spread blankets or sleeping bags across his bunk; a passenger did not dare lay naked skin against the gymnasium-issue blue pads that passed for mattresses on the *Seeker*. There are romantic smells at sea, but a cushion kippered by years of sweaty, salt-watered divers is not among them.

On this night, while Nagle and Chatterton worked in the wheelhouse, the remaining divers slept in the salon. They were:

— Dick Shoe, forty-nine, Palmyra, New Jersey; administrator, Princeton University plasma physics lab

— Kip Cochran, forty-one, Trenton, New Jersey; policeman
— Steve Feldman, forty-four, Manhattan; stagehand, CBS
— Paul Skibinski, thirty-seven, Piscataway, New Jersey; excavating contractor
— Ron Ostrowski, age unknown, background unknown
— Doug Roberts, twenty-nine, Monmouth Beach, New Jersey; owner, cosmetics business
— Lloyd Garrick, thirty-five, Yardley, Pennsylvania; research chemist
— Kevin Brennan, thirty, Bradley Beach, New Jersey; commercial diver
— John Hildemann, twenty-seven, Cranford, New Jersey; owner of excavation company
— John Yurga, twenty-seven, Garfield, New Jersey; dive-shop manager
— Mark McMahon, thirty-five, Florham Park, New Jersey; commercial diver
— Steve Lombardo, forty-one, Staten Island, New York; physician

Some of these men had arrived in pairs and planned to dive together: Shoe with Cochran, Feldman with Skibinski, Ostrowski with Roberts, McMahon with Yurga. The others preferred to dive solo, many for safety reasons—a partner can't panic and kill you, they reasoned, if he's not your partner. Most knew one another from previous deep-wreck trips, or at least by reputation. All had searched for "mystery numbers" before. Collectively, they had discovered several garbage barges and rock piles for these efforts.

The Atlantic was kind to the *Seeker* through the evening. Around sunrise, loran readouts showed the boat just a half mile from the target site. Nagle cut the autopilot, throttled back the twin diesels, and swiveled to face the bottom finder. In the salon, divers began to awaken, the new quiet of calmed engines an alarm clock to eager men.

Nagle nudged the boat closer to the numbers. A shape appeared on the bottom finder's electronic display.

"There's something on the numbers," Nagle called to Chatterton.

"Yeah, I see it," Chatterton replied. "It looks like a ship on its side."

"Christ, John, it also looks like it's deeper than two hundred feet. I'm going to make a couple passes over it to get a better look."

Nagle cut the *Seeker*'s wheel hard to port, throwing her stern starboard and pulling the boat around for a second pass, then a third and a fourth—"mowing the lawn," as they call it. All the while, he watched the mass at the ocean bottom morph in and out of the bottom finder's screen. On some passes, the instrument showed the object at 230 feet; on one it read 260 feet. Brennan, Yurga, and Hildemann climbed the ladder and entered the wheelhouse.

"What do we got, Bill?" Yurga asked.

"This is deeper than I was expecting," Nagle told them. "And whatever it is, it's lying low—there's not a lot of relief. I think it might be a two-hundred-and-thirty-foot dive."

There were no experienced 230-foot divers in 1991. Even those brave enough to test the *Andrea Doria* almost never went to her bottom, at 250 feet; most stayed near that wreck's high point, around 180 feet, with the very best divers testing 230 feet perhaps once or twice a year. But Nagle kept saying that the mass on his bottom finder looked to be at 230 feet. Worse, it seemed to rise only about 30 feet off the sand.

Chatterton was capable of diving to 230 feet. He and Nagle devised a plan. Brennan and Hildemann would throw the hook. Chatterton would splash and check out whatever was on the bottom. If it looked worth diving and the depth was reasonable, he would tie in the anchor line. If it was some crappy barge or pile of rocks, or if the depth really was 260 feet, he would trip loose the hook, return to the surface, and call off the dive. Nagle agreed.

By now, the other divers had gathered on the deck below the wheelhouse, awaiting a verdict. Nagle slid the door open, stepped out, and leaned over the rail.

"Listen, ladies, this is what I see. Whatever is down there is at two hundred twenty, two hundred thirty feet, and it's lying low. This is *Doria* diving, maybe tougher. John's going to splash first and check it out. If it's some crap garbage barge, we don't touch it—this shit is too deep to be diving a barge. If it's something decent and it's not eat-you-alive deep, we go. Either way, we wait for John. Nobody goes until John gives the okay."

Chatterton collected his gear from the rear deck and began to suit up while Nagle attempted to hook the wreck. When the anchor caught, Nagle cut the boat's engines. The *Seeker* and the mass at the ocean's bottom were now connected. Nagle climbed down to the back deck, where Chatterton was making a final check of his gauges. Before long, everyone on the boat had gathered around the dressing table. Chatterton gave some final instructions.

"Give me six minutes, then give me slack," he told Nagle. "That'll give me time to shoot down and look around. If the thing is no good or too deep, I'm gonna pop two cups. If you see two cups, that means I'm not tying in and you should take up the grapple and I'll come up with it. But if I send up one cup, that means it's worth diving and it's not too deep. You see one cup, take in the slack because I'm already tied in."

Chatterton turned to the rest of the divers.

"Just to be safe, just to make sure there's no problem, nobody splashes until I finish my deco and come back on board and brief you guys. Everyone cool with that?"

The divers nodded. Chatterton walked to the edge of the boat, placed his regulator in his mouth, pulled his mask over his face, and checked his watch. Six minutes. Nagle checked his watch. Six minutes. Nagle went back to the wheelhouse, killed the power on the loran units, and hid the bottom finder's thermal paper graphs in a drawer. He liked these guys; they were his customers and his friends. But he didn't risk his numbers with anyone. Yurga, Brennan, and Hildemann returned to the bow. Chatterton knelt on the rail and fell sideways into the ocean.

Chatterton swam just below the surface to the anchor line, then grabbed hold of the line and purged a bit of air from his wings to reduce his buoyancy. The current began swirling and ripping, and not just in one direction, so that the anchor line bent in S shapes and Chatterton found himself white-knuckling the line and forcing himself down two-handed in a fight to keep from being blown from the rope.

In normal seas, such a descent might have taken two minutes. Five minutes after he splashed, Chatterton was still fighting. "I'm getting my ass kicked and they're going to give me slack before I even get down there," he mumbled to himself. As his watch clicked six minutes, he landed on a mass of metal near the sand. White particulate matter flew horizontally past his eyes in the swirling, dark green water, a sideways white Christmas in September. In the poor five-foot visibility, he could see only specks of rust on the metal and, above him, a rounded railing and a soft corner of some kind, an oddly streamlined shape, he thought, for what was probably just a barge. But at least this wasn't a pile of rocks. Chatterton checked his depth gauge: 218 feet. The sand below him looked to be 230 feet, the outer limit diveable by the men topside. He scanned for a high point to tie into and noticed what looked to be a strut at about 210 feet. The slack arrived, lucky to reach him through the swirling waters above. Chatterton tripped loose the grapple, swam to the strut, and tied the grapple and its fifteen feet of chain until the hook was secure. He took one white foam cup from his goody bag and released it. This dive was a go.

Aboard the *Seeker*, the crew at the bow scanned the waves. When Chatterton's signal appeared, Yurga ran to the galley and threw open the door.

"He blew one cup!" Yurga yelled. "We're going diving!"

The crew hauled in the anchor line's slack, wrapped it snug to the bitt, and joined the rest of the divers on the *Seeker*'s back deck. Chatterton would likely spend twenty minutes on the bottom, meaning he would owe an hour of decompression. No one made a move for his equipment. Everyone waited for Chatterton.

At the ocean's bottom, Chatterton clipped a strobe light to the anchor line's chain. Sideways white particles continued to rush through the green-black ocean panorama, limiting Chatterton's visibility to no more than ten feet. In his headlight beam, Chatterton could make out the general shape of a ship's hull. But this hull seemed to him to have a soft roll to it, an elegant shape built not for moving cargo or pumping supplies but for gliding. At 205 feet, he reached the top of the wreck and began to pull himself forward against the current, careful to keep hold of the structure underneath to avoid being blown adrift. With every foot he moved forward, a new snapshot emerged under the interrogation of his headlight, leaving the previous scene fading to black; in this way, Chatterton's progress over the mass was more slide show than movie. He moved slowly to digest every picture. Much of the mass lay covered in white and orange anemones, dulling the shape of whatever lay beneath. A few seconds later, Chatterton pulled himself to an area overgrown in bent and rusted pipes, a tangle of chopped and frayed electric cables a sudden haircut around it. Beneath this nest of broken equipment, bolted to the wreck, lay four undamaged cylinders, each perhaps six feet in length.

"Those are pipes," Chatterton thought. "This is a pipe barge. Damn, this is probably a tanker or sludge barge."

Chatterton continued along the top of the wreck. Narcosis began to hum as Muzak from the background of his brain. A few seconds later, he spotted a hatch. He stopped. Barges did not have hatches like this. He swam closer. The hatch was angled into the mass. Hatches are not supposed to be built at angles; they are meant to allow people and things to enter ships, so they are supposed to open straight down. Who would build a hatch that angled into a ship? Chatterton pushed his head inside the hatch. The interior of the mass lit white under his headlight. This was a room. He was sure because the walls were still there. A startled fish with a wide face and fang whiskers swam past Chatterton's mask, looked him briefly in the eye, then U-turned and disappeared back into the wreck. Visibility was excellent in this enclosed space protected from ocean particulates. Against one of the walls lay a shape. Chatterton stayed motionless and took it in. "This shape," he thought, "is unlike any other shape in the world." Chatterton's heart pounded. Was he seeing things? Was he more narced than he believed? He closed his eyes for a moment and opened them again. The shape was still there.

Fins. Propeller. Cigar body. A shape from scary books and terrifying movies. A shape left over from childhood's imagination. A shape of power.

A torpedo.

A complete, intact torpedo.

Chatterton's body heaved. He began a two-man dialogue with himself, partly to check his narcosis, partly because this was too much to discuss alone.

"I'm narced," he told himself. "I'm at two hundred and twenty feet. I'm exhausted from fighting the current. I could be seeing things."

"You are on top of a submarine," he replied.

"There are no submarines anywhere near this part of the ocean. I have books. I have studied books. There are no submarines here. This is impossible."

"You are on top of a submarine."

"I'm narced."

"There is no other shape like that torpedo. Remember those rolled edges you saw on the hull, the ones that looked built for gliding? Submarine. You have just discovered a submarine."

"This is a huge dive."

"No, John, this is more than a huge dive. This is the holy grail."

Chatterton pulled his head outside the hatch. A minute ago he'd had no idea where he was on this wreck. Now the torpedo had become a lighthouse. He knew that submarines fired torpedoes from both ends. That meant he was near either the bow or the stern. The current moved in the direction the torpedo pointed. If he let go and drifted with the current, he would soon arrive at one end of the wreck. At that point it should be simple to determine whether it was bow or stern. As he released his grip, the current awoke and roared so suddenly that it seemed to have been screamed from the submarine itself, an angry exhaust from a long-asleep machine now awakened. The current flung Chatterton past the anchor line, slingshotting him toward the end of the wreck. In another second he would be blown into the abyss. Instinctively, he thrust out a glove. Something solid hit his hand. Chatterton caught hold of a bent piece of metal at the tip of the wreck. Beyond that metal, there was only ocean and sand. He breathed deeply and steadied himself. The end of the wreck was before him.

Chatterton had seen photographs of submarines before. The bows were blunted and angled downward and aft, while the sterns were streamlined horizontally at the top to make room for propellers and rudder underneath. This was the bow. This was the bow of a submarine.

He looked closely at the marine growth and the deterioration of the metal on the wreck. There was no mistaking the ship's vintage. This submarine had come from World War II. He knew from his books that there were no sunken American submarines in this area. He looked again at the wreck. For a moment he dared not think it. But it was undeniable. "I'm holding on to a U-boat," Chatterton said out loud. "I'm holding on to a World War II German U-boat."

By now, Chatterton had reached the end of his twenty-minute bottom time. He swam back to the strobe light he had clipped to the anchor line, staying close to the wreck to shield himself from the wrath of the onrushing current. As he swam, he watched the hull's rolled edges unfold below him, beautiful curves engineered for stealth, curves that still looked secret.

It was time for Chatterton to leave. His first scheduled decompression stop was not until a depth of 60 feet. On the way up, his narcosis fading, he argued against himself. "Maybe you didn't see a torpedo. Maybe you saw a fan inside a pipe barge. People come up from 230 feet saying stupid things all the time, and now you're going to be the guy saying the stupid stuff." He knew better. He had controlled his narcosis. That was a torpedo. That was the bow of a U-boat.

Chatterton made his first stop at 60 feet. The water was sunlit and warm. The last traces of narcosis had evaporated. The torpedo's image now throbbed sharp in his memory. The catalog of submarines he had studied over the years emerged as a dossier before him. Some were hundreds of miles to the north, others hundreds of miles south. None was anywhere near here. Could there be a crew on board? Could this be a U-boat with a crew on board that no one in the world knew about but him? Too fantastic. And what was it doing in New Jersey waters?

Chatterton ascended to 40 feet and began his second hang. There, he remembered a dream he'd had years ago of finding a mystery submarine. In that dream, the sub he discovered was Russian and the crew still on board. It was a glorious dream, but the part he remembered most was how immediately he realized it had been a dream, and he had realized this within a second of awakening because such a wonderful thing could never happen in real life.

Chatterton ascended to 30 feet and began another stop. He had another twenty-five minutes' decompression time before he could surface and brief the others about his find. Topside, the divers followed Chatterton's bubbles as they gurgled to the surface along the anchor line. They were supposed to wait for him to surface.

"The suspense is killing me," Brennan told the other divers. "I gotta do something."

Brennan, with his long hair, Fu Manchu mustache, and "It's cool, dude" sensibility, might have passed for a Grateful Dead roadie if he hadn't been such a meticulous diver. While every other man aboard the *Seeker* that day favored a modern dry suit that provided deep insulation from the forty-degree Atlantic bottom temperatures, Brennan stayed loyal to the tattered, epoxied, and patched wet suit he wore to retrieve sunken golf carts and fix swimming pools in rich folks' backyards. Bound by duty, other divers would break Brennan's stones about his ancient getup. "Kevin," they'd ask, "does that suit date to the Neolithic or Mesozoic era?"

"You guys want to be all toasty and warm," Brennan would counter. "I wear this same suit to the *Doria,* man. The *Doria*! I have more mobility in this thing than all you guys put together. And goddamn it, if I gotta piss, I piss. You mooks in your dry suits have to hold it in. Fuck that crap—I piss!"

Other divers would hear this explanation and shake their heads. It was forty degrees on the *Doria*. A wet suit was like wearing a T-shirt. But damn if Brennan didn't surface after ninety minutes in those temperatures clutching some killer artifact or fat lobster. Grinning ear to ear as he stepped out of his patchwork wet suit, dive after successful dive, he seemed to have a bit of Houdini in him.

As Chatterton's bubbles continued to rise along the anchor line, Brennan geared up in his trademark minimalist fashion. He didn't believe in draping himself in backup gear and the latest accoutrements—those guys looked like goddamn Christmas trees. To Brennan, the less you carried, the less that could go wrong. And the faster you could splash in case you couldn't stand the suspense any longer.

Within minutes, Brennan had flipped over the *Seeker*'s side. Seconds later he reached Chatterton, who was still hanging, still shoehorning the wonder of his discovery into the reality centers of his brain. Brennan startled him with a tap on the shoulder, then put his palms up and shrugged his shoulders, the universal "What's up?"

signal. Chatterton removed a writing slate and pencil from his goody bag, then scrawled a single word as big and bold as would fit on the tablet. It said, "SUB."

For a moment, Brennan could not move. Then he began to scream through his regulator. The words came out as if spoken from behind two pillows, but were still intelligible.

"Are you kidding, John? Are you sure? Really?"

Chatterton nodded.

Brennan yelled, "Oh, God! Oh, shit! Oh, Christ!"

Brennan could have plunged straight down to the wreck and had the submarine to himself. But this was not the kind of information decent dudes hoarded. He shot back up the anchor line, bobbed on the surface, and yanked the regulator from his mouth.

"Yo, Bill! Bill!" he called to Nagle, who was still in the wheel-house. Nagle rushed outside the compartment, thinking Brennan was in trouble—a diver wouldn't surface and scream after a minute underwater unless he was in trouble.

"What the hell happened, Kevin?" Nagle called.

"Yo! Bill! Bill! Check this out: John says it's a submarine!"

Nagle did not need to hear anything else. He ran down the wheelhouse stairs and gathered the remaining divers.

"Chatterton says it's a sub."

Until this point, many of the divers had held deep reservations about exploring a new wreck at 230 feet. The word *sub* vaporized those concerns. The divers rushed to gear up. Only Nagle, whose alcoholism had degraded his physical condition and had made this kind of deep diving impossible, remained behind. On the anchor line, Brennan stuffed the regulator back into his mouth and headed down, pumping a pair of "Way to go!" fists as he passed Chatterton. Several minutes later, as Chatterton ascended to his 20-foot stop, the other eleven divers dropped past him on an express parade to the virgin wreck. Chatterton hadn't had his chance to brief the men on the wreck's danger or depth, but he would have had to lie about the submarine to prevent any of them from diving that day, and Chatterton didn't lie. The wreck lay at 230 feet at its bottommost point in the sand, about 210 feet at the top—the outer range of doable for a dozen men dizzy with possibility.

When Chatterton finally finished decompressing, he swam underneath the *Seeker* and climbed the aluminum ladder at its stern. Nagle waited for his protégé, hanging on the back rail until Chatterton could remove his mask and sit on the dressing table. Jim Beam had chipped away at Nagle's muscles and reflexes and had begun to turn his skin yellow, but it hadn't touched his explorer's heart, the part of him that believed an alcoholic world still to be beautiful for the stories it hid in secret places. He ambled over to Chatterton, shaded his eyes from the sun, and nodded to his friend. He wanted to say something momentous because this was the day men like him and Chatterton dreamed of. Instead the two men simply looked at each other.

"I hear we did good," Nagle finally said.

"Yeah, Bill," Chatterton said, clapping his friend on the shoulder. "We did good."

For a minute, Nagle could only shake his head and say, "Damn!" Every fiber in his failing body leaned toward the ocean in the way plants bend toward the sun. He had never so desperately desired to splash as he did at this moment. He had long since stopped bringing gear. But as he gazed at Chatterton, his mind was already in the water.

"Tell me about it, John," Nagle said. "Tell me everything. Tell me every detail, every bit of what you saw and felt and heard."

Until this point, Chatterton had never been able to tell Nagle anything new. Whatever groundbreaking work Chatterton had done on the *Doria* and other great wrecks, Nagle had been there first, and this had pushed Chatterton to explore harder and deeper, to go someday where even the great Bill Nagle hadn't gone. That day, Chatterton could see in Nagle's grade-school-big eyes, had come. He told Nagle everything.

As he finished his narrative, Chatterton expected Nagle to ask technical questions, to grill him on the wreck's level of metallic degradation or the silt buildup inside the torpedo hatch. Instead Nagle said, "This submarine can change me. This can motivate me and get my health back. This is the thing that can get me back."

As Nagle helped Chatterton undress, the other divers began their exploration of the wreck 230 feet below. The current had eased since Chatterton had departed, allowing those so inclined to swim along the hull without fear of exhaustion.

Ostrowski and Roberts studied the outline of the wreck and the flatness of its topside decking. Both pegged it for a submarine. The duo swam slowly along the top of the wreck, careful not to over-breathe in their excitement, never knowing whether they moved forward or aft. They soon reached a hole in the top of the steel hull that looked to have been blown violently inward; steel didn't bend like that willingly. They stuck their heads inside, and their lights brought to life a zoo of broken pipes, machinery, valves, and switches. They craned their necks upward and lit nests of electric cables dangling from the ceiling. Their breath quickened. This room could contain history; a quick swim in and a quick swim out and they might find the wreck's identity. Neither dared enter. This room might contain answers, but it also held a hundred ways to kill the overeager diver.

Shoe and Cochran took in the wreck's cigar shape and considered its level of deterioration. Each had experience diving World War II ships, and this wreck looked to them to be worn in just the same ways. The team spent most of its dive working to loosen a valve that interested Cochran, but the part would not budge.

Hildemann, diving alone, had a tougher time believing that the mass he stood on was a submarine. That changed as he arrived near the bow of the wreck about 10 feet off the sand, where he saw a long, narrow tube reaching into the boat. He had read books on submarines before. This was a torpedo tube—the weapon's passageway into the ocean.

Skibinski and Feldman ventured forty feet from the wreck to obtain a wider view, a bold decision at this depth and visibility. They looked at each other and nodded: a submarine. They swam back toward the strobe they had clipped to the anchor line. Both men had dived the *Texas Tower,* one of the darkest of the Northeast's deep wrecks. This wreck was darker. They stayed close to the strobe.

McMahon and Yurga remained atop the wreck. They, too, knew that this streamlined form belonged to a submarine. As they drifted higher, Yurga spotted flooding vents along the hull, the centerpiece of a submarine's diving system. A minute later, Yurga beheld the angled hatch that Chatterton had seen. He, too, pushed his head and light inside. He, too, saw the tail fins and propeller of the most notorious sea weapon ever built. The men yearned to see more, but each had agreed topside that at this depth, their first priority would be to stay near the anchor line and therefore stay alive. Yurga grabbed a lobster and joined McMahon on the ascent back to the dive boat.

Brennan, the first to arrive after Chatterton, inched forward in the current until he came to what he recognized was the bow of the sub. He allowed himself to drift farther forward until he was twenty feet in front of the wreck, then turned around to face the bow. He bled a wisp of air from his wings and sank gently to the sand, landing on his knees. He knelt there as a worshiper, reverent before this grand, unmistakable mass. The current began to howl, but Brennan stayed rooted in the sand, transfixed.

"I can't believe this," he thought. "I know this is a U-boat. I know this thing is German. Look at it! It's coming right at me, like in the opening scene in *Das Boot*. I can hear the music from the movie."

From behind his wonder and narcosis, an inner voice managed to remind Brennan about the current. He swam back, fighting the water every kick of the way until he reached the anchor line, deeply narced, winded, and light-headed. "I'll never let go of that wreck again," he promised himself. Then he began his ascent back to the *Seeker*.

Between 1939 and 1945, Germany assembled a force of 1,167 U-boats. Each one, for its ability to stalk enemies invisibly, became the most perfect and terrible reflection of man's first fear—that death lurks silently and everywhere, always. Some U-boats crept with impunity to within a few miles of American shores, close enough to tune in jazz radio stations and watch automobile headlights through their periscopes. In one month in 1940, U-boats sank 66 ships while losing only one of their own. Bodies of men killed aboard ships sunk by U-boats washed up on American shores during World War II. The sight was gruesome. The implication—that the killers could be anywhere but could not be seen or heard—was magnitudes worse.

Of those 1,167 U-boats, 757 were either sunk, captured, bombed in home ports or foreign bases, or fell from accident or collision. Of the 859 U-boats that left base for frontline patrol, 648 were sunk or captured while operating at sea, a loss rate of more than 75 percent. Some were sunk by enemy vessels and aircraft that could not confirm the kills, others by mines, still others by mechanical or human failure. Because most U-boats died beneath the water's surface, as many as 65 disappeared without explanation. In worlds of unsearchable water, U-boats made the perfect unfindable graves.

This day, as the divers began to surface and board the *Seeker*, they rushed out of their gear and into debate. Each of them was giddy to have discovered a virgin submarine. Each of them already had a theory. It could be *U-550*, a U-boat supposedly sunk in the far North Atlantic but never recovered. It could *not* be the American *S-5*; numerous divers had searched for and researched that sub for years and were certain it lay near Maryland. The crew could have escaped—a hatch looked to be open, though it was hard to tell. Something violent might have happened to the submarine—no one had seen the conning tower, the distinctively shaped observation post and entryway atop submarines that houses the periscopes and serves as the commander's battle station. A refrain began to build: Where the hell was the conning tower?

Then, Yurga. He had stopped, by chance, at a naval bookstore the day before to pick up some light reading for the trip. His choice: *The U-boat: The Evolution and Technical History of German Submarines*. When he produced the book after surfacing, the divers crowded over his shoulder to compare their memories to the book's detailed schematic diagrams. Chatterton recognized the cylindrical bottles he had seen on the wreck. Yurga saw the flooding vents. This thing had to be German. This thing had to be a U-boat.

As the divers continued their discussion and book study, Chatterton and Nagle drifted from the group and climbed into the wheelhouse. The crew pulled the anchor. Nagle set a course back for Brielle, fired the diesels, and pulled away from the site. Then he and Chatterton began a private discussion.

This was a historic dive, they agreed, but discovery was only half the job. The other half, the everything half, lay in identification. Both men scoffed at divers who guessed at the identity of wrecks they had found, who didn't understand the slovenliness of saying, "Well, we found a piece of china with a Danish stamp, therefore the wreck is Danish." Were Nagle and Chatterton simply to announce that they had found a submarine, what would that really tell anyone? But to announce with certainty the identity of the submarine you discovered, to give the nameless a name—that is when a man writes history.

To Nagle, there were also more worldly reasons for making the identification. Even in his broken-down physical state, the captain retained his appetite for glory. Identifying this submarine would guarantee his legacy as a dive legend and extend his reputation to the outside world, a place that didn't know from the USS *San Diego* or even the *Andrea Doria* but always paid attention to the word *U-boat*. A find like this would make him famous. A positive identification would mean customers. In those rare instances when a dive charter captain discovered a shipwreck, he came to own that wreck in the minds of divers; they wanted to travel with the guy who'd found the missing, to attach themselves to history through the man who had looked inside it.

Nagle and Chatterton believed it would take just another dive or two to pull a positive piece of identification from the wreck: a tag, a builder's plaque, a diary, something. Until then, there was sound reason not to utter a word of the discovery to anyone. A virgin sub—especially if it was a U-boat—would attract the attention of rival divers everywhere. Some might attempt to shadow the *Seeker* on its next trip in order to pick off the location. Others might guess at the general vicinity of the location, then try to sneak up on the *Seeker* while she was anchored with divers in the water, unable to cut away and run. Once a rival had the numbers, he could rush in and steal the *Seeker*'s credit and glory; there would be no shortage of pirates looking to make their bones on such a once-in-a-lifetime discovery. But in the minds of Chatterton and Nagle, the gravest threat came from a single source, and neither man had to invoke the name to know against whom they had to guard this wreck with their lives.

Bielenda.

In 1991, the eastern seaboard featured only a handful of big-name dive charter boats. The *Seeker* was one of them. Another was the Long Island–based *Wahoo,* a fifty-five-foot fiberglass hull captained by fifty-five-year-old Steve Bielenda, a barrel-chested, cherubic-faced man who looked to be accordioned under his two-hundred-fifteen-pound frame. A 1980 *Newsday* feature had dubbed Bielenda "King of the Deep," and he seemed unwilling to allow a day to pass without reminding those who would listen—and especially those who would not—of the coronation.

From the moment Nagle entered the charter business, in the mid-1980s, he and Bielenda despised each other. No one, including the captains themselves, seemed certain how the hard feelings started, but for years they lobbed accusations at each other, verbal grenades filled with reputation-piercing shrapnel: Nagle was a drunk has-been who endangered his divers and berated customers; Bielenda was a do-nothing blowhard who was just following the money, going with the established wrecks, doing nothing new. Customers often found themselves forced to choose sides; a diver became either Stevie's boy or Billy's boy, and pity the soul who confessed to diving with both. "You're diving the *Wahoo* next week?" an incredulous Nagle would ask customers. "What kind of fucking guy are you? He'll break your balls and steal your money. You're cattle to him." It was equally unpretty on the *Wahoo,* where the crew would join Bielenda in a dressing-down of anyone foolish enough to admit enjoying the *Seeker*. "Hose this guy off," *Wahoo* crewmen were heard to say loudly of paying customers. "He stinks like the *Seeker*." After one *Wahoo* customer admitted to a fondness for Nagle, he found the hardcover book he had brought along at the bottom of the boat's bilge. By 1991, the Bielenda-Nagle feud had become notorious.

To Nagle's supporters, the foundation of Bielenda's bitterness was basic: Nagle was a threat to Bielenda's title. Nagle drank too much, sure, but he remained an explorer, an original thinker, a researcher, a dreamer, a man of daring. And he was, as his growing customer base noted, a bit of a diving legend. To many, Bielenda seemed to do little of what made Nagle great, little of the pioneering that should have been protein to a true king of the deep. Next to Nagle, Bielenda appeared to play it safe, a guy who would always sit out bad weather at the dock while Nagle challenged angry seas. As Nagle's reputation for exploration grew, customers drifted to his boat. Bielenda's business could easily withstand the migration; what he seemed unable to tolerate was the affront to his throne.

It wasn't Bielenda's words, however, that worried Nagle as the *Seeker* bobbed above this mystery submarine. It was his certainty that Bielenda would stop at nothing to claim-jump the wreck. He had heard stories about Bielenda—that if you crewed for him on the *Wahoo,* you might be expected to give him a choice of whatever artifacts you recovered; that he half-jokingly told customers that should they ever recover the *Oregon*'s bell while diving from the *Wahoo,* they had better be prepared to gift it to the King of the Deep or swim the thirteen miles back to shore with the artifact; that Bielenda had friends, and they seemed to be everywhere—in the Coast Guard, on other charters, on fishing boats, in the Eastern Dive Boat Association, of which he was president. Nagle was convinced that if word leaked of the U-boat discovery, Bielenda would head straight for it and his goals would be threefold and deadly: identify the wreck; raid the artifacts; take the credit.

Chatterton figured that even if the *Wahoo* didn't jump the wreck, other divers looking to make their bones would try. Secrecy, therefore, would have to be paramount.

"The *Seeker* is booked for the next two weeks," Nagle told Chatterton. "Let's come back on the twenty-first, a Saturday. We invite only the guys on this trip, no one else, not a goddamn other person, because these guys took a shot and that'll be their reward. We make a pact. Nobody on the boat breathes a word to anyone. This is our submarine."

"I'm with you," Chatterton said.

Chatterton left Nagle to steer in the wheelhouse and walked down the steep white stairs to the rear deck. He called the divers together and asked them to step into the salon for a meeting. One by one, the divers gathered on bunks, on the floor, by the toaster, under the *Playboy* centerfolds, their hair still slicked with salt water, a few clutching pretzels or Cokes. Chatterton addressed the group in his booming, Long Island–tinged baritone.

"This is a huge dive," he said. "But finding it isn't enough. We need to identify it. We identify it and we rewrite history.

"Bill and I have made a decision. We're coming back to the wreck on September twenty-first. It's a private trip—only you guys are invited. No one else comes. There are a lot of great divers out there, guys who are legends, who would kill to come with us. They aren't coming. If you decide not to attend, your bunk stays empty.

"But we gotta keep this thing secret. Word gets out that we found a submarine and we'll have two hundred guys crawling all over our asses out here."

Chatterton paused for a moment. No one made a sound. He asked the men to swear an oath of secrecy. Every diver on the boat, he said, had to swear silence about what they had found this day. If others asked what the men had done today, they were to say they dove the *Parker*. He told them to eliminate the word *submarine* from their vocabularies. He told them to say nothing to anyone until they identified the wreck.

"This must be unanimous," Chatterton said. "Every one of you guys needs to agree. If even a single guy in this room isn't comfortable keeping this secret, that's cool, that's fine, but then the next trip becomes catch-as-catch-can, an open boat, anyone welcome. So I gotta ask you now: Is everyone in?"

Deep-wreck charters are not communal events. The divers' presence together on the boat is a matter of transportation, not teamwork; each devises his own plan, seeks his own artifacts, makes his own discoveries. Deep-wreck divers, however friendly, learn to think of themselves as self-contained entities. In dangerous waters, such a mind-set enables them to survive. Now Chatterton was proposing that fourteen men become a single, silent organism. Agreements like this simply did not occur on dive charters.

For a moment there was silence. Some of these men had only just met on this trip.

Then, one by one, the divers went around the room and spoke.

"I'm in."

"Me, too."

"I'm not saying shit."

"Count me in."

"My mouth is shut."

In a minute it was done. Every man had agreed. This was their submarine. This was their submarine alone.

* * *

The *Seeker* glided back toward Brielle on a cushion of hope and possibility. Divers passed around Yurga's U-boat book and tried to contain themselves, fashioning responsible rejoinders like "We know this will take time to research and will likely be complex, but with solid work we should be optimistic about identification." Inside, they were jumping on trampolines and dancing in sandboxes. As evening fell, they allowed themselves to invent scenarios to explain their submarine, and in the heady triumph of the journey home, all theories were credible, every idea a possibility: *Could Hitler be aboard this sub? Isn't there some rumor he tried to escape Germany at the end of the war? Maybe the wreck is filled with Nazi gold.* Six hours later, at about nine P.M., Nagle eased the boat back into its slip and the divers gathered their gear.

One diver, Steve Feldman, stayed back, waiting for Chatterton to emerge from the wheelhouse. Of the fourteen men aboard this boat, Feldman was the newest to the sport, with about ten years of experience. He had discovered diving later in life, at thirty-four, after a painful divorce. So hopelessly had he fallen in love with scuba that he had virtually willed himself to become an instructor, and of late had been teaching diving classes in Manhattan. Many of the divers on board, including Chatterton, had never seen Feldman before this trip; he dove most often in warm-water resort locations or for lobsters on Captain Paul Hepler's famous Wednesday bug runs off Long Island. As Chatterton made his way down to the back deck, Feldman stopped him.

"John, I want to thank you," he said. "This trip has been so cool. And it's important, it's really important. I can't wait until we go back. I mean, I'm really excited to be returning, and I just want to thank you and Bill for including me on something like this. This is like a dream come true."

"It is for me, too, pal," Chatterton said. "This is the thing you dream about."

The *Seeker*'s secret lasted nearly two full hours. Around midnight, Kevin Brennan dialed his close friend Richie Kohler, a fellow Brooklynite.

At twenty-nine, Kohler was already one of the eastern seaboard's most accomplished and daring deep-wreck divers. He was also a passionate amateur historian with a keen interest in all things German. To Brennan, it would have been disloyal to keep such exciting news from his friend. Kohler, in fact, would have been invited on the *Seeker* trip but for a history of bad blood with Chatterton. Kohler had been one of "Stevie's boys," and though he had since had an angry falling-out with Bielenda, his history with Chatterton and Bielenda virtually guaranteed that he would not have been welcome on this trip.

The phone rang in Kohler's bedroom.

"Richie, man, Richie, wake up. It's Kevin."

"What time is it . . . ?"

"Listen, man, wake up. We found something really good."

"What'd you find? What time is it?"

"That's the thing, Richie—I can't tell you what we found."

Kohler's wife rolled over and glared. He took the phone into the kitchen.

"Kevin, cut the shit. Just tell me what you found."

"No, man. I took an oath. I promised not to tell. You can't make me tell."

"Look, Kevin. You can't call here at midnight, tell me you found something great, then expect me to go back to sleep. Let's have it."

"I can't, man. Richie, come on, don't bust my balls. I'll tell you what: take a guess. If you guess right, I won't say no."

So Kohler, in his underwear and still bleary-eyed, plopped down at the kitchen table and guessed. Is it a passenger liner? No. A barge? No. The *Cayru?* The *Carolina?* The *Texel?* Nope, nope, nope. The guessing ballet continued for another five minutes; always Brennan's answer was no. Kohler rose and paced the room. His face turned red.

"Kevin, give me a hint, you bastard! You're breaking my shoes here."

Brennan thought it over. Then, in a thick, almost cartoonish Italian accent, he said, "It's-a-not-a-MY boat, it's-a . . ."

"What?" Kohler asked.

"That's your hint," Brennan said. Take it or leave it. "It's-a-not-a-MY boat, it's-a . . ."

"Have you been drinking, Kevin?"

"That's your hint, Richie."

For five minutes, Brennan repeated the clue. For five minutes, Kohler paced and cursed his friend, conjuring expletives and variations of expletives only another Brooklynite could reassemble. Then it came to him: It's-a-not-a-MY boat, it's-a-YOU boat. A U-boat.

"You found a U-boat?"

"Shit, yes, Richie, we did."

Kohler sat down. A U-boat? There were no U-boats in New Jersey waters.

"It's gotta be the *Spikefish*," Kohler finally exclaimed, referring to the World War II American submarine sunk in the 1960s for target practice. "If anything, you found the *Spikefish*."

"No, Richie! I was kneeling in the sand in front of it, I was looking up, and I could hear the music from *Das Boot*—da-da-DA-da! You can't tell anyone. This is top, top secret."

"I'm calling Bill Nagle right now," Kohler said. "I gotta be on the next trip."

"No! No! Don't do that, Richie! You can't say anything."

Kohler finally agreed to keep the secret. Like Brennan, he went to sleep that night rerunning scenes from *Das Boot*.

The same evening, Nagle hit the bottle in celebration of the discovery. With each sip, the notion of keeping such a secret seemed selfish, even criminal. Ice clinking in his glass, he called Danny Crowell, a mate on the *Seeker* who, because of a business obligation, had been unable to make the trip. He didn't bother with clues. "We found a U-boat," he slurred. "Don't tell a fucking soul."

The next morning, as John Yurga punched in at the dive shop where he worked, he received a call from Joe "Captain Zero" Terzuoli, a friendly dive boat captain. Terzuoli was the store's best customer.

"Yurga, hey, it's Zero. How was your trip?"

"Oh, it wasn't too bad. It was a rock pile, so we moved on and dove the *Parker*."

"Oh, well, you took your shot," Zero said. "Catch you soon, buddy."

Five minutes later, the phone rang again. Yurga answered.

"This is Zero! I just talked to Ralphie, who talked to Danny Crowell, who says Bill Nagle told him it was a U-boat!"

Yurga's stomach pounded. He liked Zero. It sickened him to lie. But he had sworn an oath.

"I don't know what you're talking about, Zero. It was rocks, man. Call Bill."

Yurga hung up and raced to dial Nagle before Zero could do it.

"Bill, this is Yurga. What the hell is going on? Did you open your mouth?"

"That fucking Danny Crowell!" Nagle exploded. "I told him not to tell!"

The remaining divers seemed better able to keep the secret. A few told family or nondiver friends, while others were unwilling to risk it even with wives. Soon, word of Nagle's indiscretion reached Chatterton. He knew his friend's weakness and was not surprised. He suggested that Nagle make several outlandish claims—to say on Monday that he had discovered a U-boat, on Tuesday that he had found the *Corvallis*, on Wednesday the *Carolina*, and so on, until no one believed any bit of it. Nagle mumbled that he would try. Chatterton heard the ice clink. The men would need to stand guard with that much more vigilance to prevent getting jumped on the wreck the next time out.

Two weeks was an agonizing wait for divers so alive with mystery. Landlocked for eternity, many did the next best thing to diving— they hit the books.

Most worked independently from their homes or local libraries. They consulted area shipwreck chronicles, U-boat histories, and World War II naval records. Their strategy: find any submarines recorded sunk anywhere near where the mystery wreck lay. Two U-boats leaped from the pages.

In April 1944, Allied forces sank *U-550* at a location of 40°09′N latitude and 69°44′W longitude. Those numbers sounded distinctly New Jersey to the divers. They rushed to their navigational charts and traced their fingers along the lats and longs until they reached a point about a hundred miles north of the mystery wreck's general location, still in New Jersey waters but not a great match. Still, no one had ever found *U-550*. To most of the divers, the hundred-mile discrepancy might be explainable; perhaps *U-550*'s sinking location was recorded imprecisely; perhaps *U-550* had only been wounded by Allied forces and then limped underwater to the mystery wreck site before sinking. Perhaps anything—*U-550* was the only submarine recorded sunk in New Jersey waters. She became the divers' odds-on favorite.

Close behind was *U-521,* which had been sunk in June 1943 at a position of approximately 37°43'N latitude and 73°16'W longitude. Again, the divers consulted their navigational charts. This location lay in Virginia waters, about ninety miles east of Chincoteague Bay. Though not in New Jersey waters, the site was just 120 miles south of the mystery wreck. As with *U-550,* the divers considered such a discrepancy to be explainable. As with *U-550,* the *U-521* remained undiscovered.

Divers called each other breathlessly to announce their findings: it is either *U-550* or *U-521*—no doubt about it.

Yurga sent a letter to the National Archives in Washington, D.C. He made this request: "I'd like all the information you have on U-boats, please," then gave his name and address.

A week later, Yurga received a letter from an archivist.

"Mr. Yurga, we have forty-three linear feet of floor-to-ceiling shelves of U-boat documents. This does not include drawings, just text. Perhaps you might be interested in visiting here to do your research."

For his part, Nagle had done a bit of research into *U-550* and *U-521.* He trembled with excitement as he digested these stories and processed their implications. Both U-boats had been reported sunk relatively close to the mystery wreck site. Neither U-boat had ever been found. To Nagle, this was proof that the submarine they had discovered was either *U-550* or *U-521.* He phoned Chatterton and asked him to drop by the *Seeker* after work.

Around dusk, Chatterton pulled into the Horrible Inn's parking lot. Nagle was on the *Seeker*'s back deck, standing watch over the pile of research papers he had accumulated.

"John, come on board, you gotta see this," Nagle called to him. "Are you ready for some stories?"

For the next hour, Nagle walked Chatterton through the sinkings of *U-550* and *U-521*. With each detail, Chatterton became more convinced that neither U-boat was the mystery sub. When Nagle finished, Chatterton shook his head.

"Bill, no way."

"What do you mean, no way?"

"It's not either of those U-boats."

"The hell you mean? Why not?"

"Bill, look at the reported sinking location for *U-550*. It's a hundred miles from our location. That is a huge distance—"

"The Allies must have gotten the location wrong," Nagle interrupted. "It was the heat of battle. Someone made a mistake. A slip of the pen—"

"Didn't happen, Bill. You've got three destroyers there. They agree on the location—look at these attack reports. Are you telling me that three separate warships made three separate but identical mistakes? Are you telling me these destroyers knew how to find Northern Ireland but couldn't accurately record their location in American waters?"

Nagle breathed hard for a minute but said nothing. Chatterton shrugged his shoulders in apology. Nagle's eyes grew angry.

"Well, then our wreck must be *U-521*," Nagle said. "If it's not the *550*, it's the goddamned *521*."

"It's not the *521* either," Chatterton said. "Again, we're talking about a United States Navy ship relatively close to the coast. Are we supposed to believe that the navy can't tell if they're off Baltimore or Brielle? The navy can't tell where they are? How can you be sixty miles offshore and not know where you are?"

The veins in Nagle's forehead popped out.

"Okay, wiseass! Which U-boat is it then?"

"I don't know, Bill. But I'm pretty damn sure it's neither one of those."

A few days later, Chatterton decided to take a trip. Chicago's Museum of Science and Industry was the permanent home of *U-505*, a type IXC U-boat captured by the Allies off Africa in 1944. The submarine had been kept in pristine condition and was open to the public.

"I want to walk through the submarine and feel it," Chatterton told his wife, Kathy. "I know nothing about U-boats. But I want to go inside, stand in it, and absorb things."

The airlines demanded a fortune to fly midweek with no notice. Chatterton paid it. He would take a day off from work, stay in Chicago for several hours, then fly home the same night.

Chatterton arrived at O'Hare airport on Wednesday, September 18. Only three days remained until the *Seeker*'s return to the wreck site. He took a taxi to the gargantuan museum and followed signs inside to the U-boat. He stood in line alongside restless schoolchildren on field trips, vaguely interested retirees, and a few military buffs. Then he calculated how many times he might repeat this tour before his return flight to New Jersey.

CHAPTER FOUR

JOHN CHATTERTON

IN WAYS, it amazed Chatterton that he was still alive to visit museums. He had lived a life of startling decisions, many of which he'd known could kill him, and all of which would have been unfathomable to the tourists with whom he stood in line. Now that he was forty years old, married, and ideally employed, his past sometimes seemed to belong to someone else. Still, in unexpected places like this museum, small things hurtled him back in time. Drab gray paint on a waiting area display evoked 1970, a year that still lived hot in his bloodstream. Photos of a giant ocean hung on nearby walls tossed him onto the waters of an unlikely boyhood. Today, he might have looked like everyone else standing beside him. But none of them had come close to a life like his.

That life began on a leafy September in 1951, when Jack and Patricia Chatterton welcomed their first child into their lives. The scene was 1950s perfect: Jack was a Yale-educated, up-and-coming aerospace engineer for the Sperry company, a fantastical-sounding job in an era when the word *aerospace* conjured images of Martians and death rays. Patricia was a twenty-four-year-old, newly retired fashion model who had twirled her willowy shape and waterfall of brown hair on international runways.

When John was three, his family moved to a new ranch-style home in Garden City, a tony Long Island suburb populated by Manhattan executives, local business owners, and jockey Eddie Arcaro. Few could imagine a better place to raise a child. Garden City was safe and quiet, its tract homes and color televisions promising Americans a new and better way of living.

When John was four, Patricia gave birth to another son, MacRae, named for Patricia's father. As the boys grew into school age, Garden City's fortunes grew with them. Four Long Island Railroad stations served the town in a time when most communities were lucky to get one. The Chattertons enjoyed a large TV and electric heat. John's bicycle had training wheels that didn't squeak.

Patricia made the beach her priority. She drove her two boys forty minutes to Gilgo Beach, along a stretch of barrier islands off the South Shore of Long Island. There, she turned John and MacRae loose to run like untied balloons, their bare feet on fire against the blazing sand until they had to rush into the Atlantic for relief. John's father never joined the family there. He was busy. He didn't like sand and salt water.

It was the salt water that gave John his feeling. At home, he was thrilled by little. School was okay. Books were so-so. Mickey Mantle was all right. But when he stood in the Atlantic up to his knees and looked out over the horizon, he felt as if he could see a different world, a world that no one talked about. At home, he would push his T-shirts against his face and smell the salt water, and that also gave John his feeling.

At home, John's life was different from those of his friends. His mother spoke to him without filters, expressing viewpoints without dumbing down her ideas or dialogue. John's father liked to have fun, but not the ball-tossing, fishing-trip recreation that television fathers favored. Jack would spend hours behind his desk at home, studying aerospace equations and smoking through his daily four packs of Kents. Two martinis, and he was ready to put on a gorilla mask and run around the neighborhood.

When Jack began to drink heavily, Patricia tried to coax him into becoming a proper father. He countered by upping his working, smoking, and drinking. Patricia decided then that as long as her own father was still alive, she was going to leave Jack out of things.

* * *

Patricia's father was Rae Emmet Arison, a retired rear admiral and navy hero who had commanded submarines for ten years in the 1930s and led battleships in World War II. To Patricia, who had idolized her father since girlhood, there was no better model of courage, decency, and immersion in life than Admiral Arison. He had since moved to South Carolina—near the beach. She arranged visits and began a campaign to steep her boys in her father's example.

She told her sons of her father's love of submarines, about how each man depended on every other for his life, so that the greenest enlisted man had been as responsible for the survival of the submarine as had her father, and she told them that her father found honor in this idea. Occasionally, she told stories of Admiral Arison's battles in the Pacific during World War II. But mostly she told the boys about how her father had distinguished himself as a man. She told them that after the war, her father had hobbled on crutches across America to visit the families of every man who had perished under his command because it was the right thing to do, that he needed to tell them in person that he appreciated their sons. She also told them that her father had helped the families of enlisted men with money and encouragement. She told them, sometimes daily, that her father valued excellence and persistence above all, and that life could be unlimited for a man who aimed high and never gave up.

In third grade, John played the Brave Prince in a school play. He wasn't the star; that was Prince Charming. He didn't get the girl; that was also for Prince Charming. He got killed in the final act. But he loved the role. As opening night approached, he found himself thinking, "I really am like the Brave Prince. I'm not handsome like Prince Charming. Girls don't really like me. But if I have one special thing, it's courage. Being the Brave Prince is better than being Prince Charming because I get to have courage."

As John turned ten, his parents argued constantly. He played harder at the beach and developed a dry sense of humor and a deep belly laugh that stopped even adults. "Your kid is like one of us," friends told Patricia. That summer, some neighbors allowed John to try their simple scuba setup. The tank was buoyant, so the boy could only float. But his head was in the water and he was breathing—breathing inside water!—and he could see rays of sunlight beaming through the water and pointing to the bottom, and he wanted desperately to go down because he couldn't see far enough. But the neighbors had said no diving, so he thought very hard while he breathed inside water. He thought, "If I could get down there, that is where it's happening."

One summer day when John was twelve, he and his friend Rob Denigris hitchhiked a ride out of Garden City, an adventure still considered safe in 1963 America. They got fifty miles from home, to a rural outpost in Suffolk County. John and Rob began walking down a country road, looking for whatever neat stuff was supposed to be on country roads. They came upon an old Victorian-style house. The place appeared abandoned: the grounds were overgrown in weeds, loping tree branches veiled shuttered windows, and the inside looked dark and still, as if sunlight had stopped bothering. The boys approached slowly. They had seen enough horror films to know better, yet each believed there to be stories inside. They tried a door. It opened.

Upstairs, they found piles of decades-old newspapers, still unfolded, and they sat on splintery crates and read the stories aloud to each other, tales of strange people from another time who had concerns that didn't entirely make sense today. In the basement, John discovered jars of preserved fruit—it had to be a few years' supply—and he was struck by the optimism of these jars, that the people who'd lived here had hoped to be around for a long time, that they had expected to enjoy eating something sweet in the future. The boys passed hours in the house. Neither considered hurting the place or disturbing its belongings. As dusk fell, they replaced their discoveries, even the newspapers, in the way they had found them.

As the boys hitchhiked home, they constructed scenarios to explain the house and its tenants: the preserves indicated the presence of a woman; the windows had not been boarded up because the tenants had left unexpectedly; the newspapers might have been left by a relative years after the last people lived there. Time disappeared while they made these theories.

They tried to hitchhike back to the house a few days later, but could not explain to the person who picked them up exactly where they had been. The boys walked a country road but came up empty. They tried again the next day and the next. Each time, they failed to find the house.

They desperately wanted to go back. They tried a half dozen times. They drew maps. But they could never find it; they never knew where they had been. The boys hitchhiked a lot after that. But they never found a place that great again.

John entered Garden City High School in 1965, the year the first marines landed at Da Nang. He had grown into some of his tallness and, with his short blond hair and squaring jaw, looked every week more man than kid. He made friends easily, especially among guys who appreciated his wild side, a side that could hitchhike fifty miles or rebuild a motorcycle's suicide shifter.

John's academic averageness continued in high school. But as sophomore year unfolded, he began to get a handle on impressions that had been just vague companions since grade school. Garden City was isolated, he thought, enveloped by a protective bubble that shielded residents from all that was going on in the rest of the world. People's concerns seemed small—they worried about who owned the best vacation house or whether Dad would pop for the Auxiliary Air Spring Kit for their new Mustang. Neighbors claimed to favor civil rights and even went out of their way to invoke the positives of having a "black boy" in the high school, but there were no minorities or working-class folks living in Garden City.

As John became an upperclassman, he continued his love affair with the beach. Still, he never dreamed of becoming a world-class fisherman or a champion surfer or the next Jacques Cousteau. Aside from his grandfather, he had no heroes. He didn't even have a nickname, a fact that he believed kind of summed it up about him in high school. But he always thought big about the ocean. Every time he looked at the Atlantic he marveled at the vastness of the world that must lie beyond Garden City.

In 1968, John's junior year, reports poured in about unthinkable war casualties all around Vietnam. Everyone had an opinion, and

John listened to all of them. But the more John absorbed these view-points, the more he suspected that these people didn't really know. It was not that he doubted their conviction; in fact, he admired their passion and felt invigorated by the era. But he asked himself about the lives of the people behind the opinions, and the more he asked, the more he became convinced that few of them had ever gone out and looked for themselves.

By this time, John's parents had divorced and his father had moved to California. One evening, John's father called home and asked his son about his future. John knew what his dad wanted to hear—that he would apply to Yale and then pursue a field worthy of the mind. Instead, John found strange words pouring out of his mouth. He told his father that he intended to explore the world, not as a tourist or an intellectual, but in search of answers. He told his father he didn't know where he was going, just that he had to go, that he had to see for himself.

"The hell you are!" his father exploded. Jack had started his own business and had just invented the circuitry for the Bar-O-Matic, the device that allows bartenders to pour several sodas from a single hose. He was riding high. He had money. John would come work for him.

"That's your plan. That's not my plan," John said.

"If you don't do it, John, you will end up a common laborer."

John hung up the phone.

Early in 1969, during John's final semester of high school, a girl attended one of his classes wearing a black armband. B-52 bombers had conducted recent heavy raids against targets near the Cambodian border. American protesters were demanding that the United States leave Vietnam. The girl made strong statements that day; she believed in her antiwar message. John pictured himself as a soldier risking his life in combat and wondered whether he would appreciate this girl and her armband and her fist, but he could not decide; he did not have enough information. And this was John's central problem in life, right there in the classroom, right next to the girl with the armband and students chanting, "Right on!" He didn't have answers. He had never gone and seen for himself.

John hit on an idea: the military could take him into the world; by joining the military he could see for himself. He asked himself if he could kill a person or fight for a cause he might come to despise. Again, he had no good answer. Then he had an epiphany: he could volunteer as a medic. No matter how ugly things got, as a medic he could help people instead of killing people. He could stay positive and still have a first-person experience with the most important questions in the world.

He first considered the navy, his grandfather's branch. But the navy made provisions for the grandchildren of heroes, and John wanted no special treatment. Other branches would not guarantee a specialty. Only the army promised to make a volunteer a medic in return for a four-year commitment. John enlisted.

In January 1970, the army assigned Private Chatterton to the neurosurgical ward of the 249th General Hospital in Asaka, Japan. He was eighteen. The ward existed for a single purpose: to treat the horrors of war. Every day, wounded American soldiers arrived in waves as if coming over a hill, some missing the backs of their skulls, others with torn spines, still others delirious or screaming for Mother or with sideways faces. Chatterton bathed patients, applied their dressings, turned them in bed as they tried to recover from damage done by ingeniously cruel weapons. Many of the patients were Chatterton's age. Sometimes a soldier would look at him before surgery and say, "I'm paralyzed, man." On the ward, Chatterton might let his mind wander for a moment and try to fathom life for a man suddenly without his body at eighteen.

If a soldier had it good in 1970, that soldier was Chatterton. He rode trains and drank beer and dined often in Asaka's sukiyaki houses. He liked his work—it was emotional and important. He was seeing the world. He was out of harm's way. But as he watched the parade of ruined lives delivered to the neuro ward, he began to ask questions that would not go away: What caused people to do this to one another? How is this happening to these guys? What is going on over that hill?

Chatterton studied the wounded. Mostly he watched their eyes as doctors explained about wheelchairs and breathing tubes, and their eyes always seemed to stare straight ahead, as if the men were looking through the doctor. To Chatterton, these soldiers were not "Charge of the Light Brigade" types. They looked stunned, afraid, lonely. But they also looked like they knew something Chatterton did not know.

As months passed and busloads of neurosurgical patients poured through the 249th, Chatterton's questions grew more urgent. He devoured newspapers, read books, and sought out conversations, but those sources only told him about politics; they couldn't explain how the world could have come to this. He got the feeling again, the same one he'd had on the beach as a boy, that he would have to go see for himself.

Chatterton began telling friends that he might request a transfer to Vietnam. Their response was immediate and unanimous: "Are you fucking crazy?" He tested the idea on his superiors. They pleaded with him to reconsider and explained that neurosurgical ward duty was among a soldier's highest callings. He told them that this was not about patriotism or anything noble like that—he just needed to understand. Even the wounded pleaded with Chatterton. "Don't go, man—it's a big mistake," they said. A paralyzed soldier told him, "Stay here, do your time, and go home. I'm wasted, but you're still good and you gotta stay good." But Chatterton requested the transfer. In June 1970, he was on an airplane to Chu Lai in South Vietnam.

Chatterton was assigned to the 4th Battalion 31st Infantry of the Americal Division. When he landed, he was told to report to the battalion aid station on a firebase near the Laotian border, a place called LZ West. He reached the firebase late that morning.

Around noon, a telephone rang on the base. A man answered, said nothing for a moment, then mumbled, "Shit" into the receiver. Soon everyone on the base began scrambling. An administrative officer called to Chatterton, "Get your gear! A medic in the field just got killed getting off a helicopter. You're taking his place." Chatterton wasn't sure if he heard the guy correctly. He was replacing a dead medic? On a helicopter? In the field? Then the same man began to sob and his eyes went wild, a look Chatterton had seen on those suffering nervous breakdowns in the Japanese hospital.

Chatterton stood in place as men grabbed weapons and gear and zigzagged around him. He did not know where to go or what to do. A minute later, a smallish man with scruffy brown hair grabbed his arm and told him, "Listen, I'm a medic, too. I'll get you ready to go out there." The medic looked old, at least twenty-four. He introduced himself as "Mouse."

"Follow me," Mouse said.

Mouse led Chatterton to a bunker on the firebase. It would be a few hours before the helicopter arrived to take Chatterton into the jungle. Until then, Mouse said he would show Chatterton the ropes. "If you want, man, we can talk while we work," he said.

In the bunker, Mouse stuffed Chatterton's aid bag with the field medic's tools—malaria pills, tetracycline, morphine, IV, tape, scissors, field dressings—and explained the jungle way to use them all, unhappy methods more sudden than Chatterton had learned in the hospital. In between, he spoke to Chatterton of Vietnam.

"I hate the war," Mouse said. "But I'm here. I do everything I can for the men. I'm here to be a good medic. The war is irrelevant to me. Over here, being a good medic is my life."

Mouse labeled the malaria and dysentery pills, pulled buckles around Chatterton's gear, and told him to carry a small aid bag in addition to the larger one thought sufficient by average medics. On patrol, he told Chatterton, a great medic separates his trauma supplies from the allergy and stomach-cramp shit—you don't lug antihistamines to treat a bullet wound to the head.

"These guys are your responsibility," Mouse continued. "For me, I have to do right by my men. That's the only thing that matters—the men. They're the only thing."

Chatterton asked Mouse about the .45-caliber pistol he kept on his hip—didn't field medics arm themselves better than that?

"A lot of medics carry a rifle or machine gun," Mouse said. "The only reason I carry a weapon at all is to protect a guy who's down. I'm not willing to let the enemy finish a guy I'm treating just because I'm unarmed. But I won't carry an offensive weapon. I'm no warrior. I leave the heavy stuff behind. It's symbolic in a way. It reminds me why I'm here."

For the next two hours, Chatterton lost himself in Mouse's philosophy. Mouse had ideas about courage and dedication and conviction that Chatterton had known were true but could never enunciate. For those two hours, Chatterton forgot that his life would be on the line that day.

A helicopter arrived. Someone shouted, "Let's go!" Mouse helped stuff hand grenades and a poncho into Chatterton's pack, then quizzed him a final time on which pill treated which ailment. Chatterton grabbed his helmet. He strapped a .45-caliber pistol to his hip.

"One more thing," Mouse said. "A lot of the stuff you do out there, you're going to have to live with all the way down the line. You'll have to make decisions out there. When that happens, you have to ask yourself, 'Where do I want to be in ten years, twenty years? How will I want to feel about this decision when I'm an old man?' That's the question for making important decisions."

Chatterton nodded and shook Mouse's hand. Mouse would remain at the base. Chatterton wondered if he would see this man again. He could only think to say, "Thanks a lot, Mouse. Goodbye." Then he climbed into the chopper and sat on a case of C rations—no seats, no seat belts—and the machine lifted away, disappearing above the trees and into the sun on its way to the real Vietnam.

The helicopter released Chatterton and several boxes of supplies in the jungle, then disappeared back into the sky. For what seemed an eternity, there was no one else there. Finally, Chatterton heard rustling behind a patch of trees. He turned toward the sound to see a dozen men emerging from the jungle, Western men with filthy faces, long hair, and scraggly beards. To Chatterton, it appeared as if a California motorcycle gang had materialized in Vietnam. The men walked toward him dressed in torn olive T-shirts and shredded pants. None wore a helmet or flak jacket or other military garb. As they came nearer, it seemed to Chatterton that each soldier carried the same expression, the look of a man who could no longer be surprised.

The soldiers broke open the supply boxes and began to outfit themselves. None said a word to Chatterton, including another medic assigned to the company command post. Every so often, one of them would glance up at Chatterton with a tired disgust that was an unmistakable subtitle in Vietnam: *You don't know shit. You won't be around long. If we need help, you probably won't deliver.* As the men finished packing, one of them grunted to Chatterton, "Let's go." The men made up a small platoon. They were on the move to a new location. While in transit, they were to hunt and kill North Vietnamese as necessary. The group walked into the jungle. Chatterton walked with them in the single-file line.

The men crossed rice paddies, swatted bird-sized insects, slogged through alligator-infested rivers, stepped over a machine-gunned buffalo. An hour into the jungle, shots rang out. The platoon hit the ground. Chatterton was the last man down. Bullets polka-dotted the dirt around them. Chatterton believed his heart was going to explode. When the shooting stopped, he looked around. The expressions on the faces around him had remained exactly as they were when he'd first seen them. Minutes later the men resumed walking. Chatterton pulled himself together and joined them. When his breath returned and his brain began working again, he thought to himself, "These guys are crazed killers. Nobody is talking to me. Where the hell am I? What have I done?"

The platoon spent the evening under a sweltering moon. While the others slept, Chatterton lay awake. At dawn, he saw a tiger disappear into the jungle. The next day, as the temperature broke one hundred degrees, the platoon arrived on the outskirts of an abandoned village. Reports indicated enemy soldiers in the vicinity. Other than Chatterton, the men in the platoon were heavily armed and primed for such a confrontation, none more so than John "Ace" Lacko, a twenty-eight-year-old New Jersey paperhanger whom Chatterton had pegged as the platoon's top dog. Lacko, six foot two and 220 pounds, was completing his third tour, an old-timer by Vietnam standards. He carried an M-60 machine gun with seven hundred rounds crisscrossed on assault straps slung over his chest—the era's definition of locked and loaded. Lacko had earned the nickname "Ace" for the black playing card he was said to leave on the chests of the enemies he had killed.

The platoon walked single file as they began the patrol. Before long, they came to a dried-up rice paddy that looked to provide easy passage through the otherwise hilly terrain. They entered the open area, scanning the hillside for the enemy. About fifty yards into the clearing, Lacko stepped up onto a rock to get a better view of the surroundings. Shots rang out from a hillside forward left. Five rounds, two of them armor-piercing, tore through Lacko's left hip and traveled clear through to his right hip. Stunned, he placed his gear on the ground and lay down, partially camouflaging himself in the two-foot grass. Blood began flowing from his wounds. The rest of the platoon turned back and took cover behind a ten-foot pile of dirt and rocks back near the opening to the field. Someone yelled, "Ace is hit! Medic! Medic!" Chatterton and the other medic crawled forward. They could see Lacko's outline in the grass about fifty yards away. He was in the open, a clear target. The enemy would not finish him; they were likely waiting for a medic to run out, giving them two kills for the price of one.

The platoon's other medic, Chatterton's superior, hugged close to the protective cover made by the wall of dirt.

"Fuck it, I'm not going out there," he told Chatterton.

The platoon could only glare at the man. As for Chatterton, they expected him to do even less. No greenhorn on his second day in Vietnam was going to run onto a shooting range.

"I'll get him," Chatterton said.

The platoon went silent. No one was more surprised than Chatterton. He began to remove his gear, all except for the small aid bag Mouse had packed for him.

"Christ, the kid's gonna go," someone said.

The platoon began to take position to provide cover fire. With each moment, Chatterton's vision narrowed and the jungle sounds compressed, until the only impressions in his world were his own heaving breaths and pounding heart. Chatterton had contemplated moments like this at the hospital in Japan. He believed that if he was ever faced with such a decision, he could call upon the lessons of his grandfather. Now, as he readied himself to make the naked run to Lacko, he thought to himself, "I'm going to find out what I am."

Chatterton sprinted into the open. A barrage of gunfire rang from the hillside far left. Bullets sprayed dirt around Chatterton, but he kept running. Halfway to his man, he could see Lacko lying in the grass. He ran faster. The ground in front of him staccatoed with gunfire. Behind him, he could hear his platoon returning fire so thick that the sky itself began to explode. Chatterton expected to be killed, he kept waiting to fall, but a blur of a feeling kept him from turning back, and that feeling was that he did not want to go through life knowing that he had given up. A second later he slid into the grass next to Lacko.

"I was laying there and the numbness and shock were setting in," Lacko recalls today. "And I see this new guy, here comes this new guy, and he's coming with everything he's got. I didn't know him at all, didn't even know his name. But he put himself right in the line of fire. The guy was risking his life."

Chatterton took cover in the grass beside Lacko. Bullets tore up the ground around them. Chatterton reached into his supply bag for scissors, slit Lacko's pants top to bottom, and looked for arterial damage. There was none. Lacko could be moved immediately. Now Chatterton had to get him back to the protection of the dirt wall, a distance of fifty yards that seemed to stretch across all Vietnam.

Chatterton considered throwing Lacko over his shoulders, but the wounded soldier outweighed him by fifty pounds. Chatterton sat on the ground behind Lacko and took his arms. More shots hit the dirt where they lay. Chatterton began pushing his legs backward in order to drag Lacko backward a body length at a time, all the while waiting for a bullet to strike him. Two minutes later they were halfway to the dirt wall; by now the platoon had pinpointed the source of the enemy fire and was beating back the attack on Chatterton and Lacko. Soon the men were ten feet from the wall, then five feet, then behind it. Soldiers rushed to them. Moments later, two American Cobra attack helicopters swooped in and unleashed hellfire on the enemy hillside. A Huey medevac chopper followed the Cobras in and airlifted Lacko, now in shock, to the hospital.

As the Huey disappeared, Chatterton collapsed to the ground. He was dehydrated and exhausted. He scarcely knew where he was. But he could see that something had changed in the men. They spoke to him. They rubbed his shoulders. They smiled at him. They called him "Doc."

As the platoon moved through the jungle, some of the soldiers might have wondered about the shelf life of Chatterton's courage. American medics in Vietnam walked in uniquely dangerous boots when they accompanied a squad on combat patrol. Because their job was to aid wounded soldiers, medics often found themselves running directly to where the action was hottest—around land mines, in the line of sniper fire, and over booby traps. But the medic faced an even more insidious risk: the enemy often wanted him dead more than anyone. Killing a squad's medic meant that the soldiers would be on their own when wounded, a devastating blow to a squad's morale.

In the days following Lacko's shooting, Chatterton volunteered for every patrol available to the platoon. The men chuckled and clapped him on the back and explained that a medic who walked every patrol would be pulling an impossible and deadly load. Something was rumbling inside Chatterton. He had been excellent on his first patrol, and the feeling of success was overwhelming to him. He could not imagine turning away from the first thing in his life at which he had been special, the thing at which he might be great.

Every day for the next two weeks, Chatterton walked patrol with his platoon. Every day, the men took fire. Chatterton always went to get the wounded guy. And he always went the same way. While most medics picked and crawled along the dirt to minimize their profiles, Chatterton just up and hauled ass, all six foot two of him, to hell with enemy gunfire. Soon enough, "Doc" had developed a reputation more important than any medal or honor could confer. Doc, the men said, was a crazy motherfucker.

Chatterton had been with the platoon for about two weeks when word came down: Mouse had been killed. His squad had taken prisoners and Mouse had been asked to watch the captives. An enemy sniper crept up on the location and looked for a target. He might have chosen one of several Americans in range. But Mouse, carrying his .45-caliber pistol, appeared different from the rest—to the enemy, he likely appeared as an officer. The sniper lined up Mouse in his sights and pulled the trigger, hitting the medic several times.

If Chatterton had retained any illusion about Vietnam, such folly vaporized with Mouse's killing. He traded in his .45 pistol for an M-16 rifle. He had come to Vietnam looking for answers about America and about mankind, and suddenly those answers seemed obvious: America was wrong to be in Vietnam; men killed one another because they are animals. So he had his answers, big fucking deal. Yet Chatterton still found himself volunteering for every patrol and running for every wounded guy, and when he sat against trees to catch his breath he marveled at how full life felt when a person got to be excellent, and he began to wonder if he might have come to Vietnam to answer questions of a different kind.

"People talked about this kid Chatterton," says Dr. Norman Sakai, the battalion surgeon. "I hadn't met him yet. But the first thing you heard about him was that he walked point. That seemed unbelievable to me. Medics weren't supposed to engage in war. Even going on patrol was stretching it for a medic. But walking point? You never heard of a medic walking point. I thought maybe this guy was crazy. But people said no, he was different. People talked about him all the time."

As weeks turned to months and Chatterton continued to distinguish himself, he studied himself and others in action, watched soldiers live and die and show courage and break down, paid careful attention to the behavior of men around him, all to divine further insight into the right way to live. Gradually, he distilled certain principles that seemed to him indisputable truths, and he collected these principles like so many medicines in the aid pack of his mind. As he neared the end of his six-month field obligation, he had come to believe these things:

— If an undertaking was easy, someone else already would have done it.
— If you follow in another's footsteps, you miss the problems really worth solving.
— Excellence is born of preparation, dedication, focus, and tenacity; compromise on any of these and you become average.
— Every so often, life presents a great moment of decision, an intersection at which a man must decide to stop or go; a person lives with these decisions forever.
— Examine everything; not all is as it seems or as people tell you.
— It is easiest to live with a decision if it is based on an earnest sense of right and wrong.

— The guy who gets killed is often the guy who got nervous. The guy who doesn't care anymore, who has said, "I'm already dead—the fact that I live or die is irrelevant and the only thing that matters is the accounting I give of myself," is the most formidable force in the world.

— The worst possible decision is to give up.

For four months, Chatterton thought about the right way and the wrong way to live, and he continued to contemplate his principles. As one patrol bled into another and men died, his thinking solidified, and he began to consider that it might have been for these insights that he had come to Vietnam, that when he had looked into forever over the Atlantic as a child and felt sure that there was more on the other side, it was these ideas that were calling him, ideas about how a man should live.

In June 1971, after completing his twelve-month tour, Chatterton returned home to begin a two-week leave before returning to Vietnam for a voluntary six-month extension. His mother was stunned at the sight of him. Her son would not sit in a chair or sleep on a bed but would exist only on the floor. He ate off a cocktail table while sitting cross-legged on the ground. When she asked him to speak, he said nothing for a while, then sobbed and told her about men missing the backs of their heads and screaming for their mothers, about starving, about the first time he'd killed someone, about seeing the worst things a person could see. He would go quiet again after that.

His mother picked up the phone and called a family friend with military clout. Chatterton never made it back to Vietnam. He was reassigned to the dispensary at Fort Hamilton in Brooklyn and developed a bad attitude. The army referred him to a psychiatrist, where he pretended to be what they wanted him to be until they certified him as healthy. He married a girl he knew from high school, realized it was a mistake, and had the marriage annulled a few months later. Such was his routine for two years—punching the clock, feeling angry and confused, wondering about his future—until he had completed his four-year obligation to the army.

Then Chatterton decided to leave everything.

* * *

Chatterton spent the years from 1973 to 1978 trying to find a niche. He lived in Florida, where he tried hospital work and attended college. After his father died of a heart attack in 1973 at age forty-eight, he moved to New Jersey and started a small construction business in the resort town of Cape May. None of this work afforded him the feeling of excellence he had realized in Vietnam, a feeling missing from his life since he'd returned to the States.

In the spring of 1978, Chatterton walked to the Cape May docks and approached an acquaintance for a job on a local scallop-fishing boat. A day later he was at sea. The men explained the business: The boat dragged two ten-foot-wide steel dredges along the ocean floor. Every half hour, the dredges would be hauled up and the contents of their attached bags emptied onto the deck. The crew would dig through the buffet of things that lived in the ocean, pull the scallops out, and throw the remaining junk overboard. Then the men would take the scallops into the cutting house and shuck them. When Chatterton asked which of these jobs would be his, the men replied, "All of them."

Chatterton took to scallop fishing from the start. He learned to cut and weld steel, tie knots, splice cable—in short, to do whatever it took, an instinct that resonated inside him. He ate like a king from scruffy-bearded cooks who knew scallops and lobster more intimately than chefs at five-star Parisian restaurants. But the part that moved him was watching the ocean floor come to life on the deck. The massive dredges did not discriminate in what they pulled from the bottom of the Atlantic; along with piles of scallops came Russian fishing nets, whale skulls, bombs, cannonballs, mastodon teeth, muskets. And shipwreck artifacts. Lots of shipwreck artifacts. The other crewmen viewed such artifacts as garbage. To them, scallops equaled money; everything else equaled shit that you kicked over the side. To Chatterton, the everything else was the only thing.

The boat captain paid Chatterton three thousand dollars and a ten-pound bag of scallops for the nine-day trip, a king's ransom in 1978. Better, Chatterton now had a place on the boat. He made several more trips that year, some lucrative, others a flop, none without a treasure chest of ocean artifacts to coax his mind into scenarios.

He began to tote home items until his place looked like a B-movie pirate ship—his television atop a lobster trap, a whale skull on the wall, whale bones on the roof, a Russian fishing net strung across the ceiling and booby-trapped to fall on visitors as they entered through the front door.

For two years, Chatterton earned a handsome living and learned the sea as a scallop fisherman. He often vowed to go scuba diving, but his intense and unpredictable work schedule prevented it. Chatterton promised himself that when things lightened up, he would strap on the tanks and really see the ocean.

In 1980, flush from another successful scallop run, Chatterton met Kathy Caster, a co-owner of a tiny dockside restaurant in Cape May. He knew he was interested in Kathy before they finished their first drink. While many women Chatterton knew had locked on to safe and predictable paths, Kathy's life had been creative and open-ended. She had grown up in nearby Atlantic City but had fled to test the California life after graduating from high school. She wore peasant dresses, a sheepskin coat, Stevie Nicks blond hair, and one-day-at-a-time cool. When people talked about Woodstock, she told them she had not only attended the festival but had lived in the town, too.

Chatterton loved her pragmatism perhaps most of all. Kathy did not go in for the girly activities typical of many women he knew. She disliked beauty shops and thought shopping boring. She preferred active sports and the outdoors, and respected that Chatterton made his living on the seas, with his hands.

And Kathy did not seem frightened by him. He was twenty-nine years old but had no college plans. He went to sea for weeks at a time in terrible storms. He was nowhere close to finding himself. Caster respected these qualities. When Chatterton told her he wasn't sure where he was going in life, she told him she believed in him.

Kathy and Chatterton moved in together. He bought her a .380 pistol to keep in the home for protection while he was out at sea. At the shooting range, he admired her facility with a gun; she had never fired a weapon before, but the bull's-eyes on the targets kept exploding. This was his kind of girl. Neither seemed in any hurry to marry or have children, and the union felt relaxed and open-ended. "If a woman can put up with these whale bones," Chatterton thought, "I think she can put up with me."

The couple had lived together for less than a year when, in 1981, the bottom fell out of the scallop market and Chatterton's earnings plummeted. Kathy's restaurant had closed, leaving the couple financially strained. Chatterton signed up for a grueling seventeen-day trip. When the captain wrote him a check for $85 at the end, he knew it was time to quit the scallop business.

At home, he and Kathy discussed the future. His G.I. Bill benefits expired in a year, in 1983, so if he intended to go back to school he needed to do it now. Chatterton found computers fascinating and figured them to be the future. He enrolled in a programming course and was given a starting date.

On the eve of the first class, Chatterton awoke from his sleep and sat bolt upright in bed. He shook Kathy until she awakened. She thought he was having a nightmare or a Vietnam flashback. She grabbed him without turning on the lights.

"Kathy, Kathy, Kathy—"

"John, what's wrong?"

"I can't become a computer programmer."

"What are you saying?"

"I can't spend my life sitting under fluorescent lights."

"Okay, okay. You have to be happy, John."

"I know what I'm going to do now. I'm going to be a commercial diver."

"What's that?"

"I don't exactly know. I don't know yet, but it just feels right to me . . . a commercial diver."

He fell back to sleep content.

Chatterton did not know what commercial divers did or where they worked. But he felt like the clouds had parted and the rays were coming down. The next day, he rushed out to buy an issue of *Skin Diver* magazine. Inside were ads for commercial diving schools. Now the idea seemed perfect. He had experience in carpentry, steelworking, respiratory medicine, and diving. He was a natural in the water. A school in Camden offered classes. Two months later he drove his purple Gremlin to that school to pursue his new dream.

Chatterton had been in class just a few minutes before he concluded that commercial diving was indeed his calling. The instructor said commercial divers made a career of one-of-a-kind jobs, improvising and solving problems on the spot, working in hostile and rapidly changing environments. Chatterton could barely sit still. This was the setup under which he remembered being great in Vietnam.

He took to the muscular tools of the trade—the twenty-five-pound Desco Pot helmet made of spun copper, the air hoses that connected the diver to topside air generators, the thick neoprene gloves, the dry suit—all of it felt like a second skin. As the four-month course wore on, Chatterton wondered how he had ever gone so long without knowing a man could get paid for diving.

After graduation, Chatterton signed on with a commercial diving outfit that worked in New York Harbor. In his first month he made perhaps fifty dives, each unique in its setting and challenge. In a single week he might be asked to demolish underwater concrete or install experimental pile wrap at the Port Authority Heliport or weld a rusted support beam under South Street. Every time he told his bosses, "I can do it."

Chatterton faced immense problems in the waters beneath Manhattan. He often worked in zero visibility—in tunnels or caves or under structures so dense in silt and sediment that he could not see his own glove pressed against his face mask. He was asked to pretzel himself into inhuman spaces, then do detailed work inside. His thick neoprene gloves short-circuited his tactile sense. In winter, his dry suit became Saran Wrap in the freezing New York Harbor waters. Overnight tides worked like vandals to undo his daily progress.

At home, Chatterton told Kathy, "This job was made for me." He felt centered in the water, relaxed when straitjacketed between steel beams, at peace even without his eyes. He volunteered for everything, an act that felt like an old friend.

Chatterton liked to challenge himself. On days when the visibility dropped to zero, he pressed his body against the crevices of his surroundings, assembling impressions from elbows, knees, neck, even fins until the work site came to life like a painting in his imagination. He made hands of his every body part, at once placing, say, a left calf against a wall for orientation, a right knee atop an important set of wrenches, and a boot outside a hole as a barometer for changes in current. As he spent more time in the water, his sense of touch heightened to such a pitch that he could distinguish ordinary steel from burned steel solely by the different vibrations each made against his knife. Often, he needed only brush an ankle or a weight belt against an object to deduce that object's identity and condition.

Chatterton's independence from eyesight freed his imagination. He began to visualize story lines for his dives, imagining how a shackle would fall if it slipped his grip, how he might reorient himself in a tunnel should a support beam crack, how he could slither out a cave's crack if the front end collapsed. Over the next year he came to believe that he could see with his mind and body as sharply as he could with his eyes, and this granted him an unteachable calm. When things went wrong in the water, even in total darkness or a crescendoing chaos, he didn't panic, because he believed he could see. Soon he was negotiating the tightest and most dangerous spaces in the commercial diving business, feeling with his body, feeling with his equipment, feeling with his tools, confident that he was safe so long as those paintings kept showing in his mind. Topside crews began to call Chatterton a natural.

In good visibility he watched everything. He studied the ways objects fell through water, the effect of current on sediment, the stages of metallic decomposition, the patterns in which water danced around man-made things, the orientation of wood chips as they became buried in sand. All of it was interesting to him. All of it, he believed, could be useful to him on future dives, even if he could not figure out how at the moment.

He planned relentlessly. Driving to work he rehearsed the movements of his dive the way a ballet dancer envisions his program, prioritizing procedures and even calculating the order in which he would use his tools, and he would not get into the water until he was satisfied that the plan accounted for every contingency. He remembered well what happened to soldiers in Vietnam who waited until the action started to think about how to move. In this way he minimized the need to make decisions underwater, where any number of other factors could thin his judgment.

Most of all, Chatterton refused to give up. He began to see that a commercial diver could be a top welder, an expert demolition man, a champion pipe fitter, but if he wasn't compelled by blood and instinct to finish the job—no matter what—he could never be great. "No matter what" happened every day in commercial diving, and it was for those moments that Chatterton lived, and it occurred to him that it was for those moments that he had been living for a long time. One day, he broke the welding lens in his helmet. Replacing it would hold up the project. He decided to weld without one, eyes closed—a blind welder. The men topside just stared when Chatterton came up with the broken lens and said, "Job's done, fellas." Chatterton drove home grateful that night that he had found a calling, a life's work that allowed him to be excellent again.

By 1985, Chatterton had joined the dock builders' union, moved to Hackensack, New Jersey, and was earning an excellent salary and benefits as a commercial diver. He dedicated much of his free time to scuba diving off nearby beaches, especially at a nearby Catholic retreat where two small shipwrecks, one steel and one wood, lay in the shallows just a few hundred feet offshore. Chatterton never tired of exploring them.

The small wrecks made Chatterton want to see more. He dropped in at a dive shop to inquire about other nearby shipwrecks. A clerk nodded toward a pile of green mimeographed flyers announcing the shop's upcoming charter schedule. Chatterton ran his eyes over the smudged writing, gulping wondrous names like USS *San Diego* and *Mohawk* and *Texas Tower*. Listed under trips for August was a name that stopped him: *Andrea Doria*. Chatterton could scarcely believe it—the *Andrea Doria* was famous, it was history. Television had made documentaries about the wreck. He asked the clerk if there was still space on the *Andrea Doria* trip.

"The *Doria* is Mount Everest, buddy," the clerk told him. "It's only for the best. Guys die on the *Doria*. Start with something smaller."

Chatterton signed up for charters to modest inshore wrecks. Each trip fascinated him for the history he envisioned attached to the ship. He returned from these dives so enthusiastic that Kathy found herself signing up for diving lessons. Together, they explored dozens of nearby shipwrecks, and Kathy could have been content diving these wrecks. But Chatterton got hungry. He decided to work toward his scuba instructor's certificate, the most sensible way he could think of to prepare to dive the *Doria*.

Late in the summer of 1985, a dive shop owner took stock of Chatterton's passion for shipwreck diving and suggested that he join some of the shop's more experienced divers aboard the *Seeker*, a charter boat owned and run by Bill Nagle, one of the sport's legends. The owner told him, "Nagle can be an abrasive bastard, but you two seem to share a certain spirit about diving."

The *Seeker* was revelation to Chatterton. Nagle and his customers carried double air tanks, sledgehammers, crowbars, backup lights, and three knives. They studied deck plans and traveled offshore, as far as necessary, to explore the best wrecks. Sometimes they even chased sketchy numbers in hopes of finding a virgin wreck, an impulse that floored Chatterton because it seemed so closely parallel to the spirit of the early American explorers, a group he admired.

Nagle hardly grunted toward Chatterton on their first trips together, but Chatterton drank in the captain. Nagle was a pisser— that much was clear before the boat left the dock—but he also seemed consumed with aiming big. Chatterton loitered closer to Nagle, always listening. "What kind of fucking man," Nagle would growl, "says that something's impossible? What kind of man doesn't go look?" Chatterton signed up for every *Seeker* trip available.

On weekends aboard the *Seeker* in 1986, Chatterton began to notice that the skills he had developed at work seemed to transfer naturally to the business of shipwreck exploration. He found himself willing to swim into crushed and dangerous quarters because he knew he could find his way out. He became calm in low visibility, even as mushrooming silt clouds turned shipwrecks black, because he knew that his body could see. He rolled with the unexpected—and much was unexpected on *Seeker* trips—because he believed in "No matter what." In 1986, when Chatterton volunteered to retrieve the dead diver from the *Texas Tower,* no other *Tower* virgin would have considered it. Chatterton went for the guy. Twice.

In 1987, Chatterton proposed to Kathy. Since he had bought her a pistol for home protection, Kathy had transformed her affinity for the weapon into a competitive shooting career. She traveled across the country to matches, and was on her way to owning several national records. The grind was hard on the couple, reminiscent of the days when Chatterton was at sea fishing for weeks at a time. It made them feel as if they were living separate lives. They missed each other when Kathy was on the road.

For his part, Chatterton's intense personal standards of excellence bled into his expectations for others. If a friend or family member or Kathy behaved in a way that Chatterton found wanting, or even believed something that ran counter to his core values, he might go days without speaking to that person. Once, a friend who had promised to help Chatterton rake leaves at nine A.M. arrived instead at noon. Chatterton walked away from the man, then did not speak to him for a month. "He's not reliable," he told Kathy. "I can't be living like that. Reliability is everything."

The couple married on a diving trip to Key West. A few months later, Chatterton earned his scuba instructor's certificate. He now felt ready to challenge the *Andrea Doria*. Nagle was running a five-day marathon to the great wreck, for which Chatterton signed up and chose a bunk. The trip was historic and produced several museum-quality artifacts. The *Doria* was now in Chatterton's blood. He began to dream about the wreck. There were places on the *Doria* that no diver had ever seen, places presumed out of reach. But what did "out of reach" really mean?

In the early months of 1988, Chatterton began training for a return to the *Doria* and asking himself why he was so drawn to shipwrecks. As the *Doria* trip drew closer, he believed he understood. A shipwreck was a vast repository of secrets. Some of these secrets could be uncovered through exploration; they came up in the form of artifacts. Other secrets inside the shipwreck were less tangible.

Those were secrets about the diver himself. A shipwreck gave a man limitless opportunity to know himself if only he cared to find out. He could always press further, dig deeper, find places no one had mastered. To Chatterton, there always seemed to be opportunity on a shipwreck, even the simple wrecks: the opportunity to confront the problems really worth solving, and this meant everything to him, this was the act that made his life feel worthwhile. He started to tell colleagues that wreck diving had a lot to do with finding out about yourself.

For the next three years, Chatterton owned the *Doria*. He penetrated into third class, second class, the first-class galley—all groundbreaking achievements that for years many had thought impossible. In a sport famous for hoarding, he gave away priceless *Doria* artifacts, asking fellow divers, "How many teacups does one guy need?" He gained a reputation as one of the best shipwreck divers on the East Coast; some said he might be among the best in the world. One day Nagle paid him the highest compliment by saying, "When you die no one will ever find your body."

As Nagle spiraled deeper into alcoholism and resentment, Chatterton managed much of his friend's business, so that the *Seeker* could remain viable. He seemed always in good cheer, ready with a dry one-liner and his booming baritone laugh. Yet he was capable of intense reactions when his sense of principle was offended. He could not tolerate the lazy or the immoral in others any more than he could in himself, and pity those offenders who crossed his path.

In 1990, he got word of a dive shop owner who had removed a human bone from the wreckage of *U-853*, a U-boat sunk near Rhode Island. Chatterton phoned him. By now, almost every diver on the East Coast knew Chatterton's name.

"I hear you're taking bones off the 853," Chatterton said.

"Ah, yeah, I guess word gets around," the man replied.

"You got it up in your house?"

"Yeah, I do."

"What the *fuck* are you doing?" Chatterton roared.

The man chuckled nervously.

"I'm not laughing," Chatterton said.

"Look, man, they were the enemy. Fuck the Germans. We won."

Chatterton's voice exploded through the receiver. "I'll tell you what. You're so proud of what you did, I'm going to call the newspapers and have them come over and interview you. Then you can tell them how proud you are to be a grave robber, and everyone in the state will appreciate what a hero you are for stealing bones. Let's make this a big business opportunity for you. I'll call the newspapers right now."

There was silence on the line.

"What do you want me to do?" the man finally asked.

"You know what? You fucked up. And you fucked up bad," Chatterton said. "I'm on your ass now and I'm not going to get off. Those were sailors on that submarine. That's a war grave you robbed. You're going to take that bone back and you're not going to put it on the outside of the wreck, you're going to put it inside the wreck exactly where you fucking found it. And then you're going to call me back and tell me that you did it. And only then will I be off your ass."

A week later, word had it that the bone was back inside the submarine.

By 1991, Nagle's drinking had made it impossible for him to dive. Doctors told him his alcoholism would kill him. Still, at night on the *Seeker* while customers slept, Chatterton and Nagle spoke about exploration, about how diving was really about searching, about how beautiful it would be to find something new and important, something no one knew was there.

CHAPTER FIVE

CHATTERTON STEPPED INSIDE *U-505*, the World War II U-boat on display at Chicago's Museum of Science and Industry. In every direction
fantastical mechanisms jutted from the walls and ceilings in a forest of
technology—gauges, dials, pipes, conduits, speaker tubes, plumbing,
valves, radios, sonar, hatches, switches, levers—every inch a protest
against the idea that men cannot live underwater.

The roomiest spots stretched barely four feet wide and six feet tall—
in many places, two children on the museum tour could not stand side
by side. To pass into some sections, a crewman would have had to
shimmy headfirst through a circular steel door. No one, including the
commander, had a bunk that looked long enough to accommodate his
body.

The audio tour in Chatterton's headphones told about life aboard a
U-boat. Crewmen slept in three shifts on the ship's tiny bunks. In the
forward torpedo room, the U-boat's largest compartment, perhaps two
dozen men slept, worked, and ate atop potatoes, canned goods, containers of sausages, and up to six live torpedoes. Rough seas often
turned U-boats like this one into bathtub toys, tossing crewmen from
their bunks and shaking the boat's single cooking pot from the galley's
dollhouse-like stove. In icy seas, these overhead pipes dripped with
condensation, freezing the necks and scalps of the crewmen; often, the

only escape from the chill was in the diesel motor room, where gargantuan twin engines pounded out deafening metal symphonies, creating one-hundred-plus-degree temperatures with stifling humidity and causing hearing loss to some of its operators. Wafting carbon monoxide produced by the engines chipped away at mental acuity, caused sleep disorders, and became the only recognizable flavor in whatever meal the chef could squeeze out of his postage-stamp-size galley.

Chatterton could see that ventilation was designed for survival, not comfort. U-boats quickly began to stink. Though most U-boats had two bathrooms, or "heads," one was usually reserved for extra provisions, leaving the other to service as many as sixty men. Flushing was a subtle skill taught in training; if performed improperly, ocean water could backwash into the boat and even sink it. In the war's early days, when U-boats spent much of their time on the surface, garbage was hurled overboard. Late in the war, when commanders kept the boats submerged to avoid detection, crews improvised as the trash began to reek. They stuffed waste into torpedo tubes and pressed FIRE every few days—a maneuver they dubbed the *Müllschuss,* or "garbage shot." Soon, the stink on the men exceeded the stink of the garbage. The submarine could accommodate almost no personal effects, including wardrobes. Few men owned a change of underwear, opting for "whore's undies"—a single pair of black shorts that hid the evidence of a month at sea. Chatterton thought, "I cannot believe sixty men lived inside here for months at a time while they terrified the world."

Chatterton moved slowly with the audio tour, pressing STOP on the player every few seconds to orient himself and make careful mental notes. He studied the composition of shelves, components, gauges, and floors, envisioning each as it might appear covered in sea anemones and rust after fifty years on the Atlantic floor. He craned his neck around machinery and into off-limits areas, looking for anything—a tag, a builder's plaque, a diary—inscribed with the U-boat's number so that he might search for the same in New Jersey. Everything he did annoyed other visitors. He blocked impassable aisles, backed up into children, wiggled around seniors. When a tour guide asked him to move along, he exited the U-boat, got back in line, and waited for another turn.

The next time he only pretended to push the buttons on his tape player. In the officers' quarters he took note of wood cabinets that might survive a half century underwater and hold important documents. He stopped for a full five minutes at the chart table, pretending he could not hear people complaining behind him. The chart table stood beneath shelves of navigational instruments; if he could find those instruments on the wreck he might have a prime clue in identifying his sub.

He got into line yet again. This time, his plan was to watch the *U-505* sink from underneath him. Inside the boat he played movies in his mind in which the submarine went down by gunfire, flood, internal explosion, equipment failure. During each movie he imagined how the rooms in front of him would collapse, how wall-mounted instruments might fall, how floors would accordion, how debris would billow. He imagined where the ship might crack to allow a diver access and which places he most effectively might swim through. He got into line six more times, until he knew these movies like old *Honeymooners* episodes and the tour guide smirked at Chatterton's pretension to still be using the headphones.

At O'Hare, Chatterton bought a yellow legal pad, a pen, and a pink highlighter and began sketching *U-505*. He marked in pink the places that might surrender identification tags or other useful artifacts. He made notes like this in the margins: "Builder's plaque on periscope and made of brass—could be the thing." As he boarded the airplane back to New Jersey, he thought, "I accomplished what I came here for. I got a sense, a feeling, an impression of a U-boat."

The return trip to the mystery submarine was scheduled for Saturday, September 21, 1991. The crew and passenger list remained the same but for one addition and one subtraction: Ron Ostrowski had a family obligation and could not attend; Dan Crowell, a boat captain and longtime *Seeker* crewman who had missed the first trip because of a business obligation, joined the roster. As the big date neared, the divers could scarcely sit still for their anticipation.

Some divers, like Doug Roberts and Kevin Brennan, counted down the days by safety-checking their gear and fine-tuning their setups. Others, like Kip Cochran, Paul Skibinski, and John Yurga, continued to research U-boat construction and lore, hoping for some nugget of insight that might steer them to solving the mystery. Everyone savored the buildup. Wreck divers spent careers dreaming of the chance to write history. These men were three days away.

Perhaps no one was more excited than forty-four-year-old Steve Feldman, a top props man at CBS's television studios and the diver who had thanked Chatterton at the end of the discovery trip. Feldman had taken up scuba ten years earlier after a sudden divorce had left him reeling. Feldman had become lonely, obese, and depressed. He chain-smoked Parliaments. His friends thought him a kind, unassuming man and could not stand to watch such a person ache so deeply. They suggested yoga, scuba diving, working out, anything to coax him back into the world. In his thick New York accent he would only say, "Nawww . . ."

One day he forced himself to take a scuba lesson. In the water the world opened up. He devoted every hour of free time to learning the sport. His weight dropped and his face returned—handsome Mediterranean features with a thick black mustache and gleaming blue eyes. He quit smoking and joined a gym, all to make himself a better diver.

For the next few years, Feldman kept his diving shallow and warm. The sport transformed him. The water was a more basic world to him, a place in which a man could be what he was meant to be. He found a girlfriend. He made himself a regular on Captain Paul Hepler's Wednesday "bug runs," then cooked the lobster he bagged for stagehands and soap opera actors back at the CBS kitchen. He bought a tent so that he could change into his gear on winter beach dives.

Soon he was diving shipwrecks. He rarely ventured deeper than 100 feet and he penetrated wrecks only superficially, but he was hooked on the history that wafted from these ships. He began to sign up for as many wreck dives as he could find. Like many New Yorkers, he owned no car, so he often stood on the street outside his apartment at Ninety-seventh Street between Central Park West and Columbus, two hundred pounds of scuba gear on his back and by his sides, trying to flag down a taxi, most of which would slow down to inspect the Martianlike figure before speeding away. Feldman's friends loved the image, but most of all they loved the delight he took in watching the cab drivers' faces as they passed him by, and they loved that this never upset him, even while he waited in the rain.

Feldman arrived at charter boats in what became his trademark uniform: wearing a baseball cap with no logo, jeans, and a T-shirt, and carrying a large takeout container of Cantonese noodles with peanut sauce. No matter how high the seas, no matter how brutal the dive, Feldman always ate those noodles, and the empty box in the garbage can became a sure sign on a charter that "Feld" had been along for the ride.

Before long, Feldman had made himself into an instructor. He made deeper wreck dives—to 120 feet, even to 170 feet once—but stayed mostly shallow and warm, allowing the heavy hitters of the sport to tackle the crazy stuff on the eastern seaboard. When Paul Skibinski, a buddy he knew from Hepler's bug runs, invited him along to chase Bill Nagle's numbers, he leaped at the chance. The names Nagle and Chatterton and *Seeker* were legend in the area; this was his chance to dive with the best.

Feldman returned from the discovery trip transformed. He had splashed shoulder to shoulder with the big shoes. He had touched bottom at 230 feet, far deeper than he had ever dreamed for himself. He was part of a secret group on the lip of history. And he might be the one to identify the wreck. On the Saturday afternoon of the return trip to the submarine, he bought a large box of Cantonese noodles with peanut sauce and lugged his diving gear onto the street. A decade ago he had been lost. Now, as taxi drivers gawked and passed him by, he felt like he was going exactly where he should be going, and this was the thing about diving to Feldman, and it always had been the thing: in the water, self-contained, a man could be what he was meant to be, and when that happened it was impossible to be lost.

The *Seeker* pushed away from its Brielle dock around one A.M. on its journey back to the mystery U-boat. The night was calm and made for sleeping, but everyone stayed awake for this ride. The divers had it figured this way: there were thirteen divers onboard, each of whom could make two dives; that meant twenty-six dives in which someone had a chance to score a single piece of identification. Today, someone would be the man.

Only one man was not giddy. In the wheelhouse, Nagle seemed nervous as he adjusted the loran units and guided the *Seeker* out of the inlet.

"What's wrong, Bill?" Chatterton asked.

"I'm nervous that some son of a bitch is going to jump us on the wreck," Nagle said. "Word has leaked out that we're on to something big here."

"Word has leaked out, has it?" Chatterton asked.

"Seems like it, yeah," Nagle said.

"Well, I wonder how that happened!" Chatterton laughed, his booming voice carrying into the salon below. "If you could've kept your big mouth shut for more than a day, Bill, maybe you'd be relaxed today."

"Ah, shit. I ain't the only one who talked."

"Look, Bill. No one but us goes sixty miles offshore in late September. Bielenda and those guys aren't about doing anything interesting. Even if they've heard that we're doing something great, their laziness would keep them away. They'd want us to do all the hard work first."

"Yeah, John, you're probably right—"

"Oh, wait! Bill, look!" Chatterton teased. "There's Bielenda off to starboard! He's following us!"

"Go to hell."

Six hours later, the *Seeker* reached its destination. The men geared up. Chatterton would splash first and tie in, then go about his dive. While the other divers intended to pick a spot and search for a tag or other piece of identification, Chatterton planned to swim the wreck, orienting himself according to his Chicago memories, looking for nothing but impressions. Only when he understood a wreck did he believe he could formulate a plan to approach it. The strategy made it likely that another diver would beat him to the sub's identity, but Chatterton was willing to take the chance. He staked much of his diving on the principle that preparation came first, so he would not just start digging in hopes that he might get lucky.

Chatterton moved down the anchor line. Visibility was decent, about twenty feet. As he neared the bottom, he could see that the grapple had hooked into a metal mass lying beside the submarine in the sand. Its rectangular shape was unmistakable—this mass was the conning tower, the observation post that was supposed to be atop the submarine. He swam forward a few feet. Now he could see the submarine. It lay in the sand intact and was shaped as in the photo books except for a single, striking difference—this submarine had a gaping hole in its side, perhaps fifteen feet high and thirty feet across. Chatterton understood metal. This wound could have resulted only from a cataclysmic event. This wound was what had caused the conning tower to fall and collapse in the sand. This submarine had not gone down peacefully.

The hole beckoned Chatterton. He could swim inside and search the area for identification before any of the other divers arrived, but that was not according to plan. He swam instead to the top of the wreck and then turned left, studying the boat's topography and making a filmstrip of mental notes. As he neared the end of the wreck he came upon the same torpedo-loading hatch he had seen on the first trip. That hatch, he remembered, had been on the submarine's bow; therefore, the hole torn into the boat must be on its port side. A picture of the submarine began coming together in Chatterton's mind.

Chatterton reversed course and swam the other way. He nearly reached the stern before his dive timer ordered him back to the anchor line for his ascent. The other divers, the first of whom were now descending, would certainly plunge into the hole and start digging. But Chatterton had gotten what he'd come for—knowledge. He could save exploration for his second dive, after he studied that picture in his mind and pieced together exactly where he would be going.

As Chatterton made his way up the anchor line, the next divers reached the wreck. Skibinski and Feldman got inside the hole near the fallen conning tower and began searching the debris. Skibinski found a foot-long tubular piece of equipment he believed might be inscribed with a serial number. For the next several minutes, both he and Feldman dug in earnest, enthralled by the magnitude of promising debris. But both men had sworn to start up the anchor line after just fourteen minutes, no matter how tempting the exploration. Skibinski's watch read thirteen minutes. He tapped Feldman on the shoulder and pointed up. Feldman nodded his okay. Skibinski headed for the anchor line and began his ascent. It had taken discipline to leave such a wellspring of artifacts, but the men had stuck to their conservative plan.

As Skibinski ascended he glanced down for Feldman, who appeared to be examining something on the wreck. "He better stop digging and get his ass up here," Skibinski grumbled through his regulator before ascending another few feet. He looked down again, and this time he noticed that there were no bubbles coming from Feldman's regulator. Narcosis started to hum in the background of his mind. "Something's not right," Skibinski told himself. "I gotta go down there and check." He dropped down the anchor line to his friend.

Skibinski grabbed Feldman and turned him around. Feldman's regulator fell from his mouth. His eyes were not blinking. Skibinski looked deeper into his friend's mask, but Feldman just kept staring back, he would not blink, *a man had to blink, goddamn it, please blink, Steve.* Nothing. Skibinski screamed through his regulator, "Fuck! Fuck! Fuck! Fuck!" while the jungle drums of narcosis began their stampede and he tried to replace the regulator in Feldman's mouth but that mouth just hung open, which confirmed that Feldman wasn't breathing and Skibinski screamed, "Oh, fuck! Oh, fuck!" and Feldman only kept staring at him and Skibinski's head pounded harder and he breathed harder, which made the needle on his air supply drop.

Skibinski wrapped his left arm around Feldman. Questions whizzed through his brain: Should I inflate Feldman's suit with air and shoot him to the surface? Can't do that, the bends would kill him. Should I leave Feldman behind and ensure my own safe and controlled decompression? Can't abandon a friend, can't abandon a friend, can't abandon a friend. Only one option remained: he would carry Feldman with him to the surface. Sometimes unconscious divers snapped out of it with ascent; he had definitely heard about that.

Still negatively buoyant, Feldman was lead in Skibinski's arm. Skibinski pulled with all he had, gulping air as he one-armed himself and his friend up the anchor line, Feldman arched back in the current, arms dangling at his sides, legs slightly apart, eyes staring straight ahead. With each pull Skibinski grew wearier and sucked more air. He made it to 170 feet, 165 feet, 160. Then he saw two divers, Brennan and Roberts, above him coming down.

Skibinski released the anchor line to rest for just a moment. Instantly, he and Feldman began to drift away in the current. Skibinski, knowing that he was burning air and could go lost at sea in a matter of seconds, began kicking furiously to regain the anchor line, thrashing against the current until he could no longer maintain a grip on his friend. He let go of Feldman. The limp diver began sinking rapidly, all the while on his back and staring up, his mouth moving open and closed but no bubbles coming out.

Instinctively, Roberts bolted for the body, but Feldman kept sinking. Roberts knew that by leaving the anchor line and chasing this diver he could go lost himself. But it was a reaction—he could not allow another man to drop into the abyss. At around 200 feet, Roberts thrust out his arm and caught hold of Feldman's harness, but the leaden diver was so heavy that both men continued to plummet toward the sand. Roberts righted himself and began searching desperately for Feldman's buoyancy compensator or dry-suit inflation valve—if he could pump air into Feldman's equipment he might better carry him toward the surface. But Feldman was a morass of equipment, and Roberts could not find any inflation gear under all his stuff. Roberts pumped his own suit full of air, but even that did not arrest the duo's plummet. Both divers hit bottom together. Narcosis began to bang inside Roberts. He looked into Feldman's face. He saw no life. He could not see the wreck. He could not see the anchor line. There was only sand in every direction. "We're in the middle of nowhere," he thought. "I'm in fucking never-never land. I'm lost."

As Roberts sat on the bottom alongside Feldman, a panicked Skibinski regained the anchor line at about 160 feet. His eyes turned giant and he rushed toward Brennan, making the slashing-across-throat motion that indicates a diver is out of air. Brennan had seen the look before—this was panic, the snowball. Skibinski lunged for Brennan's regulator. Brennan backed away; he could not allow Skibinski to kill them both. He reached behind him for his backup regulator and offered it to the thrashing Skibinski. Skibinski took it and started to gulp Brennan's reserve. Brennan began to ascend with Skibinski, stopping with him to do brief decompression stops at 50 feet, 40 feet, all the while thinking, "If Doug's still alive, he's gotta be lost and freaked out. He's alone down there risking his life to get a guy who's already dead. I have a responsibility to Doug. I gotta go get Doug." At around 30 feet, Brennan passed Skibinski off to another diver and bolted for the bottom to search for Roberts, thereby making himself a prime candidate to go lost.

Sitting in the sand with Feldman at ocean's bottom, Roberts checked his gauges; he had burned 60 percent of his air supply struggling with Feldman. If he stayed much longer he would incur a decompression obligation beyond his remaining air. Feldman's body lay next to him in the sand, mouth and eyes agape. Roberts's peripheral vision narrowed with his crescendoing narcosis—he could now see only in front of him. He thought, "If I don't get out of here fast, there will be two of us dead on the bottom." The anchor line was nowhere in sight. He would have to swim for the surface, even though that meant that he would likely be blown miles from the *Seeker* by the time he surfaced. He could only pray that someone topside would see him bobbing on the waves before he went lost at sea and drowned.

Just before ascending, Roberts began to tie a line to Feldman. That way, if anyone found his body, they could find Feldman, too. He strained to wrap the line around Feldman, but his motor skills were blunted and he could not make a good knot. He tried again. Finally, he secured the line and began his ascent.

Roberts did not know exactly how long he had been on the bottom. He ascended. At 100 feet the first trickles of light began to spackle the ocean around him, and he saw a miracle. Somehow, in his ascent, he had been blown back into the *Seeker*'s anchor line, a huge long shot. He tied the thin nylon rope that led to Feldman to the anchor line, then improvised a decompression stop. Brennan reached him moments later. The two of them made their way to the surface.

Brennan climbed aboard the *Seeker* first. Chatterton and Nagle saw him coming up the ladder and figured something was wrong—he had been in the water only a short time.

"There's a problem," Brennan said, pulling off his mask. "There's a guy dead on the wreck. I think it's Feldman."

Chatterton called to Steve Lombardo, a physician who had yet to splash, and asked him to stand by. Nagle rushed down from the wheelhouse. A few minutes later Skibinski climbed the ladder. As he reached the top rung, he pulled off his face mask and began sobbing, "He's dead! He's dead!" Then, before anyone could assist him, he pitched forward and fell face-first onto the *Seeker*'s wooden deck, a three-foot fall. Chatterton, Nagle, and Lombardo rushed to the mumbling diver, believing he might have broken his neck. They moved Skibinski gingerly, trying to remove his gear. Skibinski could only say, "He's dead! I couldn't breathe! My regulator! He's dead!" Chatterton removed the diver's hood. Skibinski was covered in vomit.

"Paul, listen to me," Chatterton said. "Did you do your deco?"

"I don't know . . ."

"You must answer me," Chatterton said. "Did you do your deco?"

"Steve's dead!" Skibinski cried before vomiting again.

"DID YOU DO YOUR DECO?"

Skibinski managed to nod confirmation that he had decompressed.

Roberts surfaced next.

"Feldman's down there! You gotta go get him!" he yelled.

Chatterton did not move. He studied Roberts's face.

"Come on, get going!" Roberts yelled at Chatterton. "Feldman is down there!"

Chatterton noticed blood on Roberts's face. His medic instincts took over. "Let me look in your mask," Chatterton ordered. "You might have embolized."

Chatterton took the mask. It was full of blood. Roberts coughed up more blood through his mouth and nose. Someone yelled, "Get a chopper!" Chatterton retracted into a new level of calm. He looked deeply into Roberts's mouth and nose; the bleeding had stopped.

"I think he busted a blood vessel," Chatterton said. "There's no embolism. Give him oxygen as a precaution. We don't need a chopper."

As he breathed oxygen and settled down, Roberts confirmed that Feldman had been without a regulator for close to thirty minutes, that he had tied Feldman to the line from his reel, and that the reel was now tied to the anchor line at about 100 feet.

Chatterton gathered Nagle and Danny Crowell.

"Before we do anything, we have to get everyone back on the boat and make sure everyone's okay—no injuries, no nervous breakdowns," Chatterton said. "Then we have to go get the body."

"Who's going to go?" Nagle asked.

"Danny and I will go," Chatterton said. "We're crew. We'll go get him."

Crowell nodded. He and Chatterton figured they would have to wait another two hours before they had off-gassed enough nitrogen from their first dives to return safely to the water. Nagle returned to the wheelhouse and locked the door. He had his own decision to make.

Coast Guard rules required boat captains to radio immediately whenever a diver went missing. But nothing said that a captain had to drop everything to radio news of a dead diver. Ordinarily, Nagle or any other captain would have called in Feldman's death straightaway; it was the decent thing to do and would expedite the Coast Guard's mandatory investigation. Nagle just stared at his radios. If he called the Coast Guard now, hours before Chatterton and Crowell could even attempt to recover Feldman's body, he would be broadcasting the wreck's location to every boat and seaman in a thirty-mile radius, any of whom could use a direction finder to zero in on and steal the wreck site. Worse, he believed that Bielenda had moles in the Coast Guard; if he revealed the location—now or ever—it would be just a matter of time before Bielenda raided the submarine and stole the *Seeker*'s glory.

Nagle made a plan. He would radio the Coast Guard only when the *Seeker* was ready to pull up anchor and head back to shore. Even then, he would give them just an approximate location of the accident. "Why the hell do they need to know exactly where this happened?" he reasoned. "They aren't coming out here one way or the other for a dead guy." He left the wheelhouse without touching the radios.

Two hours after Skibinski surfaced, Chatterton and Crowell geared up and went to get Feldman. At around 100 feet they found Roberts's line tied to the anchor line. Feldman should be attached to the line at the bottom of the ocean. Chatterton descended to retrieve the body. He reached the bottom. Connected to the line were Feldman's mask and snorkel, but no body.

Chatterton knew what had happened: in the tunnel vision and slowed motor skills of narcosis, Roberts had tied the line to Feldman's head instead of to his harness or tanks. As the current had tumbleweeded Feldman across the sand, the line had slipped over his head, caught on his mask and snorkel, and come free. Feldman was still somewhere on the ocean bottom. Chatterton and Crowell, however, were out of time and could not continue to search for him. They returned to the boat and gathered the other divers.

"Listen," Chatterton said. "We gotta go down and try to find this guy. He was negatively buoyant, so we know he's not floating on the surface somewhere. He's in the sand and he's off the wreck. I don't know that we can find him. But we gotta look."

The divers held their breath, hoping Chatterton would not say what he said next.

"We gotta do sand sweeps."

Wreck diving offers few more dangerous propositions than the sand sweep. The technique is simple enough: a diver ties a line from his penetration reel to the wreck, then backs up in the direction of the current. When he reaches a distance of, say, twenty feet, he walks a 180-degree arc in the sand, searching for scallops or artifacts—or lost divers. If the search is fruitless, the diver lets out more line, backs up farther, and sweeps a bigger arc. The diver's life depends on his line. If he loses the line—if it gets cut on debris or slips from his grip or frays against the wreck—he is gone, a nomad in a featureless landscape without any direction back to the wreck. He then must free-ascend, risking a sloppy decompression and the likelihood that he will surface miles from the dive boat and go lost at sea.

Chatterton asked for volunteers. It was no small request. The day was getting late and everyone's nerves were shot, a petri dish for narcosis. And no one could help Feldman, anyway.

Many divers still had two or three hours of off-gassing obligation and could not get back into the water before dark. Nagle was in no physical condition to dive. That left just four or five candidates.

Brennan shook his head.

"The guy's already dead," he told Chatterton. "I'm not getting bent or going lost to help a dead guy. I already almost drowned from Skibinski panicking, and I cut my deco short. The current is whipping now. There's nothing I can do for the guy. I'm not risking my life."

Chatterton would not risk sending Roberts back into the water. Skibinski was an emotional wreck. John Hildemann and Mark McMahon stepped forward. They would do the sweeps. Hildemann would go first—he was the only diver who had not yet been in the water. If necessary, McMahon would follow.

At the bottom, Hildemann attached a strobe to the anchor line. Visibility was perhaps thirty feet. The current blasted past his face. He paid out some line. He walked his arc and scanned the ocean floor. In every direction he was alone. The bloody green of the water grew more eerie with each pass. He found broken pieces of wood but nothing else.

McMahon was next. He tied his penetration line to the top of the wreck, then backed up slowly, allowing forty feet of line to unspool from his reel, never taking his eyes off the wreck. When the line went taut, he began sweeping, hovering ten feet above the ocean bottom to broaden his perspective. Nothing. He let out another twenty-five feet and began drifting backward. The wreck faded into wavy shadow, then disappeared. Now, wherever he looked, McMahon saw only dirty green water, sideways white particulates, and his one-eighth-inch white line stretching into the darkness. But no body. The jungle drums beat louder. He let out another twenty-five feet. A crab popped out of the sand and spoke to him.

"Keep coming, Mark," the crab said. "Keep coming, man."

McMahon was startled. But he was also enchanted. He stopped sweeping and looked closer. More crabs popped out of the sand. They all waved their claws to him. Each of them spoke perfect English.

"Over here, Mark, over here," they said. "Keep coming . . ."

McMahon wondered if he should follow the crabs out to sea. He took a deep breath. He started talking to himself. "I gotta get outta here," he said. "Crabs are talking to me. When a crab talks it's time to go home."

On board, McMahon told the divers that he, too, had come up empty. By now, Feldman could have drifted five miles from the boat. Dusk was approaching. It was a terrible thing to leave a diver behind, and it would be crushing for his family. But Chatterton and Nagle had reached a limit. "Someone is gonna get killed if we keep looking," Chatterton said. He and Nagle agreed to pull up anchor and head back to shore.

In the wheelhouse, Nagle radioed the Coast Guard and reported a dead diver. It was four P.M.—five hours since he had first heard that Feldman had died. When the Coast Guard asked why he had not called sooner, Nagle told them he had been busy getting divers out of the water and then organizing the underwater searches. When they asked him for the accident location, he gave them rough coordinates, within a few square miles of the site; that would keep claim jumpers—and especially Bielenda—away from what rightfully belonged to the *Seeker*.

The Coast Guard ordered Nagle to Manasquan, New Jersey, where it said it would meet the *Seeker* at the pier. The five-hour ride was melancholy and quiet. Some divers tried to console Skibinski, assuring him that he had done everything possible for his friend. Many speculated as to what had caused the accident, the consensus being that Feldman had succumbed to deep-water blackout, a not-uncommon condition of sudden unconsciousness that afflicted divers for reasons science still did not understand.

The *Seeker* arrived at the U.S. Coast Guard Station in Manasquan Inlet at about ten P.M. Each man aboard the boat was taken inside and asked to write an account of the incident, then was released. Driving home that night, Skibinski thought back to a conversation he'd had with Feldman over dinner the night before. They had been discussing the trip—who was going, what they might find, the submarine's identity, and especially how happy they were for the opportunity. Out of nowhere, Feldman had said, "If I ever die, I want to die diving because I love it so much." Now, nearing home,

Skibinski reached into his wallet for a phone number. At an Exxon station he called Feldman's close friend Buddy and told him the bad news.

Most of the divers called wives and girlfriends from the dock and told them about Feldman. They did so to let the women know they were okay and because they needed someone awake when they got home.

Brennan returned after midnight. After his girlfriend went to sleep, he called Richie Kohler. This time, he played no Italian-accent guessing games with his friend.

"Richie, man, it's Kevin. Something terrible happened."

Brennan's voice sounded so flat Kohler barely recognized it.

"What time is it, Kevin?"

"You know Feldman?"

"No. Who is he?"

"He's dead."

"Who's Feldman?"

"Paul's partner. He's fucking dead. Oh, man, Richie . . ."

"Kevin, what happened? Go slow and tell me what happened."

Brennan could choke out only the most basic details.

"I gotta go, Richie. I'll call you tomorrow and tell you the whole story."

Kohler hung up the phone. He felt bad for the dead diver. But he had just one thought as he climbed into bed, and that thought hung over him until morning: he had to replace Feldman on the next trip.

Brennan called back the next day and told Kohler the whole story. At the end, Kohler spoke frankly; the men were tight and always Brooklyn direct with each other.

"Kevin, you gotta get me on the next trip."

"I know, Richie. I'll talk to Bill today."

Brennan pitched Kohler that afternoon. To Nagle, the idea seemed perfect. Kohler was smart, tough, and relentless, one of the best wreck divers on the eastern seaboard. He had steeped himself in World War II history and knew German lore and artifacts. He was at home in crazy-deep water. And he would not go and get himself killed—the last thing Nagle needed after the Feldman accident.

Ordinarily, Kohler would have been included from the start of the expedition. But there were issues. First, Chatterton disliked Kohler, not just personally but for what he represented. Kohler was a member of the infamous Atlantic Wreck Divers, a hard-core and exclusionary dive gang that wore matching skull-and-crossbones patches sewn onto their denim jackets and raised hell on the boats they chartered. They were fearless and first-rate wreck divers—Chatterton would give them that—but he despised their overriding lust for tonnage, a collective instinct to take every last piece of crap from a wreck until their goody bags bloated with artifacts and their supposed manhood. None of them seemed to Chatterton to love diving for knowledge or exploration or for what the sport might reveal to a man about himself. They wanted shit and lots of it, period.

If Kohler's membership in Atlantic Wreck Divers was his only failing, Chatterton could have forgiven that; he dove often with a few of the gang's members and liked those men personally. But Kohler had committed a far graver sin, maybe the worst sin, and it was this black mark that lingered with Chatterton. Two years earlier, Kohler and others had set out on a mission that would fuck the *Seeker*.

Late in 1989, Chatterton had squeezed through a tiny opening that led to the third-class dining room on the *Andrea Doria*. Many divers had spent years trying to access third class, but none had succeeded. Inside, Chatterton saw mountains of glistening white china, more than *Seeker* divers could haul out in years. Chatterton considered it a big opportunity for Nagle: divers would kill for a place on *Seeker* charters for access to these artifacts. The problem was that few besides Chatterton had the skill to shimmy through such a tight opening. He proposed a wild solution: he could use a Broco underwater torch on the next trip and burn away one of the steel bars blocking the opening. After that, anyone could swim in. Nagle told him, "You are one amazing son of a bitch."

On a special *Seeker* run to the *Doria*, Chatterton assembled the torch and rigged its onboard oxygen cylinder and the hoses that delivered its fuel. Underwater, he changed into a diving mask to which he had taped a welding shield and fired up the Broco. The torch spit blinding red and white sparks as its ten-thousand-degree Fahrenheit rod boiled the ocean around it. That day, *Seeker* divers hauled perhaps a hundred bowls and dishes from the *Doria,* the first artifacts ever to come out of third class. One of the divers took video to commemorate the historic occasion. At the trip's end, Nagle gathered the divers.

"It's too late in the season to come back," he said. "But first thing next year, we come back and kick ass in third class."

A short time later, someone from the *Seeker* turned traitor. A copy of the videotape was leaked. Kohler and some other members of the Atlantic Wreck Divers watched the tape, astounded as Chatterton used the Broco to burn his way in—impossible! As the bar fell away and the hole opened up, the video showed a white mountain of dishes inside that looked piled by Walt Disney himself. More than one man muttered, "Holy shit."

The video lasted just a few minutes. Kohler had never seen a bounty like this. Every cell in his body lusted for the easy ransom glistening in the room that Chatterton had opened. But there was bad news: word had it that Chatterton and Nagle were planning to go back to the *Doria* early the next season, long before most boats would even consider tackling that wreck. Their mission: to haul every last artifact from the area and leave nothing for Bielenda or the *Wahoo.*

Often, a ribbon of salvation runs through the lives of deep-shipwreck divers. This time, that ribbon weighed two hundred and fifteen pounds. Bielenda had planned his own trip to the *Doria,* a charter scheduled just two days before the *Seeker*'s. Kohler and the others could be there just in time to waltz into Chatterton's area and take away as much as they could carry, leaving the site damn near empty by the time the *Seeker* got there. Knowing the bad blood between Bielenda and Nagle, Kohler believed this to be a heaven-sent opportunity for Bielenda. But the idea of beating Nagle to the *Doria* grinded against Kohler's ethic: you don't jump another guy's claim. Still, the video was irresistible, the china so magnificent and endless. Kohler had met Chatterton just once, briefly, so he was not concerned about the skinny guy with the blowtorch. He liked and respected Nagle, and had had only positive experiences aboard the *Seeker*. He also believed Bielenda a blowhard and a follower, not a doer. He snickered at the name "King of the Deep." But the china was so beautiful and stacked like snowy mountains, and his fellow AWD guys were going and . . .

"Sign me up," he told Bielenda. Kohler could not remember ever seeing Bielenda so ravenous to lead a charter.

Bielenda's trip was scheduled for June 23. Kohler kept his mouth shut about the charter. But someone's conscience had kicked in. The plan was leaked to Nagle, including the date of the *Wahoo* trip. Nagle called Chatterton, drunk and furious.

"Those motherfuckers!" he screamed into the telephone. "We gotta do something!"

Chatterton devised his own plan. He and Glen Plokhoy, an engineer and frequent *Seeker* diver, would build a metal grate to block the opening Chatterton had burned into third class. The *Seeker* would go to the *Doria* two days before Bielenda's trip. They would fill their bags with china. Then Chatterton and Plokhoy would install the grate. When the *Wahoo* divers arrived they would find the hole closed.

The plan sounded perfect to Nagle. But Chatterton never stopped at phase one of any plan. He formulated additional criteria:

— He and Plokhoy would design a grate that they could open and close; simply welding a grate in place would lock out everyone, including *Seeker* divers.
— The grate must appear to the *Wahoo* divers to be loose and easily removable so that they would waste time and look foolish struggling with it.
— The grate must still allow a diver to pass through the tiny opening Chatterton had originally wiggled into so that anyone wanting to work to get in, as Chatterton had, retained that opportunity.

Chatterton and Plokhoy went to work on the design in a local dive shop's classroom. They studied the videotape and took reference measurements, then sketched plans for a five-by-six-foot, three-hundred-pound iron grate. Rather than weld it into place, they would chain it down, so that the grate would shake and the *Wahoo* divers would believe it was loose. They engineered a device that could be unlocked only by a custom-made wrench, and then had a friend make the wrench. Finally, they squirted grease into the grate's recessed bolt assembly to disguise the custom nature of the lock—the divers on Bielenda's boat would be like monkeys trying to open the grate with standard wrenches.

The *Seeker* set out for the *Doria* forty-eight hours before Bielenda's scheduled trip. For two days, the divers were Christmas elves, stuffing their bags with third-class china until they could not carry any more. On the afternoon of the second day, Chatterton and Plokhoy suited up to install the grate. They told Nagle that they planned to leave a sign for Bielenda and the *Wahoo* divers, something clever and subtle that would make their point. Nagle's face turned red.

"You should write, FUCK YOU, BIELENDA, YOU PIECE OF SHIT!"

"I don't know if that's exactly our point," Chatterton said. "Anyway, we've already prepared a message."

The installation of the grate was flawless. It shook but did not give. It looked easy but was bulletproof. Chatterton reached into his bag for the slate and tie-wrapped it to the grate. In block letters he had written:

CLOSED FOR INVENTORY
PLEASE USE ALTERNATE ENTRANCE
THANK YOU
CREW AND PATRONS OF *SEEKER*

Bielenda's boat set out that evening for the *Doria*. As the *Wahoo* settled over the great wreck, two crew members splashed to set the hook as close to the third-class hole as possible. Bielenda then had divers draw straws for the chance to enter the hole first. Kohler and fellow Atlantic Wreck Diver Pete Guglieri won. They made a simple plan: fill as many bags as humanly possible. As Kohler splashed, he could not remember ever having been more excited.

The divers hit the wreck a minute later and came face-to-face with Chatterton's sign. For a time they simply hung there flabbergasted. Then they got mad. Guglieri shook the grate. Kohler pounded it with his sledgehammer. They inspected the grate from every angle, trying to figure a way to beat the lock. Both men worked in construction and understood how things came apart. They tried every trick they knew. Nothing worked. Kohler nearly lost consciousness from anger. Once his air supply was depleted, he could do nothing more than cut off the sign Chatterton had left.

When the divers returned to the *Wahoo,* Bielenda and the others crowded around for the first report.

"How'd we do?" Bielenda asked.

The divers described the grate.

"Those cocksuckers!" Bielenda screamed.

Furious, Bielenda paced and stomped and screamed. Someone suggested chaining the *Wahoo* to the grate and yanking it off. Bielenda rejected the idea, reminding them that the *Wahoo* was just a forty-nine-ton boat.

As Kohler and Guglieri undressed, Guglieri began to laugh.

"What is so fucking funny?" Kohler asked.

"Give them credit," Guglieri said. "They found it first. And that grate is some piece of work. More power to them."

For a moment Kohler glared at his partner. Then his eyes turned up at the corners. A second later he was laughing full out with his friend.

"You're right," Kohler said. "We tried to fuck them and they fucked us first."

Now, more than a year later, Nagle could forgive Kohler. Diving was a carnivorous business; these things happened every so often and had to be allowed to blow over. Kohler, in the interim, had had a nasty falling-out with Bielenda and had sworn off the King of the Deep forever. To Nagle, Kohler seemed the only natural choice as Feldman's replacement.

Chatterton was another matter. A man of honor and principle, he would feel differently about sharing such an important dive with a person who had once set out to screw him. Nagle balanced the concerns in his mind. He respected Chatterton more than anyone. But this dive was too big; it was history. He needed the best divers in his arsenal. He told Brennan to give Kohler the green light.

Word of Feldman's death ricocheted through the wreck-diving community. Divers everywhere now knew that the *Seeker* had discovered a submarine. As the workweek began, Nagle's phone rang off the hook with requests from divers, including many who had passed on the discovery trip, to join the team. He invited two of these divers along: Brad Sheard, an aerospace engineer and underwater photographer, and Steve McDougal, a state trooper. They would replace Lloyd Garrick, who took some time off from diving shortly after the incident, and Dick Shoe, who remained willing to dive the *Doria* and other deadly wrecks but vowed never to return to something so dangerous as this submarine.

Nagle planned a return trip to the wreck site for September 29, just eight days after the Feldman incident. Kohler arrived at the dock at around ten P.M. dressed in full gang colors—denim jacket, skull-and-crossbones patch, and "Atlantic Wreck Divers" logo. Chatterton was already aboard and tying down his gear. "Ay! A little help ovah hee-ah?" Kohler asked into the air with an accent atomized from the stoops of Brooklyn. "How's the wauta look? Any of yooz seen Kevin?"

Chatterton, already aboard and joking with another diver, went silent. Without looking up, he knew that this was the sound of East Coast gang diving, the noise of the artifact pirate, the voice of the guy who had tried to screw him on the *Doria*. He turned away from his conversation and took a step toward the dock where Kohler stood. A half dozen conversations around the boat faded to hush. Nagle, who lived for a good blood feud, pressed his face against the glass of the wheelhouse above. Kohler stepped forward so that the toes of his tennis shoes hung over the water. Each man shot his convictions into the other's stare. Kohler's shoulders twitched, just enough to give life to the "Atlantic Wreck Divers" patch spread winglike across his back. Chatterton hated the jacket and took another step forward. Ordinarily, either of them might have pressed the plunger then. Tonight, however, neither moved farther. Feldman was just eight days dead and still missing. Brennan stepped forward and said, "Here, Richie, hand me your shit." With that, Chatterton returned to packing his gear and Kohler stepped onto the *Seeker* for his first trip to the mystery U-boat.

The *Seeker* left Brielle around midnight. Kohler and Brennan remained on deck, watching the shoreline disappear and debating the wreck. Kohler believed, as he had on first hearing of the discovery, that the divers had found the *Spikefish,* the World War II American submarine sunk in the 1960s for target practice. Brennan insisted it was a German U-boat and told Kohler, "When you get down there you'll know. You'll hear the music."

Chatterton splashed first and tied in the grapple. His plan was trademark: shoot video, forgo artifacts, return with knowledge. He often used video cameras, which picked up underwater nuances that were beyond the human eye, then watched the tapes topside, learning wreck topographies and planning his second dive. At home, he watched the tapes dozens of times more.

Chatterton swam into the gaping hole in the submarine's side and turned his camera in all directions, careful to record the way in which the mechanical chaos splaying from the boat's wounds might catch and trap a diver. He then backed out and swam over the wreck, first toward the forward torpedo-loading hatch, then to the stern area, where, except for a portion of one blade, the propeller lay buried in the sand. When his time ran out, he returned to the anchor line and began his ascent. Once again, he would finish a dive without recovering an artifact.

Kohler and Brennan followed. Immediately, Kohler recognized the narrowness of the wreck for a submarine. The divers swam aft and above the ship until reaching an open hatch. The sight stopped Kohler in his tracks—submarine hatches were supposed to be closed. He shined his light inside. A ladder led downward into darkness.

"Someone had to have opened that hatch," Kohler thought. He envisioned water flooding in and men screaming and scrambling up the ladder and opening that hatch to escape.

Kohler pulled his head out of the hatch and he and Brennan began their ascent to the surface. Kohler had hoped to find some artifact, anything, written in English to prove that the submarine was the *Spikefish,* but he'd found nothing. When he climbed aboard the *Seeker,* he undressed and sat down for lunch in the salon. Nearby, Chatterton studied his videotape on the room's tiny television. Other divers discussed their findings. No one, it turned out, had recovered anything meaningful.

Around noon, Chatterton dressed for his second dive. Brennan, slightly bent and achy in his joints from his dive, packed his gear away and called it a day. Kohler geared up by himself and would make his second dive alone. He and Chatterton never considered diving together, but the two of them splashed within minutes of each other.

This time Chatterton intended to penetrate the submarine. He swam toward the fallen conning tower, which lay beside the submarine like a mobster gunned down beside his car. A single pipe connected the fallen tower to the body of the submarine. From diagrams he had seen, Chatterton recognized the pipe as one of the ship's two periscopes. He drifted inside the conning tower, where the periscope's other end remained in its protective metal housing, a kind of armor shaped like a Spartan's helmet with a section cut out for the lens. Chatterton recalled having seen a builder's plaque attached to the periscope housing in photographs of the *U-505.* He doubled back to the control room and searched for the plaque inside this cramped conning tower but found nothing—whatever identification might have existed here had been eaten away by nature or disintegrated through violence. At the top of the conning tower he saw the hatch that allowed crewmen to enter and exit. The hatch was open.

Chatterton reversed field and exited the conning tower. He now faced the submarine's gaping hole. He swam inside and then through a small circular hatch, the one through which crewmen ducked when traveling between the control room and the officers' quarters or the sound and radio rooms. The bulkhead that connected the hatch to the submarine's body was blown out on the port side, a condition Chatterton knew must have resulted from a devastating force. He finger-walked forward, meticulously avoiding the forest of bent pipes, jagged metal, and traumatized electrical cables that blurted from walls and ceiling. The water inside the submarine was still, the particulates scarce and hovering. The submarine's ribs, intact and visible, arched across the curved ceiling. Chatterton was likely now in the sound and radio rooms and across from the commander's quarters. He continued forward, jutting left through one rectangular doorway and right through another, until he came to an area filled with elbow-shaped pipes and cracked metal flooring. Something tugged at his instincts. He studied his Chicago memories, the movies he had made of *U-505* collapsing around him. There might be a cabinet here, he thought, though it likely would not look like a cabinet anymore. He swam left and shined his light. Dark fish with white whiskers scurried away. He stopped moving and allowed his eyes to adjust. A cabinet shape appeared before him as if from a vapor. He still did not move. The rims of bowls and plates seemed to protrude from the cabinet. He swam forward and reached for the china. Two bowls came loose. He brought them to his face. The fronts were white with green rims. On the backs, engraved in black, was the year 1942. Above that marking were the eagle and the swastika, the symbol of Hitler's Third Reich.

At the same time, Kohler was completing his second dive. He had swum to the open hatch inside the U-boat's hole, but by this time Chatterton had disturbed the visibility enough so that Kohler did not dare enter. Instead, he ventured inside the fallen conning tower and found a piece of speaker tube, the kind a crewman would talk into, but it revealed no writing. He stuffed it in his goody bag and began his ascent to the surface.

Chatterton checked his watch and saw that it was time to go. Foot by foot he retraced his path, until he emerged from the submarine and found the anchor line. He was exuberant as he ascended—his planning and homework had paid off. He would give Nagle one of these bowls. The look on the captain's face would be priceless.

For nearly an hour, both Chatterton and Kohler ascended and decompressed, each unaware that the other was nearby. At 30 feet, Chatterton caught up to Kohler and settled just below him. Kohler angled his head sideways to steal a glimpse at Chatterton's bag. Kohler could not contain himself—he lived for artifacts and was powerless at the sight of a bulging goody bag. He released the anchor line and drifted down to Chatterton. The divers were now eye to eye. The unmistakable bone white of china seemed to light the ocean around Chatterton. Kohler's face flushed and his heart pounded. There was history in Chatterton's bag; he could smell it. He reached for the bag.

Chatterton snatched the bag away and turned his shoulder to block Kohler. The divers' bodies tensed. Their eyes locked. No one moved for what seemed like minutes. The men did not like each other. They did not like what the other represented. And you don't touch a guy's shit. But as Chatterton searched Kohler's eyes he could not find anything sinister in them; the man was just flat-out excited to see the china. Chatterton opened his shoulder, slowly at first, and pushed the bag forward. Through the mesh Kohler could see the eagle and swastika and he erupted, screaming through his regulator, "Holy shit! You did it! I can't believe this! You did it!" For a minute he danced like a child as he held the bag, twirling and kicking and punching Chatterton in the arm, looking away and then back again to make sure he was seeing what he thought he was seeing. Now there was no doubt. The divers had discovered a German U-boat.

Chatterton did his best to block Kohler's celebration punches as the two ascended to their next stop. On board the *Seeker*, Nagle held the bowls and could only repeat, "Fuckin'-A . . . fuckin'-A . . ." The other divers slapped Chatterton's back and snapped photos of him holding the bowls.

As the *Seeker* steamed home and many of the divers retired to the salon to sleep, Chatterton and Kohler found themselves sitting together atop a cooler. The trip had overwhelmed Kohler; it had brought together, in a single day, his passions for naval history, submarines, exploration, and artifacts. It had made him feel a part of history. For a while, he and Chatterton discussed the U-boat's construction, its damage, those open hatches. Neither of them mentioned Atlantic Wreck Divers or Bielenda or the past.

"You know, this was the most exciting dive of my life," Kohler told

Chatterton. "The whole thing was once in a lifetime. But the part I liked best was the time we spent in the water just looking at those dishes. For a while, you and I were the only two people in the world who knew this was a U-boat. The only two in the world."

Chatterton nodded. He understood what Kohler meant. He could tell that Kohler was not talking about diving now, he was talking about life, and he thought it would not be a bad thing to get to know this man better.

CHAPTER SIX

RICHIE KOHLER

IF EVER A PERSON had been born to dive a virgin U-boat, that person was Richie Kohler.

In 1968, Richard and Frances Kohler moved with their three young children into a house in Marine Park, a close-knit Italian and Jewish neighborhood in Brooklyn where kids ran chores for elderly widows and immigrants grew figs in their narrow backyards. Richard, a twenty-eight-year-old owner of a glass business, was of German descent and proud of it. Frances, twenty-seven, had her roots in Sicily and was equally proud of her heritage. Each aimed to instill their sense of culture in the children, especially in six-year-old Richie, who was now old enough to appreciate such flavors. As the Kohlers raised Richie, however, they noticed that something unusual was going on with their boy. He read voraciously, but not the big-print kiddie stuff typical of first graders. Instead he studied *National Geographic,* war histories, and anything concerning outer space. When nothing remained in the house to read, he started over and read everything again. His mother asked if he might not rather be outside playing with other kids and rolling around and getting dirty. He asked his mother to subscribe to *Popular Mechanics.* Frances did not know whether to celebrate or call a doctor. She had never met a person—child or adult—so relentless in his pursuit of answers.

Frances bought her son more books, and Richie kept reading—military biographies, battle narratives, weapons manuals, and anything that celebrated bravery. Before long, Frances had to force Richie outside.

When Richie discovered the Apollo program, the idea of penetrating an alien environment and then mastering it seemed too wonderful to believe. He read about Neil Armstrong and that settled it—he would be an astronaut. He drank Tang for energy, dressed his G.I. Joes in homemade tinfoil "space suits," and pleaded with his mother to buy Swanson TV dinners—the closest facsimile to space food available in Brooklyn.

All the while, his father worked grueling hours building his glass business. In between, he committed himself to the proper raising of his children. He appreciated Richie's love of reading, but he also wanted the boy to toughen up, to learn the kinds of lessons no one published in books. He taught his son to do physical things—at home, at his shop, on his boat—and he assigned him important responsibilities. Richie could cut glass at seven, and had mastered the circular saw by eight. When Richie faltered, Kohler would rail, "Are you stupid?" or "Don't be so dumb!" and Richie's chin would drop to his chest—he worshiped his father, and it crushed him to disappoint the strongest man in the world. Richie's mother recoiled from the words. "How could you say that?" she'd ask. "You know how your own father hurt you with those words. How could you do the same to your son?" Richard Kohler could not answer her.

Soon Richie wanted to please his father even more than he wanted to be an astronaut. When his dad asked, "You play with G.I. Joes? With dolls?" Richie switched to building models of warships and fighter planes. When his father took him boating and gave him important jobs, he trembled at the idea of tying the wrong knot or steering too close to an obstruction—the idea of being called stupid virtually caused the rope to fall from his hands. Yet he was tying and steering by himself on the open ocean with his father—what seven-year-old kid in his neighborhood did that? Before long, Richie could do things teenagers could not, all because his father believed he could and made certain he could.

Even as Richie continued to gobble history, another kind of education was taking hold in him. Each of his parents leaned harder into teaching him to be proud of his heritage. The smell of Frances's Sicilian cooking, her family's instinct to hug and pinch cheeks and leave lipstick marks, the forgoing of meat on Fridays, the embrace of open emotion, the sounds of neighbors screaming to kids in Sicilian dialects—these were the marks of Richie's Italian roots. He looked the part, too. His thick black hair, sculpted to the side Donny Osmond style, was shag carpeting against a brush's drag. His skin was the olive color at the bottom of his mother's imported bottles of extra-virgin oil, his eyes the brown of playground bark. His eyebrows drooped at the ends like the arms of a football player being helped from the field, but they were storytelling eyebrows, the kind that cock and dip into action when the passionate describe their lives. When he was young, Richie's eyebrows were always in motion, even when he read.

Richie's father countered that as Germans, he and Richie were part of a hardworking and honest people who accepted neither handouts nor grief. His overarching philosophy was "If you want more, you have to be more," and he imparted this to Richie relentlessly. He warned Richie to be proud of his heritage and never to allow anyone in this "Guinea" neighborhood—or the world for that matter—to tell him he was less for being German. Richie had already developed a foundational German pride from reading books and watching history programs, and he noticed from these sources that whatever people thought of Germans, they always respected their instinct for excellence.

Most indelible, perhaps, were his father's memories of Mr. Segal, a neighbor he had idolized as a boy. Segal, a German immigrant, had been the strong man in a German circus and had traveled the land several times before fleeing as Hitler rose to power. Segal had told Richard Kohler of the country he had loved, a land of craftsmen who built beautiful things, of leading scientists and artists, of storybook villages with ancient traditions, of quiet pride and a deep work ethic. Before Mr. Segal, Kohler never thought to consider his heritage. After Mr. Segal, Kohler was German. Sometimes Richie's father seemed to lose himself in these memories of Mr. Segal, as if he were a kid himself again, and young Richie could hear then that his father considered Mr. Segal his hero, and this idea overwhelmed the boy, the idea of a man so strong as to be a hero to his hero.

Richie began to focus his reading on German history, especially World War II. On television he noticed that Germans were often portrayed as sneaky rats, and he wondered why people thought Germans were so bad when it was this one monster, Hitler, who had hurt the country. He read about Germany before the war and how Hitler had come to power. Whenever school required a research project or book report, he wrote about the German side. The name Kohler, he told people in his neighborhood, came from the German word for "coal miner."

As Richie gulped more history, he noticed that he thought differently about things than his peers did. Many of them liked to read about war and battles, but only Richie seemed interested in the lives of the soldiers. He wondered about weird things his friends never considered—about the letters soldiers wrote when pinned down in a bunker, about why privates always seemed to long for the little stuff at home the most, about the childhood of a fighter pilot, about how a family felt when they got word that their son had been killed. When he saw photographs in books of soldiers lying dead on the battlefield, he hoped that the book was not available in those soldiers' hometowns.

Though Richie's father worked grueling hours, he made certain to spend time with his children on weekends. He was not, however, the type of father to toss a baseball or attend school plays. If Richie wanted to be with his dad—and he did very much—he would have to do so on his dad's terms, which always meant on the boat.

Often he quivered while his father watched him tie the bowline or wax the chrome handrails because he knew that if he faltered his father might call him names or say "Don't be so useless!" When he did things right, however, he was elated. His father allowed him great responsibility aboard the boat, and soon Richie began to absorb his father's "no matter what"—the idea that if he set his mind to it, there was nothing he could not do.

Offshore, the world expanded before the seven-year-old's already wide eyes. Richie's father loved to fish and, like all fishermen, owned a book of numbers, a passport to secret places. Often they fished the shipwrecks, and while they watched their poles Kohler told his son that row after row of wrecks lay beneath them courtesy of the German U-boats, fantastic hunting machines that had thrived in the most hostile environments on earth. To Richie, who had dreamed of conquering the alien environment of outer space, the idea of such a machine operating decades ago, in his own neighborhood, seemed more amazing than the science fiction he watched on TV. When their boating trips took them through the Rockaway Inlet, Richie asked about the circular stone pillar built into the water, equidistant from Brooklyn and Breezy Point; it looked like a castle. His father explained that the Army Corps of Engineers had used the structure to string steel nets underwater to block the U-boats from entering Jamaica Bay. "Can you believe that, Richie?" his father asked. "The Germans came right here. Look, you can see the Verrazano Bridge. That's how close the U-boats came." Richie reveled in the information, but did not breathe a word of it to friends. To him, knowledge of U-boats on America's front porch was a secret only fishermen like him and his father should share.

After his father told him about those steel nets, Richie went to the store and bought a U-boat model, and he painted that model until it looked as if it had been caught up in those steel nets itself. When he studied his father's navigational charts he was amazed to see a sunken U-boat, *U-853*, off Block Island in Rhode Island listed along with a thrilling red-letter entreaty: WARNING—UNEXPLODED ORDNANCE. A quarter century since the U-boats had sailed and there was still something alive about them.

On a sunny and warm day when Richie was eight, his father took him on a waterskiing trip to Dead Horse Bay in the Mill Basin waters off Brooklyn, a small area around which boats pulled waterskiers. During one of Richie's runs, the line went slack and he fell into the water—his father had cut the engines. Kohler made a U-turn, yelling to Richie, "Get in the boat! Get in the boat!" and then plucked his son out of the water. He then began making slow circles around an object. Kohler told Richie, "Get inside the cuddy and don't look." Richie's life was devoted to looking. He went into the cabin only halfway and kept watching, following the object his father circled until he could tell that it was a body, a woman—he knew it was a woman because he could see her bikini bottom. His father called the Coast Guard and continued circling. Richie looked closer. The woman was facedown, her long hair floating on the water, her legs spread, her buttocks peeking out from beneath her bathing suit, several symmetrical white flesh wounds chopped across her back and thighs. Her body bobbed in the wake of his father's boat. Richie's heart pounded, but he could not stop looking. He did not cry. He did not hide. He wondered how a person could be left in the ocean without anyone knowing she was there.

As the boating season drew to a close, Richie's father decided to learn scuba. At home, Kohler allowed Richie to assemble and disassemble his tank and regulator—he believed in making his three children feel comfortable with mechanical equipment, to make them unafraid to touch things. He threw the equipment to the bottom of the family's above-ground backyard pool, then told Richie to swim down, assemble it, and begin breathing. The idea that Richie was able to conquer this underwater world put him on par with the divers he watched in *20,000 Leagues Under the Sea*.

All the while, Richie continued to read. Had an observer known only his academic side, he might have pegged the kid for an egghead. Richie joined no sports teams and did not play outside with the regularity of most neighborhood boys. He spent much of his free time reading or building World War II models, which he customized with increasing detail. Yet Richie was no softie. When Richie's father heard that a towering, Afro-headed bully named Vinnie had beaten Richie up after school, he walked the block with Richie until he found the culprit and forced his son to pummel the boy. Neighborhood kids saw Richie differently after that fight. Now word had it that if you messed with Richie Kohler he could go wild. No one bothered him much after that.

The summer when Richie was nine, he, his father, and a dock mechanic took the family's thirty-five-foot Viking Sport Fisherman, the *Lisa Frances,* for a day of party boating. By now, Richie was allowed to navigate, swim in the ocean, even mix pitchers of vodka gimlets for the adults; he was an important part of the crew. Kohler gave Richie the helm and allowed the boy to steer out of the inlet and into the Atlantic. Just ten minutes from the dock, Richie cut the wheel hard, shaking his father to attention.

"What are you doing?" his father called out.

"There's a tire ahead and I didn't want to hit it," Richie replied.
Kohler leaned over and looked into the water.

"That's not a tire," he said.

Richie squinted for a better look. As the boat drifted forward, he could see that the shape he believed to be a tire was in fact a man's body. The person was facedown, arms straight out to his sides, legs dangling in the water, a black windbreaker blown over his head like a shroud. As the boat passed, the water's wake shook the man's head back, and Richie could see his face. His eyes were closed and he was clean shaven. His hair was in his eyes and he wore a light-colored turtleneck beneath the windbreaker. The man's skin was white. He was dead.

Richie's father took the wheel and swung the boat around. "Get in the cabin and don't look!" he ordered. Richie left the wheelhouse but kept looking. His father and the other man took a ten-foot gaff and fished the body toward the boat. The water was rough and kept tossing the corpse up and down, but the man's arms never changed shape; they stayed in the crucifix position, away from his sides. Kohler called the Coast Guard.

"Bring the body on board," ordered the dispatcher.

"Absolutely not," Kohler responded.

Kohler knew that by taking a body on his boat, he would be involved in a prolonged investigation, and he had no time for that. Instead, he chose to stay with the body and wait for the Coast Guard. While the authorities sped to the scene, Kohler and his friend indulged in gallows humor: "Check him for a wallet!" "Does he have any diamond rings?"

When the Coast Guard boat arrived, it radioed to Kohler.

"Pull the body onto your swim platform and follow us in."

"No way," Kohler replied. "I'm going to let the body go unless you come and take it."

That idea terrified Richie more than the sight of the body. He could not endure the prospect of a dead man going adrift at sea and lost forever. He knew his father was serious. He prayed that the Coast Guard would take the body.

The Coast Guard boat maneuvered closer in the rough water. Richie continued to stare at the dead man's face and those arms spread at his sides. As the Coast Guard boat passed, Kohler handed off the gaff to the guardsman, who vomited at the sight. The Coast Guard boat ordered Kohler to follow it back to shore. When everyone arrived at the Coast Guard station, the body was moved to a gurney. Water dripped from the dead man's mouth. A boy about Richie's age ran to the gurney and cried, "My dad! My dad!" Richie trembled, using all his powers of toughness to keep from sobbing. A few minutes later, someone told the Kohlers that the victim had been caught in a storm in a sailboat and had been knocked overboard and drowned. The man, they said, was a minister.

All the way home, Richie thought about what would have happened if he and his father hadn't found the minister. It had been a year since he had seen the dead woman in the water, but Richie had never stopped wondering how people could be left in the water when they had loved ones at home who needed to know where they were.

When Richie was eleven, his father finally took him diving. The men went to the dock where Kohler kept his boat. Richie checked his gauges, spit in his mask to keep it from fogging underwater, and patted his side to make sure his knife was still in place. When everything felt right, he rolled backward into the water as he had seen actors do on the TV series *Sea Hunt*. The New York water was dotted with foam cups and cigarettes, its surface splotched with oil and a broken umbrella, but Richie could hardly believe the beauty beneath the surface—horseshoe crabs crawled by, minnows darted, and a jellyfish drifted past on the current—and as he moved about this place where human beings were not supposed to go, where the U-boats had glided under the noses of the world, he understood that he had penetrated another realm, that he had made that astronaut leap for which he had always yearned.

By the time Richie turned twelve his parents had separated and his father had begun dating another woman. One night in February 1975, Frances tiptoed into Richie's bedroom, where the boy lay asleep. She woke him and handed him suitcases and told him to pack his belongings and to help his brother do the same.

"Where are we going?" Richie asked his mother, rubbing his eyes.

"We're going to Florida," Frances said. She was surprised at her answer. She had never thought about Florida before this moment.

At two A.M., Frances put the three children into her black Buick Riviera and headed south on the New Jersey Turnpike. At a gas station, she bought maps and put Richie in charge of navigation. When daylight came, she pulled over at a rest stop and napped with the children. Then she continued the drive until the family arrived at her mother's house in New Port Richey, Florida. She hadn't told her mother she was coming. Rosalie Ruoti kissed her daughter and squeezed her grandchildren. Frances knew then that she was never going back to New York.

A few weeks after leaving New York, Richie celebrated his thirteenth birthday at his grandmother's home in Florida. Frances soon bought her own house nearby. By phone, Richie told his father, "I love you and you're not here for me," and Kohler could only say, "You know, buddy, I can't do anything. Your mother and I don't get along." After a few of these calls, Richie knew that he would do the rest of his growing up in Florida.

At fourteen, Richie enrolled in Hudson Senior High School, near his home. One day while outside for gym, a hulking muscleman of a classmate began pushing around a tall, skinny, blond kid Richie recognized from his algebra class. Richie walked over and advised the big guy to stop the bullying. The bully said, "Mind your fucking business or I'll . . ." Richie reached his right fist back to Thirty-third Street and put it across the kid's chin. The bully collapsed to the concrete, where he began whimpering and talking gibberish. Richie's father was right: always swing while the other guy is telling you how he's going to kick your ass.

The skinny kid thanked Richie and introduced himself as Don Davidson. He invited Richie to his house after school. Don's bedroom was revelation. Hanging from the ceiling were a half dozen models of World War II fighter aircraft, each detailed so finely they could have been mistaken in close-up photographs for the real thing. Richie lay on his back and took in the scene above him, and soon he was under bleeding Filipino skies in 1944 at the Battle of Leyte Gulf, machine guns shredding enemy wings and pilots bailing out of burning cockpits. Don was cool about Richie lying on the floor because he did the same thing all the time. On Don's bookshelves were at least two dozen books on the Luftwaffe, Hitler's air force. "I'm German," Don told Richie. "I'm really into the technology of World War II—especially German engineering and their superior weapons." Richie told Don about the Kriegsmarine—the German navy—and about how U-boats had come to New York's doorstep, just a mile or two from his own front door. Richie told Don he was German, too. The boys were best friends already.

After Richie and Don turned fifteen, they signed up for scuba classes and earned their junior certification. They dove constantly, spearing fish and even tangling with sharks. Richie felt every bit the astronaut underwater, free to explore worlds off-limits to the kids who sat, bored, next to him in biology class or study hall. He reveled in the finely tooled equipment that acted at once as shield and as portal to the sea. He thrived on the feeling of independence that came with spearfishing; hunters like Don and himself spent as much as an hour alone in a boundaryless world without fathers, relying only on themselves.

Richie's high school junior year found him drifting to the rowdy crowd. The time he had devoted to bookish study for so many years increasingly gave way to chugging Miller High Lifes on the beach, stashing weed in plastic thirty-five-millimeter film containers, and customizing his black 1974 Oldsmobile Cutlass Supreme. He wore the uniform of the 1970s burnout: hair to his shoulders, light mustache, cutoff shorts, black rock-concert T-shirt silk-screened with glitter. In the Florida sun, his already olive skin darkened to toast. His jawline continued to square. Girls wanted to touch him. His eyebrows kept talking and talking.

In the classroom, Richie pulled A's and B's, but teachers inscribed his report cards with caveats like "Doesn't apply himself" and "Does just what he needs to do." The street toughness stitched into him by his father showed itself eagerly. Once, when his fourteen-year-old brother, Frank, confessed to being terrorized by an adult bully, sixteen-year-old Richie pummeled the grown man until he cried. On another occasion, Richie and four junior-varsity foot-ball teammates decided to pull a prank on some seniors by lighting their gym clothes on fire through the metal grates in their lockers. The school pressed charges. In court, the judge told the boys that if they stayed out of trouble, the record would be expunged. After that, Richie kept clean.

As the year wore on, Richie began to think about his future. He wanted no more of school—for all the pleasure he took in learning, he needed to be in the world doing, not behind more desks listen-ing. An idea took shape in his mind. He could join the navy. In that way, he could live on the water, travel the globe, and work with the most spectacular fighting machines in the world. Maybe—and this is when his heart really started fluttering—he could work aboard an attack submarine. Not a lumbering nuclear missile sub but a sleek, fast, hunter-killer submarine.

Late in Richie's junior year, a U.S. Navy recruiter visited his high school as part of Career Day. Richie asked a lot of questions. The man told him there were officer-training programs available to the highest scorers on the Armed Services Aptitude Test. Those pro-grams guaranteed training in a recruit's area of choice—including submarines. Richie signed up for the test and took it cold. He scored at the ninety-eighth percentile. The United States Navy said they would love to have him. He asked again about submarines.

The recruiter assured Richie that if he gave the navy a six-year commitment, the navy would guarantee him service aboard a sub-marine. He presented a contract that memorialized the obligation. Richie and his mother signed the papers. It had been years since his astronaut dreams had fizzled. Now, though it sounded strange, he told himself, "I'm back in the game."

After graduating from high school, Richie and several dozen other new recruits were taken by bus to a Florida naval air station for induction. Navy jets roared overhead. The recruits were sworn in. Richie was a member of the United States Navy.

Later that day, an officer in a blue jacket called Richie into a room and asked him to sit down.

"There's a problem, son," he said. "You lied on your application."

"What do you mean?" Richie asked.

The officer explained that they had found a record of Richie's high school arson incident. The navy had no intention of allowing anyone connected to arson to serve on board a navy ship. Ever.

Richie's stomach fell. He explained the prankish nature of the incident and that the judge in the case had expunged the record. The officer was unmoved. He offered to allow Richie to stay in officer training with the understanding that he could never serve aboard a naval vessel, and asked him to sign a document to that effect. Richie would not sign. A few hours later Richie was on the street, heartbroken and disoriented. He had been a member of the United States Navy for a day. Now his plans for a remarkable future had been smothered in rules and a youthful mistake. He wandered around for the next few days, taking stock of his life and wondering how he might ever replace such a lost opportunity. When he could think of nothing else to do, he decided to move back to New York to work for his father.

For three years, Kohler worked long hours and built the mirror division of his father's company. Not once did he touch his dive gear, which remained in storage in the basement at Fox Glass. One day he was called to a window-repair job at the Wantagh South Bay Dive Center, a scuba shop on eastern Long Island. While working, he noticed a photograph of a diver on a shipwreck. The man in the picture looked to be excavating faucets from a bathtub. Kohler asked the shop owner, a man named Ed Murphy, about the photo.

"That's the *Andrea Doria*," Murphy said.

Kohler had read books about the *Andrea Doria* and knew that the ship had sunk off New York, but he had never processed that anyone could dive it. Murphy pulled out piles of *Doria* snapshots. This was not the kind of wreck Kohler had seen in Florida, the type shredded by nature and surrendered to sea life. The *Doria* looked like a Hollywood shipwreck, with intact rooms and identifiable plumbing and echoes of life and tragedy.

"I want to dive that," Kohler blurted. The suddenness of his declaration surprised him—he had thought nothing about diving for three years.

"Oh, no, no, no, no," Murphy scolded. "The *Doria* is something you work up to. It's at two hundred and fifty feet. It's only for the best divers."

"I was the best," Kohler said. He told Murphy about his Florida spearfishing experience.

"This ain't spearfishing, friend," Murphy said. "But I'll tell you what. I got a group of customers going out this weekend to a wreck called the USS *San Diego*. It's a World War I cruiser laying in the sand, sunk by a German mine. It's a good wreck. You can come along. It's at a hundred and ten feet—you should be able to handle it. Bring your gear."

"I'll be there," Kohler said.

Kohler rushed to the basement at Fox Glass. His equipment was dusty and mildewed. He unpacked and hosed off his tank, regulator, mask, and fins. The smell of mummified neoprene wafted from his suit.

That weekend, Kohler set sail for the *San Diego*. When the dive boat reached the wreck site, he began to gear up. The other divers snickered and coughed. Kohler had no gloves, no hood, no boots— just a Farmer John–style wet suit that did not even cover his arms. Someone asked if he had planted corn that morning.

"It's freezing down there," a diver told him. "Florida's a long way off, kid."

"Ah, I'll be all right," Kohler said.

A minute into the dive, Kohler was shivering. The green-gray water was no more than fifty degrees. When he reached the wreck he realized it was upside down, or a "turtle." He swam along the side, looking for a way in, and finally found a compartment open to the ocean. Kohler had no training in digging or sifting or the other fine arts of excavation. He just stuffed his hand into the silt and came out with dozens of bullets. Amazing. His body began to shake from the cold. He checked his watch—he had been down only five minutes. He began his ascent lest he die of exposure. On the way up he stared at the bullets. The ammunition had traveled directly from World War I into his hands. He was hooked.

After that, Kohler began to buy proper Northeast wreck-diving gear: dry suit, gloves, a fifty-dollar knife. He signed up for all the dive shop's charters. He seemed to gravitate instinctively to areas rich in artifacts; often, he recovered items others had spent years passing by. He moved fearlessly about the *Oregon,* the *San Diego,* and other wrecks, and penetrated areas that scared instructors. Diving was back in his bloodstream. The fall and heave of the ocean, the grumble of the charter boat's engines, the gray-blue of inlet waters, the white smear of the Milky Way's reflection in the midnight water—it all reminded him of the good times he'd enjoyed as shipmate to his father, the summer years when his dad was giant and the water could take a kid anywhere.

It seemed to Kohler that in wreck diving, a person could still go anywhere. He read in a dive magazine about a group of men who had chartered a boat in 1967 to dive the *Doria.* One of those men, John Dudas, had recovered the ship's compass. To Kohler, Dudas seemed of another species. In a day when divers had no gauges, froze in wet suits, and prayed that their wristwatches did not flood, Dudas had gone to 250 feet and had taken the binnacle from inside the *Andrea Doria.* To Kohler, who was beginning to understand the jackhammer of narcosis and the true meaning of the word *cold,* Dudas was astronaut, mercenary, gladiator, and porpoise all rolled into one.

As he accumulated experience, Kohler evolved his own brand of bravery. On one *San Diego* dive, he squeezed through a rotted hole into a room black with oil. In zero visibility, he filled his green mesh bags with china, lanterns, telescopes, and bugles, then divvied up the bounty to colleagues topside. The dive earned him notice in enthusiast magazines. On other wrecks—the *Oregon,* the *Relief,* the *Coimbra,* the *Resor*—he dug into silt and swam into collapsed spaces, a prescription for disorientation. He always exited with air in his tanks. More often than not, he swam out with spoils from these dangerous rooms. All the while, he developed an insatiable appetite for artifacts. The more he recovered, the more he lusted for.

One day, Murphy called Kohler aside for a private conference. He told him of a group of six divers—a gang, really—that he believed to be Kohler's kindred spirits. The gang had no formal name, but others called them the Thugs. They were fearsome, Murphy said, in their appetite for artifacts and their reputation for hard living. But they were also among the best divers on the eastern seaboard.

"They dive crazy deep, Kohler," Murphy said. "They go places no one else goes. They're your kind."

"Can you introduce me?" Kohler asked.

"Listen. Some people consider them pirates raping the ship-wrecks—"

"Now you *have* to introduce me," Kohler said.

Murphy invited the gang on one of the dive shop's charters to the *Oregon*. Kohler signed up, too. Murphy made the introductions. The Thugs comprised six men—five blue-collar workers and an aerospace engineer—each of whom had at least ten years of deep-wreck diving experience. They were loud and rowdy aboard the boat, but on the shipwreck they became transformed. Kohler watched as the gang melded into a single entity, flashing hand sig-nals and lining up for what was obviously a plan. They stuffed one member, Pinky, into a tiny hole in a cargo hold on the stern, then took turns bagging the portholes, moonshine jugs, dishes, and other artifacts Pinky extracted. Every member seemed to anticipate every other member's movement, so that no motion was wasted and the maximum tonnage poured forth into their coffers. Kohler had never seen such teamwork. As a kid who had grown up admiring beauti-fully built machines, he felt as if he could watch these men work forever.

Topside, the Thugs celebrated their haul by pounding beers, swearing at the heavens, and consuming enough cold cuts to open a floating delicatessen. Kohler showed them the two gargantuan lob-sters he had captured aboard the wreck. They scoffed. "Where the hell are your artifacts? If you want to catch lobster you can stay on the goddamn jetty." Kohler smiled and asked if he could dive with the gang again.

The Thugs did not like outsiders, but they liked Kohler. The kid had matched them drink for drink, and he hated the same charter captains they did. Best of all, he seemed at one with their pirate sen-sibilities. They made him a proposition. "You're the beermeister," they said. "You bring the beer and you can come along on our next charter."

Kohler brought waterfalls of beer, and he continued bringing it for a year. He'd never known men who partied so hard. The gang raised hell in pizza joints before dives, mooned passing family vessels, wore plastic pig noses and snorted at enemy boat captains, all the while consuming booze and food in quantities that would shame a frat house. In between the fun, the gang threw an education into Kohler the likes of which a diver could not purchase for any price.

Like army sergeants, the men stripped Kohler of his civilian equipment and began to outfit him in the gear of the great wreck diver. His harness? It sucked—buy this kind. His lights? Trash the Florida shit and buy brighter—this is the Atlantic, for Christ's sake. His fifty-dollar knife? Too goddamn fancy; use a cheapo you won't chase and drown for if you drop it. The lessons were clear: if a diver was going to go places no other men dared, he had better have the hardware to do it.

Then the men set about to strip him of old thinking. They pushed him to study deck plans and photographs in order to determine a wreck's meatiest locations; divers who barreled in and dug blindly for prizes never bagged up like a man with knowledge. They preached a group ethos whereby the gang worked together and shared the spoils; Kohler should always expect to bag another guy's stuff or finish another's hard labor or do whatever else it took to maximize the haul. And Kohler's cutthroat attitude toward artifacts? Beautiful, baby, but not inside the group. Inside the group, remember this: we never fuck each other.

The Thugs did their best teaching on the way to the wrecks, and their method was ancient and indelible. They discussed how a wreck's tilt betrayed where its artifacts lay. They revealed the beauty of using brains and a steel wedge over brawn and a sledgehammer. They were living encyclopedias of dive accidents. They studied the sport's close calls, bends hits, and drownings, deconstructing each incident until they understood its genesis and could intuit its prevention. After years of absorbing how other men had fucked up and died, they believed, a diver was that much less likely to do it himself.

The divers battered Kohler with talk of survival. They taught him that so long as he was breathing he was okay. They taught him to answer a rising panic by slowing down, falling back, and talking himself through the situation. They branded into him the horror of shooting to the surface without decompressing, and when they said, "I'd rather slit my throat than take that kind of bends hit," he believed them because they had seen men climb aboard a boat with their blood foaming and their hearts choking. They warned him—relentlessly—about the "snowball effect," the process whereby a diver ignores a minor problem or two only to encounter other problems that combine with the earlier ones to doom him. "Always answer the first problem immediately and fully," they said, "or you're fucking dead."

Kohler took in every word. When they brought him to the most dangerous wrecks he held his own, bagged up, and stayed safe. Over the next year, he signed up for every charter the gang booked. To these men, Kohler was the young Turk, but he brought a package to the table unlike any they had seen. The kid knew no skepticism or cynicism; no goal was impossible to Kohler, no idea too grand. He believed, for Christ's sake, that the gang could take the bell off the bow of the *Coimbra,* even though that wreck was four hundred feet long and in 180 feet of freezing water and no diver had ever been to the bow before. "That's a great way to get us killed, smart-ass," they told him, pelting him with beer cans. Yet as much as the men laughed at the scope of Kohler's vision, as much as they broke his balls and delighted in the shades of red he turned while insisting "It's possible!" they found themselves challenged to ask why Kohler might not be right. A month after Kohler proposed the hunt for the *Coimbra*'s bell, the gang armed itself with extra tanks, devised a teamwork-driven battle plan, and became the first divers ever to explore that shipwreck's bow. (To this day, no one has recovered the bell from the wreck.)

One day on the way back from a dive, the divers' discussion turned to solidarity. If the gang could add members and organize themselves, they could charter their own boats, thereby saving money and dictating destinations. It would require a commitment—a member would pay for charters whether he attended or not—but in that way the group could build real power.

One by one, the men on the trip said, "I'm in." The gang would need an official name. Someone suggested "Atlantic Wreck Divers."

Perfect. Someone else recommended matching windbreakers. "We're not a goddamned bowling team" was the collective reply. How about matching denim jackets with skull-and-crossbones patches? That was more like it. Now the six original members had to elect an additional four, and the vote had to be unanimous. Only the very best divers were nominated, matching souls who had dived with the gang and shared their mind-set. When Kohler's name was offered, four thumbs went up and two went sideways. His heart sank. No one said a word. When the two members with sideways thumbs were convinced they had sufficiently traumatized Kohler, they turned their thumbs to the sky. "Ballbreakers to the end," Kohler thought. Beer flowed. Oaths of loyalty were sworn. The Atlantic Wreck Divers had been born.

Around the time Kohler became an Atlantic Wreck Diver, he heard through the grapevine that his father was dating his ex-girlfriend, a woman Richie had lived with the year before. He confronted his father, who admitted it was true and that the relationship had been going on for months. Richie was devastated. For a minute he could not speak.

"How could you?" he finally choked out.

"I'm your father and I can do what I want," the elder Kohler said. "If you don't like it, there's the door."

The door. If Richie walked through it there would be no coming back. In his father's world a person who took the door could never come back. Richie's throat lumped and his forehead flushed. His breath howled as it rushed through his nostrils. He could back down now—he could mutter some face-saving obscenity and save his job and his future and his relationship with his father, and besides, he did not love the girl anymore, and who the hell was she to push him through the door? He looked into his father's eyes. The man did not blink. If Richie walked now he would lose this man, this strong man who knew the ocean and understood business and had toughened him to the world. Could he do it? Kohler knew his life. He could stick with anything if he knew it was right.

"I'll take the door," he told his father.

That day, Richie removed his possessions from the basement at Fox Glass. It would be years before he would see his father again.

Now Richie had to find work. A glass salesman tipped him to a company paying top dollar and looking for someone with his experience. A few days later he was working as a mechanic for Act II Glass and Mirrors, a business that served New York's Orthodox Jewish community. He hit it off with the owner, and four months later he was the company's foreman.

Over the next two years, Kohler worked hard and provided a vision for the company. The owner rewarded the effort by making Kohler a partner. Life was good again. During summers, he committed to the Atlantic Wreck Divers. The ocean had never seen anything quite like that gang before.

Food was religion on AWD charters. Members brought along the finest cold cuts, cheeses, pepperonis, and pastries, and they did so in quantities worthy of Roman orgies. If one man brought his wife's special tomato-and-mozzarella salad, another man would outdo him the next week with his wife's slow-cooked pork tenderloin. The divers might even barbecue steaks, chicken, and the occasional speared flounder on the back of the boat.

Rascality was prized even above gluttony. Often, without warning the boat captain, the gang would yell "Swim break!" and get naked and jump into the ocean, never letting go of their beer cans as they bobbed in the water. Members brought along guns and slung stuffed animals into the air for target practice. When a black-tie party boat passed, the gang would throw beer cans at the vessel and break into their trademark ditty:

> Cat's ass, rat's ass, dirty old twat;
> Sixty-nine douche bags tied in a knot;
> Cocksucker, motherfucker, dicky licker, too;
> I'm a fuckin' scuba diver, who the fuck are you?

If the passing partygoers seemed insufficiently offended, the gang would seal the deal by mooning the boat.

Every AWD member was known by a nickname. Pete Guglieri, the oldest and most levelheaded member, was "Emperor." Jeff

Pagano was "Hateman" for his negative outlook. Pat Rooney was "Hammer" for the tool he carried underwater, John Lachenmeyer "Swingin' Jack" for his tendency to walk around naked, while Brad Sheard, the aerospace engineer, went by "Dick Whittler" because of the piece of driftwood he'd tried to whittle into a sailboat that had turned out looking more phallic than maritime. Kohler had earned his moniker during a discussion about Richard Pryor's freebasing accident. Because his work took him into the most drug-infested sections of Brooklyn, he'd been able to explain to the gang the difference between cocaine and crack. After that, he was Crackhead.

Around this time, Kohler met Felicia Becker, a dark and pretty sales clerk for one of Kohler's glass-business customers. She understood his passion for diving. They married in the fall of 1989, and shortly after the wedding Felicia became pregnant.

One night that year, Kohler stopped for dinner at a Spanish restaurant in Brooklyn. He was alone. As he sat at the bar he felt a slap on his back. It was his father. The two had neither seen nor spoken to each other in five years. The elder Kohler asked if he could sit down. Richie told him he could.

"You're going to be a grandfather," Richie said. His father did not even know his son had married.

Richie and his father spent hours catching up on their lives and families. Neither man mentioned Richie's old girlfriend. His father asked him to come back to Fox Glass. Richie told him he could not work for anyone after having been a partner in his own business. His father proposed that they become partners and open their own glass company in New Jersey, and Richie accepted. He had stuck to his resolve; it was his father who had moved. He was happy to be back in the family business. He was happier to know that if he committed to something, even something so wrenching as leaving his father, he could see that decision through.

In 1990, Kohler and Felicia celebrated the arrival of their first child, a son. Kohler worked grueling hours, then devoted his free time to Atlantic Wreck Divers. Their handmade, photocopied schedules were collector's items in the dive community. The single-page calendar was strewn with pornographic images taken from cheap men's magazines. Phone numbers such as 1-800-EAT-SHIT were listed as contacts. One schedule promised "beer tasting sessions, pig calling lessons, lesbian watching, automatic weapons, more beer tasting sessions, greenhorn bashing . . . as well as some great fucking diving." Another said, "If you don't have our numbers, we don't want you fucking diving with us." In the center was a list of dates, boats, and wreck destinations. Often the vessel the gang had chartered was the *Wahoo*, Steve Bielenda's boat.

For a while, Kohler had no problem using the *Wahoo*. But recently Kohler had clashed with Bielenda, one time nearly coming to blows. Now Kohler needed a new boat to get to the *Doria*. He had dived several times with Nagle on the *Seeker*—to the *Durley Chine*, the *Bidevind*, and the *Resor*—and had long admired Nagle's legend. And while Nagle had a reputation for crudeness and impatience, he had always treated Kohler with respect. Kohler signed up for several *Seeker* charters in 1990 and 1991. Though Chatterton was practically running Nagle's business by then, he and Kohler never found themselves together aboard the boat.

In the fall of 1991 Kohler heard word of the virgin U-boat discovery. The news stopped his life. For days, he was a blur of longing and desire, pacing the floors at home and at work, distracted from family and friends, unable to sort out the details of his yearning. Then Brennan called and said, "You're in," and the words lifted Kohler back to the days when his father told stories of Mr. Segal and he became proud of his last name and the way Germans built machines, and it carried him across the thousands of pages he had read about World War II and the courage of men and steel nets stretched across New York, and it ferried him over the sailboat he and his pal Don had designed to circle the world, above the navy man who had promised a submarine, beyond the gear he had used to penetrate alien worlds, and he knew that he had to be part of this virgin U-boat because for twenty-nine years it had been part of him.

CHAPTER SEVEN

HORENBURG'S KNIFE

THE SWASTIKAS on the dishes Chatterton recovered from the U-boat reached through time and chokeholded his imagination. A person could spend a lifetime studying Nazis and U-boats, and in the end it was all just information. The dishes were heavy. The swastika's angled arms rubbed rough against a person's fingertips; even with closed eyes one could detect the infamous shape. No one had cataloged or curated or even touched this china since the U-boat fell; the dishes had traveled from Hitler's Third Reich directly to Chatterton's living room, and for that unbroken path they still seemed treacherous on his mantel.

If there were a few in the diving community who still had not heard of the mystery wreck after Feldman's death, that changed with the discovery of the dishes. Now it seemed that every conversation in every dive shop along the eastern seaboard involved the U-boat and its possible identity. Chatterton and Nagle were certain that such attention would grind against Bielenda's ego; the King of the Deep could not abide pretenders to his throne, and while he likely did not yet know the sub's location, they believed it would be only a matter of time before he wrested it from his Coast Guard connections and set sail to raid their wreck. Ordinarily, the *Seeker* would have been back to the submarine the next week—the men were sure that with another dive or two the U-boat would surrender her name. But it was now hurricane season, the time of year when windows of opportunity were measured in hours rather than months. Landlocked, Nagle renewed his vow to get sober and work his body back into diving shape for next season. Chatterton returned to his research. If he could not penetrate the wreck from the ocean, he would try to get inside it through history.

While a few of the divers had thumbed library books looking for insight into the wreck, Chatterton continued to research as he had from the beginning—by submitting written requests to an archivist at the Naval Historical Center in Washington, D.C. The NHC was the Fort Knox of naval war records, and it was from the archivist's expertise that Chatterton hoped to mine hidden nuggets. But replies took weeks, and when they did arrive they consisted of one-page general-information synopses. If Chatterton was going to penetrate beneath history's crust, he would have to make the research more personal and immediate.

Chatterton was not the only man engaged in serious investigation. From his home in New Providence, New Jersey, Kohler barrel-rolled into his collection of U-boat books, devouring titles past midnight even when his glass company demanded that he be fresh before dawn. Mornings, he used one eye to shave and the other to choose additional titles from his Naval Institute Press catalog, then wrote checks to the company for sums he hoped his wife would never notice. He introduced himself at a German-American club on Route 130 in Burlington, New Jersey, where he told the elderly membership the story of the mystery U-boat and recruited volunteers to help him translate the German books he had purchased.

One day he called a dive charter captain who had once mentioned knowing a U-boat crewman. He asked the captain to seek out this U-boat man and see if he had any suggestions that might help identify the wreck. The captain spoke to the veteran and then called Kohler.

"Search the boots," the captain said.

"Huh?"

"Search the boots. If you can find boots on the wreck, look inside them. The guy says they all wrote their names inside their boots so no one else would wear them. They hated when other guys wore their boots. And they put their watches and jewelry in their boots, too, and some of that stuff also had their names."

Kohler resolved to search the boots. None of the other divers would think to look inside a rotting old boot; they would likely swim past footwear in search of more dishes or a builder's plaque or some other glamorous artifact. If he could, Kohler would search every boot he saw.

Then Kohler hit upon another idea, this one maybe his best. He had heard that a retired U-boat commander, Herbert Werner, lived in America. But Werner was not just any commander. He had written *Iron Coffins*, a memoir that had become a classic in the genre. Kohler poked around library white pages until he hit gold. Werner not only lived in America, he lived in ever-loving New Jersey. Kohler got his number and, trembling, dialed one of the great U-boat commanders.

A man answered in a light German accent.

"Hello, I'm looking for Mr. Herbert Werner," Kohler said.

"This is Herbert Werner."

Kohler's heart raced. He might have the answer to the U-boat mystery before he hung up the phone.

"Sir, my name is Richard Kohler. I'm a diver. My colleagues and I found a U-boat off the New Jersey coast. Sir, the reason I'm calling—"

"Everything I have to say I said in my book," Werner stated in an even and measured tone. "I have nothing more to say."

"But if I can just ask—"

"Good-bye," Werner said pleasantly, then hung up.

Kohler held the receiver to his ear for a minute before he could bring himself to replace it.

Weeks had passed since the dishes came out of the wreck. The divers had put in dozens of hours of research, and one fact screamed above all the rest: no U-boat had ever been recorded sunk within one hundred miles of the wreck site. To Chatterton, it seemed as if his research with the archivist at the Naval Historical Center was moving backward. And he and Nagle could virtually hear Bielenda warming up the *Wahoo*'s engines. Chatterton hit upon an idea: Why not put out news of the U-boat discovery to the world? Surely there were historians or experts or governments who knew the wreck's identity; why not expedite the research by going to those who know? The *Seeker* would still enjoy the glory and fame of discovery, Bielenda and others would be precluded from claim-jumping the wreck, and the mystery would be solved through the *Seeker*'s research. There was risk in the idea—namely that someone else would get credit for making the identification. Chatterton decided he could handle that scenario. He pitched Nagle on writing a press release. Nagle loved the idea. "Put my name and phone number at the bottom," he told Chatterton.

At the local library, Chatterton found a book on how to write press releases. At home that night, he came up with this:

FOR IMMEDIATE RELEASE—OCTOBER 10, 1991

DIVERS DISCOVER MYSTERY U-BOAT
OFF NEW JERSEY COAST

Captain Bill Nagle and the divers from the Brielle, New Jersey charter vessel *Seeker* have located a World War II German U-boat sunk only 65 miles from the New Jersey coast, at approximate latitude 40, longitude 73.30. The wreck lies upright and is essentially intact, though it shows damage from an apparent depth charge attack.

The U-boat is in 230 feet of water, making it accessible to only a select few experienced deep wreck divers. The submarine was located on Labor Day, during a *Seeker* expedition to identify undiscovered wrecks. On a subsequent trip to the wreck, *Seeker* crew member John Chatterton recovered two china dishes from deep within the wreck, each emblazoned with the Nazi swastika and dated "1942," proof of the sub's origin.

The items recovered from the wreck prove it is a World War II German U-boat, but which one? No German submarines were ever reported sunk within 150 miles of this location, and German records contain no accounts of U-boats being lost in

New Jersey waters. Divers from the *Seeker* will continue to cautiously probe the wreck to discover its identity, and unravel the mystery of why it is where it is. A small piece of naval history may have to be rewritten.

Contact: Captain Bill Nagle

Kevin Brennan gave Chatterton a black-and-white photo of one of the dishes to include with the release. Chatterton made a list of all the media outlets he knew, a total of ten names, including local newspapers, the Associated Press, UPI, and diving magazines. He mailed a press release and photo to each address.

A day passed without a reply. Then a few days. Chatterton checked Nagle's phone several times. He called the phone company and asked that they check Nagle's line. The phone was working fine. Finally, Chatterton called Nagle.

"Well, that didn't work," he said.

"Looks like it," Nagle grumbled.

Several days later, Nagle's phone rang. He referred the call to Chatterton. It was from a reporter at the Newark *Star-Ledger,* an important New Jersey daily newspaper. The man sounded weary and uninterested. His questions dripped with skepticism, as if he were being forced to interview yet another Billy Bob who had discovered a spaceship in his backyard.

"So, you supposedly found some mysterious U-boat, huh?" the reporter asked.

Chatterton said that he had. The man asked more questions. To each, Chatterton provided a detailed answer. By the end of the conversation, the reporter asked if he might visit Chatterton's home. A day later he was there taking notes and handling the china. He said he thought the story might be good enough to run on page one.

The next morning, Chatterton walked in bathrobe and slippers to the end of his driveway and picked up the *Star-Ledger.* At the bottom was a headline: U-BOAT WRECK FOUND OFF POINT PLEASANT. Alongside the story was a photo of Nagle and Chatterton inspecting the dishes. Chatterton ran inside and called Nagle. The story summed it all up: the dangers of deep-wreck diving, the ominous

146 • ROBERT KURSON

presence of U-boats in American waters, Feldman's death, the ongoing mystery of the sub's identity. It also quoted Professor Henry Keatts, an author and U-boat expert. "They have definitely found a German U-boat," Keatts told the paper. "The mystery is how it ended up where it is today. . . . None is supposed to be in this area."

The *Star-Ledger* story unleashed a media frenzy. That evening, Nagle's and Chatterton's phones rang nonstop with interview requests from radio, television, and print reporters. International media ran the story of the mystery U-boat discovered off the New Jersey coast. CNN sent a crew. Television reporters had Nagle and Chatterton hold the dishes up, swastika side out, while they interviewed the pair aboard the *Seeker*. Even the tabloid *Weekly World News* ran a front-page item: NAZI SUB CAPTURED BY U.S. NAVY SHIP! The story, fantastical even by that publication's standards, told not only of the New Jersey U-boat but of a second U-boat, one that had sailed from Germany into a time warp and had surfaced only today, its still-youthful crewmen convinced that Hitler ruled Germany. It quoted a "Washington-based Navy officer" who said, "I don't know all that much about time warps, but that seems to be the only explanation for this whole situation."

Chatterton's phone, which had sat silent for two weeks after the press release, now rang so relentlessly it threatened his sleep and his meals. His mailbox overflowed. Packages were delivered to him addressed simply "John Chatterton—Diver—New Jersey."

Many of the contacts came from people who claimed to know the identity of the U-boat or the explanation for its sinking. Sons, mothers, brothers, and grandchildren swore that loved ones had attacked and sunk a U-boat on a secret mission that the government still refused to acknowledge. Others called claiming to have classified U-boat information. Still others told of seeing U-boat crewmen swimming onto American shores to buy bread or attend dances. One elderly caller told of meeting an old German man while fishing as a teenager. "The guy looked at the spot on our chart we'd been fishing and said that's where he'd lost his U-boat," the man told Chatterton. "It was at the same spot you found your wreck." Several widows called saying that their husbands had sunk U-boats but had never received credit. A scholarly-sounding man called and said that the mystery could be solved simply by wiping the dirt from the conning tower, as U-boats had their numbers painted prominently on the side.

One man called and spoke in a heavy German accent.

"I am looking for ze diver who found ze U-boat," the man said.

"Okay, that's me," Chatterton said.

"Vat ken you tell me about ze diver who died?"

"Well, he was a pretty good diver. It was a terrible accident."

"His name vas Feldman?"

"Yeah."

"How do you spell det?"

"F-E-L-D-M-A-N."

"Vas Feldman a Jew?"

Chatterton hung up after that.

On another day, he received a call from a different man with a thick German accent.

"Your bubbles are disturbing ze sailors' slumber," the man said before hanging up abruptly.

Chatterton researched many of the stories he heard, even the ones that seemed loopy. Stories of U-boat men mixing into the American population turned out to be the product of terrified imaginations; on only a few occasions did men move from U-boats to American soil, and in those cases the men were saboteurs and spies. U-boat conning towers did sport the U-boat's number, as is evidenced in photographs, but only before World War II began; after that, any such markings were erased or painted over. So far, none of Chatterton's leads had inched him any closer to knowing the mystery submarine.

Kohler, too, was receiving phone calls. His name had been mentioned in some of the newspaper stories, and like Chatterton, he heard from family members seeking credit for a supposed U-boat kill a relative had made fifty years ago. He also began to hear from collectors.

"Are there human remains on the boat?" one man asked.

"We don't know that yet," Kohler said.

"I'd like to buy a Nazi skull."

"I don't do that."

"I'll give you two thousand dollars for a skull."

"I told you, I don't do that."

"What the hell do you mean you don't do that? We *won*. Are you some kind of Nazi lover?"

So-called collectors, Kohler found, got angry fast. He learned to hang up on them even faster.

Not every contact with Chatterton came from family or fanatics or conspiracists. Early on, he received a letter from the German embassy in Washington, D.C. It was written by Dieter Leonhard, a captain in the German navy. The letter began cordially, acknowledging Chatterton's discovery and offering assistance in researching the wreck. Farther down the page, however, Leonhard made plain Germany's position:

> The Federal Republic of Germany retains ownership of the submarines, regardless of whether the present position of the wreck is within national territorial waters or not. Sunken German warships are principally defined to be "tombs of a seaman's grave." Diving and exploring the wreck is therefore not permitted without government approval, which has been denied in each case to date. To keep a wreck a tomb, the FRG prohibits any violation to a World War II sub and will enforce this condition through legal means.

Chatterton called the phone number on the stationery and was transferred to Leonhard. Chatterton told him that he had received the letter and would be grateful for assistance with documents and research. Leonhard said he would be happy to help. Chatterton then popped his big question.

"Do you know the identity of the wreck?"

Leonhard said that the German government often relied on a man named Horst Bredow at the U-boat Archive in Cuxhaven-Altenbruch as a repository for such information. He offered Chatterton the contact information. Then Leonhard reiterated what he had written in the letter—that Germany did not permit diving on sunken U-boats.

"Which U-boat is it?" Chatterton asked.

"The one you found," Leonhard replied.

"Yes, but what is the specific U-boat designation?"

"I do not know."

"What about the exact location?" Chatterton asked.

"I do not know that, either."

"I'm going to be honest with you," Chatterton said. "I want to be respectful. You don't know what wreck this is, and therefore you can't lay claim to it. My goal is to identify the wreck, to put a name on the tombstone. I'm going to continue diving it until that happens."

"You understand our position, Mr. Chatterton. We do not want divers descending on this U-boat and scattering any human remains that might be on board and desecrating the wreck," Leonhard said. "We cannot and will not allow that."

"I understand that and I don't intend to allow that to happen," Chatterton said. "It's my first priority to be considerate and respectful. You have my word on that."

By now, Chatterton understood Leonhard's position. The man could not formally grant a diver permission to explore a war grave. He sensed, however, that Leonhard—who had kept an even and pleasant tone throughout the conversation—would not make official trouble for him so long as he treated the wreck with respect. The men thanked each other for their time and ended the call.

About a week after the first U-boat story appeared, Chatterton began to compile several promising leads. One of the first came from Harry Cooper, the founder and president of Sharkhunters International, a thousands-strong group based in Florida and "dedicated to preserving the history of the U-Bootwaffe," as their motto read. Chatterton had seen the group's text-crammed, exclamation point–filled newsletters—homemade-looking publications that mixed interviews, intrigue, history, editorials, criticism, and even the occasional classified ad. Despite the wild look of its mailings, Sharkhunters counted American historians, former U-boat commanders and crewmen, professors, U.S. naval veterans, and other experts among its members. Cooper urged Chatterton to join Sharkhunters, saying that the group had deep and far-reaching contacts he believed could help solve the mystery. Cooper asked questions no one yet had: Does your wreck have saddle tanks? Does your wreck have two stern torpedo tubes or only one? The answers could easily be gleaned while diving, Cooper explained, and would reveal much about the U-boat's type and the year it might have sailed. Chatterton resolved to inspect the wreck for that information on the next dive and report back to Cooper with the answers.

One morning, a man phoned Chatterton claiming to have sunk a U-boat from a blimp in 1942. A month earlier such a claim would have sounded like another bit of lunacy to Chatterton. But in his research, Chatterton had learned that blimps had been a formidable force in keeping U-boats submerged and in escorting ships along the eastern seaboard; that at one point during World War II more than fifteen hundred pilots had manned blimps considerably larger than the current versions used for advertising; that the blimps carried sophisticated antisubmarine technology; and that a blimp had even fought it out with a surfaced U-boat, a battle that had resulted in injury to the U-boat and the blimp plummeting from the sky. So Chatterton listened.

"I'm an old man and my mind ain't so good," the man said. "I don't remember all the details. But I know I sunk a U-boat from a blimp."

"Go ahead, sir, I'm listening. I really appreciate the phone call."

"Well, I was based out of Lakehurst, New Jersey. I attacked the U-boat close to there. I sunk it with a depth charge. I'm sorry, but that's all I remember. I hope that helps."

Chatterton recorded the man's story on his legal pad and made a note to research any reports his contact at the Naval Historical Center might find for him about blimp attacks on U-boats in the area of the wreck.

Another morning, Chatterton drove to the Naval Weapons Station Earle in Monmouth County, New Jersey, and showed a videotape of the wreck to experts in weapons, ordnance, and demolition. They watched the tape again and again. They talked among themselves and used technical words and physics terms in their discussions. They arrived at this consensus:

— the damage to the U-boat's control room looked to be caused by explosion rather than by collision;

— the shape and direction of the damaged metal indicated that the explosion likely occurred from outside the submarine; and

— the damage was likely caused by a force far greater than a depth charge, the weapon used so often by Allied forces against U-boats.

Chatterton took notes on everything. He asked the men if they might be kind enough to fashion a guess as to what had caused such cataclysmic damage.

"We can't be certain," one of the men said. "But if we had to guess, we would guess it was damaged by a direct torpedo hit."

A direct torpedo hit? Driving home, Chatterton turned the idea over in his mind a hundred times. Who would have fired such a torpedo? An account of an American submarine that had sunk a U-boat would have made every history book, yet there had been no such incident anywhere close to the wreck site. Could another U-boat have mistakenly sunk a friend? It had happened before, but mostly among U-boat wolf packs—groups of U-boats that hunted enemy ships together—and there was simply no record of a wolf pack anywhere near the wreck site. One thing was certain: the idea that a U-boat had limped from some other location with such an injury—as Nagle and some divers left room to believe—seemed impossible. To Chatterton, whatever had blown up that U-boat had done it at just the place in the ocean where the divers had found it.

The *Star-Ledger* story was barely a week old and already Chatterton had gathered reams of information from sources great and small. The best, however, were still to come.

One arrived in the form of a meeting at Nagle's house attended by Nagle, Chatterton, and Major Gregory Weidenfeld, a Civil Air Patrol historian who had contacted Nagle through a newspaper reporter. Chatterton had heard of the CAP; they were a group of civilian pilots organized in 1941 by New York's Mayor Fiorello La Guardia and others to fly small, privately owned airplanes to help defend coastal shipping. On any given night, a deli counterman or an accountant or a dentist might patrol the skies along the New York and New Jersey coasts, hunting U-boats with a pair of minibombs jury-rigged under the plane's wings. So patchwork was the weapon system that pilots were sometimes told not to land with the bombs still attached, as the explosives might trigger from the jolt; instead, they were often advised to drop the bombs whether or not they had spotted a U-boat. Weidenfeld explained that over the course of the war the CAP had detected more than 150 subs and had dropped depth charges on several of them.

"We sank two U-boats," Weidenfeld said. "But we never got credit for either of them."

"I've read about those incidents," Chatterton said. "You guys believe the navy didn't want to credit civilians."

"That's right," Weidenfeld said. "The navy didn't want to acknowledge it because it would have terrified the public to think that average civilians were needed to fight the U-boats, and that the U-boats were coming so close to our shores. Anyway, one of the kills was off the Florida coast. The other was in New Jersey."

Chatterton got out his pen. Weidenfeld told the story.

"On July 11, 1942, two of our pilots in a Grumman Widgeon spotted a U-boat about forty miles off the coast just north of Atlantic City. The guys chased the U-boat for four hours until it began to rise to periscope depth. When it finally surfaced, they dropped a three-hundred-twenty-five-pound depth charge, and the bomb exploded—they could see an oil slick streaking on the surface where the sub had been. They dropped the other depth charge right into the oil slick. It was a kill, absolutely. The pilots are both dead now. But I've been working for years to get my guys credit for this. I think you found their U-boat."

Chatterton was enthralled by the account. Weidenfeld had provided an exact date and a location only about twenty-five miles from the wreck site. If Chatterton could find a list of U-boats lost in American waters in July 1942—even if the boat was recorded sunk some distance away—he might find a way to explain its movement to the wreck site and solve the mystery. He thanked Weidenfeld and promised to do all he could to resolve the question of whether the lost sub was the one the Civil Air Patrol had killed nearly fifty years ago. A day later, Professor Keatts said of the story to the *New York Post,* "This is the most reasonable account I've heard so far. It could very easily be the same U-boat."

At around the same time, another unusual phone call came in, this one from a collector of Nazi memorabilia. This hobbyist, however, made no offer to buy artifacts.

"Among other things I collect photos of U-boat commanders," the man told Chatterton. "I correspond with a lot of these guys. One of them is Karl-Friedrich Merten, the eighth-most-successful U-boat ace of World War II. He read your story in a German newspaper with great interest and has some information he would like to share with you by mail if you'd be kind enough to provide your address."

"Absolutely," Chatterton replied.

Over the next several weeks, letters arrived from Germany. In them, Merten thanked Chatterton and the divers for their efforts. He also told a singular tale.

His colleague Hannes Weingärtner had also been a U-boat commander, and like Merten had been promoted to training flotilla commander, a prestigious land-based position. Weingärtner, however, still had battle in his blood and in 1944, at the advanced age of thirty-five, walked away from the desk and back down through the hatch of a U-boat. His assignment: to take *U-851,* a Type IXD2, or "U-cruiser," U-boat designed for the longest-range patrols, to the Indian Ocean to carry supplies to Far East German bases and deliver cargo to the Japanese navy.

The assignment, Merten speculated, might not have been what Weingärtner had in mind. He believed Weingärtner to have been "a submariner of the first hour," meaning that the man's early war roots and instincts—to aggressively hunt and kill enemy ships—had never withered.

"I had the impression that Weingärtner considered the position of the U-boat war not very different from his last command [of] Sept. '39," Merten wrote. "I don't know the text of his patrol order, but *U-851* was certainly not destinated [*sic*] for the Indian Ocean but for the U.S. coast."

To Merten, it seemed reasonable that the tameness of Weingärtner's assignment might have coaxed his colleague toward New York.

"I myself am pretty sure that the wreck you have found will be that of *U-851*," Merten wrote.

The words "I myself" danced off the air-mail stationery and into Chatterton's imagination. In Merten's letter, he now possessed genuine inside information delivered direct by a U-boat ace, a theory that bypassed textbooks and historians and got right to the heart of the matter. Merten knew his friend, and now Chatterton knew Merten, and for this Chatterton could not remember a time when he felt more excited.

As with all the information Chatterton had gathered, he told Kohler nothing of his contact with Merten. Though he had admired Kohler's enthusiasm aboard the boat, he still viewed him as just another guy along for the dive, a man whose artifact lust likely precluded any appetite for history or artistry. Instead, he shared his findings with Yurga, who continued to study the hard-core technical aspects of U-boat construction and layout, and who provided sound scientific counterpoint to whatever theories Chatterton entertained.

Through it all, a thrilling idea had begun taking shape in Chatterton's thinking. In the course of two weeks he had contact with a U-boat ace, a blimp pilot, a historian, and the president of a U-boat club. Each gave accounts of history unavailable in books and sometimes at odds with books. To Chatterton, who had hungered since childhood for better explanations, for the chance to see for himself, this stretching of history's canvas was a revelation.

While Chatterton continued to field phone calls, Kohler studied U-boats like an undergraduate before a final exam. He dedicated every free moment to understanding the U-boat—its construction, its evolution, its command chain, its lore. Much of his study was driven by an overriding motivation: to position himself to haul tonnage from the wreck. In his diving lifetime, he could not recall a moment like the one he'd experienced when he'd first laid eyes on Chatterton's Nazi china. As he'd held that dish in his hands he'd understood that he had possession of something transcendent. He hadn't been able to enunciate it to himself at the moment, but he'd known what he was feeling. In a single piece of china, every quality that made a shipwreck artifact great—history, symbolism, beauty, mystery—seemed to come together to a brilliant point.

As the days passed and Kohler delved deeper into his U-boat studies, he found himself paying closest attention to those books about the lives and times of the U-boat man, and this surprised him because his mission was so forcefully committed to identification and artifact recovery. Reading about men did not seem like book work to Kohler. Instead, he found himself transported; he could feel the inside of a U-boat not just as a machine but as the backdrop to a human being's life. He could feel the grueling and claustrophobic conditions under which these soldiers waged war, the coldness of a live torpedo next to a man's sleeping face, the smell of six-week-old underwear, the spittle in the expletives of men crammed too close to one another for too long, the splatter of a single icy condensation droplet on the neck of an enlisted man finishing a six-hour shift. Technical information interested him, yes, but technology did not make his heart pound—nothing did—like the idea of a U-boat man waiting helplessly while Allied depth charges tumbled through the water toward his submarine, the ominously dainty *ping . . . ping . . . ping . . .* of Allied sonar a prelude to imminent explosion. For years, Kohler had believed the U-boats to be nearly invincible. Now he began to learn of "Sauregurkenzeit" or "Sour-Pickle Time," the year when Allied ingenuity and technological and material superiority reversed the course of the U-boat war so decisively that U-boats sometimes went weeks without sinking a single enemy ship, when the hunters became the hunted. One source said that no fighting force in the history of warfare had taken the casualties the U-boat men had and still kept fighting. As October wore on, Kohler found himself wondering if any crewmen were still aboard the mystery U-boat, and he wondered also if their families knew that they were there.

As Chatterton continued to field the rush of phone calls and letters, he got word of a black plan. Bielenda had secured the exact location of the U-boat wreck site. He was planning to hit the wreck any day. Worst of all, the numbers were said to have come from Nagle.

The plan, as Chatterton heard it, was this: Bielenda had organized a dedicated mission to the wreck site to recover Feldman's body. Another captain had offered his boat and fuel for the trip; Bielenda was to supply the divers, who would search the area for the corpse. Chatterton doubted that Bielenda or the others would make even a perfunctory search for the body; it had been a month since the accident, the tides had been strong, and Feldman had never been inside the wreck in the first place. He called Nagle at home. He heard ice clinking in a glass.

"Ah shit, John. I gave up the numbers," Nagle admitted.

The way Nagle explained it, he had received a late-night phone call from another dive boat captain and longtime friend. Nagle had been drinking. The captain had announced that he had three sets of numbers and knew one of them to be the U-boat's location. Nagle listened as the captain recited the numbers. The captain was right—one of the sets was correct. Nagle suspected, even in his drunken haze, that Bielenda had wrung the general location from his Coast Guard cronies, then had asked this captain to check his voluminous book of numbers for anything close. Now the captain, who was supposed to be Nagle's friend, was leaning on him to reveal the exact location. Ordinarily, Nagle would have chewed off the captain's head for the attempt. But in his stupor, still guilty over Feldman's death and the *Seeker*'s inability to bring the diver home, Nagle mumbled something about location number two "possibly" being correct.

"I knew I was fucked as soon as I hung up," he told Chatterton.

Shortly after Chatterton spoke to Nagle, his own phone rang. Bielenda was calling. He told Chatterton that he had organized a mission to recover Feldman's body. He invited Chatterton to come along.

Chatterton's face flushed. For a moment he entertained the idea of accepting the invitation, certain that Bielenda would skip the rescue aspect of the mission and allow the divers to go straight into the U-boat for artifacts. He demanded to know Bielenda's true intentions. Bielenda insisted that the mission was dedicated to recovering Feldman's body. Chatterton pressed, asking where the *Wahoo* captain intended to look for the body. Bielenda told him that he would search around the wreck. This was too much for Chatterton, who believed that Bielenda's only intention was to dive the U-boat. He told Bielenda what he thought of the plan. Bielenda protested, but Chatterton would hear none of it. Spewing out a stew of expletives, Chatterton told Bielenda he wanted nothing to do with the so-called recovery mission and hung up.

A few days later, Bielenda and several divers made the trip. Some of the divers did, in fact, make a good-faith search for Feldman. Others just dove the wreck. No one saw a corpse. According to one of the divers on the trip, many went home that night with an over-riding impression: This wreck is lunatic dangerous. This wreck is going to eat people.

Word of the recovery mission reached Chatterton and Kohler a day later. They had a single question for their sources: Did anyone on the trip identify the U-boat? The answer was that no one had come close. Neither Chatterton nor Kohler was surprised. But each of them suspected that Bielenda would be coming back. So long as Nagle and the *Seeker* remained in the spotlight, they believed, the pirate flag of Bielenda's intention would fly at full mast.

On a Monday in early November, just after the recovery mission, the skies bathed New Jersey in sunlight. The sight rejuvenated Nagle, and he called Chatterton.

"We can make it to the U-boat one more time," Nagle said. "We can go Wednesday. We can identify this thing Wednesday. Are you in or out?"

"Have I ever been out?" Chatterton asked.

Nagle and Chatterton made phone calls. The trip was planned for November 6, 1991. Since Feldman's death, some of the divers from the discovery trip had decided not to tempt the U-boat again. Everyone else was in. Two empty bunks remained for Wednesday. Nagle called some legends.

Tom Packer and Steve Gatto were perhaps the most formidable deep-wreck diving team on the eastern seaboard. In a sport in which the buddy system was often shunned for its potential dangers, Packer and Gatto seemed to exist as a single organism, intuiting the other's moves and needs in ways usually reserved for identical twins. Many in the wreck-diving community referred to the team as "Packo-Gacko" for the unity with which they negotiated their dives. Packer had been part of Nagle's team when that crew took the bell off the *Doria*. Gatto had recovered the *Doria*'s helm a few years later. They rarely gave up on a wreck without getting what they had come for. They told Nagle they were coming to identify the U-boat.

The divers gathered on the *Seeker* for a head count near midnight. Again, Kohler had arrived decked out in his gang colors— denim jacket, skull-and-crossbones patch, "Atlantic Wreck Divers" logo. Chatterton shook his head at the sight. Kohler shot back his own look, one that said, "You got a fuckin' problem?" Neither spoke a word. Memories of Feldman still arched over the *Seeker*. Each diver answered "Yeah" or "Yo" when his name was called, then made his way to the salon without much of the usual carousing and joking.

Lying in their bunks on opposite ends of the salon, Chatterton and Kohler mentally rehearsed their dive plans. Chatterton would use his first dive for two purposes. First, he would follow the advice of Harry Cooper of the Sharkhunters club and inspect the submarine for saddle tanks, the externally affixed compartments primarily used for fuel in Type VII U-boats, the most common of the German fleet. If he had time, he would also look to see if the submarine contained two stern torpedo tubes, the narrow cylinders by which the fired weapon left the boat. Cooper had suggested that a U-boat so configured was likely one of the larger Type IX models, while the Type VIIs contained just a single stern torpedo tube.

For his part, Kohler had the eagle and swastika in his crosshairs. Every day for six weeks he had imagined recovering a Nazi dish of his own, of reaching into a mystery and pulling out a witness to a time when the world could have gone either way. He would not tolerate another day without ownership of such history. He was going straight for the dishes.

Chatterton dressed early the next morning. He, Packer, and Gatto would set the hook, then dive the wreck first. They would enjoy pristine visibility but would create silt and sediment clouds for subsequent divers, making artifact recovery more difficult. Kohler got wind of the plan. He stormed the stairs to the wheelhouse, where Chatterton was shooting the breeze with Nagle.

"Bill, what the hell is going on with this guy?" Kohler asked, pointing to Chatterton.

"What's wrong, Richie?" Nagle asked.

"He's gonna fuck the viz for me. I'm going forward for dishes. He went first last time. Let me go first today."

"John's going to videotape," Nagle said. "You splash after him. And don't go forward and mess up his viz. He needs clean water to shoot in."

"What? Why does he automatically splash first every time? He eats all the good viz while the rest of us get silt and clouds. Where's our fair shot?"

"Listen, Richie," Chatterton interjected. "You don't know what it's like down there yet—"

"You're right," Kohler interrupted. "No one knows what it's like because we can never go down there in good viz. I planned to go forward today, I'm looking for dishes. Now Bill tells me I gotta go somewhere else. That's a little unfair, don't you think?"

"John's going first, he's a captain," Nagle said. "There's plenty of room on the U-boat, Richie. Go somewhere else on your first dive."

Kohler shook his head and returned to the deck, muttering patchwork expletives that all ended in the word "Chatterton." He hated Nagle's decision but would respect the word of a captain on his own boat. He would go somewhere else on the wreck.

The water was calm and the skies partly cloudy when Chatterton, Packer, and Gatto splashed. They tied into the wreck just above the damaged control room, then waved good luck to one another and parted ways. Chatterton swam along the side of the submarine, searching for the saddle tanks Cooper had spoken of. He saw none. This was good evidence that the submarine was not a Type VII, and an invaluable piece of information in further researching the wreck. He would inspect the stern torpedo tubes later; to swim that distance now would consume too much valuable dive time. Instead, he would enter the wreck in the control room below him and videotape his push toward the forward torpedo room.

As Chatterton moved to go inside the wreck he could see Packer and Gatto still hovering outside the U-boat's torn-open control room. He knew the body language of excellent divers; the team had taken measure of the sub's tangle of interior dangers and had decided against challenging the wreck straightaway. "Smart guys," Chatterton thought to himself as he drifted inside. At least for now, Packer and Gatto were not going to identify the wreck.

The control room, for all its ground-zero devastation, looked like home to Chatterton. He had studied videotapes of his last dives the way a football coach watches film, memorizing formations and openings, envisioning jogs and hopscotches that might deliver him past the myriad obstacles. He had not been to the U-boat for six weeks, but he saw order in the chaos for all his video study, and that feeling of mastery was what he had come for.

Chatterton glided forward through the control room, crocheting himself between dangling cables, juking around dead machinery, and pointing his camera in every direction until he had passed the commander's quarters on the port side and the sound and radio rooms to the starboard. He moved easily past the galley to the officers' quarters, the place where he had found the dishes in late September. Now it was time to push toward the forward torpedo room, the U-boat's forwardmost compartment. But the navigational videos he had memorized from previous trips went snowy in his brain; he had never been this far forward. If he was to continue forward, he would have to do so by guts and instinct.

Video camera raised high in the compartment, Chatterton moved his fins and inched forward. A wooden partition materialized before him; the path to the torpedo room was blocked by a fallen piece of cabinetry. Chatterton swam closer. He allowed the water around him to still. Slowly, he raised his right arm to shoulder level and opened his palm, then held the position motionless, as if he were a python about to strike at prey. When everything in the compartment settled, he thrust his arm forward, crashing his hand into the partition. The wood exploded, spitting a cloud of sawdust and debris about the room. Chatterton froze and allowed the dying wood its fall. When the bulk of the particulate matter had sunk to the floor and some of the visibility returned, he could see the circular hatch leading to the torpedo room at the front end of the U-boat. He moved his fins and again crept forward.

Now he hovered in the noncommissioned officers' quarters, the place where crewmen like the navigator, chief machinist, and senior radioman slept. Chatterton remembered from Chicago that there might be dishes and other artifacts in the compartment. He scanned the debris and sediment piled on the port-side floor area for the familiar white of china. He saw the white. He inched closer. This was a different white. He moved still closer, until the white became a round shape with eye sockets and cheekbones and a nasal cavity and an upper jaw. This was a skull. Chatterton stopped. He allowed some silt to settle. Beside the skull lay a long bone, perhaps a forearm or shin, and beside it several smaller bones. Chatterton recalled the open hatches atop the submarine. If men had attempted to flee this U-boat, at least some of them had never made it out alive.

Now Chatterton faced a decision. He had been advised by some to search pockets, boots, and other personal effects he might discover inside the sub—those were the likeliest places to find a silver wristwatch or a wallet inscribed with a crewman's name, or maybe a cigarette lighter or cigarette case a crewman had taken to a silversmith to have his U-boat's number engraved on it. Chatterton knew that clothes and personal effects often lay near bones. He did not move. If he searched for personal effects, however carefully, he might disturb the human remains, and he was not willing to do that. He had contemplated this possibility after discovering the dishes and realizing that the boat had likely sunk with crewmen aboard, and in every iteration he came out resolved the same. This was a war grave and these were fallen soldiers. He knew firsthand what fallen soldiers looked like and what a fallen soldier meant in a world of wars and maniac leaders; he had seen life pass from young men defending their country and knew that whatever the politics or justness of a country's cause, a soldier deserved respect in death. He also understood that he might someday have to answer to a family about the bones before him, and he was unwilling to say that he had shuffled those remains in order to identify a shipwreck and maybe gain himself a little glory.

Chatterton turned his head away from the skull so as not to stare. He kicked his fins and moved forward, allowing the remains to fade back to blackness behind him. A moment later the forward torpedo room took shape in the distance. As Chatterton drifted closer, he could see that the room's round hatch—the hole through which crewmen had moved in and out—was open but blocked by a piece of fallen machinery. Chatterton lifted the obstruction, moved it aside, and swam into the compartment. Two torpedoes, including the one he had seen from atop the submarine on the Labor Day discovery trip, lay poised and pointed forward, seemingly as ready for firing as they had been during World War II. Only the top two of the room's four torpedo tubes were visible; the other pair lay underneath several feet of silt and debris that had piled up and into the middle of the room. Chatterton knew from research that the torpedo-tube hatches were sometimes marked by identifying tags. He also recalled that the torpedomen often wrote their nicknames or the names of girlfriends and wives on the outside of the hatches. He swam forward and searched for such evidence, but any trace of a tag or writing on the hatches had been eaten away by time and seawater. This wreck, even at its tip, refused to surrender its secret.

Chatterton panned his camera around the room in slow motion, capturing as much detail as possible for later study. The bunks that had once hung from the port and starboard walls no longer existed. The boxes of food and supplies that the torpedomen slept beside or atop in this compartment had vaporized long ago. The rigging, used to move the massive torpedoes into their firing tubes, lay fractured in the sediment. A white speck caught his eye. He aimed his light at the shape. Fish scurried through cracked machinery to escape the brightness. In the light he saw a human bone, then another, then dozens more. Many men had died in this room, the place farthest from the cataclysmic control-room damage. "Jesus, what happened to this ship?" Chatterton mumbled through his regulator. He turned around to leave. Before he could begin his swim out he came face-to-face with a femur, the largest and strongest bone in the human body. He averted his gaze and drifted past it slowly until he had exited the torpedo room.

The postscript to Chatterton's entrance was a swirling black silt that reduced visibility to zero. To exit the wreck, he would have to follow a map that existed solely in his brain. Chatterton began picking and finger-walking his way through the compartments, reversing memorized pathways and anticipating remembered dangers. Passing through the noncommissioned officers' quarters, he hugged the sub's starboard side in order to leave undisturbed the human remains he had seen while coming in. In nearly total darkness he moved through spaces other divers would not tempt on foot in a well-lit gymnasium. Again, he survived by favoring learning over artifacts. Again, preparation delivered him from a web of obstacles and traps. Chatterton exited the wreck through the control room, swam toward the flashing strobe he had clipped to the anchor line, and began a ninety-minute ascent to the surface.

Still steaming over Chatterton's dibs on the U-boat's forward section, Kohler decided to explore aft instead. Remembering an area of damage on top of the wreck's stern, he wondered if he might gain entrance to an unexplored section there. His instincts were excellent. The damaged area had been blasted open by some external force—he could see that much because the metal had been forced down and into the U-boat—and while the damage was nowhere near as extensive as that in the control room, it left enough room for a courageous diver to drop in and land where he might. Kohler hovered above the open wound, burped a breath of air from his buoyancy compensator, and sank into the U-boat.

As Kohler settled into the wreck, he detected the outline of two adjacent torpedo tubes in the haze of his white light. At once he understood where he was and the implication of his discovery: this was the aft torpedo room inside what was likely a Type IX U-boat, the kind built for patrols of longer range and duration. Though Chatterton had intended to inspect the stern torpedo tubes himself, Kohler had beaten him to it. In just a half hour, the two divers had answered the two most important technical questions about the mystery U-boat.

Kohler shined his lights about the room. Under some fallen debris he found a metal tag and an escape lung, the combination life vest and breathing apparatus used by crewmen to escape a submerged U-boat. Kohler's pulse raced. These were just the kinds of items that often bore identifying marks. He pulled them close to his mask. Any writing that might have been embossed on the tag, however, had been eaten away by nature. The lung, small technical marvel though it was, came up blank as well. Kohler packed the items in his goody bag and began a short swim aft to get a closer look at the torpedo tubes. Like Chatterton, he knew that the tube hatches had often been tagged and sometimes bore the names of the crewmen's loves.

Kohler never got to the tubes. During his swim, he noticed the edge of a white dish protruding from the debris on the floor. Pay dirt! He would score some china after all. He crab-walked toward the dish, careful not to raise any more silt than was necessary. Would the china contain the eagle and swastika? Could this be his greatest discovery of all? Kohler had to force himself not to lunge forward and start grabbing. *Slowly, slowly, slowly.* Finally, he completed the ten-foot swim. He suggested his hand forward and put the gentlest of squeezes on the china. The dish bent forward. Kohler let go. It sprung back into shape. Kohler understood at once. He had made the prize-winning discovery of a Chinette plate, something not invented until thirty years after the last U-boat had sailed. New divers are often surprised to find such modern objects aboard old shipwrecks, but a veteran like Kohler had seen Budweiser cans, plastic prescription-medicine bottles, a Kotex applicator, even a Barney the Dinosaur balloon on hundred-year-old wrecks, and he understood that such objects had been dropped off passing boats and had drifted along the ocean bottom until they got caught up in a wreck. Kohler removed the plate and stuffed it in his goody bag, the underwater equivalent of picking up a hot-dog wrapper in a park. Silt spilled around the hole he made. Another white object came into view. This one was no paper plate. This one was a femur.

Kohler went cold. Unlike Chatterton, he had rehearsed no plan for dealing with human remains. He had never seen bones on a wreck before this. And he had never faced a moral decision at 230 feet with narcosis banging. He knew this: he was no grave robber. He would not disturb bones to get artifacts. But should he dig nearby? That was a different story. Nearby was different. He looked again at the femur. He turned even colder. His breathing became more rapid.

Kohler backed away several inches, and in his movement the silt swirled black and buried the bone as quickly as it had been revealed. He had spent the last six weeks learning about U-boat men. He had come to sense the punishing and tedious nature of their work, the constant peril of their patrols, the hopelessness of their late-war situation. All that, however, was an experience of the mind. Here was a femur, the strongest of human bones, torn free from what had once been a human being. That bone was the bridge between book and imagination, and it stopped Kohler. Soon his coldness was replaced by a pall of regret. He found himself thinking, "I didn't mean to disturb you" as he watched the area where he had seen the bone. He decided to return to the *Seeker*. Kohler worked his way forward until he was under the damaged opening at the ceiling, injected a bit of air into his wings, and ascended out of the U-boat.

A few minutes later he began his ninety-minute ascent up the anchor line. For a while, he contemplated the fate of a U-boat in which men had died so far away from the boat's epicenter of damage. But as his decompression continued, the crescendo of his frustration with Chatterton renewed. He could not tolerate the idea of this diver stealing the visibility in a gold mine of artifacts under the pretext of shooting video. A mystery U-boat full of china and the guy is shooting video!

As Kohler climbed aboard the *Seeker*, divers gathered to inspect the tag and escape lung he had recovered. Some told him of Chatterton's push to the forward torpedo room. Kohler had heard enough. He decided to have another word with Nagle.

In the wheelhouse, his dry suit still dripping, Kohler explained to Nagle that his culture was Atlantic Wreck Divers to the core, an ethos in which divers worked as a team for the good of the group, none of this me-first-every-time bullshit. Chatterton entered the room behind him. Kohler rolled his eyes. Chatterton shut the door and spoke in a near whisper.

"I saw skulls up front," he said.

"I saw a long bone, a femur, in the back," Kohler answered.

"There are a lot of bones up front," Chatterton said.

"Did you videotape the skull?" Kohler asked.

"No. I didn't videotape any of the bones."

"What? You didn't videotape the bones? You steal the viz so you can shoot video, then you come across human remains and you don't tape them? What the hell were you doing down there?"

For a moment Chatterton said nothing. Nagle waved his hand as if to say, "Leave me out of this."

"I deliberately did not video them," Chatterton said. "It's a matter of respect."

Kohler begrudgingly nodded his agreement and left the wheelhouse. In the salon, he fixed himself a peanut butter and jelly sandwich and relaxed. He would need to spend three hours off-gassing his body's built-up nitrogen before he could splash for a second dive. Chatterton entered a few minutes later, popped his videotape into the VCR, and studied his first dive. Neither said anything to the other.

Chatterton was the first to return to the water. His goal was to search the area around the galley and the noncommissioned officers' quarters for cabinets that might contain the ship's logbook, maps, or other written materials like those he knew had been safely stored in wooden furniture on the Chicago U-boat. He would avoid the forward section of the NCO quarters so as not to disturb the human remains he had seen there.

Chatterton had little trouble reaching his target area. He got purchase on some low-lying machinery and began digging, feeling around for cabinet shapes. He found none, but he did run his hand along a smaller object he took to be a box. A moment later he had unearthed the item from beneath a pile of silt and sediment. It appeared to be a silverware drawer about eleven inches by eight inches, with sections for knives, spoons, and forks. A gelatinous black mud had cocooned the drawer and had sealed its contents. Chatterton looked closer and saw the outline of spoons in one of the sections. He nestled the silverware drawer into his bag and turned back for the anchor line. Perhaps there might be a date or year stamped on one of the utensils inside.

Not long after Chatterton had departed the sub, Kohler entered. This time, he beelined to the forward part of the wreck, exactly where Chatterton had recovered the dishes on the last trip. If he had to deal with Chatterton's silt, so be it. He was going to bag up.

The visibility was not as bad as Kohler had expected; he could see landmarks, and to an Atlantic Wreck Diver landmarks meant life. He navigated through the last remnants of Chatterton's haze and into the noncommissioned officers' quarters, a penetration only he and Chatterton dared risk on so virgin a wreck. He poked through sediment and debris, looking for the rounded white corners and feeling for the smooth surfaces that meant china to savvy divers. He found a four-inch-tall cologne bottle imprinted with a German word, *Glockengasse*, which he took to be a brand name. He remembered that U-boat men splashed cologne on themselves to battle the body odor inevitable on hundred-day patrols in broiling boats in which showers were unavailable. But he had not come for cologne; he had come for dishes. He resumed his search in earnest, running his hand through silt and sediment the way a child works a sandbox. He found nothing. He dug farther. As he cleared some debris he came upon what he could only describe to himself as a boneyard: skulls, ribs, a femur, shins, a forearm. That cold settled over him again. "I'm standing in a mass grave," he told himself. "I need to leave now." He packed the cologne bottle into his bag and turned around. The silt worsened from haze to black. Kohler breathed deeply and shut his eyes for a moment. Navigate. As long as you can breathe you're okay. He remembered his way and reversed it in his mind. He maneuvered back out of the U-boat as if following a trail of lighted bread crumbs. The Atlantic Wreck Divers had taught him well.

Back near the surface, Chatterton clipped his goody bag to a line attached to the boat—he dared not climb the *Seeker*'s ladder in bouncy seas holding such delicate bounty. On board, he undressed and dried, then fished his bag from the ocean. Divers gathered to inspect the haul. Chatterton took the silverware drawer from his bag and reached into the gelatin. A methane smell of rotten eggs and petroleum burst from the artifact, a final protest at being wrested from its peace. Various expletives ushered forth from the onlookers.

The first items out were silver-plated forks, stacked one atop another. Only these forks had been consumed so fully by electrolysis that all that remained was the rice paper–thin shape of the fork, the *form* of the fork. Nagle stepped forward. He had seen this kind of artifact before and understood that the slightest jolt could cause it to crumble into powder. He reached to spread the forks across the table for closer inspection. His hands shook from years of heavy drinking and hard living. He stopped and gathered himself and seemed to be asking a favor of his body, if only this once, to settle down long enough to be part of such a moment. His hands went quiet. He reached forward and took the forks and, without breathing, separated each from the others and laid them on the table. Each of the forks was stamped, on the underside of its handle at the widest part, with the eagle and swastika. Nagle moved them around delicately, searching for any other identifying mark. When he found none, he backed away and began breathing again. His hands began to shake so badly that he struggled just to put them in his pockets.

Next out of the drawer came several stainless steel spoons, these still sturdy enough to use for breakfast cereal. The spoons were spread on the table for inspection. They bore no marks. That left only one section of the silverware drawer: the knives. Chatterton looked closely. Only one utensil appeared to be in that section, a knife with a stainless steel blade and wood handle. He fished into the remaining gelatin and pulled out the utensil.

The knife was covered in mud. Chatterton dunked it in a bucket of fresh water and began rubbing the handle between his thumb and forefinger to remove the dirt. As the mud flaked away, he began to feel the imprint of letters beneath his thumb. He dunked again and rubbed harder. More letters pressed against his thumb. The hair on the back of his neck stood up. The other divers crowded closer. Chatterton kept rubbing. The final crusts of clay fell to the table. Beneath his thumb, carved into the knife's handle in handwritten letters, was a name. It said HORENBURG.

For several seconds, no one moved or said anything. Finally, Brad Sheard, the aerospace engineer, stepped forward and clapped Chatterton on the back.

"Well, that's it, man," Sheard said. "You've identified the U-boat. All you have to do is find crewman Horenburg. Congratulations."

"This might be the best artifact I've ever taken from any wreck," Chatterton told the divers. "This guy actually carved his name into the knife. It's not like a tag that was made in a factory. This is like a personal message. All I need to do is find Horenburg and the U-boat is identified."

By this time, Kohler had climbed aboard the boat. He and the other divers took turns inspecting the knife and congratulating Chatterton, each of them gracious but also disappointed that he had not been the one to identify the wreck. "Call me tomorrow when you find Horenburg and let me know which boat this is," the divers told Chatterton. Packer and Gatto, who had penetrated only the wreck's stern on their second dive, shook Chatterton's hand.

As the *Seeker* steamed back toward shore, Chatterton joined Nagle in the wheelhouse and took over the helm, and the two began a postmortem on the day. A few minutes later, Kohler walked in. Nagle offered him a beer and invited him to stay. Kohler mumbled additional congratulations to Chatterton. Nagle sensed that Kohler was still sore about Chatterton's decision to dive first, and perhaps a little jealous over the knife. Never one to pass up a potential confrontation, especially after a few beers, Nagle elbowed the divers in trademark Nagle fashion.

"Richie, if you don't like John splashing first, maybe you should put up a grate and lock him out," Nagle said, cackling. "Maybe you should leave him a sign on the grate that says 'Closed for Inventory.'"

Nagle's ear-to-ear grin looked half-satanic, half-schoolboy. Both divers knew that the captain adored confrontation, and each hated to be a pawn to this appetite. But the subject of the *Andrea Doria* grate had been festering since Kohler had joined the U-boat trip, and Nagle, the clever bastard, had lit a fuse.

"Maybe we should get things out in the open," Kohler said.

"Fine," Chatterton replied. "I'll tell you this. I don't like you Atlantic Wreck Divers. You tried to fuck me on the *Doria*."

"Yeah, okay, we did," Kohler said.

"If it wasn't for one honest guy from your little club, we would never have known. I'm not going to tell you who it is, but it's obvious only one of you guys has a conscience."

"Look," Kohler said. "I already came to terms with Bill on the grate. We did try to fuck you, yeah, I admit it. Do you want an apology? Do you want me to start crying and beg your forgiveness? Is that what you want?"

"I don't need an apology," Chatterton said. "We beat you at your own game. That grate was the best revenge. For me, it ended there."

"So you won," Kohler said. "I'm not going to flog myself. It ends there for me, too. And by the way, I don't like your kind either. Everything is so serious with you about diving. At least we know how to have fun."

"Mooning families on passing boats and making up pornographic dive schedules and wearing little matching uniforms is fun?"

"Hell yeah, it's fun. You should try it."

"That's the problem with you guys—"

"We got no problems—"

"Oh, you got plenty of problems—"

"Ah, fuck it," Kohler said, downing the last of his beer. He left the wheelhouse for the deck, where he found a seat on top of a giant cooler. A few minutes later, Chatterton came down the ladder and sat beside him. For a while, neither spoke.

"Listen, Richie," Chatterton finally said. "I don't need to be the first one to splash every time. If you don't mind setting the hook, you're welcome to go first next time. But remember, tying in is a gamble. If you run into trouble, you can blow your whole dive while you fix things."

"I don't mean to be a prick," Kohler said. "I respect you. I just want a fair shot."

Again neither spoke for a few minutes. Then Kohler began to tell Chatterton that he was feeling like the U-boat meant something more to him than the chance to load up on Nazi artifacts. He explained that he had been buying and reading books like a man possessed since his first trip to the wreck; that maybe something in his German heritage was connecting with this mission; that while he was eager to recover artifacts from this U-boat, he also found himself captivated by the history of the U-boat war and the men who had fought it. He asked if Chatterton had yet read Günter Hessler's book *The U-boat War in the Atlantic, 1939–1945,* then provided a detailed review. To Chatterton, these were not the typical leanings of an Atlantic Wreck Diver.

Chatterton walked into the salon to get a package of peanut butter crackers. He came back and sat beside Kohler again.

"Listen," Chatterton said. "I got a lot of calls and letters after the media got hold of this story. I think you might really find some of them interesting."

For the next three hours, Chatterton regaled Kohler with news of the last few weeks: of hearing from the Civil Air Patrol, of the blimp pilot, of the families and kooks and self-professed experts, of Harry Cooper of Sharkhunters, of U-boat ace Merten and the story of his colleague Weingärtner, who might just have had the gumption to flout orders and take his Type IX submarine to New Jersey instead of to the Indian Ocean. Kohler gulped the information and asked endless questions, all of which Chatterton found incisive and open-ended. As night fell and the *Seeker* made its way into the inlet near Brielle, the divers walked toward the salon to pack their belongings. Inside, Chatterton asked Kohler for his address.

"You going to send me something?" Kohler asked.

"I'd like to send you the videotape I shot today, and some others," Chatterton said. "You have to promise me that you won't show them to anyone or let them out of your hands—I've been burned by that before, as you know. But I think it can really help you navigate the wreck. I'm going to trust you with this."

"Thanks, man," Kohler said. He jotted down his address. "You have my word."

That night, Chatterton took the knife he had discovered and placed it on his desk. The name HORENBURG looked as clearly carved as the day the crewman had inscribed it.

"Who were you?" he asked as he gazed at the knife. "What happened to your U-boat, and who were you?"

He closed the lights to his office and made his way to his bedroom.

"Just another day or two," he said to himself. "Just another day or two and I'll have the answer to the mystery of the U-boat."

CHAPTER EIGHT

NOTHING AT THAT LOCATION

THE MORNING after Chatterton recovered the knife, he set out to find Horenburg. To this end, he wrote a letter detailing his discovery and mailed it to four experts, each of whom he believed could trace Horenburg and thereby identify the mystery U-boat. Those experts were:

— Harry Cooper, president of Sharkhunters, whose connections ran deep in the U-boat world
— Karl-Friedrich Merten, the U-boat ace in Germany with whom Chatterton had been corresponding (and who believed the mystery sub to be *U-851*, the one commanded by his colleague)
— Charlie Grutzemacher, curator of the International Submarine Document Center in Deisenhofen, Germany, a renowned repository of U-boat information
— Horst Bredow, a U-boat veteran and founder of the U-boat Archive in Cuxhaven-Altenbruch, Germany, the world's leading repository of personal U-boat information and the place to which the German government often referred researchers

By Chatterton's calculation, it should take no more than a week to receive the answer. For his part, Kohler continued to rampage through historical texts, learning the patrols of America-bound U-boats. In

these pursuits—Chatterton with the knife, Kohler with the books—
each was answering to more than a mystery. Each believed that once
the U-boat was identified, he had a responsibility to the families of
the fallen soldiers and to history to explain why the U-boat was in
American waters, how it had slipped through history's cracks, and
how it had met its end. And if there was a Mrs. Horenburg, she deserved to know why her husband lay buried off the New Jersey coast
and why no one in the world knew that he was there.

A week passed without reply. Then another week. Chatterton sat
beside his phone willing it to ring. He checked between the pages of
junk-mail flyers for the pale blue of an airmail envelope. A month
passed without a reply. He wrote to his sources again. Each told him
the same thing: There's been some confusion—we're still working
on it. Just after Christmas, nearly two months after his initial in-
quiry, Chatterton's phone rang. It was a U-boat enthusiast with
whom Chatterton had recently become acquainted. The man had
news.

"The knife is a dead end, Mr. Chatterton. You have to go back to
the wreck."

"What do you mean it's a dead end?"

"There was only one man in the U-boat service named Horenburg. And he never served in the western Atlantic."

"What U-boats did he serve on?"

"He doesn't remember."

For a moment Chatterton could not speak. Only the sound of
telephone static convinced him that the man was still on the line.
Finally, he choked out the question.

"Horenburg is alive?"

"He's alive," the man said.

"He survived the sinking?"

"I didn't say that."

"What did Horenburg say?"

"He said it's a dead end."

"What's a dead end?"

"The knife. He doesn't remember the knife."

"What else did he say?"

"Forget it, Mr. Chatterton. You should move on."

"Wait a minute. I would like to talk to Horenburg—"

"That's impossible. He talks to nobody."

"Please. Tell him I'd like to speak to him. This is everything to me. If this is his knife I'd like to return it to him."

"He doesn't want to talk."

"Can you at least tell me what U-boat he was on?"

"He doesn't recall anything. You need to go on from here. I'm sorry I can't help you further. I must go. Good-bye."

Chatterton sat stunned, unable to hang up. Horenburg is alive? He doesn't remember the knife? He talks to nobody? Chatterton held the phone to his ear, oblivious to the phone company's recorded warnings while he processed the impossible: *A knife with a crewman's name—the best artifact I have ever found—and it's a dead end?*

For the next several days, Chatterton thought obsessively of Horenburg. The man had survived the war, lived into old age, and was in a position to announce the answer to the mystery. Yet he wouldn't talk. Why not? What reason could he have for not at least providing his U-boat number?

A few days later, Chatterton received replies from Merten, Bredow, and Grutzemacher. Each of them had reached the same conclusion: there had been only one Horenburg in the German navy— Martin Horenburg, a *Funkmeister,* or senior radioman, in the U-boat service. His last patrol had been aboard *U-869,* a U-boat sunk by Allied forces off Africa in 1945. That U-boat's entire crew, including Horenburg, had been killed in the attack. It was the only patrol *U-869* had ever made. It had happened 3,650 miles from the mystery wreck site.

Now Chatterton was furious. He was certain that his three German sources—all respected experts—were correct about Horenburg. That meant, however, that the U-boat enthusiast had not spoken to Martin Horenburg, if he had spoken to anyone. On the spot, Chatterton wrote the man off and resolved never to speak to him again. Still, he remained unconvinced that his German sources had pursued the matter to the ends of the earth, as he would have. Perhaps there had been another Horenburg they had overlooked. Chatterton had heard about a U-boat memorial in Germany inscribed with the names of U-boat veterans killed in action. If he traveled to Germany, he could inspect that memorial himself, every last listing if necessary, in search of another Horenburg. Yes, if he went to Germany, he could study that memorial, visit the U-boat museum, and have at Bredow's archive himself. He checked his calendar. March would be a good month to do this right.

Chatterton invited Yurga and Kohler to accompany him to Germany. Yurga accepted. Kohler, who ran his own business, could not free himself for the weeklong expedition. But the invitation moved him. Chatterton was serious about this mission and would not have included anyone he did not respect or whose help he could not rely on.

"I'll work stateside," Kohler told Chatterton. "I'll keep my end going here."

As the March trip approached, Chatterton received a telephone call unlike any since the media storm had begun. An elderly gentleman introduced himself as Gordon Vaeth, a former intelligence officer for the Atlantic Fleet airships during World War II—the blimp squadrons. He had read of the divers' discovery and asked about any research Chatterton had undertaken. Chatterton told him of his slow correspondence with the Naval Historical Center.

"If you'd like to come to Washington, I would be more than happy to introduce you to the heads of the center, who are my friends," Vaeth said. "Maybe they can help you find what you're looking for. I don't intend to insinuate myself, but if I can help in any way it should be my pleasure."

Chatterton could scarcely believe his good fortune. Vaeth had been on the spot for antisubmarine warfare, in intelligence no less. And he had connections at the NHC. They made a date to meet in Washington for late February. As Chatterton hung up, he wondered if the trip to Germany would be necessary anymore. If anyone knew the answer to the mystery, it had to be the American government. Now, with Vaeth's help, he would be escorted straight to the source.

A few days later, Chatterton made the four-hour drive to Washington, D.C. He was due to meet Vaeth at the Naval Historical Center at 10:00 A.M. He arrived an hour early and pulled into the vast

Washington Navy Yard, an ancient-looking complex of trolley tracks, cobblestoned roads, libraries, and classrooms. A retired navy destroyer moored in the Anacostia River peeked at Chatterton from behind a stone building as he made his way to the NHC, storehouse for many of the navy's historical documents and artifacts. Inside, a snowy-haired man dressed in a tweed jacket rose to greet Chatterton. He introduced himself as Gordon Vaeth.

The men became acquainted, and Vaeth outlined his plan for the visit. He would introduce Chatterton to Bernard Cavalcante, the head of operational archives and a world-renowned U-boat expert, and Dr. Dean Allard, the director of the center. Those two men, Vaeth suggested, had access to nearly everything the United States knew about U-boats. Chatterton breathed deeply. He now believed himself minutes away from the answer to the mystery.

Vaeth escorted Chatterton into Cavalcante's office. These rooms, Vaeth explained, contain the vast majority of American naval records, and it is Cavalcante, a passionate historian born for the job, who oversees them. "And he's particularly expert in U-boats," Vaeth whispered as Cavalcante, a slightly built, middle-aged man in a checked sport coat and drooping reading glasses, emerged from an adjacent room. Cavalcante greeted the men warmly but with a cocked eyebrow, as if to say, "Oh, jeez, another U-boat nut in my office."

The men sat down and Vaeth asked Chatterton to tell his story. Chatterton was direct and economical. He and other divers had discovered a World War II U-boat about sixty miles off the New Jersey coast. They had recovered artifacts proving as much, yet had not been able to identify the submarine. They had checked the history books but found no mention of any U-boat within one hundred miles of the wreck site. The divers had used loran to return to the site three times, so the location was solid. They had shot videotapes, a compilation of which he had brought along.

For a moment there was only silence. Cavalcante looked to Vaeth with the vaguest grin, then to Chatterton. He reached into his desk and pushed some papers forward for Chatterton to sign—if the NHC was to accept the video, it had to be bequeathed properly. Chatterton had never felt so important signing his name. Cavalcante took the tape, then looked Chatterton in the eye.

"We are the United States Navy, sir," Cavalcante said. "We know a good bit about what lies in the ocean. But we cannot necessarily reveal that information. You understand that, Mr. Chatterton, correct?"

"Absolutely, sir, I do."

"We have an accounting of shipwrecks off the East Coast. We track this for military reasons, not for historical reasons, not for researchers or . . . if you'll excuse me, for divers. We have this list here. But I cannot show it to you. I'm sorry."

Chatterton's heart sank. The answer was on the other side of Cavalcante's office, and the man would not open the door. Vaeth remained seated, erect and dignified, but said nothing. Cavalcante said nothing. Chatterton wondered if the meeting was over. He was not willing to allow for that possibility.

"Mr. Cavalcante, I don't have to see the list," Chatterton said. "I'm just interested in this particular wreck at this particular location. This has become very important to me. Putting a name on this grave is the right thing to do for the families, and it's the right thing to do for history. There are dozens of dead sailors down there, and no one seems to know who they are or why they are there."

Cavalcante settled his chin between his thumb and forefinger. Vaeth cocked his head slightly as if to ask, "Well, what now, Bernie?" Cavalcante nodded slightly.

"Well, I suppose I can look it up," he said. "But you cannot have any photocopies of the information, and you cannot take any photographs with you."

"That's fine, thank you," Chatterton replied. "I will be satisfied with you verbalizing to me whatever information you might have about this wreck."

Chatterton wrote down the U-boat's latitude and longitude and handed them to Cavalcante, who excused himself into a fortress of documents. Vaeth grinned and gave Chatterton a nod that said "Nice going." The answer was moments away.

Several minutes later Cavalcante returned, a massive binder under his arm, and sat at his desk. He looked at Chatterton with that cocked eyebrow again.

"Are you sure about that location?" he asked.

"Positive," Chatterton replied. "We've been there three times."

"Well, we do not appear to have anything at that location. There is no U-boat—or anything else—at that location."

Vaeth's grin, kept in check throughout the meeting, surrendered to a smile.

"This is fascinating," Cavalcante said finally. "This is absolutely fascinating. Let's take the videotape to Dr. Allard and watch it together. He has to see this. I have to tell you, Mr. Chatterton, we hear from an awful lot of people who believe they've discovered a U-boat or have secret U-boat information. It's almost always nothing. But this is just fascinating."

Cavalcante ushered Vaeth and Chatterton into a stately office. Soon the men were greeted by a middle-aged man with wavy salt-and-pepper hair parted in the middle, wire-rimmed glasses, a bow tie, and a tweed jacket. The man introduced himself as Dr. Dean Allard, director of the center, and asked his visitors to sit down.

Cavalcante launched into the story. Mr. Chatterton, he said, had found a U-boat off the New Jersey coast: location definite, vintage definite, casualties definite, videotape available. All the while, Allard listened through weary ears. He had heard such claims a thousand times. Always, they were groundless.

Cavalcante paused a bit for effect.

"Here's the thing, Dr. Allard," Cavalcante continued. "I've checked the books. There's nothing there."

Allard nodded slowly.

"I see," he said. "I understand you have a videotape, Mr. Chatterton. May we view it?"

As Cavalcante prepared the tape, Allard called William Dudley, his second in command, into his office. Allard dimmed the lights and the five men viewed scenes of Chatterton moving about the conning tower, then forward toward the torpedo room. Various murmurs—"Fascinating," "Unbelievable," "Astonishing"—wafted through the office until the forty-minute tape had finished.

"I can't believe there's a World War II German U-boat out there and we don't know anything about it," Allard said. "Mr. Chatterton, if I can get a navy ship and divers to go to your location, would you be willing to work with the navy to identify this U-boat?"

It took Chatterton a moment to process the magnitude of the

offer. He was a New Jersey guy with a couple of scuba tanks fighting the ocean in an eleven-knot boat. Now Allard was offering to send a team of hard-hat divers and the muscle and resources of the United States Navy to solve his mystery. He began to fashion a sophisticated acceptance to fit the grandeur of the moment. Instead, he could only utter, "Definitely!"

Dudley stepped forward. He was the only one in the room not smiling.

"Dr. Allard, I'm sorry, we can't do that," he said. "As you know, the U.S. has filed a complaint against France in international court over the Confederate ship *Alabama*. The heart of that case is that the French are diving on an American warship we argue has protection for being a war grave. We can't at the same time be diving a German war grave in America. Our position in court would be weakened."

Allard contemplated the argument for a moment.

"Well, you're right, Bill," Allard said. He turned to Chatterton. "I'm disappointed. But if we can't actively go out there and help you with the diving, Mr. Chatterton, we can still provide you with whatever you need in terms of research assistance here."

Allard stood and removed his jacket and rolled up his sleeves.

"In fact, let's start right now. Bill, would you get the pamphlet explaining our resources for Mr. Chatterton?"

Dudley escorted Chatterton to his office. He closed the door behind himself, turned, and looked Chatterton in the eye.

"I don't like you," Dudley said. "I don't like divers who touch things on shipwrecks."

Chatterton knew what was unfolding. Some scholars despised divers for their willingness to disturb shipwreck artifacts. Chatterton had resolved this with himself long ago. If he were to discover, say, a Viking ship from a thousand years ago, he would surrender it to archeologists; there are things to be learned and preserved from a Viking ship. But a World War II vessel about which everything is known and meticulously documented? Chatterton believed he was on good paper with Allard and Cavalcante and the NHC. He would not force the issue with Dudley.

"Okay, that's fine," Chatterton said.

Dudley returned with Chatterton to Allard's office, where the men thanked Chatterton for bringing "a genuine mystery" to the

NHC. Vaeth and Cavalcante then showed him to the archives, where they introduced him to Kathleen Lloyd, an archivist and Cavalcante's right-hand person, who would assist Chatterton in whatever way possible. Chatterton thanked Allard, then disappeared with Lloyd and Vaeth into a research area filled with active-duty military personnel, authors, veterans, historians, and professors. There, Lloyd told Chatterton about four critical research tools available to him. Each struck Chatterton as a revelation. They were:

1. Anti-submarine Warfare Incident Reports (ASW): A daily chronology of underwater contact between Allied forces (ships, airplanes, blimps, Civil Air Patrol, armed guards aboard merchant vessels, etc.) and enemy vessels believed to be submarines. Reports could include battles, chases, sightings, sonar contacts—anything related to the hunting of U-boats. If a report told of a battle, a more detailed account—called an "attack report"—could be referenced.

2. Eastern Sea Frontier War Diaries (ESFWD): A daily chronology of interesting activity or observations made by Allied personnel along the American eastern seaboard. Such activity could include anything from the appearance of an oil slick to a mysterious puff of smoke to the discovery of a life jacket. Unlike the ASW reports, these reports did not have to involve submarines.

3. BdU KTBs: A daily summary written by German U-boat Control (BdU) detailing U-boat activity around the world. These contained a U-boat's orders, its radio communications to headquarters, and its engagements. Only BdU KTBs written before January 16, 1945, survived the war; those from later months were destroyed by the Germans.

4. Individual U-boat Files: Dossiers of U.S. Navy–compiled information on specific U-boats. These might contain files on the U-boat's type, its orders, its patrols, intercepted communications, intelligence reports, photographs, and survivor interrogations, as well as biographical information on its commander.

Lloyd suggested that Chatterton begin by searching the ASW incident reports, checking for any Allied underwater engagements in the area of the mystery wreck site. If he found any incidents near the wreck site, he could request detailed files about those incidents. He could also check the incident's time frame against the German U-boat diaries to see which subs had been sent to America then. She brought him the first boxes of reports labeled 1942. Vaeth smiled and wished him luck.

"I'm going to look at every piece of paper in this place if I have to," Chatterton said.

With that, Chatterton sat down and opened the first box of 1942 ASW incident reports. He began at January 1 and skimmed the page for latitudes and longitudes within a fifteen-mile radius of the wreck site.

Several hours later he finished with 1942. He had scanned more than a thousand incidents. None of them had occurred within a fifteen-mile radius of where the mystery U-boat lay. He was due home that night. He called his wife and told her he would be staying another two days. The next morning, he was first in line at the archives, asking for 1943.

Chatterton made his way through every incident report for the entire war. In four years, not a single Allied force had engaged a submarine within a fifteen-mile radius of the wreck site.

Chatterton asked Lloyd if he might next inspect the Eastern Sea Frontier War Diaries—these would yield information about *anything* that might have happened in the wreck area, whether or not it dealt with U-boats. She presented him with another mountain range of files. As he'd done with the incident reports, Chatterton bulldozed through the war years, hunting for any speck of activity near his wreck site. Two days later he was finished. During the war, not a single incident—not a piece of flotsam, a washed-up life jacket, the body of a sailor, an oil slick, even a puff of smoke—had occurred anywhere near the wreck site. It was as if that section of the ocean, where several dozen crewmen lay dead in this mystery U-boat, had vanished from existence during the war.

Chatterton asked Lloyd if he might spend the final few hours of his trip browsing some of the archive's other files. Soon he was lost behind a great wall of binders and boxes. While others around him tore into the masses of information, Chatterton was more feline in their company. He studied the labels without opening containers, flipped through research guides to learn what lay inside, orienting himself to the archive's myriad offerings so that he could return with vision and with a plan. In this way he negotiated research as he negotiated a shipwreck, by small initial penetrations designed to set up the later home run. As Chatterton lifted boxes and unlooped the strings from manila envelopes, he was twelve years old again and back in that fantastical house he had discovered after a day's hitchhiking, surrounded on all sides by stories and the dust of history. It was only when Lloyd tapped his shoulder and said, "Mr. Chatterton? Mr. Chatterton? We're closing now . . ." that he realized that he had forgotten to go home. He thanked her for all the help over his three-day stay and made his way to the parking lot, believing that he could come back to this wonderful place and find his answer, that he could learn to see into those records, which had so far denied him, that he could do it tomorrow if only he had the time.

Two weeks later, Chatterton and Yurga landed in Germany. The divers bought a large bouquet of mixed flowers, then headed to the U-boat Memorial in Möltenort, near the port city of Kiel. Here, listed on eighty-nine bronze plaques, were the names of the thirty thousand U-boat crewmen killed in action in World War II, each according to the submarine on which he died. Freezing rain needled into their necks and made mascara of the ink on the pages of notes they had brought along. For three hours the men traced their fingers down plaques to the letter *H* in search of Horenburg. They could find only one—Martin Horenburg, the *Funkmeister* who had perished with his crew on *U-869* off Africa, just as the experts had said.

That night, still chilled after a scalding shower, Chatterton placed a call to Merten, the U-boat ace with whom he had been corresponding. He knew that Merten had recently taken ill, but he hoped the eighty-six-year-old commander might be well enough to receive visitors and brainstorm about the mystery wreck. A young person answered the phone and apologized—Herr Merten could welcome no visitors; the once-great U-boat ace was sick and did not wish anyone to see him in such a weakened condition.

That left Bredow's U-boat Archive in Cuxhaven-Altenbruch. By this time, Chatterton had come to understand more about this unusual private repository. A U-boat veteran, Bredow had converted his own home into the archive, cramming files, photos, records, mementos, artifacts, and dossiers next to his kitchen and beside his appliances. Only a massive anchor in his yard distinguished Bredow's from the other homes on the block. The operation had come to be viewed by the German government and by historians as the country's premier U-boat archive, especially for information about the men who'd fought the war. Bredow possessed one-of-a-kind items, including letters, diaries, and photographs. His was a living museum focused on the men. When serious researchers looked to solve mysteries, it was to Bredow that Germany often referred them.

Chatterton and Yurga rang the doorbell as the clock struck 9:00 A.M. A short, balding, bespectacled sixty-eight-year-old man with a white beard opened the door and said in a heavy German accent, "Ah! Herr Chatterton and Herr Yurga—welcome to the U-boat Archive. I am Horst Bredow." Above Bredow's shoulder were file cabinets standing sentry over the house, artifacts laid on felt in glass cases, and dozens of framed photographs of U-boat crewmen in more hopeful days. As the divers stepped inside, they could barely remove their coats for their nerves—they believed themselves moments from the answer to their mystery.

"Everything you see here I have built from a single piece of paper!" Bredow exclaimed, spreading his arms. "All the answers you are seeking are here. You need go no other place."

Chatterton inhaled deeply. Bredow was about to identify the wreck.

"But first, before I give you the answer, I shall show you the archives," Bredow said.

Chatterton nearly burst from his skin. Instead, he and Yurga managed to say, "Oh, that sounds . . . wonderful."

For the next ninety minutes, Bredow took the divers through every room in the house. For ninety minutes, the divers continued to say, "Oh, very nice," and "Oh, how interesting," fighting to stay in their shoes while Bredow rambled on, in no hurry to present the solution.

Finally, Bredow sat behind a desk and asked the divers to sit across from him. He took a narrow, typewritten scrap of paper from inside a drawer. Chatterton's heart raced. Bredow pushed the paper across the table, facedown.

"Here is your answer," Bredow said.

Chatterton's hands shook as he received it. He turned over the paper. On it, Bredow had typed the names of seven U-boats.

Chatterton went numb. Yurga could not move. This was a list of U-boats lost off the American East Coast—a list available in public library books. One of the U-boats listed was a Type VII and therefore could not be the mystery sub. Others had been sunk several hundred miles from the wreck site. Still others had yielded survivors or other ironclad evidence of their identity. One, *U-853*, off Rhode Island, had been dived for years. These were the U-boats the divers had eliminated first.

Chatterton took a deep breath. "There are problems with all these boats, sir," he said. "It cannot be any of these."

"It must be one of those boats," Bredow said. "Your location must be wrong."

"No, sir," Chatterton said. "The location we gave you is very accurate. We have returned to it many times."

Bredow's forehead furrowed into narrow trenches. His cheeks turned red.

"You can look through my files if you like," Bredow said gruffly. "I do not know what else to say."

Chatterton and Yurga excused themselves to another room, out of sight of Bredow, and put their heads in their hands. With little left to do, the divers began to copy crew lists of every Type IX U-boat sent to America's eastern seaboard. Two hours later, they had done all they could. They were leaving virtually empty-handed.

On the way out, Bredow offered a bit of personal advice.

"If you can recover an escape lung from the wreck, perhaps the owner has written his name on it. We used to do this quite often."

Chatterton thanked Bredow for the tip and wished him a good day. In the hotel lobby that night, Chatterton bought a postcard and addressed it to Kohler. On it, he wrote, "We know more than they do. We must go back to the wreck." Kohler received it a few days later. He showed it to his wife.

"This postcard really means a lot to me," he told her. "It was a very personal thing to do, not typical for Chatterton's personality. I think we're going to be working together for a long time. I think we're becoming a team."

After Chatterton returned to the States, he phoned Yurga and Kohler and called a meeting at his house. It was time to take matters into their own hands.

It took Kohler all of eight minutes to reach Chatterton's place. The two had lived five miles from each other for years and had never known it. In Chatterton's living room, he and Yurga briefed Kohler on the Germany trip, each competing to do the best impression of Bredow's confounded expression when told that his list did not solve the mystery.

"I gotta say, this is a mystery like you read in a book," Kohler said. "A German U-boat comes to our doorstep in New Jersey. It explodes and sinks with maybe sixty guys onboard, and no one—no government or navy or professor or historian—has a clue that it's even here."

Chatterton recounted his research in D.C. "I went through the entire war, page by page," he said. "My glasses were sideways on my face. The room started spinning. Not a single thing happened anywhere near our wreck site during the entire war. Nothing."

A pizza and a six-pack of Cokes arrived. Kohler paid and forgot to ask for change. No one risked reaching for plates for fear of interrupting the flow. The divers were grooving now.

"I think we all know from our research that the stuff you hear about U-boats coming up on the beaches and the crewmen attending costume balls and buying bread at the local market are bullshit fantasy," Kohler said, pacing the room and using his triangular pepperoni slice like a professor's pointer. "But I'm going to confess something. You know the stories and rumors you read about how the Nazis tried to smuggle gold out of Germany at the end of the war? Or even the stories about how Hitler fled in a U-boat as Berlin fell? Well, think about it. If our U-boat was used for something like that, there sure as hell wouldn't be any record of it, would there?"

"Whoa! Whoa! Whoa!" Chatterton and Yurga called out from the couch. "Are you saying Hitler might be on our U-boat?"

"I'm not saying anything definitive," Kohler replied. "What I am saying is that we need to expand our thinking. We need to start conceiving of scenarios that might explain why no one in the world has a clue that this U-boat and these dead crewmen are in New Jersey. If we don't consider every possibility, even ones that sound outrageous, the answer might slip right past us. Because I gotta tell you fellas, this mystery is already pretty damned outrageous."

For a moment no one spoke. Kohler's eyebrows twitched at the corners with possibility—he was ready to see this thing through no matter what. Chatterton, who had returned from Germany deflated, basked in the innocence and single-mindedness of Kohler's resolve. Kohler stood his ground and kept his eyes locked on Chatterton's, nodding ever so slightly, as if to say, "We can do this." Chatterton found himself nodding back. He had last seen this kind of spirit in Vietnam, a place where a person could run through bullets for no other reason than that it was the right thing to do.

"Okay, it's about scenarios," Chatterton said, getting up from the couch and allowing Kohler the seat he had vacated. "I propose we start painting them."

Chatterton reminded the divers that two theories remained strong. First, that the U-boat had been sunk by the Civil Air Patrol on July 11, 1942. Second, that the wreck was *U-851,* the submarine Merten believed his maverick friend had taken to New York in violation of orders. Chatterton laid out his plan. Two months remained until dive season began. The divers would use that time to return to D.C. and research these two theories.

Near ten P.M., the divers called it quits. As they were pulling on their jackets at the door, someone said, "Do you think there really might be gold on board?" Another said, "Can you imagine if Hitler is aboard?" The third said, "Heck, at this point, I wonder if the *Weekly World News* was right—maybe our U-boat sailed in a time warp from Germany." Everyone laughed at that one. Then Chatterton said, "Whatever the answer is, it's going to be amazing." No one laughed this time because they all knew that it was true.

* * *

A few days after the caucus at his house, Chatterton returned to the NHC in Washington. On his first visit, he had searched the historical records for any activity that might have occurred within a fifteen-mile radius of the wreck site. He had come up empty. This time, he would expand that search to a thirty-mile radius, then to a sixty-mile radius if necessary. The research lasted four days.

He found nothing. Not a single event or observation had been recorded within sixty miles of the wreck site.

On his next trip, made with Yurga, Chatterton focused on *U-851*, the boat Merten believed his colleague Weingärtner had commandeered to New Jersey in an effort to more actively hunt enemy ships. Chatterton shared Merten's theory with Cavalcante, the head of the archives, who took an immediate interest in the idea and began his own bit of research.

While Chatterton waited for Cavalcante's findings, he turned his attention to the Civil Air Patrol theory. He posited a basic question: Had Germany sent any U-boats to the American East Coast during early July 1942, when the CAP claimed to have sunk one off New Jersey? The answer would lie in the BdU KTBs, the diaries kept by German U-boat headquarters. Chatterton requested those diaries from the research room.

Bingo. Several U-boats, it turned out, had been hunting in American waters then. According to the diaries, all but two of those U-boats—*U-157* and *U-158*—had returned safely to Germany. Both *U-157* and *U-158* were Type IXs, just like the U-boat the divers had found. Chatterton requested the attack reports associated with the sinkings of *U-157* and *U-158*.

According to the navy, *U-157* had been sunk northeast of Havana on June 13, 1942, by a U.S. Coast Guard cutter, killing all fifty-two men on board. The incident had happened nearly two thousand miles from the divers' wreck site. The attack report was ironclad—there were several witnesses, and debris had been recovered from the wreck, indicating that the sub sank where it was attacked. Chatterton therefore determined it impossible that *U-157* was the mystery U-boat. He next checked the attack report for *U-158*. That

188 • ROBERT KURSON

proved more interesting. On June 30, 1942, an American amphibious airplane spotted *U-158* off Bermuda, with perhaps fifteen of its crew suntanning on deck. As the submarine crash-dived, the pilot dropped two depth charges, one of which lodged inside the U-boat's conning tower—a nearly impossible bull's-eye. As the U-boat submerged, the bomb detonated and, according to the report, destroyed the submarine, killing all fifty-four men on board. According to the attack report, there was just one witness—the attacking airplane— and no debris had been spotted or recovered. That left room for the possibility that *U-158* had not been sunk where it had been attacked. The archive was closing for the weekend. Chatterton copied the documents and placed them in a manila envelope marked RICHIE. Kohler would be the perfect man to investigate the last days of *U-158*.

Chatterton and Yurga had been in Washington for three days. As they were packing to return to New Jersey, Cavalcante stopped by the research room and dropped a bombshell.

"As you know, I've been doing some research on *U-851*, the one that belonged to Merten's friend," Cavalcante said. "During the war, our spy network in Germany produced some very precise intelligence on what that U-boat had in cargo."

The divers held their breath. Just days ago they had speculated about hidden gold stored aboard U-boats.

"Turns out *U-851* was loaded with many tons of mercury to be delivered to Japan," Cavalcante said. "They did a cost analysis at the time. At 1945 prices, that mercury was worth several million dollars."

Chatterton and Yurga nearly collapsed. They were both commercial divers. They began envisioning plans to pump the mercury from the wreck. They thanked Cavalcante and practically sprinted to their car. Before Chatterton could put the key in the ignition both divers exclaimed, "We're rich!" During the drive home, they formulated a plan. Yurga would research the current price of mercury. Chatterton would contact an attorney to work out the legalities of salvage. They discussed the challenges of being new millionaires. Hours later, they looked up and saw a sign welcoming them to Pennsylvania. Their new status as tycoons had caused them to miss the exit for New Jersey.

The next morning, Yurga called his father, who dealt with scrap-metal dealers, and asked if he might research mercury's current value. An hour later, his father called back. Mercury was now considered a toxic waste. You had to pay others to get rid of it. Chatterton and Yurga had been millionaires for exactly twelve hours.

Armed with the attack report for the sinking of *U-158*, Kohler set out for Washington to do his own research. Rather than duplicate Chatterton's work at the NHC, Kohler went instead to the National Archives and Records Administration, storehouse for the Declaration of Independence, the Constitution, and the majority of America's most important records, including many naval documents. He had learned that many of the captured German records resided with the N.A., and he hungered to examine whatever information had survived about this U-boat and its commander.

At the sign-in desks, in various research rooms, Kohler recognized the names of several authors and historians whose work he had admired since childhood—unbelievable for a Brooklyn kid who'd never spent a day in college. He requested information on *U-158*. Staff members brought stacks of files and boxes of microfilm, and asked that Kohler wear white gloves while inspecting photographs. Much of the information was in German, causing Kohler to tap other researchers on the shoulder to ask, "Does this word mean 'machine gun'?" to which they might reply, "No, that word means 'parakeet.'" He kept at it, copying reconstructed logs from *U-158*'s doomed mission and diaries from its earlier patrols in hopes of seeing into the mind of Erwin Rostin, its commander. On the way out, he was forced to wait while officials stamped his research DE-CLASSIFIED—a touch of cloak-and-dagger that made Kohler think, "I'm back in the game."

A few nights later, Kohler called a meeting for Chatterton's house. With Chatterton and Yurga settled on the couch, he proceeded to weave a singular tale from his research. On June 30, 1942, as they knew, an American amphibious airplane patrolling off Bermuda had dropped a depth charge directly into the conning tower of *U-158*. According to the pilot, when the U-boat dove to escape, the bomb detonated and sank the submarine, killing everyone aboard.

"But what if," Kohler asked, whirling on his heels, "*U-158* is only injured? Or she escaped damage completely? Let's say her conning tower is damaged but she still is able to move. What would she do?"

"She'd try to make it back to Germany," Yurga said.

"Exactly," Kohler agreed. "Especially since she was at the end of her patrol and out of torpedoes. But in this case, she has an even better option. My research says she was scheduled to rendezvous with a 'milk cow'—one of those resupply U-boats—in the open Atlantic. So you'd expect *U-158* to head northeast to the milk cow for fuel and supplies, right?"

"Right," Chatterton said.

"Are you ready for this?" Kohler asked. "I say she never headed for Germany or for the milk cow. I say Commander Rostin thought to himself, 'I'm within striking range of New York City. I'm going to New York to sink American ships with my deck gun.' So he takes the U-boat north toward New York. He gets as far as New Jersey when the Civil Air Patrol spots him and lets him have it. Now *U-158* is really wounded. She hobbles a few dozen miles before the conning tower finally separates and she sinks—right at our wreck site. The Civil Air Patrol never gets credit because the first airplane claimed the kill."

"Hold everything," Chatterton said. "What commander in his right mind is going to take an injured U-boat without torpedoes and head north to New York when he has the chance for repair or escape to the east?"

"I'm going to tell you about that commander," Kohler said. "I've learned a lot about him. His name was Erwin Rostin. A few months before this, on his first war patrol, he sank four ships. On this patrol, the guy sank thirteen ships. No U-boat commander in history had a deadlier two-patrol total. This guy Rostin, he's a certified bounty hunter. He's killing Allied ships like it's target practice. He machine-gunned a Spanish vessel and took the captain prisoner! I've read about the great U-boat commanders, how they never gave up, how this generation was all piss and vinegar. Rostin is so unstoppable they award him the Knight's Cross by radio while the U-boat is still at sea! Rostin is not limping home, no way. He's only a thousand miles from New York. He's still got enemies to kill."

Chatterton and Yurga argued against Kohler's scenario. They insisted that a commander so low on fuel would never risk his ship and his men to fire his deck gun at enemy ships. They called him Tom Clancy for suggesting that this U-boat had been injured twice before finally dying at the mystery wreck site. Kohler never wavered. He asked them to imagine a time in which the world considered U-boats invincible. He asked them to envision an era in which U-boat commanders were the subjects of legend-making books, stories, radio programs, memoirs, newsreels, and parades. Chatterton did not necessarily agree with Kohler's scenario, but he found himself swept up in the man's enthusiasm, and as he watched Kohler wave his arms and clench his fists, it occurred to him that Kohler's overarching instinct was dead-on, that if one did not accept written history as gospel, worlds of possibility opened.

It was Chatterton's turn to speak. He acknowledged that Kohler had made an intriguing case for the wreck being *U-158* and for the Civil Air Patrol dealing the death blow. Now it was time for him to make the case for the wreck being *U-851,* the boat commanded by Merten's colleague Weingärtner.

"Merten knows his man," Chatterton said. "He knows the guy still was a hunter in his heart. Richie, you talked about the importance of knowing the man. Well, we are personally being told by one of the great U-boat aces that he knows the man—and he is convinced that the man came to New York. That's why there's no record of *U-851* in our wreck area—the boat was ordered to the Indian Ocean. Weingärtner disobeyed the orders. When he disappears, Germany presumes he sank where they'd sent him."

"I don't believe it," Kohler shot back. "No commander is going to go against orders like that. They'd be shot for that. Taking a U-boat to New York when you're ordered to the Indian Ocean? It's too egregious. I've read about a lot of U-boat commanders. I never heard of one who'd disobey like that."

Now it was Yurga's turn. He specialized in the technical end. That's what he delivered.

"We've got two favorites," Yurga said. "Richie likes *U-158.* John likes *U-851.* It sure looks like it's gotta be one or the other. I know how to settle it. According to my research, *U-158* was built with a deck gun. But some Type IXs were not. Next time we hit the water, we look for evidence of a deck gun. If our U-boat was built without one, it can't be *U-158*. Period.

"Now, as to *U-851*. It was a Type IXD, a special model they called a U-cruiser. U-cruisers were about thirty feet longer than typical Type IXs. All we need to do is drag a tape measure across the wreck. If it's two hundred and eighty-seven feet, it's a U-cruiser. If it's shorter, it ain't *U-851*. Next time we splash, we do a little looking, a little measuring, and we'll know where we stand with both these theories."

The divers shook hands and called it a night. Later that evening, at around midnight, Kohler tiptoed out of bed and into his kitchen. He found Chatterton's phone number stuck to the refrigerator door. It was too late to call. He dialed anyway.

"John, it's Richie. Listen, man, I'm sorry for calling so late. . . . When I was at National Archives, I came across some photos."

Kohler described the pictures he had seen: of a U-boat man's arm lying on the deck of an American ship—just his arm—with his tattoo still clear as day on his biceps; of a smiling British seaman holding a bucket of guts with a caption that said something like, "10 feet of human intestines; one human lung recovered from debris of sunken U-boat"; of a human liver next to a chocolate tin from a German mess kit. He told Chatterton he had been reading about U-boats for a long time and that for some reason, he'd had this pretty little picture about how a submarine sinks—that it cracks, starts dropping, the crewmen scratch once or twice, and then everyone drowns quietly. Now he told Chatterton that he knew better. He said these pictures got him thinking about the guys on their U-boat, and he asked Chatterton what he thought the sailors were thinking in the thirty seconds before their world blew up.

Chatterton told Kohler he'd been seeing the same kinds of photos. He described one that showed thirty U-boat crewmen in a life raft reaching their arms out to the enemy ship that had just rammed them. He told of snapshots showing the horrific damage done to U-boats by depth charges. The worst part, he told Kohler, was that a lot of these photos were from late in the war, when these sailors had gone out in their submarines knowing they had almost no chance of returning home. He told Kohler he could not imagine what a man might be thinking then.

For a few moments there was only silence on the line. Then Kohler apologized for calling so late, and Chatterton told him that the call was no problem at all.

CHAPTER NINE

A HEAVY TOLL

THE SEASON'S FIRST TRIP to the U-boat was scheduled for May 24, 1992. By now, the divers had taken to calling the wreck *U-Who,* but no one expected the mystery to last much longer. Especially Chatterton. In the off-season, between research trips to Washington, he had gone and messed with voodoo.

For decades, scuba divers had breathed good old-fashioned air from their tanks. In recent months, however, a group of cutting-edge warm-water divers had ditched air in favor of a mixture of oxygen, helium, and nitrogen known as "trimix." These divers had not invented trimix; rather, they had taken military and commercial diving technology and then tinkered with it to suit their purposes. As Chatterton heard it, trimix offered a fantasyland of advantages over breathing air in deep water:

— widened peripheral vision
— sharpened motor skills and coordination
— longer bottom times
— shorter decompression times
— reduced risk of oxygen toxicity and deep-water blackout
— elimination of narcosis

Chatterton believed that any one of these benefits could revolutionize wreck diving in the Northeast. Together they could turn a wreck diver into a superhero. Imagine working the U-boat without the pounding, narrowing fear of narcosis—and being able to do it longer, better, and safer than ever. When a Florida diver offered a trimix workshop in New Jersey, Chatterton and Yurga rushed to sign up.

Kohler, however, stayed away. He, too, had heard about trimix. He believed that if something sounded too good to be true, it was. "This is witchcraft, it's black magic," he told Chatterton. "You're going to 'experiment' at two hundred and thirty feet? Inside a U-boat? No one knows the effects of that gas on the brain or the body. You're going to get bent. Or paralyzed. Or killed."

Chatterton and Yurga attended anyway. The workshop was taught by Billy Deans, a Florida dive shop owner. For a fee of one hundred dollars, attendees received a loose-leaf binder with photocopied articles and tables. The principle behind using trimix—known as technical diving—struck Chatterton as sound. By replacing some nitrogen with helium, a diver could diminish his risk of nitrogen buildup—the culprit for so much of what goes wrong in air dives. The benefits were said to be quantum leaps in safety and productivity.

But there were potential downsides. First, there were no technical diving classes or certification agencies; a diver experimenting with this new art was on his own. Second, divers could make just one dive per day, not two as was customary, because the intricacies of off-gassing helium while topside were not fully understood. Third, because divers breathed a separate gas, called "nitrox," during decompression, they had to add nitrox tanks to their rigs, thereby carrying more gear. Fourth, northeastern dive shops did not stock trimix; if a diver wanted the stuff, he had to mix it himself. Finally, there existed almost no dive tables to instruct a technical diver on how long to decompress; this, too, would be a matter of improvisation and experimentation.

When the workshop ended, Deans told Chatterton and Yurga, "If you guys go forward, you'll be practically the only ones in your part of the country doing it. We don't know exactly how this works in cold water. You'll have to be pioneers."

By now, Chatterton was willing to pioneer. He believed he was just a dive or two from pulling evidence of the *U-Who*'s identity from the wreck. He believed in his ongoing responsibility to the crewmen's families and to history. He believed in looking beyond, and technical diving seemed the first true beyond since Cousteau.

Kohler feared for his friends' lives. He begged them to reconsider—so much productive diving had already been done on the wreck, why risk it? He warned Chatterton that working with pure oxygen under such high pressures could result in disaster—a single spark could cause an explosion or fire. Chatterton could only say, "When it comes to the U-boat, Richie, trimix is the future."

In February, as the divers steadied themselves for the business of brewing their own trimix, word arrived from the Coast Guard: a fishing boat about a hundred miles off Atlantic City had pulled up a human body dressed in a diver's dry suit and scuba tanks. The corpse's face had been eaten away by scavengers, leaving just a brown, waxy substance over the skull. Five teeth remained attached to a dislocated lower jaw. The Coast Guard identified the corpse as Steve Feldman. His body had been recovered perhaps five miles from the U-boat. He had been missing since September.

In January 1992, Chatterton and Yurga set out to mix their own gas. They rented five-foot-tall bottles of helium and oxygen from the local industrial gas supplier and purchased high-pressure hoses, delicate connectors, and finely tooled pressure gauges. They would mix the gas in Chatterton's garage. To give himself a chance at survival in case of an explosion, Chatterton would stand outside the garage and reach his left hand through the window to manipulate the valves. "I'm a righty," he explained to Yurga. "If this thing blows, it's better that I lose my left hand."

For weeks, Chatterton mixed gases in his garage, reaching his left hand through the window, holding his breath, waiting for an explosion. Soon, he and Yurga were expert at preparing the mixture of 17 percent oxygen, 30 percent helium, and 53 percent nitrogen they hoped would revolutionize their diving. They purchased dive tables from an engineer who wrote them as a hobby—he was one of maybe three people in the country who even attempted it—then used imagination and daring to extrapolate those tables so that they might make two dives in a single day. They purchased new and larger scuba tanks. When the weather warmed, they took the new rigs with their newfangled gas and splashed in a Pennsylvania quarry, adjusting buoyancy, tweaking rigging, and learning to breathe the magic gas. In the quarry's shallows, their minds remained crystal clear, their coordination precise. The bottom of the Atlantic, however, would be another matter. And the inside of a sunken U-boat another matter still.

On the evening of May 23, 1992, divers gathered at the *Seeker* for the season's first trip to the *U-Who*. Backs were slapped, new gear inspected, off-season stories swapped. Everyone asked trimix questions of Chatterton and Yurga. They always answered the same way: "Yes, I think we'll live." Kohler was among the last to show. Next to Chatterton's new rig, Kohler looked as if he'd stolen his gear from the 1958 set of the television show *Sea Hunt*. On his back were the skull and crossbones of the Atlantic Wreck Divers.

"You're a dinosaur, Kohler!" Chatterton yelled from the boat.

"Maybe," Kohler shot back, taking in the sight of Chatterton's new gas, "but I ain't heading toward extinction."

A few minutes later, Nagle emerged. Few had seen the *Seeker*'s owner since the end of last season, when he had vowed to quit drinking and work himself into diving shape. It took a moment for the divers to process the sight. Nagle's skin was spotted with jaundice, his hair greasy, his body like a rumpled suit on a wire hanger. He smelled bad. He had brought along no dive gear. People scurried to avoid staring.

The rumble of the *Seeker*'s diesels was comfort to these divers, who never slept quite as well at home as they did on these thin, stained blue pads that delivered them to where they belonged. In the wheelhouse, Nagle and Chatterton took turns steering. Chatterton updated Nagle on the two favorites—*U-158* and *U-851*—and how Crowell and Yurga planned to measure the wreck and search for evidence of a deck gun, two simple tests that would pronounce on these original theories. Nagle stared straight ahead, the liquor spots on his face lit red by the instruments. For several minutes he said nothing.

"The *Seeker* is bigger than me," Nagle said finally. "Diving is bigger than me. The *Seeker* will go on long after I'm gone."

Chatterton said nothing. Ocean mist spattered the windshield. Nagle continued to steer a course for the *U-Who,* the greatest shipwreck a diver could ever find.

The divers awoke the next morning to a glorious day. The sun shone and the ocean was glass. Bottom visibility, they speculated, would be one hundred feet at least. Chatterton and Kohler began dressing. They had decided weeks ago to dive together and now rehearsed their plans. According to Chatterton's research, torpedo-tube hatches—the circular doors that swung closed after a torpedo had been loaded into its firing chamber—contained on their faces a tag bearing the U-boat's number. On his first dive, Chatterton would slither through the sub and into the forward torpedo room, video-taping his navigation for study topside. On the second dive, he would return, penetrate to the end of the torpedo room, and remove the tags from the hatches. With any luck, the tags would reveal the wreck's identity. The plan was classic Chatterton: tape, study, and return. For his part, Kohler planned to explore the stern, searching the aft torpedo room for torpedo-hatch tags and any other useful artifacts. Measuring the wreck would be left to Danny Crowell. Yurga would search for evidence of a deck gun. By day's end, mysteries would be solved.

Chatterton and Kohler splashed just after sunrise. Neither had seen the Atlantic so still and limpid, as if the ocean had dressed for this promising day. Chatterton's trimix flowed into his lungs and brain as theory had promised, keeping his thinking sharp and the enemy narcosis at bay. At 100 feet, in this miraculous visibility, they could see the submarine end to end. But for the mortal wound to its side it looked ready for war, an eel of steel, torpedoes, and guns, still stealthy and deadly. Before this, Chatterton and Kohler had seen only twenty-foot patches of the wreck in the swirling ocean. Now they saw a war machine. The divers descended farther. At 150 feet, the cataclysm of the U-boat's final moments screamed from the gaping hole in the control room. Only now, in such pristine visibility, could the full extent of the violence done to this U-boat be digested. Chatterton and Kohler looked at each other. Each mouthed the words "Oh, Christ."

The divers continued to the wreck and secured the grapple. Chatterton remained astounded at his clarity of vision and nimbleness of hand. He felt no narcosis. Kohler watched him for signs of delirium or other symptoms that might occur when one dabbles in the black arts. Chatterton smiled and gave him the okay. The divers went their separate ways.

Chatterton made his way into the control room, through the commander's quarters, and into the noncommissioned officers' quarters. Again he saw piles of human remains—skulls, femurs, ribs, shins. This time, after a winter's research, he felt a connection to the bones, as if he were returning to the home of a family he had known. He had read crewmen's letters and had seen their faces in photographs as they drowned on sinking lifeboats. For the first time, Chatterton felt as if the men might not mind his efforts to find their names.

Chatterton corkscrewed himself through more obstructions, dodging hanging wire and jagged metal until he arrived at the forward torpedo room. Breathing trimix, he felt invincible and was tempted to push through and go right for the identifying tags he believed were attached to the torpedo tubes. But he stuck to his plan and videotaped the inside of the room, knowing that the camera would catch navigational traps worthy of topside study. After a few minutes of filming, he turned back, made his way out of the wreck, and ascended to the surface.

At the stern, Kohler worked into the aft torpedo room and began to search for artifacts. As before in this place, he saw a femur, then a skull and several other bones. Last year, the sight of these remains had thrown a cold chill through Kohler. This year, after he'd burrowed into the lives of the U-boat men, the room began pulsing. As Kohler looked at the skull and bones he could envision the checked bedsheets on which the sailors had slept, and he could hear the singing of their songs.

Kohler spent twenty minutes searching for clues but found nothing. Back on board the *Seeker*, he and Chatterton compared notes. Each had been in the water for about ninety minutes. Chatterton's trimix, however, had enabled him to stay on the wreck for thirty minutes, while Kohler had stayed only twenty-two before needing to decompress.

"It was like diving in the Caribbean, Richie," Chatterton said. "Clear head. Sharp motor skills. No narcosis."

"I'll stick with the stuff that got me here, thank you," Kohler replied.

By this time, Crowell was preparing to splash and measure the wreck, and Yurga was dressed and ready to dive for evidence of a deck gun. Yurga had brought along a customer from the dive shop where he worked, a personable emergency-room physician named Lew Kohl, who had also outfitted himself to breathe trimix.

"You sure about him?" Chatterton whispered to Yurga.

"He's used trimix on some shallower dives this year. He says he's ready. And I'll be diving with him," Yurga replied.

Kohl adjusted his mask, bit down on his regulator, and flopped sideways off the gunwale. Chatterton and Kohler could not believe what happened next. Rather than bob to the surface as most divers do after the splash, Kohl plummeted like an anchor toward the ocean bottom. The topside divers knew at once what had happened: Kohl had not adjusted the buoyancy for his new trimix equipment. He had become what divers called a "dirt dart."

Dirt darts were in deep shit. The furious increase in water pressure that came with their plunge squeezed their suits into a second skin. Rapid compression caused their regulators to free-flow, exploded their sinuses and blood vessels, burst their eardrums, and induced vomiting and vertigo. And that was before they hit the bottom.

"Oh, shit, he's gone," Kohler said. "Lew Kohl's dead."

But Chatterton could see that Kohl had landed and was still breathing—he could see his bubbles. Chatterton's mind slowed to 16 rpm, the speed of the Vietnam medic under pressure.

"Look at his bubbles. He's wandering around looking for the wreck, which means he's alive," Chatterton said. "Yurga, I'm going to give you a line. Follow his bubbles and go get him."

"John, this is too dangerous," Yurga said. "This is my first trimix dive and—"

"I'm going to give you a line that I'll have with me up here at all times. Richie and I cannot get back in the water now. You must go in the water, follow his bubbles, and get him."

Yurga splashed. As he spiraled downward around Kohl's bubbles, Kohl managed to drop his weight belt. Now positively buoyant, he began to ascend. At 150 feet, however, he ran out of gas—nothing was coming from his regulator. At that point, he lost interest in proper dive protocol. Kohl decided to rocket toward sunshine. Seconds later he broke the surface.

"Now he's a Polaris missile!" Kohler shouted. "He's gonna be bent for sure if he lives."

Kohl began flailing and thrashing on the surface. But he was not vomiting or trembling, evidence to Chatterton that he had not yet been seriously bent.

"He's only been in the water maybe ten minutes," Chatterton yelled. "He's got a chance."

Kohl was not able to swim. Tom Packer and Steve Gatto dived into the ocean, dragged him up the ladder, and put him on the dressing table. "Get me a stethoscope and the crash kit," Chatterton ordered. Kohler cut off Kohl's dry suit. Chatterton took Kohl's vital signs and began recording dive and medical information doctors would later need. As he made notes, he asked flatly, "Lew, are you in pain? Lew, can you hear me?"

Kohl could not respond. Chatterton told Nagle to call the Coast Guard rescue chopper. He shoved aspirins down Kohl's throat, forced him to drink massive amounts of water to reduce the gas volume in his blood, and put an oxygen mask over his face. He used the stethoscope to listen for the gurgling of an embolism in Kohl's blood vessels. A minute later, Kohl began to come around, almost as if he had been reanimated in a mad doctor's laboratory.

"Lew, we're calling a helicopter for you," Chatterton said.

"Oh, no, don't do that," Kohl replied. "I'm fine. I'm coming around. I'm not even symptomatic—"

"You're fine for the moment," Chatterton said. "But we're treading water here with this aspirin and oxygen. You're going to become bent. You can't do what you did without problems. We gotta get you to a hospital."

Chatterton shined a flashlight into Kohl's eyes.

"I see no signs of neurological damage," Chatterton said. "But you're gonna be bent. It's just a matter of time."

The divers continued to comfort Kohl and keep him stable on oxygen and water. With each minute, Kohl seemed better and healthier. Several minutes passed. Nagle poked his head from the wheelhouse and announced that a Coast Guard chopper was en route.

"Ah, jeez, I'm really sorry, guys," Kohl said. "Everyone's trip is on me. I pick up the tab for everyone."

Chatterton smiled and allowed another diver to stay with Kohl for a while. He then moved to the back of the *Seeker* to help Yurga climb aboard. Still about two hundred feet from the stern of the boat, Yurga waved to Chatterton. Chatterton began to wave back, but his arm froze. Stalking Yurga from behind was an eighteen-foot monster.

"Shark!" Chatterton yelled. "Yurga! Behind you! Shark!"

Yurga whirled around just as the shark submerged.

"What?" Yurga yelled. "I don't see anything!"

The shark surfaced again, moving closer to Yurga.

"Shark! Behind you!" Chatterton yelled.

Again, Yurga turned. Again, the shark submerged.

"Quit busting my balls!" Yurga screamed. "Come on. Get serious!"

Now, even as the shark bore down, Chatterton could not help laughing.

"Swim, Charlie, swim!" he screamed, quoting a line from the movie *Jaws*.

Yurga swam. The shark followed. Yurga swam with all he had. The shark finally turned away and disappeared.

Nagle cut the anchor line and headed to meet the Coast Guard helicopter. Kohl continued to improve. The chopper took him away. He would suffer joint pain as a result of the bends but would recover fully. Most likely, only his relatively brief time on the ocean bottom saved him; had he stayed down longer and then shot to the surface without decompressing, his adventure as a dirt dart probably would have killed him. The divers, however, had lost the most perfect day any of them had ever seen. Crowell had never had a chance to measure the wreck. Yurga hadn't checked for a deck gun. And Chatterton hadn't gone inside the torpedo room to get his tags. The season, however, was young. That was another thing about wreck diving. So long as you were alive, there would always be another trip.

Nagle booked the next *U-Who* trip for June 9, 1992. Dr. Kohl had seen enough of the U-boat for one lifetime. He was replaced by two divers unlike any Chatterton and Kohler had known before.

Chris Rouse, thirty-nine, and Chrissy Rouse, twenty-two, were father and son, though with their identical wiry builds and Mediterranean features, the men were often mistaken for brothers. Smiling, they almost appeared to be twins, their pupils turning leprechaun under dark eyebrow forests of naughtiness. They smiled a lot. They argued even more.

The Rouses bickered incessantly, flinging insults, epithets, and crudities at the slightest provocation—and preferably no provocation—no matter the place or occasion.

"The best part of you was the stain I left on the mattress," Chris would say in front of a boat full of divers.

"You old fucking man, you can't keep up with me," Chrissy would reply.

"You're lucky you got my good looks or you wouldn't get anywhere with women," Chris would say.

"Ah, you just got lucky with Mom, you old douche," Chrissy would answer.

And on and on, until the Rouses came to be known as the Bickers. Some divers were horrified by the exchanges. Many more were entertained. Chatterton and Kohler watched in amazement.

Yet the Rouses were excellent divers. They had made their bones as cave divers, a branch of scuba known for its meticulous and unrelenting safety training. Cavers often shunned wreck diving because of its unpredictability and harsh conditions, but the Rouses were drawn to wrecks for the history to be uncovered and the artifacts to be taken. Cavers who challenged shipwrecks often did so stubbornly, refusing to warehouse their long-held mantras and techniques. The Rouses had no such issues. They were ravenous in seeking new skills and burned to apply them. Like many cavers, they had experience with technical diving and breathing trimix, and were eager to discuss theory and ideas.

When the Rouses hit water it was clear they were blood. They dove as a team and had developed a sixth sense between them, the kind of anticipation born of a lifetime of living under the same roof. Underwater they remained absolutely loyal, each willing to sacrifice himself for the good of the other. This single-mindedness—this love—made the Rouses perhaps the most formidable team in diving.

When Nagle invited the Rouses to join the *U-Who* expedition, Chrissy vowed to solve the mystery. He told Chatterton that by identifying the wreck he would immortalize the Rouse name and contribute a page of history to the world. His father did not bicker with him about this.

"They're more than talented and capable enough to do it," Chatterton told Kohler. "They may be the ones who get this done."

The weather for the June trip was not nearly as perfect as it had been in May, but the divers' plans remained the same. Chatterton would search the forward torpedo tubes for numbered tags. Kohler would hunt for identifying artifacts. Crowell would measure the wreck. Yurga would determine if the *U-Who* had been built with a deck gun. As for the Rouses, they would penetrate the wreck and begin to learn the U-boat.

As before, Chatterton and Kohler dove together and set the hook. This time, Kohler swam forward with Chatterton, his eyes scanning the areas where crewmen kept records and personal belongings. Chatterton moved through the forward section of the U-boat, into the torpedo room, and up against the torpedo-tube hatches. Where he had once seen nothing in this spot, he now saw a white, tag-shaped patch of encrustation on the hatch. He grabbed his knife and pried the blade under the encrustation. White flakes fell away, revealing the perfect outline of a tag. Except no tag remained. Corrosion had eaten away the metal so that only the imprint of the tag had survived. Chatterton's heart sank. He inspected the other three torpedo-tube hatches. Same story. A half century of salt water and storms had gnawed away the answer. As Chatterton turned to end his dive he felt profoundly disappointed. He had developed concrete evidence for the tags' existence and had designed a well-researched plan for their retrieval, only to find them eaten by nature.

Just behind Chatterton, Kohler was having better luck. While in the noncommissioned officers' quarters he discovered a closetful of boots and shoes, still lined up neatly—left-right, left-right—just as the crewmen had left them. He took one of the boots, believing a crewman might have written his name inside. "It doesn't look like you guys were wearing these, so I'm going to take one," he explained to the roomful of remains around him.

Kohler moved next to the conning tower lying broken in the sand beside the U-boat. Inside, he discovered a bicycle-type seat. At once, he recognized the piece as the chair on which the commander sat while manning the attack periscope. "This might be where the commander died," he told himself. "If this U-boat was attacking when it was sunk, this is where the guy would have been sitting." The chair, however, bore no identifying marks, so Kohler left it alone. He met Chatterton on the anchor line. Each man shook his head. Neither had solved the mystery.

While Chatterton and Kohler decompressed, Crowell and Yurga set about their missions. To measure the wreck, Crowell attached one end of a surveyor's tape measure to the U-boat's bow, then swam aft, allowing the tape to unspool from its reel as he moved. He had affixed a tag to the tape at the 250-foot mark before leaving on this trip, the length of the typical Type IX. If this U-boat was any longer than that, it would be powerful evidence that the wreck was *U-851*, the rare Type IXD U-cruiser commanded by Merten's rebel colleague Weingärtner.

Crowell allowed the line to unspool slowly as he began his journey along the wreck's top. Line spun free of the reel. As the tip of the U-boat came into view, the reel hiccuped. Crowell looked down. His marker had come up. The wreck was about 250 feet long. U-cruisers were 287 feet long. This could not be *U-851*.

While Crowell prepared to ascend, Yurga settled in just forward of the damaged control-room area. He had made a careful study of Type IX deck plans and knew exactly where to look for the deck gun mount, a known feature of *U-158*, the submarine commanded by the daring Erwin Rostin. Yurga crab-walked along the top of the wreck and envisioned the blueprints he had devoured like pulp-fiction novels during the off-season. He surveyed the relevant area. The evidence was plain as day: this U-boat had been built without a deck gun mount. This wreck could not be *U-158*. In the course of twenty minutes, the divers' two leading theories had been sunk.

The men regrouped topside. Each seemed more shell-shocked than the next. A winter of intense research had come to naught. None of them could fathom any viable contenders other than the two they had just eliminated. They halfheartedly inspected the inside of the boot Kohler had recovered. As befitting the day, it contained no information. The Rouses surfaced soon after. Neither father nor son had found much of significance. Chatterton and Kohler made another dive but found little. As the boat headed back to Brielle, the divers knew that summer was upon them, meaning that Nagle would begin running the *Seeker* to the *Andrea Doria,* his money trips. None of them knew when the boat might again be available to take them to the *U-Who.*

The day after returning from the *U-Who,* Chatterton wrote a letter to Karl-Friedrich Merten. He explained that divers had measured the wreck and determined that it could not be *U-851*, the boat Merten believed his colleague Weingärtner had commandeered to New York. Merten wrote back expressing gratitude for Chatterton's efforts and acceptance of his conclusion. Chatterton did not phone Major Gregory Weidenfeld of the Civil Air Patrol; though the divers had ruled out *U-158*, they still allowed that the wreck might have fallen to the CAP.

For the next three months, Nagle ran to the *Doria,* and even when he had an open date for the *U-Who,* the weather interfered. Chatterton still could not believe that the sub's torpedo-tube hatch tags, which he had thought were made of resilient brass, had been eaten away. He tracked down an elderly U-boat veteran in South

Carolina who had also built U-boats in Germany's naval yards. The man explained that as brass had become scarce, tags had been made of leftover materials, a metal stew that could not survive long in the marine environment. Chatterton thanked him for the information and began to say good-bye.

"One other thing, if I might," the old U-boat man said.

"Of course. What is it?" Chatterton asked.

"Thank you for what you are doing. Thank you for caring about those boys down there. They don't have anyone else."

Caring for the fallen crewmen had figured into much of Chatterton's and Kohler's thinking since the last *U-Who* trip. Though neither spoke of it, a truth had begun pounding at their awareness: they would stand a far better chance of identifying the wreck by digging through the human remains. Many of the bones were still dressed in clothes, the pockets of which might contain wallets, coins, a personalized money clip, love letters, an engraved pocket watch, anything. Items like these survived for decades on shipwrecks. Frustrated and with no promising leads, Chatterton and Kohler fantasized about the answers that lay mixed among these bones.

Chatterton called Kohler and set up a meeting at Scotty's Steakhouse, a popular nearby restaurant.

"You want to talk about the men, right?" Kohler asked.

"Right," Chatterton said. "It's time."

The next evening, the divers sat down for rib eyes and baked potatoes. They discussed the prospect of digging through the crewmen's remains. The bones appeared to be well preserved. Personal belongings were likely still among the bones. The only question was how to deal with those remains. Each man announced his decision.

"I say we leave the remains undisturbed no matter what," Kohler said.

"I agree," Chatterton said. "We don't touch them. Even if it means we never solve the mystery."

For a moment, the divers sat in silence, startled by the finality and similarity of their thinking. Slowly, each explained his reasoning until it became clear that they had arrived at their conclusions for identical reasons. Their discussion lasted for hours. Their resolve pivoted around five principles:

1. Respect for the crewmen. The U-boat men were sailors. They had risked their lives to serve their country. By doing that, they had earned a respect that entitled them to rest undisturbed.
2. Respect for the families in Germany. Neither diver could bring himself to tell a crewman's family that he had solved the mystery by rummaging through the pockets of their loved one's corpse. Nor were they willing to lie to a man's family and say that they had not done so if in fact they had.
3. Honoring the brotherhood of the deep. As submariners, the U-boat men had embraced the risks of living below the ocean's surface. The divers existed in the same place, abided by the same laws, and faced many of the same perils, all of which generated a feeling of brotherhood and a sense of protectiveness toward the remains.
4. Protecting the image of wreck divers. The *U-Who* had become international news, Chatterton and Kohler emissaries of wreck diving. Their behavior would reflect on the sport for years.
5. Doing the right thing. The commitment to solve the mystery had originated in the instinct to do right by the crewmen. To violate their remains in order to find an answer would defeat the dedication to dignity with which the project had been undertaken.

Chatterton and Kohler agreed on a simple guideline. If they saw a piece of identification lying behind, say, a skull, they could move that skull to retrieve the tag. But they would not search remains for evidence, even if they believed such a search would be productive. Moreover, they would create an environment of peer pressure to urge—even coerce—other divers to behave similarly.

Driving home that night, Chatterton contemplated a final reason why he had determined to leave the remains undisturbed, a reason that seemed too personal to share with Kohler. More than ever, diving had become a reflection of life to Chatterton. The principles by which he had made himself a great diver were the same principles by which he lived. If he were to lower the bar now because he was frustrated, who would he be?

Kohler, too, had kept a reason to himself. His German heritage, so much a part of his identity since childhood, had been reawak-

Bill Nagle in 1991, with a major score from the second-class area of the *Andrea Doria*.

The *Seeker* was built for a single purpose: to take scuba divers to the most danger-ous shipwrecks in the Atlantic Ocean.

"It was the salt
water that gave
John his feeling."

John Chatterton, preparing for one of his first wreck dives, West Long Branch,
New Jersey, summer 1983.

"Richie never stopped wondering how people could be left in the water when they had loved ones at home who needed to know where they were."

Richie Kohler, "tonnage king" and Atlantic Wreck Diver.

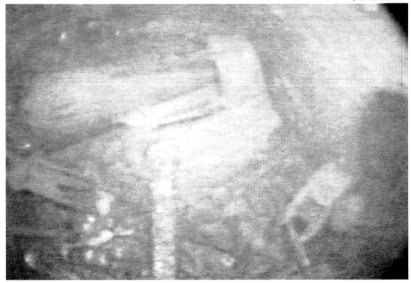

The torpedo (*upper left*) discovered by John Chatterton inside a wreck he and others had believed was probably just a pipe barge.

Topside view of the wreck's antiaircraft gun mount.

Steve Bielenda,
"King of the Deep."

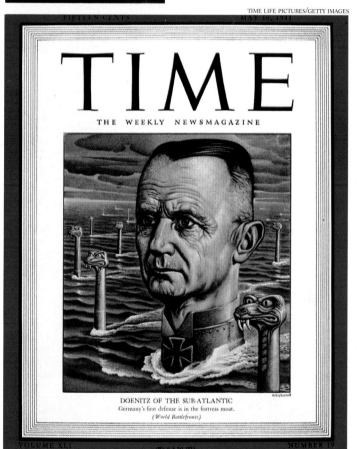

Karl Dönitz and the U-boat terror, *Time* magazine, May 10, 1943.

Richie Kohler gears up on the *Seeker*'s dressing table. Note the German-style lettering on his tank, a Kohler trademark even before the discovery of the mystery U-boat.

Steve Feldman

The first clue: a dish recovered by Chatterton, marked with the eagle and swastika, dated 1942.

Richie Kohler after bagging up on the mystery U-boat wreck.

John Chatterton and Richie Kohler with two excellent *U-Who* artifacts. Neither piece, however, revealed anything about the wreck's identity.

John Yurga, left, and John Chatterton aboard the *Seeker*.

The U-boat's periscope, which lies on the ocean floor beside the wreck.

Rubber-soled shoe amid the wreckage in the officers' quarters. Crewmen wore soft shoes during attacks in order to stay silent to enemies.

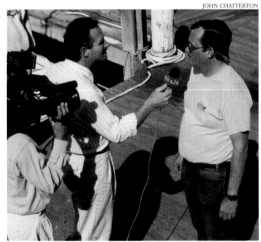

Bill Nagle, captain of the *Seeker*, grants another interview after the 1991 discovery of a mystery German U-boat in New Jersey waters makes international news.

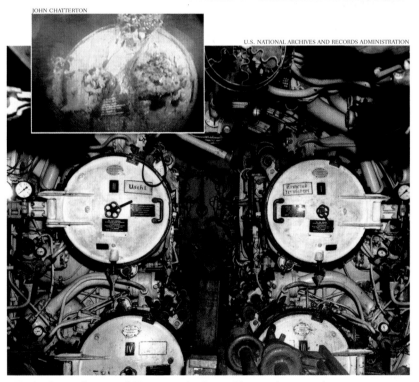

Forward torpedo room of *U-505*, on display in Chicago. It was in this compartment on the wreck that Chatterton expected to recover an identifying tag. (*Inset*) A torpedo tube hatch on *U-Who*.

Mud-entombed silverware drawer recovered by John Chatterton. At the bottom lies a knife with a crewman's name hand-carved into the handle.

John Chatterton holding Horenburg's knife.

A closer view of Horenburg's knife.

A valve from the U-boat's interior.

Metal schematic diagram discovered by Chatterton. It was this artifact that confirmed the U-boat's type and the shipyard at which it was built.

A few of Richie Kohler's *U-Who* artifacts, including a metal schematic diagram, the face of the diesel motor room telegraph, directions for use of a survival kit, and a glass bottle for cologne, which submariners used to mask the odors of months at sea.

One of the U-boat's steel hatches, likely blown open by the force of an immense explosion.

Tight squeeze: Richie Kohler entering the diesel motor room through a control room hatch.

Chris Rouse, left, and son Chris Rouse, Jr., aboard the *Seeker* after diving the *Andrea Doria* in 1992.

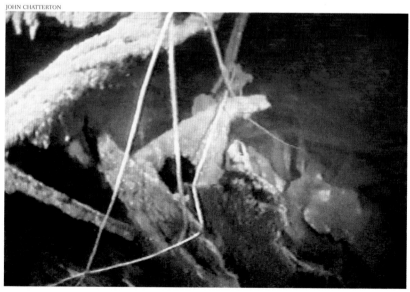

Chrissy Rouse's penetration line, tangled after his desperate attempt to escape the U-boat.

One of the Rouses' scuba tanks, still lying on the wreck after their fateful dive.

Reunited. Richie Kohler and John Chatterton in the summer of 1996, after Kohler's self-imposed exile from diving.

ened in these brushes with the fallen crewmen. He never kidded himself about the U-boat's purpose or about the madman who had sent it. As an American, he would have attacked the U-boat himself had he been patrolling the Atlantic. But he also recognized these fallen men as Germans. "These men," Kohler thought to himself, "came from where I'm from."

It took three months for the *Seeker* to set sail again for the *U-Who*. In September, the divers had to make the most of their opportunity; the weather would be unpredictable come fall, and this might be the last U-boat dive of the season.

Optimism aboard the boat was muted this time around. Chatterton and Kohler had exhausted their leading theories and had whiffed in their hunt for an identifying artifact. Their disappointment, however, did not extend to the Rouses. From the moment father and son boarded the *Seeker* they began their high-octane bickering, sniping at each other's equipment, sexual prowess, age, diving ability, sandwich choice, and—particularly odd to eavesdroppers—family ancestry. As before, Chris said little about what he hoped to accomplish on the U-boat. Chrissy was more forthcoming.

"I'm going to identify the wreck," the junior Rouse told Chatterton. "I'm going to be the one to do it."

As before, Chatterton and Kohler splashed together and tied in the anchor. This time, Chatterton swam toward the stern and dropped into the blown-out deck section that led to the aft torpedo room. His off-season research had revealed that this room contained an auxiliary steering station possibly marked by a brass tag. But when he began to look around, he saw a boot, then a life jacket, then several skulls, femurs, and other remains, a boneyard before him. It was possible that the answer to the mystery lay within the remains. Chatterton turned and swam out.

Kohler, in the meantime, had chosen to explore forward. As he entered the noncommissioned officers' quarters, he spotted the cuff of a dark blue shirt that appeared to have spilled from a cabinet. Since it lay far from the human remains in the compartment, Kohler felt comfortable tugging at the shirt. Black silt billowed from the cuff. When the cloud cleared, he saw an arm bone in the sleeve. He let go of the shirt and apologized aloud, saying, "I'm so sorry. I had no idea." He replaced the shirt where he had found it and began to leave. A few feet later, as he neared the galley, he shined his flashlight under a piece of wood. The eye sockets from a skull stared back into his. Kohler's heart pounded. This was a bad day. He apologized again and made his way from the wreck.

Chatterton and Kohler's second dive was equally unproductive. The Rouses, however, had better luck. In the galley, Chrissy had discovered a canvaslike fabric imprinted with German writing.

"I don't know what the words mean," Chrissy told Chatterton and the other divers topside. "All I know is I gotta dig the thing out. It's stuck in there. But it looks important. I think I can get it on the next trip. This could be the thing."

The Rouses, however, would have to hope that the weather held. Rough seas and violent storms could mess with anyone's project over the course of a long off-season. As Nagle fired the diesels and turned the *Seeker* back toward Brielle, every diver on the boat wished for just one more trip before winter.

In early October 1992, Nagle booked the *Seeker* for the season's final journey to the *U-Who*. It would be a two-day venture, held over the Columbus Day weekend. The divers would have a final shot.

The day before the trip, Nagle called Chatterton and begged out of the trip.

"I just don't feel like it," Nagle grunted.

"Bill, this could be the time. We need you," Chatterton said.

"Don't you get it?" Nagle exploded. "After I'm dead nothing matters! Fuck the U-boat!"

Chatterton tried to reassure his friend, but he had seen this transformation building all summer. Nagle had begun the season reflectively, taking comfort in the idea that even if he were unable to sober up and rebuild himself for diving, the *Seeker*'s legacy would outlive him. Now jaundiced and sicker than ever, a failure at countless rehabs, he could not bring himself to take his own boat to one of the biggest dives ever.

"You and Danny take the boat," Nagle said, ice clinking in the background. "I don't give a shit. Go without me."

On the night of October 10, the divers gathered at the *Seeker's* Brielle dock. No one had to ask why Nagle was not in the wheelhouse.

While the other divers tied down their gear, the Rouses began their bickering. This time their argument was a bit more serious than usual. Neither father nor son could afford trimix for the trip—they would be forced to breathe air, a savings of a few hundred dollars.

"Chrissy was supposed to buy the mix this time," Chris sniped.

"No, it was the old man's turn," Chrissy countered.

"Was not."

"Was too."

"Cheapskate."

"Miser."

And so on into the evening.

The next morning, Chatterton and Kohler splashed first, as had become their custom. While Kohler explored the NCOs' quarters, Chatterton returned to the forward torpedo room in search of more tags. He found a few made of plastic, but none with identifying information. On the way out, he spotted a bent piece of aluminum about the size of a tabloid newspaper lying amid a pile of wreckage. Ordinarily, he would have ignored such junk. This day, something urged him to pluck it from amid the garbage and drop it into his bag. Chatterton gave the artifact no more thought as he began his ascent to the *Seeker*.

Topside, Chatterton emptied his bag. The aluminum piece, Swiss-cheesed by rust and splotched with marine growth, clanged onto the dressing table. Yurga walked over to inspect it. Chatterton opened the bent metal as if it were a magazine. Engraved on the inside were technical diagrams—a schematic illustrating the mechanical operations of some part of the U-boat. Chatterton grabbed a rag from a bucket of fresh water and wiped it across the artifact. The sea growth lifted easily, revealing small German inscriptions along the tattered bottom edge. Chatterton pulled the schematic toward his face. He read, "Bauart IXC" and "Deschimag, Bremen."

"Hold everything," Yurga said. "Deschimag-Bremen was one of the German U-boat construction yards. That means this wreck was a Type IXC built at Deschimag-Bremen. There couldn't have been more than a few dozen Type IXs built there during the entire war. This is huge for our research."

Kohler surfaced a few minutes later. Like Yurga, he understood the magnitude of the discovery.

"This is really going to narrow things down," Kohler said, slapping Chatterton's back. "All we have to do is go home, check our books, and we'll have the short list of IXCs built at Deschimag. It's gorgeous."

The divers splashed again that day but found little. Their minds, in any case, were on Chatterton's spectacular find. That evening over dinner, as the *Seeker* rocked in the waves while anchored to the U-boat, the Rouses admired the schematic and told Chatterton about their day. They had nearly excavated the piece of canvas covered in German printing and believed they might be a dive away from bringing it topside. Optimism echoed off the salon walls. The divers wished one another a good night. In a single day, a season of dead ends had transformed itself.

The Atlantic recused itself from the divers' optimism. As men slept aboard the *Seeker,* the ocean turned the vessel into a bathtub toy, tossing some divers from their bunks and forcing the captains, Crowell and Chatterton, to consult the weather radio. Conditions were snotty with five-foot waves, and the forecast had changed for the worse. At 6:30 A.M. Chatterton walked down to the salon and roused the divers.

"It's getting nasty out there," Chatterton said. "Anyone thinking of diving best get going now. After that, we're pulling the hook and going home."

"You diving, John?" someone asked.

"Not on a day like this," Chatterton said.

Of the fourteen divers on the trip, just six moved from their bunks to gear up. Kohler was first and dressed without hesitation. A half hour later he rolled into the ocean. The dive team of Tom

Packer and Steve Gatto followed, as did New Jersey State Trooper Steve McDougal. The Rouses also rolled out of bed.

"I'm not diving, forget it," Chrissy said, peering out a cabin window. "Too rough out there."

"You pussy!" his father bellowed. "You got no backbone, kid."

"Didn't you hear, old man?" Chrissy asked. "Chatterton said the weather's nasty and getting worse. Can't you feel it out there?"

"If you can't dive these conditions, you got no business being out here," Chris said. "I can't believe you're my son. You're an embarrassment!"

"Okay, you old crow," Chrissy said. "You want to go diving? We'll go diving. Let's go."

For a moment Chris said nothing.

"Ah . . . that's okay," Chris finally said. "I was just jerking your chain. It really is too rough. Let's pass."

"Too rough? Maybe too rough for you, you old geezer," Chrissy said, taking the offensive. "If you're too soft to go diving, I'll go myself. You stay here with the women."

"You're not going without me," Chris said. "If you go, we both go."

"You guys are too much." Chatterton laughed, leaving the salon. The Rouses continued bickering as they decided what to have for breakfast, whether to shave, how long their dive should last. Chris jokingly ordered Barb Lander, the only woman aboard, to fix his breakfast and wash his dishes.

As the Rouses geared up they reviewed their plan. Chrissy would return to the galley to free the piece of canvas containing the German writing. It was stuck beneath a floor-to-ceiling steel cabinet. Chris would wait outside the wreck, his lights a beacon for his son's exit. Chrissy would work for twenty minutes before exiting the wreck. At the dressing table, the Rouses affixed their trademark hockey-style helmets and started for the gunwales. Waves battered the *Seeker's* stern, knocking the flipper-footed Chrissy onto his side like an overtired toddler. Yurga forklifted him under the arms and stood him upright. Another wave rocked the boat. This time Chrissy did a face-plant onto the deck.

"Hey, Chris," Yurga yelled. "Your kid keeps missing the ocean!"

Finally, Chrissy made it over the gunwale, his father followed, and their dive was under way. It took just a minute or two before the team hit the wreck and made their way from the anchor line to the opening gouged in the control-room area. There, Chrissy unfastened the two small stage bottles he would breathe from on his ascent and laid them on the U-boat's deck. Next, he clipped one end of a nylon line to the torn-open entrance of the U-boat and slithered into the wreck, allowing the line to unspool from a reel attached to his harness. This way, even if the visibility dropped to zero or he became lost or disoriented, he could follow the line out of the U-boat and back to his father. Cave divers like the Rouses called this technique "running a line" and made it their religion. Wreck divers, however, did not believe in depending on nylon lines—or anything else—that could become tangled or cut inside a wreck's jagged guts.

It took Chrissy just a minute or two to snake into the galley and begin his work. The pillowcase-sized piece of canvas he had worked on for so long still lay buried under the skeleton of a floor-to-ceiling cabinet made of heavy-gauge steel. Chrissy could not hope to move the massive cabinet. To free the artifact he would have to dig beneath the cabinet into the rotting debris until enough space had been cleared to pull the canvas out. For perhaps fifteen minutes, Chrissy burrowed with his hands, creating a silt tornado that blackened the room and dropped the visibility to zero. He kept digging and pulling. The canvas began to loosen from beneath the cabinet. Chrissy pulled harder. Mushroom clouds of silt exploded within the compartment. The jungle drums beat louder. He pulled again. More canvas came free, then even more, and it kept coming, like the scarves in a magician's trick, while the drums pounded louder and Chrissy grew closer to solving the mystery. Perhaps just seconds remained in the dive. Chrissy pulled again. The steel cabinet, now deprived of its bottom support, began to collapse, hurtling several hundred pounds of steel atop Chrissy's head and burying his face in the hole he had dug. Chrissy tried to move. Nothing happened. He was trapped.

As the gravity of his situation sludged into Chrissy's consciousness, the feral dog that is narcosis leaped from its cage and set upon him with fangs fully bared. His head throbbed. His mind narrowed. He believed, more certainly than he knew his name, that a monster was on top of him, pinning him. He tried again to move but could not—in its collapse, the cabinet had wedged between other debris and had become part of an interlocking sarcophagus atop the diver. Outside, Chris checked his watch and saw that his son was overdue. He had not planned to penetrate the U-boat. He was unfamiliar with the area in which Chrissy was working. He swam into the wreck.

Chris reached his son and began working to free him from the trap. Chrissy struggled to climb out but only burned faster through his remaining air and deepened his narcosis. Chris kept working. Finally, after several minutes, Chrissy came free of the cabinet. Father and son now needed to exit the wreck. Chrissy checked his watch. It read thirty minutes. He and his father were ten minutes over on their time.

Ordinarily, the Rouses would have followed Chrissy's nylon line out of the wreck and to the tanks they needed to breathe from to make their ascent. But in Chrissy's struggle to free himself, the line had become tangled around the canvas until it was a morass of knots. Narcosis banged like an industrial press inside Chrissy's brain, tunneling his peripheral vision and lighting the panic fuse of his instincts. He and his father swam in the direction of the control room and managed to exit the submarine through a crack between its skin and bulkhead. The tanks and the anchor line were now in front of the divers and just forty feet away. All the Rouses had to do was swim aft, locate the bottles, and begin their ascent. In the struggle, however, Chrissy had likely become disoriented and believed himself to be facing the wrong direction. He turned around and swam toward the bow—directly away from the tanks and anchor line. His father followed.

The Rouses searched frantically for their tanks. Chris, who had dropped only one of his stage bottles outside the wreck, gave the remaining one to Chrissy. A minute passed and the Rouses kept searching, but they were now 150 feet from their stage bottles and their narcosis was spiraling deeper by the second. Two minutes passed, then three, then five—still, they could not find their tanks. They searched for another five minutes, never knowing that they were turned around and nowhere near the stage bottles or anchor line. Chrissy checked his watch. He had been underwater for forty minutes. The Rouses were now twenty minutes over their dive time. Their required decompression, originally sixty minutes, had now expanded to two and a half hours. Neither had enough air to breathe for that long.

A clear-thinking diver breathing trimix likely would have used his remaining gas to eke out the best decompression possible. The Rouses, however, had made this trip without trimix and were breathing air. Chrissy, terrified at losing his stage bottles and lost on the wreck, made a decision that divers spend a lifetime dreading—to bolt for the surface. His father shot up after him. Nagle had a saying about divers who rocketed to the surface after so long down deep. "They're already dead," he would say. "They just don't know it yet."

The Rouses missiled toward the surface. At about 100 feet they intersected a miracle. Somehow, in their explosive ascent, they spotted the anchor line, swam to it, and held on. Now they had a chance. They could fashion a decompression from their remaining air, then switch to the oxygen tank the *Seeker* dangled at 20 feet for emergencies.

Chrissy switched from his main tanks to the stage bottle his father had given him. He sucked from the new tank and gagged—the mouthpiece had torn and was delivering water, not air. That was enough for Chrissy. He switched back to the main tanks on his back and bolted again for the surface. Again, his father followed. This time, Chrissy would stop for nothing.

In the *Seeker*'s wheelhouse, Chatterton, Kohler, and Crowell checked the weather and shivered—brutal seas and nasty winds were rolling in. A minute later they saw two divers pop to the surface about a hundred feet in front of the boat. Chatterton looked closer. He saw the hockey-type helmets of the Rouses. They had come up an hour ahead of schedule.

"Oh, Christ," Chatterton said. "This ain't good."

Chatterton and Kohler tore down the wheelhouse steps and onto the *Seeker*'s bow. Chatterton raised his arm and put his fingertips on his head, the universal "Are you okay?" signal to divers. Neither man responded. Six-foot waves threw the divers closer to the boat. Chatterton and Kohler looked into the men's faces. Both father and son had the wide, rapidly blinking eyes of the newly condemned.

"Did you complete your decompression?" Chatterton yelled.

Neither diver answered.

"Swim to the boat!" Chatterton yelled.

Chrissy moved his arms and inched closer to the *Seeker*. Chris also tried to swim, but he flopped sideways and half-kicked like a sick goldfish.

"Chrissy! Did you complete your decompression?" Chatterton pressed.

"No," Chrissy managed to yell back.

"Did you come straight to the surface?"

"Yes," Chrissy said.

Kohler went ashen at the answer. He remembered the Atlantic Wreck Divers' mantra: *I would rather slit my throat than shoot to the surface without decompressing.*

Chatterton grabbed two throw lines to fling to the Rouses. The *Seeker* rose and fell on the raging waves like a carnival ride, each undulation threatening to launch Chatterton and Kohler into the Atlantic. An eight-foot wave pushed Chrissy under the *Seeker* as her bow lifted off the ocean like an executioner's ax. The *Seeker* fell from the darkening sky, Chrissy helpless to move away. Chatterton and Kohler held their breath. The boat's splash rail hurtled downward and bashed the regulator on Chrissy's tanks, just inches from his skull, splitting the brass mechanism and releasing an explosion of rushing air from the tanks. Chatterton threw the lines. Each of the Rouses managed to grab a rope. Chatterton and Kohler pulled the divers along the side of the boat, towing them out from under the *Seeker* and toward the stern. Crowell ran into the wheelhouse.

He radioed the Atlantic City Coast Guard repeatedly but got no reply.

"Fuck this," he thought to himself. "I'm calling a Mayday."

"Mayday! Mayday! Mayday!" Crowell called into his handheld microphone. "This is the vessel *Seeker*. Requesting immediate helicopter evacuation. We have injured divers. Please acknowledge." The Brooklyn Coast Guard station responded. They were sending a chopper.

Chatterton, Kohler, and other divers continued to tow the Rouses toward the back of the boat as the *Seeker*'s bow rose and fell with thunderous booms. Chris came around nearest the ladder. Chatterton rushed toward him.

"Chris, get up the ladder!" Chatterton yelled.

"Take Chrissy first," Chris grunted.

Chatterton began to insist but stopped himself when he looked into Chris's widened eyes. In them, he saw only fear and knowing—the kind of knowing that occurs when one's fate is certain and moments away.

"Okay, Chrissy, come up!" Chatterton yelled to the younger Rouse, who was holding on to a line about ten feet behind his father. The divers pulled Chrissy to the ladder. He screamed in pain.

"I can't move my legs!" Chrissy yelled. "Monkeyfuck! Monkeyfuck! It hurts! It hurts so bad!"

Chatterton knew that serious decompression bends were already upon the divers. He and Kohler straddled the gunwale on either side of the ladder and put their arms under Chrissy, grabbing the underside of his tanks for leverage. The *Seeker* rose and fell with nature's onrushing tantrum, each explosion against the ocean threatening to catapult the divers overboard and crush Chrissy under the stern. The lactic acid in Chatterton's and Kohler's muscles burned as they willed themselves to hang on to the stricken young diver. Between impacts, they managed to lug Chrissy up the ladder until he thudded onto the deck like a netted tuna.

"Get him onto the dressing table!" Chatterton ordered. Kohler and others dragged Chrissy to the table and began cutting off his gear. Barb Lander, a nurse by profession, force-fed Chrissy aspirin and water and put an oxygen mask over his face.

"I fucked up, I fucked up, I fucked up!" Chrissy yelled. "I can't move my legs!"

Lander cradled his head.

"You're okay, Chrissy," she said. "You're on the *Seeker* now."

Chrissy thrashed and screamed and tried to tear the oxygen mask from his face.

"I can't breathe!" he screamed. "I'm burning! A monster pinned me! I was trapped!"

At the ladder, Chatterton turned his attention to Chris.

"Chris! Chris! Come on, you're next. You can do it! Let's go!" Chatterton yelled.

Chris looked into Chatterton's eyes.

"I'm not going to make it," he said. "Tell Sue I'm sorry."

Chris's chin dropped to his chest and his head flopped into the water. Chatterton and Kohler, both dressed in street clothes, leaped into the freezing ocean. Chatterton lunged for Chris's head and lifted it into the air.

"Get me a knife!" Chatterton yelled. The *Seeker* bashed up and down in the Atlantic, hurling Chatterton and Kohler underwater. When the boat rose, Chatterton yelled, "I gotta cut his rig off!"

Kohler pointed to a knife sheathed on Chris's shoulder. Chatterton grabbed it and slashed at the diver's harness until Chris's rig fell away. Chatterton then muscled Chris into a fireman's carry and brought him up the ladder, straining to hang on as the *Seeker* heaved and exploded into the ocean and sent salt water spraying into the men's eyes. Kohler looked inside Chris's mask, praying to see more dread because dread would mean that Chris was still alive. Chris only stared straight ahead. The men dragged him onto the *Seeker*'s deck, his fins sloshing along the sea-soaked wood. Chatterton began CPR on the elder Rouse.

For a few moments, Chris did not respond to Chatterton's efforts. His skin began to turn blue. Kohler murmured, "Come on, Chris, don't let go . . . don't let go . . . don't let go . . ." Chatterton kept relentlessly at his CPR. Suddenly, Chris threw up into Chatterton's mouth, and Chatterton could taste the Pepsi he and Chris had shared that morning. Kohler sprang to his feet, hopeful that the vomiting indicated revival. Chatterton looked up at Kohler with eyes from 1970 Vietnam.

"Richie, go in the wheelhouse," Chatterton said with a calm that seemed to Kohler to mute the raging ocean. "Get pencil and paper. Write down times and events. Be sure to get everything Barb's doing on that table and everything Chrissy is saying. Make sure she gets vital signs on him. Record everything. We'll need to send this information with the Coast Guard."

Chatterton continued the CPR, but with each compression he

felt increasing resistance, evidence that Chris's blood was turning to foam and clotting in his body. After five minutes, Chris's heart stopped and his skin turned from blue to coal gray. The whites of his eyes were bloody. Chatterton knew he was dead. He kept pumping anyway. You did not give up on a human being just because he was dead.

At the dressing table, Lander pushed Chrissy's long brown hair out of his face and held his head in her lap as he writhed and screamed and drifted in and out of lucidity.

"The monster got me!" he screamed. "A monster pinned me. Monkeyfuck! It was a monkeyfuck!"

Kohler bit his bottom lip and took notes.

"My father! How is my father?" Chrissy asked.

Kohler and Lander looked toward Chatterton as he pumped away on Chris's lifeless body. They knew Chris had died.

"John's with your father," Kohler told him. "He's on oxygen. He's gonna be fine. Hang in, Chrissy. Can you tell me what happened?"

Chrissy went calm and for a moment spoke with a crystalline mind. He told Kohler that something had fallen and pinned him inside the wreck, that his father had come in and freed him, and that while they were ascending he had run out of air. Then, just as quickly, Chrissy spiraled back into delirium.

"I was in the wreck and fuck this! I'm cold! I'm hot! I can't feel my legs!"

Lander stroked his head.

"Please shoot me!" Chrissy begged. "It hurts so bad. Someone find a gun and shoot me. Please kill me. Dad! Dad!"

For the next ninety minutes, Chatterton and others continued CPR on Chris's dead body. Crowell, who had cut the anchor line, headed thirty degrees into the wind as instructed by the Coast Guard, then began a head count. Each diver called out, "Here." Crowell dropped the *Seeker*'s antennas to allow the helicopter to approach unobstructed. He ordered everyone into life jackets, then demanded that any loose items be moved into the salon or secured to the deck; the helicopter's prop wash could turn a loose face mask into a deadly missile or suck up a sleeping bag into its rotors and crash.

On the horizon, the divers could see the orange-and-white Coast Guard chopper speeding toward them. All but Chatterton, Kohler, and Lander ran into the salon to stay out of its way. As the chopper lowered its shoulder and swooped toward the *Seeker,* the whine of its jet engines blanketed the sky and its rotors made an upside-down rainstorm of the water still sloshing on the deck. The chopper settled to a hover just over the *Seeker*'s bow and strained to hold its position in the roiling winds. From the side door, a muscular search-and-rescue swimmer dressed in a Day-Glo orange dry suit, gloves, hood, goggles, and fins jumped feetfirst toward the ocean, one hand stretched across his stomach, the other holding his mask, a perfect dart into a violent sea. As he surfaced, he threw a medical bag onto the *Seeker*'s deck and climbed aboard the boat. He made no introductions and offered no welcome gestures. Instead, he strode directly to Chatterton.

"You're a little slow on those chest compressions," the swimmer said from behind rounded goggles. "It should be one-two . . . one-two . . ."

"I've been doing CPR on this guy for ninety minutes," Chatterton answered, still pushing into Chris's chest. "He's dead."

The swimmer pivoted and looked at Chrissy, who still had color in his face and was writhing in pain.

"Okay, we're going to take both these guys—one at a time," the swimmer said.

"Listen to me," Chatterton told the swimmer. "I'm telling you this guy is dead. We need to take all our prayers and fucking hope and energy and throw it into that kid, who's still alive. Forget the old man. If he were to sit up, he'd tell you the same thing."

"That's not the way we do it," the swimmer said. "We're taking both of them. One at a time."

Now Chatterton was in the Vietnamese jungle. Bullets flew past his ears and staccatoed the dirt. Long-atrophied triage instincts flared to life.

"Taking the old man will cost you twenty minutes," Chatterton said. "Take the son and rush him to a recompression chamber as fast as possible. The time you waste with the father might cost the kid his life. I'm begging you. Forget the father."

"Not possible," the swimmer said. "We take them both. One at a time."

The swimmer radioed to the chopper to move in and drop the basket. A moment later, the metal stretcher was being lowered by cable toward the *Seeker*.

"No one touch anything!" the swimmer yelled. "This thing has a static charge that can blow you off your feet. Let the basket hit the boat's rail and discharge first."

The basket pendulumed in the howling winds before hitting a rail on the *Seeker* and exploding with the discharge of static electricity. The swimmer ran to the basket, unclipped it, and waved the chopper away to ease the effects of its prop wash.

The swimmer pulled the basket toward Chrissy, who was now bundled in a blanket, still screaming for his legs, still telling stories about monsters. He placed Chrissy inside and crossed his arms mummy-style. The helicopter dragged its cable through the water until it hit the boat. Chatterton, Kohler, and the swimmer lifted Chrissy's basket onto the gunwale and attached the cable. A moment later, the helicopter was heaving Chrissy into the sky.

"Look, I'm begging you," Chatterton told the swimmer. "Leave now. The kid's life depends on this. It's going to take twenty minutes to get that basket back down here to load up a guy who's already dead."

"Not possible," the swimmer said.

Chatterton whirled toward Kohler.

"Richie, take all the information you gathered—all the vital signs and notes and dive profiles—and put them in a waterproof bag. Then go into the salon and get the Rouses' wallets—it will be hectic and messy in there, but you will be able to find them if you stay with it. Put the wallets in the bag, too. Make certain that this swimmer leaves with that bag."

Kohler bolted for the salon. He tore through sleeping bags, dumped duffel bags, and overturned suitcases until he found both wallets, then rifled through the kitchen drawers until he found a Ziploc bag. Lander gave him the vital signs, notes, and dive profiles, and he packaged everything and made true the seal. As he opened the salon's door, he was blasted by seawater and winds from the chopper's blades. He pushed forward and pressed the bag into the swimmer's hands.

Now the basket was coming down for Chris. Chatterton continued his chest compressions, muttering, "Son of a bitch, son of a bitch . . ." In the jungle he could have run to save Chrissy—he always ran—and even when the grunts shook their heads he ran anyway, because it was the right thing to do and because it had always been in him to run. Here, as the chopper sent a basket for a dead guy while a live kid's blood foamed and choked his heart, Chatterton had nowhere to run, and that finality drowned him, because he had never in his life been unable to run.

It took twenty minutes to load Chris onto the chopper. After both Rouses were aboard, the helicopter lowered the basket a final time for the swimmer. The jet engines screamed as the chopper swooped away and raced toward the recompression chamber at Jacobi Medical Center in the Bronx.

One by one the divers made their way from the salon and toward Chatterton. Each thanked him or hugged him. Everyone knew that Chris was dead. Everyone believed Chrissy would make it.

The trip back to Brielle was somber but hopeful. Hospital recompression could take hours; the divers hoped to get word of Chrissy's condition by the next morning. The metal schematic, which had held so much promise and which had brought such optimism, lay forgotten, wrapped in a towel in a Tupperware container.

That evening Lander called Chatterton at home.

"Chrissy didn't make it," she said. "He died in the chamber."

Chatterton put down the receiver. In thirty-six years, there had been several thousand dives on the *Andrea Doria,* the most dangerous of all shipwrecks. Six people had died. In a single year, the *U-Who* had claimed three lives. Chatterton walked into his office. For months he had come here to gaze at the Horenburg knife and ask, "Who are you? What happened to you?" This time his eyes went through the knife. He sat for hours, not asking much of anything.

SHORTLY AFTER THE ROUSES DIED, Chatterton and Kohler set out for the *U-Who* to retrieve the fallen divers' equipment. They had heard reports of Chrissy's recompression-chamber experience at Jacobi. The bubbles in his system had turned his blood into sludge. Kohler smoked thirty cigarettes on the way to the wreck and wondered how long he could continue refusing the voodoo of trimix in favor of air.

Inside the wreck's galley, Chatterton shot footage of the fallen cabinet and shelves. The tangled penetration line Chrissy had relied on for navigation had been twisted around the ten-foot-long piece of canvas he had worked to excavate. In the now-pristine visibility, Chatterton recognized this canvas as part of a life raft. Its German writing gave generic instructions for use. Outside the wreck, Kohler discovered the three stage bottles the divers had not been able to find in their confusion. Each was marked "Rouse." None of them was inscribed with a first name; the tanks were interchangeable between father and son.

At home, Chatterton and Kohler returned to the business of research. Now armed with the information from the schematic, they tore into their reference books in search of Type IXC U-boats built at Germany's Deschimag-Bremen shipyard. Fifty-two such U-boats, it turned out, had never returned from patrol. That list of fifty-two, the divers agreed, could easily be narrowed. Over rib eyes at Scotty's, they agreed on two exclusionary parameters:

1. Eliminate any U-boat in which crewmen survived the sinking. If there were survivors, the U-boat's identity would be known and accurate in the historical record.
2. Eliminate any U-boat built with a deck gun. The divers had already determined that the *U-Who* had been built without a deck gun; any Type IX constructed at Deschimag-Bremen with that weapon, therefore, could not be the *U-Who*.

Chatterton and Kohler set out for Washington to begin the elimination process. Reference books indicated that there had been survivors on twenty-two of the fifty-two U-boats on their list. That left thirty U-boats to consider. Of these, ten had been built with deck guns. The list was now down to twenty possible U-boats.

"One of these U-boats on this single piece of notebook paper is our sub," Kohler said.

"We are now looking at the answer," Chatterton said. "We just have to narrow this list down further."

Neither man could remember having been so excited. This was original research. This was exploration.

Back in New Jersey, the divers took their usual table at Scotty's and began to brainstorm. They needed additional exclusionary criteria to further narrow the list of twenty. They quickly settled on a plan. They would return to the BdU KTBs—the German war diaries—to inspect where U-boat headquarters had ordered and plotted each of the remaining U-boats on their list. Any submarine the Germans believed to be operating more than a few hundred miles from the U.S. East Coast would be eliminated from the list of twenty. After all, the Germans would know better than anyone where their U-boats were patrolling.

The divers planned to return to Washington the next week. Chatterton would research half the boats, Kohler the other half. At midnight the night before the trip, Kohler's phone rang. The caller did not speak. The only evidence of another person on the other end was the sound of ice clinking in a glass. That sound meant the caller was Nagle.

"Hey, Richie, it's me," Nagle said. "Think we'll ever figure out this U-boat?"

"Sure, Billy, we will," Kohler said. "What's going on? It's midnight."

"Ah, I'm sitting here alone just thinking about the U-boat. You know, Richie, sometimes I just want to end it all . . ."

"What are you talking about, Bill?"

"This is bullshit, Richie. I got my gun right here. I should blow my fucking head off right now."

"Whoa, Bill, hold on. You got everything in the world, man. You got a boat, a beautiful family back in Pennsylvania, money, a nice house. All you gotta do is run a boat. That's a nice life. I'll take that life."

"Ah, you ain't got no clue!" Nagle exploded. "Feldman's dead. The Rouses are dead. My old friend John Dudas is dead. I see all these dead guys in my dreams, Richie. I gotta go . . ."

Nagle hung up. Kohler's fingers pounded out Chatterton's phone number.

"John, it's Richie. Bill's gonna kill himself—"

"He does this sometimes," Chatterton said, still groggy. "He's in a terrible way. I've tried to intervene. His family has intervened, his girlfriend, too. I've taken him to rehabs. You know what he does? He takes a few weeks off. He gets himself just well enough to enjoy drinking again, checks himself out, then stops at the liquor store on the way home. I don't think he'll kill himself, at least not with a gun. I think Jim Beam's the weapon of choice."

"Can we do anything?" Kohler asked.

"We've all been trying for years," Chatterton said. "I don't know what else anyone can do."

The divers returned to Washington and attacked the U-boat Control diaries. According to the German records, eighteen of the twenty U-boats on the divers' list had been operating in or ordered to areas so distant from New Jersey as to be unworthy of further consideration.

That left two U-boats—*U-857* and *U-879*. According to the diaries, each of these submarines had been ordered to attack targets of opportunity on the American East Coast. As the divers read further they came upon a bombshell. Both of these submarines had been docked in Norway, in early 1945—the same place and roughly the same date as Horenburg's boat, *U-869*.

"That could explain the knife!" Kohler said.

"Exactly," Chatterton said. "Maybe Horenburg lent the knife to a guy on the U-boat next to his. Maybe he lost it and it ended up on a nearby boat. Maybe someone stole it. Any way you look at it, the knife now makes sense. One of these two submarines has got to be the *U-Who*. It's either *U-857* or *U-879*. We're down to two U-boats."

The divers rushed to their history books. According to these texts, *U-857* had been sunk off Boston by the USS *Gustafson*, while *U-879* had been destroyed off Cape Hatteras, North Carolina, by the USS *Buckley* and USS *Reuben James*. That seemed to leave no chance that the mystery wreck was either *U-857* or *U-879*.

"Let's do this," Chatterton said. "Let's check the files for the sinkings of these two subs. Let's see for ourselves what the navy says about how these two U-boats were killed."

"Are you saying these two U-boats might not have been sunk where the history books say they were?" Kohler asked.

"I'm saying we have to check," Chatterton said. "I'm getting the feeling we have to check everything."

It was evening by now, so the divers packed their gear and found a thirty-five-dollar motel room on the city's outskirts. The next morning they returned to the NHC, drooling to get at the navy files for their remaining two U-boats, one of which had to be the answer to their mystery.

The divers looked first at navy files for the sinking of the *U-857* off Boston, which gave this account: While patrolling Cape Cod on April 5, 1945, *U-857* fired a torpedo at the American tanker *Atlantic States*, wounding but not sinking her. American warships were dispatched to the area to hunt and kill *U-857*. Two days later, one of those warships, the destroyer USS *Gustafson*, obtained a sonar contact on an underwater object near Boston. It fired several Hedgehog bombs into the ocean toward the contact. Crewmen reported hearing an explosion shortly thereafter, and then smelling oil.

And that was it. No evidence of a U-boat had floated to the surface. No blobs of oil had been spotted on the surface. The divers could not believe what they read next. Navy assessors who analyzed the *Gustafson*'s attack had written the following conclusion:

> It is considered that although a submarine, known to have
> been in this area, may have been lost, it was not lost as a result
> of this attack. It is therefore recommended that this incident
> be assessed "E"—probably slightly damaged.

"Wait a minute," Kohler said. "The grade on this attack report says B—probably sunk."

"Yeah, but look here," Chatterton said, pointing to the report. "The original grade of 'E' is crossed out. Someone changed it to a 'B.' "

The divers knew what the alteration meant.

"Son of a bitch," Kohler said. "The postwar assessors upgraded this report!"

Chatterton and Kohler had only recently learned about the postwar assessors. As navy investigators, it was the assessors' task after the war to make a final report on the fate of all U-boats. In most cases the evidence was clear-cut and the assessors' job simple. In rarer instances, when a U-boat could not be accounted for, the assessors stretched for an explanation—they were loath to leave question marks in the history books.

"That must have been what happened here," Chatterton said. "The *Gustafson* never sank *U-857*. The U-boat survived the Hedgehog attack, continued past Boston, then sank somewhere else. After the war, the assessors needed an explanation for the loss of *U-857*. So they looked at this really dubious attack by the *Gustafson* and said, 'Let's upgrade it from an "E" to a "B." ' They didn't care that the original navy assessors knew the *Gustafson* hadn't sunk a submarine. They just wanted *U-857* accounted for so they could move on with their business."

For a moment the divers could only shake their heads.

"Well, if the *Gustafson* didn't sink *U-857* off Boston," Kohler finally asked, "what happened to that submarine?"

"We gotta figure that out for ourselves," Chatterton said.

The divers checked various German documents. An hour later they had their answer.

According to German diaries, *U-857* had been ordered to proceed south along the American East Coast. She had last attacked a ship off Cape Cod. That meant New York and New Jersey lay two hundred miles away—to the south.

Neither Chatterton nor Kohler could move. Here was a U-boat that fit every criterion they had established, had possibly been docked beside Horenburg's sub, had likely survived the *Gustafson*, and was believed by the Germans to be on her way toward New Jersey.

"It's gotta be *U-857*," Chatterton said.

"I think we've got our U-boat," Kohler said.

The divers, however, still had to inspect the box of files for *U-879*. Again, they found history mauled.

Over the last half century, various assessors had ascribed three fates to *U-879*: they first pronounced her lost without a trace; then sunk off Halifax in Canadian waters; then sunk off Cape Hatteras, North Carolina. As the divers studied further, they recognized that the current assessment by German naval historian Axel Niestlé—that *U-879* had been sunk off Cape Hatteras—was correct. But the lesson was stark and by now familiar: written history was fallible. Sloppy and erroneous assessments had been rushed into the official record, only to be presumed accurate by historians, who then published elegant reference works echoing the mistakes. Unless a person was willing, as Chatterton and Kohler were, to ditch work and sneak off to Washington, chisel away at mountains of opaque original documents, sleep in fleabag motels, eat street-vendor hot dogs, and run outside every two hours to shovel quarters into a parking meter, he would presume the history books to be correct. As they left Washington for New Jersey that night, Chatterton and Kohler celebrated their detective work—original research that virtually proved that the *U-Who* was *U-857*. Along the way, each marveled at how easy it was to get an incomplete picture of the world if one relied solely on experts, and how important it would be to further rely on oneself.

Now armed with abundant evidence that their wreck was *U-857*, Chatterton and Kohler determined to use the rest of the 1992–93 off-season to complete the proof.

For his part, Chatterton placed a classified ad in *Proceedings* magazine, a publication of the U.S. Naval Institute, seeking information on the sinking of *U-857* by the USS *Gustafson*. Several *Gustafson* crewmen, now in their seventies, replied to the ad. Chatterton interviewed them about the day they attacked the U-boat off Boston.

While the accomplishment had been a source of lifelong pride, none could offer any more evidence of the sinking today than they had in 1945. They had fired Hedgehogs and smelled oil. And that was it.

Chatterton did not have the heart to inform these men, soldiers who had gone to hunt U-boats in defense of America, that the sinking of which they had been proud for so long had likely never happened.

During one interview, a crewman invited Chatterton to their upcoming "Greasy Gus" reunion. He asked Chatterton to speak about his research. As Chatterton considered the invitation, he was struck by the oddest thought. He had run to fallen men in Vietnam bullet-storms. He had swum under a thousand pounds of dangling steel inside a crushed submarine. But contemplating speaking before these elderly men at their celebration, he found himself afraid. He felt sure that he could not attend their reunion and tell these men that the story they had told their grandchildren about sinking the U-boat was wrong, that history had been mistaken, that the Greasy Gus had missed. Chatterton thanked the crewman for the invitation but told him he would be unable to attend.

For his part, Kohler set out in search of the grandmaster of U-boat knowledge. For decades, Robert Coppock had been caretaker to Britain's U-boat records—including captured German records—and he still worked for the Ministry of Defence in London. According to an archivist Kohler had met, no one had a more comprehensive understanding of U-boat records than did Coppock. And no one had deeper connections into the sometimes murky world of U-boat historians, thinkers, and theorists.

"He still works his job?" Kohler asked.

"Since forever," the archivist replied.

Kohler called London the next day.

An English-accented woman speaking over pillows of static answered the telephone.

"Scotland Yard. Can I help you?"

Kohler believed he had misdialed, but did not dare hang up; the idea of being connected to the legendary crime-fighting headquarters was too thrilling to abandon. For a moment he just listened to the static, imagining men scurrying in deerstalker hats crying, "It's murder!"

"This is Scotland Yard. Is anyone on the line?"

Kohler finally said, "I must have the wrong number. I was trying to reach Mr. Robert Coppock at the Ministry of Defence."

"One moment and I'll connect you to Mr. Coppock," the woman said.

Kohler was beside himself waiting for Coppock. This was the first time he had ever spoken to anyone with an English accent. Across the Atlantic, in a cavernous office lined with floor-to-ceiling gray filing cabinets, institutional furniture, and frosted windows, the silver-haired Coppock settled in among his U-boat history and took the phone. Kohler introduced himself.

"Ah, yes, the diver from New Jersey," Coppock said. "I know of you, sir. I have been following your adventure with great interest. I find the mystery most intriguing."

Coppock asked detailed questions of Kohler—about the divers' research, the *U-Who*, the contacts they had made, about Horenburg. Kohler answered them all, flattered that Coppock spoke to him as a colleague rather than as a guy from Brooklyn late to replace a window at a Kentucky Fried Chicken franchise, which he was. When Coppock asked if the divers had fashioned any theories, Kohler laid out the case for *U-857*.

Coppock listened intently, then agreed that Kohler had made a persuasive argument for *U-857* as the New Jersey wreck. He asked if Kohler would like him to consult his records and sources and look into the matter further.

Kohler nearly blurted, "Hell yeah!" Instead, he managed, "Yes, sir, I'd be grateful for that kind of help. Thank you very much."

As he sped to fix the window at KFC, Kohler called Chatterton from his truck.

"John, I talked to Coppock. The guy must be seventy-five years old but he's totally on the ball. And he works at friggin' Scotland Yard!"

"What'd he say?" Chatterton asked. "You're killing me here—"

"I laid out the case for *U-857*. He said it sounded 'persuasive.' He really liked it. He's going to look into it on his end."

"Beautiful," Chatterton said. "What an amazing adventure we're on."

"That's what it is," Kohler said. "An amazing adventure."

Shortly after Kohler spoke to Coppock, the divers contacted Horst Bredow and Charlie Grutzemacher in Germany and made the case for *U-857*. Each of the archivists absorbed the evidence, pulled out his own records, asked a few questions, then agreed—the *U-Who* almost certainly was *U-857*. Kohler redialed Scotland Yard (really Great Scotland Yard, a different place from the fabled police station) to follow up with Coppock. This conversation was brief. Coppock told Kohler that he had consulted records and considered further the divers' theory. As before, he believed it likely that the divers had discovered *U-857*.

As the early months of 1993 wore on, Chatterton and Kohler continued to meet for steaks or pizza. They no longer speculated, however, about the *U-Who*'s identity; that question was settled. Instead, they began to imagine how the U-boat had met its end. By now, they had conferred with several munitions experts. All evidence pointed in a single direction: the U-boat had been destroyed by a massive explosion, the kind most likely caused by a torpedo.

But whose torpedo? If an Allied sub had fired on the U-boat, there would have been a record of the incident. If another U-boat had fired and inadvertently hit the sub, that too would have been recorded. Could one of the U-boat's own torpedoes have exploded accidentally from within? Impossible, as the blast damage showed a strike from outside the sub. That seemed to leave a single explanation. The divers had read about occasions in which a torpedo's steering system malfunctioned, causing the weapon to reverse direction in the water and head back toward its own submarine. Those derelict torpedoes were called "circle-runners" and had turned on several of their own U-boats.

"Imagine you're Rudolf Premauer, commander of *U-857*," Kohler said to Chatterton one night at Scotty's. "You've made it through icy waters and past swarms of Allied aircraft all the way from Norway to the United States. You've narrowly escaped a hunter-killer group off

Boston and now you're in New Jersey, a few miles from Manhattan. You spot a target steaming in the distance. You order your men to their battle stations, climb into the conning tower, and raise the attack periscope. You've got your target locked. You give the order— 'Fire torpedo!' The torpedo flies out the tube. Everyone's silent and hopeful, waiting for an explosion in the distance. Nothing happens. Then, from the sound room, the radioman says, 'Circle-runner! We have a circle-runner! Our torpedo is bearing down on us!' Premauer orders the sub to crash-dive; it's their only hope. Now it's a race, the U-boat against her own torpedo, and there's only one question: Can the U-boat submerge before the torpedo strikes? The men are doing everything humanly possible to drop that boat. Do they have twenty seconds? Five seconds? They don't know. They give it everything they've got. Too late. The torpedo hits. Seven hundred pounds of TNT. It's too goddamned late."

"And that explains why there's no incident report from the area," Chatterton said. "It's probably night. It's winter. When the torpedo hits the U-boat, no one on the target vessel is going to hear it because it occurs underwater, and even if they do hear a muffled explosion, hell, it's wartime—muffled explosions are everywhere. The U-boat sinks and no one has a clue she went down."

For a minute, each diver poked at his food but said nothing.

"Imagine the feeling that radio guy has the moment he realizes the torpedo's coming back," Kohler said.

"Imagine the certainty that either your life will end violently in a few seconds or the circle-runner's going to miss," Chatterton said. "There's no middle ground. You know it's one or the other."

The next morning, Chatterton searched through the piles of crew lists he had copied at Bredow's archive in Germany. On the bottom was that of *U-857*. He scanned the roster, fifty-nine men with names like Dienst and Kausler, Löfgren and Wulff. Some of these men were nineteen or twenty years old. The senior radioman was Erich Krahe, born on March 14, 1917. If a circle-runner torpedo had killed this U-boat, perhaps he had been the first to realize it was coming. Kohler searched his books for photographs of twenty-five-year-old commander Premauer. Chatterton and Kohler still had two months before the start of the 1993 dive season, time enough to learn about the last year of the U-boat war, the year that had delivered the men they had discovered.

By 1993, Kohler had built a collection of U-boat books worthy of a university library. Now he spread those books on his living room floor like a kid's baseball-card collection and divided them in half. He would lend Chatterton one pile for study and keep the other for himself. Between them, they held in their hands the story of the men who'd waged the final campaign of the U-boat war, the men who lay dead in their wreck.

Chatterton and Kohler settled into their reading chairs at home and began with page one: primitive submarines had existed during the American Revolution. Each fidgeted with page two: the torpedo was invented by an English engineer in 1866. Neither waited around for page three. The divers needed to know what had happened to their men. They flipped their books to the final chapters. They found hundreds of pages soaked in blood.

By the war's end, more than thirty thousand U-boat men out of a force of about fifty-five thousand had been killed—a death rate of almost 55 percent. No branch of a modern nation's armed forces had ever sustained such casualties and kept fighting. The U-boats had kept fighting. But it was worse than that. The late-war U-boat man, it turned out, had had it perhaps deadliest of all.

A U-boat sent to war in early 1945—as U-857 had been—stood only a 50 percent chance of returning from its patrol. A crewman's statistical life expectancy in that period was barely sixty days. Those ordered to American or Canadian waters almost never came back. Over the years, the divers had read dozens of war books, but none had affected them as deeply as the final pages of these volumes. As Chatterton and Kohler pored over the body counts, they found themselves hoping for a better ending, not for the Nazis or for Germany but maybe for a crewman or two, for one of these kids whose shoes were still lined up neatly on the mangled U-Who, and when the divers could not find hope for the late-war U-boat man, they called each other and agreed that they had never turned a book's pages like this because they'd never before felt as if they had been reading about men they knew.

By nearly every account, the late-war U-boat man had not just fought through the final hours of World War II but had done so nobly and bravely, all the while knowing the grim odds against his survival. The Allies had predicted mutinies aboard these doomed U-boats. That never happened. The Allies had expected surrender from these doomed U-boats. That never happened, either. In January 1945, even as the Allies hunted and killed U-boats with unflinching regularity, Churchill summoned top military commanders and warned them of the "much more offensive spirit" displayed by U-boats at sea. It was this idea—that the beaten U-boat man was doing more than just trying to survive—that kept Chatterton and Kohler reading.

In October 1940, at the peak of what German submariners called the "Happy Time," U-boats sank sixty-six ships while losing only one of their own. The U-boats enjoyed a second "Happy Time" in early 1942 with Operation Drumbeat, a surprise attack on American ships off the U.S. East Coast. In that offensive, U-boats pushed up against American shores so closely that crewmen could smell the forest from their decks, watch automobiles drive the parkways, and tune in American radio stations playing the jazz so many of them loved. The first weeks of Drumbeat were a slaughter as U-boats torpedoed unprotected ships. Body parts, oil, and wreckage washed up along the eastern seaboard. Five months later, just a few U-boats had sunk nearly six hundred ships in American waters at a cost of just six of their own, the worst defeat ever suffered by the U.S. Navy. In Germany, U-boats were welcomed back to harbor by bands, flowers, and lovely ladies. Churchill wrote, "The only thing that ever really frightened me during the war was the U-boat peril." It was no longer safe to be Goliath in a world where David could turn invisible.

The Americans, however, did not remain vulnerable for long. The navy began running convoys, an ancient maritime strategy whereby armed escort vessels protected groups of boats sailing together. Now when a U-boat fired on an Allied ship, the convoy escorts would be there to spot, chase, and kill it. As convoys increased, sinkings by U-boats dropped to near nothing.

Scientists joined the war effort from U.S. laboratories and universities. One of their most potent weapons was radar. Even in total darkness or a violent storm, radar-equipped airplanes and ships could detect a surfaced submarine at great distances. While submarines had long enjoyed the luxury of operating primarily on the surface, where subs moved considerably faster than they could while submerged, they suddenly found themselves pounced upon by Allied aircraft that seemed to appear in the sky as if by magic. For a time, Karl Dönitz, the commander in chief of the U-boat force, did not fully appreciate the radar threat. His submariners continued to die. Even when Germany finally grasped the situation's gravity, the U-boats could do little but submerge and stay underwater, which protected them from radar but made them too slow to catch or evade enemies.

The underwater environment presented its own perils. An Allied ship that suspected there was a submerged U-boat in its vicinity could use sonar—the broadcast of sound waves—to sniff it out. Once sonar echoed off the submarine's metallic form, a U-boat was tagged for death—unable to outrun the enemy while underwater, a fish in a barrel if it chose to surface and fight it out with its guns.

U-boats relied on radio to communicate with German headquarters. Allied brains pounced on the dependence. They developed a radio detection system known as "Huff-Duff" (for HF/DF, or high-frequency direction finding) that allowed Allied ships at sea to fix the position of U-boats. Now a submarine using its radio—even to report the weather—was as much as announcing its location to the enemy. The Allies wasted little time dispatching hunter-killer groups to U-boats so exposed.

Perhaps the deadliest Allied breakthrough came in the form of code breaking. Since the war's beginning, the German military had encrypted its communications through a cipher machine known as Enigma. A boxy, typewriter-like device capable of millions of character combinations, Enigma was believed by the German High Command to be invincible, the strongest code ever created. Allied code breakers estimated the odds against a person cracking Enigma without knowing the code to be 150,000,000,000,000,000,000 to 1. They tried anyway. Building on years of pioneering work by Polish cryptanalysts, and with the help of a captured Enigma machine and key documents, teams of cryptographers, mathematicians, Egyptologists, scientists, crossword puzzle experts, linguists, and chess champions spent months attacking Enigma, even building the world's first programmable computer to aid in the effort. The mental strain and pressure could have overwhelmed them. They kept at it. Months later, with the help of covert intelligence, they cracked it—one of the great intellectual achievements of the twentieth century. By late 1943, the Allies were using intercepted Enigma messages to direct hunter-killer groups to unsuspecting U-boats. Dönitz suspected that Enigma could be compromised, but was constantly assured by experts that Enigma was unbreakable. The Allies continued to read the German mail. U-boats continued to die.

By spring 1943, the fangs of Allied technology had encircled the U-boats, leaving no safe areas in the ocean. In May of that year, forty-one U-boats were destroyed by Allied forces, a disaster that came to be known as "Black May" and which Dönitz described as "unimaginable, even in my wildest dreams." The "Happy Time" had yielded to Sauregurkenzeit, or "Sour-Pickle Time." The hunters of the early war had now become the hunted.

By early 1945, U-boats stood a greatly reduced chance of inflicting damage or even surviving. Younger crews replaced the elite, handpicked service that had threatened in the early war to dominate the world. Allied bombing devastated German cities. France had been lost. The Russian army had crossed onto German soil. Aboard a U-boat, surrounded by killers who might know its every move in advance, a U-boat crewman could not even dream of safe haven back home. His Germany was falling.

As Chatterton and Kohler digested the late U-boat war, each discovered a new pride for Allied ingenuity and tenacity, for the ability of the United States to dig deep into its instinct for freedom, rise up against one of history's most terrifying threats, and pound it down until the world was safe again. Yet neither of them could put out of his mind the crewmen lying dead in their wreck. They did not speak to wives or coworkers or friends about these thoughts. Instead, they made a plan to meet at Scotty's.

The conversation that night was different from the others the divers had shared over dinner. Before, Chatterton and Kohler had talked in broad terms—about research, theories, strategies—large thoughts about solving the *U-Who* mystery. Now, educated in the hopelessness of the late U-boat war, they found themselves thinking on a smaller scale, a scale that envisioned the lives of men with whom they had become intertwined.

Over and over, they asked each other, "How could these men have kept fighting?" Part of the answer, for Chatterton and Kohler, lay in Dönitz's own characterization of a U-boat crew. He had called them a *Schicksalsgemeinschaft*—a community bound by fate—in which each man "is dependent on the other, and is thereby sworn to one another." To the divers, such a band of brotherhood seemed about the most noble of human instincts, and as they nursed after-dinner coffees, that instinct seemed also to describe their friendship.

There was another answer, one that each of the divers had been contemplating but about which neither spoke. Most men, it seemed to them, went through life never really knowing themselves. A man might consider himself noble or brave or just, they believed, but until he was truly tested it would always be mere opinion. This, more than anything, is what moved the divers about the late-war U-boat man. Despite knowing his efforts would be futile, he had gone to sea determined to strike a blow. As the divers said good night that evening, each wondered if he might not be moving toward the same kind of test. The *U-Who* had already killed three divers. Chatterton and Kohler could back out now and abandon their search for conclusive identification—they already were certain of the sub's identity. But as each man drove home that night he wondered: What will that say about me if I quit? What will it mean if life tests me and I do not try to strike a blow?

CHAPTER ELEVEN

A MISSED SIGNAL

IN LATE MAY 1993, as the residents of Brielle rubbed winter from their eyes, the divers booked the *Seeker* for the season's first U-boat trip. By now, Chatterton and Kohler had taken to calling the wreck *U-857* and even announcing their finding to dive show audiences. Many people asked the divers why they planned to continue searching such a dangerous wreck now that they had deduced its identity. The divers responded that until they pulled proof from the wreck, everything else was mere opinion. They had not come this far, they said, to stand on mere opinion.

The first U-boat trip of 1993 was scheduled for May 31, Memorial Day. As Chatterton and Kohler drove their cars to the *Seeker's* dock, neither could remember having felt so content. Chatterton had made every important discovery inside the wreck and had gone places on the submarine no other diver had. He had been relentless in his research until his thinking had produced a solution even the world's great U-boat minds did not dispute.

Kohler felt a similar satisfaction. Two years ago, he had been a ferocious tonnage king and Atlantic Wreck Divers fundamentalist. He'd lived to haul shit and raise hell in between. But as he'd come to know the U-boat and feel its crew, as he'd watched Chatterton dedicate entire dives to shooting video for later study, as he'd done original research that had corrected written history, the jaws of habit had loosened and he'd come to feel himself not just a diver but an explorer, a pass-holder to the landing place of his childhood dreams.

Not everyone celebrated this evolution. During the off-season, some of Kohler's Atlantic Wreck Divers mates had lashed out at the betrayal. "So, you're diving with your new buddies, are ya?" they'd ask when Kohler found time to make their charters that spring. "How's it feel diving with that asshole who put up the grate on the *Doria*?"

For a time, the criticism hurt Kohler. These friends had delivered him into deep-wreck diving; their guidance had kept him alive. Chatterton could see how deeply the barbs cut Kohler. He spoke up on those occasions.

"Your friends have plans this season," Chatterton told Kohler. "Diving the *Oregon* again. Diving the *San Diego* again. What do they want, another plate from the *Oregon*? Another bowl like the one they got twelve bowls ago? That's bullshit, Richie. That's against the spirit of diving. You don't buy it. If you did, you wouldn't be diving the U-boat."

Kohler always answered the same way: "You're right, John. Things have changed for me."

Things had changed so much, in fact, that Kohler had dedicated part of his off-season to converting to trimix. He had seen Chatterton's and Yurga's diving transformed by the safety and benefits offered by the new gas. And he believed the Rouses had died for a onetime decision to breathe air. Kohler had committed himself so fully, in fact, that he had given up smoking so he could optimize his abilities underwater.

The parking lot at Brielle looked emptier than usual to the arriving divers, though none found himself surprised. If Feldman's death had suggested the *U-Who*'s reputation as a death trap, the Rouses' demise had cemented it. Word in the diving community had it that there were a thousand ways to die on this wreck, that if the depth didn't kill you the sub's dangling steel or anarchy of wires would. The trip was expensive—$150 just for the ride. Mantel-worthy artifacts were virtually nonexistent. The media had long since gone home. Divers capable of this depth wanted prizes, and they wanted to live. Most said "No thanks" to the *U-Who*.

On board the *Seeker*, the gathered divers shook hands and compared off-season notes. Near midnight, a skeleton wobbled from the Horrible Inn toward the *Seeker*. No one spoke. The figure drew closer, feet dragging the dirt parking lot as it approached the pier. "That's Bill," someone whispered.

Nagle's face was yellow from jaundice and splotched with purple bruises. His hair was oily and his T-shirt grimy. He weighed perhaps 120 pounds, skin dripping from his legs, the remaining bump of his potbelly the only evidence of a man of former appetites. Under his arm he carried the cowboys-and-Indians sleeping bag he had used since boyhood, the one he'd brought along when he had taken the bell off the *Andrea Doria* in the days when he ruled the world.

The divers screwed on their best faces. "Hiya, Bill," someone said. "The *Seeker*'s looking beautiful, Bill," said another. As the boat left the dock that night, everyone on board gave thanks that Chatterton and Crowell—two capable and sober captains—were also on hand.

As the *Seeker* steamed for the *U-Who*, the divers made a final review of their strategies. Packer and Gatto, perhaps the country's finest wreck-diving team, would penetrate the diesel motor room. In addition to housing the submarine's massive diesel engines, this compartment contained gauge panels, telegraphs, and other equipment possibly engraved with the U-boat's identity. Until now, the diesel motor room had been inaccessible, its entrance blocked by massive air-intake ductwork that had fallen from the upper casement of the submarine. Packer and Gatto, however, had prepared to forcibly remove the obstruction, even if it required using a rope and several lift bags, a risky operation in close quarters. Such access would yield an additional benefit. By gaining entry to the diesel motor room, the divers would also have a clear shot into the adjoining electric motor room, the only other remaining compartment inaccessible to divers.

Chatterton's plan was simpler. He would return to the wreck's forward section—the radio room, sound room, commander's quarters, and officers' quarters—areas he had already explored. Once there, he would become nearly motionless.

"This is a matter of seeing," he told Yurga on the boat. "This is a matter of looking at a big pile of garbage until one little thing in the pile starts to look a little different than the rest. I'm looking for a glimmer of order in the chaos. I think if I just start digging, I'm never going to see more than the pile. But if I just stay quiet and look long enough, I think I'll see something."

Kohler's plan was similar. His off-season research had uncovered dozens of photographs in which U-boat crewmen held lighters or pocket watches or wore hats emblazoned with a U-boat number or logo. Like Chatterton, he believed important items would be located in the forward part of the wreck, where the crewmen had slept and stored their personal effects. Unlike Chatterton, however, he was willing to dig, trusting his hands to become his eyes in the black silt clouds raised by his activity, willing to reach anywhere he was certain did not contain human remains.

The morning sun was a brilliant alarm clock. As they had the previous season, Chatterton and Kohler splashed together. Kohler inhaled his trimix, the voodoo gas he had sworn would kill its heathen users. He continued living. At 100 feet Kohler checked his mind for narcosis, and Chatterton checked Kohler checking himself. No drums. At 200 feet Kohler stopped on the anchor line to process the scene. On air at this depth, his vision would have already narrowed. "Unbelievable," he thought. "This is the difference between watching a portable kitchen TV and going to a movie theater." He flashed Chatterton an okay sign. Chatterton grinned. The two divers wriggled inside the wreck and swam forward toward the sections where so many crewmen had died, the section where vision would be key.

Kohler penetrated farthest, landing in the noncommissioned officers' quarters, the place he knew as a boneyard. Chatterton settled into the commander's quarters. He had not said much to anyone, but he believed that he stood a chance of recovering the ship's log, the KTB, in this area. Artifacts with legible writing had survived shipwrecks older than this one, and the KTB would be the ultimate find: a first-person account of the sub's mission, targets, hopes, fears, and dying. If the KTB still existed, only quiet eyes would find it. Chatterton began to go still.

At first, the wreckage in the commander's quarters appeared as the junk pile Chatterton expected. He settled in and absorbed the scene.

Still, junk. As minutes passed and he stayed locked on the scene, however, specks of order began to dance in and out of the chaos.

"That shape is not random," Chatterton thought as he reached forward into the pile of rubble. He pulled out a pristine leather boot.

"That speck of metal is smoother than the rest," he considered as he pushed his hand into another wreckage heap. He pulled out a signal flare.

"That brown is not from nature," he speculated as he fidgeted his hand into a mound of splintered wood. He pulled out a crewman's escape lung—complete with small oxygen tank, breathing apparatus, and vest.

In twenty minutes, Chatterton had salvaged three prime artifacts he had overlooked on earlier dives to these forward rooms. Each likely contained writing. The escape lung seemed the most promising. In Germany, Horst Bredow had urged the divers to recover this device—a mini–scuba tank and rubberized mouthpiece used by submariners to exit a sinking U-boat—because crewmen often wrote their names inside them. As Chatterton made his way up to the *Seeker* he found himself unusually proud, though for most of the hour he could not put his finger on why. At 20 feet, when he saw the dive boat swaying above him, he understood. In detecting beauty camouflaged in wreckage, he had done the very thing that had made Nagle great, and it had always been his dream to dive like Bill Nagle. When Chatterton climbed aboard, Nagle dragged himself over to inspect the artifacts. Chatterton could smell his body odor and see the dirt in his hair. He put his arm around Nagle and asked the captain to help him undress. It was a good feeling, Chatterton thought, to still dream to dive like Nagle.

Kohler followed Chatterton onto the boat and threw off his tanks. He had recovered only some pieces of a coffeepot, so he rushed to the dive table to join in the inspection of Chatterton's finds. The divers placed the leather boot, the flare, and the escape lung in a bucket of fresh water and sloshed them around. Nagle removed the boot first and dabbed a towel at the grime. The divers crowded in, each of them looking for a name or initials or other writing. The boot was barren—its owner had written nothing.

Next, Nagle pulled the shotgun shell–shaped flare from the

bucket. This is what the crewmen would have fired into the air from a pistol in case of distress. He rubbed it in soft, genie-lamp circles. German writing appeared in answer. The words, however, provided just a manufacturer's name and the flare's gauge size.

Only the escape lung remained. It consisted of a brownish rubberized canvas life vest, a black corrugated rubber tube, an orange rubber mouthpiece, and a thermos-sized aluminum oxygen cylinder, from which crewmen could breathe in emergencies. Of the three artifacts, it was in the worst condition. Much had eroded in the ocean environment. The oxygen bottle was dented in the middle and bent out of alignment. Nagle wiped at the apparatus. Mud fell away. There was no writing. Nagle rubbed further. This time, from the handle of the mouthpiece, a tiny eagle and swastika materialized.

"Is there a name written anywhere?" Kohler asked.

Nagle wiped some more.

"No name," Nagle said. "Looks like it coulda belonged to any of 'em."

Chatterton's hopes drifted off the *Seeker* and evaporated in the midmorning breeze.

"Zero for three," he said. "This wreck is one tough S.O.B." He took the escape lung and placed it in his cooler. "May as well take it home, clean it, and let it dry," he told Yurga. "Who knows? Maybe I'll see some writing if I let the canvas dry completely."

At the ladder, Packer and Gatto surfaced with promising news. The fallen ductwork that had blocked entry to the diesel motor room had disappeared during the off-season, a gift from a winter storm. Inside, the team had seen several instruments and pieces of equipment, any one of which might be engraved with the U-boat's number. Another dive and they would have time to begin inspection.

"How much of the diesel motor room did you see?" Kohler asked.

"Not much," Packer said. "We only got about ten feet inside. There's another huge obstruction that blocks the rest of the way. You still can't reach the electric motor room. But I think we got in far enough to hit it big."

"Congrats," Chatterton said. "I think you guys have done it."

Rough seas and plummeting visibility cut short most of the second dives. As Nagle pulled up anchor and coaxed the boat to life, many of the divers fantasized aloud about the wonders Packer and Gatto would yank from the diesel motor room when next they got the chance. At first Chatterton led the discussion, recounting the treasures he had seen in the same room on *U-505* in the Chicago museum. But as the divers kept talking, Chatterton fell quiet, looking instead at his cooler and imagining the tattered escape lung inside, wondering if there might be order inside that broken artifact, and wondering about this U-boat in which nothing was exactly as it seemed.

Chatterton returned home from the Memorial Day dive near midnight. He unpacked his gear quietly, careful not to awaken his wife. When only the cooler remained, he fished out the escape lung and walked it into his garage. Shelves everywhere held the overflow of shipwreck artifacts from Chatterton's house, making the garage a museum of his underwater daring. He found a spot for the battered lung alongside several years' bounty of *Andrea Doria* serving bowls, silverware, and china. He figured it would take several days for the piece to fully dry. Inside his house, Chatterton washed his face and thought, "Packer and Gatto are going to be the ones to recover proof of the wreck's identity."

A few days later, Chatterton went to his garage to check on the escape lung. He stood dumbfounded at the door. Broken china lay strewn across the floor. Shattered glass had been shrapneled against the walls and ceiling. A thick wooden shelf lay broken and dangling.

"Someone blew up my garage," Chatterton said aloud. "Someone came in here with a bomb."

Dazed, he searched for a broom and began sweeping. Virtually nothing on the garage shelves had survived. He kept sweeping. In the rubble, he spotted a metallic silver shape. He picked it up. This was the escape lung's oxygen bottle, but it was no longer cylindrical and closed. Now it was flattened, like a toothpaste tube sliced open.

"Goddamn," Chatterton said. "The oxygen bottle exploded. The thing was still live. The escape lung blew up my garage."

Chatterton looked closer at the flattened cylinder. The explosion had blasted away a half century's encrustation, the part that could not be removed with simple wiping. Chatterton pulled it close to his face. Stamped onto the flattened metal was a bit of writing. It said: 15.4.44.

Chatterton knew right away what the numbers meant. He ran into his home and called Kohler.

"Richie, man, the oxygen bottle blew up my garage," he said.

"What?"

"The escape lung. Remember the oxygen bottle? It was still charged. I let it dry in my garage. The corrosion must have caused it to blow. All my *Doria* stuff in the garage is destroyed. My garage is like a war zone. But listen to this: the explosion produced a clue. The bottle has a date on it—*fifteen-dot-four-dot-forty-four*—that's European for April 15, 1944. That's the hydrostatic test date, the date the bottle was examined and certified to be good."

"That means our U-boat sailed after April 15, 1944," Kohler said.

"Exactly."

"I'll be right there."

Chatterton returned to the garage. He picked up the broom but could not sweep. Only now did it occur to him how lucky he had been while handling the escape lung. He had carried the artifact in his goody bag for his hour-long decompression, eyeballed it on board the *Seeker*, stored it next to his pickup truck's gas tank, moved it around on his garage shelves. As he awaited Kohler's arrival, two thoughts tolled inside his mind. First, it seemed more certain than ever that the wreck was *U-857*, which had departed for war in February 1945. And second, perhaps the divers were getting too close—that, crazy as it sounded, maybe the dead crewmen were beginning to fight back.

A few hours after finding his garage blown up, Chatterton called Major Gregory Weidenfeld, the Civil Air Patrol historian who had dedicated himself to proving that two everyday civilians in a private plane had sunk a U-boat off New Jersey in 1942.

"Listen, Greg," Chatterton said. "We found a hydrostatic test date that proves the wreck sailed sometime after April 15, 1944. That excludes the chance that this is your U-boat. I'm really sorry."

For a moment, Chatterton believed he could hear Weidenfeld struggling to compose himself. He could not remember a time when he had met someone so loyal to the memories of the slighted.

"Thank you, John," Weidenfeld said. "That means there's another U-boat out there you'll have to find."

A few days later, Chatterton received word that his friend the U-boat ace Karl-Friedrich Merten had died at age eighty-seven. The news was not unexpected, as Merten had been ill for some time. But Chatterton knew that Merten's passing, together with his own good-bye to Weidenfeld, meant that a chapter in the divers' quest had closed. For a year, Chatterton, Kohler, and Yurga had considered *U-158* (via the Civil Air Patrol) and *U-851* (via Merten's information about his colleague Weingärtner) as the likeliest solutions to the mystery. They had cut their research teeth on these theories, and had considered the men friends.

Weather and scheduling prevented the *Seeker* from returning to the *U-Who* until July 31, two months after the season's first trip. The divers practically had to sit on their hands to contain themselves when the boat finally departed for the wreck. This would be the trip when Packer and Gatto would begin to make their haul from the diesel motor room.

The next morning, Chatterton and Kohler splashed and headed toward the sub's forward compartments, areas they still thought likely to yield identifying artifacts. As before, Chatterton studied the debris field, quieting his mind to acclimate his eyes to the shapes of order. In the commander's quarters, lying in plain view, he spotted a pair of binoculars.

"I've been here a dozen times and there were no binoculars in here," Chatterton thought. "There's no way I would have missed that."

Chatterton lifted the binoculars to his mask. Some optics were missing, and much was encrusted in sea growth. He placed the piece in his bag. If the pair had belonged to the commander, perhaps his name lay inscribed underneath the muck. The remainder of Chatterton's search produced little. All the while he thought about how poetic it was to have recovered binoculars in a dive dedicated to seeing.

Kohler continued to dig in the noncommissioned officers' quarters. He had been meticulous in avoiding the closet in which the crewmen's shoes lay neatly arranged, as well as other areas near the compartment's abundant human remains. In a silt pile he spotted what appeared to be a bowl and brought it to his mask for inspection. It took just a moment for Kohler to realize he was holding a skull. Silt poured from the eye sockets and nasal cavity. A year ago he might have panicked and flung the skull back into the debris. Today, he held it and looked into its eyes.

"I'm going to do my best to figure out your name," Kohler said aloud. "Your families should know where you are."

It was time to leave the wreck. He took the skull and gently placed it in such a way as to allow it to look out over the compartment and its mates.

Topside, Chatterton and Kohler washed the binoculars. The apparatus was unmarked. Now they could do no more than await the arrival of Packer and Gatto, who had gone to work inside the promising diesel motor room. An hour later that team climbed the ladder. Packer's goody bag bulged. He opened the mesh container and removed a pressure gauge the size of a dinner plate—one of the instruments Chatterton and Kohler had seen in books stamped with a U-boat's identity. The divers pressed in for a closer look. Etched on the gauge's aluminum face was the eagle and swastika. The rest of the face, however, contained only generic words and numerals. Packer wiped the gauge's body. It nearly crumbled in his hands. As with the torpedo room tags, this instrument had been constructed with the cheap metal porridge used by Germany during its late-war raw-materials shortage. The implication was grave: other artifacts inside the diesel motor room—including identifying tags—were probably made of the same low-grade materials and had likely not survived the ocean environment.

Ripping currents made short work of most second dives. That night, as the *Seeker* cut through the blue-black Atlantic on her way back to Brielle, few of the divers found themselves with much to say. In the wheelhouse, while Nagle muttered, "This goddamned

U-boat . . . ," Chatterton made a short entry in his logbook. It read "Where to next?"

The *Seeker* made four trips to the U-boat over the next six weeks. Packer and Gatto continued their work inside the open portion of the diesel motor room. They gathered beautiful and interesting artifacts: a gauge panel, plastic tags, even a telegraph, the instrument used to signal orders like ALL STOP, FULL AHEAD, and DIVE. All the marks were generic; none identified the wreck. Further access into the compartment was blocked by a massive steel pipe that lay angled in the narrow walkway between the two diesel engines. Kohler recognized this pipe as an escape trunk, a vertical tunnel with an interior ladder through which crewmen could flee a sinking U-boat. Now wedged between the engines and reaching from floor to ceiling, the escape trunk blocked any further penetration into the diesel motor room and the adjoining electric motor room. The loss did not seem severe—if the smorgasbord of items Packer and Gatto had thus far recovered revealed nothing about the U-boat's identity, it was unlikely that the remainder of these technical rooms held the answer.

Chatterton and Kohler devoted their dives to the U-boat's forward section. They recovered various artifacts—bowls, cups, shoes, gauges—not a bit of which contained identification. Chatterton pulled two gems from the wreck, museum-quality pieces that drew gasps from his fellow divers. One of them, lying fully exposed in an area Chatterton had combed a dozen times before, was a surgeon's kit, a collection of stainless steel medical instruments complete with instructional diagrams—printed in still-brilliant red and black inks—on linen canvases. None of it, however, revealed the wreck's identity.

"You guys can have all these instruments," Chatterton told the other divers. "I'll keep the diagrams for my house."

"Christ, John, that surgeon's kit is a gorgeous find, one of a kind," someone said. "You can't give it away."

"I'm looking to identify the wreck," Chatterton replied. "The kit doesn't do it. It's yours."

250 · ROBERT KURSON

On the next trip, Chatterton recovered the chronometer—the U-boat's precision clock—from the commander's quarters. It was another major score. As with the surgeon's kit, he had found the chronometer lying in the open in an area of the commander's quarters he had searched repeatedly. Topside, he inspected the handsome instrument for evidence of the wreck's identity. Except for the markings of the eagle and swastika, there was none. Chatterton moved to throw overboard the chronometer's wooden box.

"What the hell are you doing?" Kohler asked, rushing forward.

"The box tells us nothing," Chatterton said.

"It's a spectacular find! Are you crazy? That's a career find!"

"That's not what's important."

"Give me the clock and the box," Kohler said. "I got a restoration guy. Give it to me and I'll make it beautiful for your house."

"Whatever you want, Richie."

"Christ, John, what's going on with you?"

Riding back to Brielle that night, Chatterton told Kohler what was going on with him. He had begun the dive season with a ferocious optimism, certain that his brand of hard work, preparation, and instinct—his artistry—would pay off in a positive identification of the wreck. Now, four months and six trips later, he found himself with all kinds of crazy thoughts. He worried for the first time that a greenhorn diver would climb the *Seeker*'s ladder with an identification tag stuck to his fin, becoming the accidental but official discoverer of the *U-Who*'s name.

"It's not that I care about who gets the credit," he told Kohler. "It's that it would mean my approach hadn't worked."

He worried about how he and Kohler had missed major artifacts in earlier explorations only to find them lying in the open on later dives.

"It's like the crewmen are putting stuff out for me," Chatterton said. "But it's not the stuff I want. It's like they're saying, 'Hey, let's put out the binoculars for him; that'll really get him going.'"

Kohler put down his beer.

"Listen, John, we can do it," Kohler said. "If I have to row us out here in a canoe I'll do it. I'm with you. I believe in what we're doing. Let's keep pounding. You tell me what you need and I'm there. We ain't quitting."

It was then that Chatterton fully understood what Kohler had meant to the project. He was a first-rate diver, one of the best, and a passionate and creative researcher. But deeper than that he was a believer, and as Chatterton watched Kohler reach for a handshake, he knew that this was the most important thing of all, that in a quest in which men were asked to really know themselves, an unflinching belief in the possible survived all. Chatterton shook Kohler's hand.

"We ain't quitting," he said.

Even as October's autumn settled over New Jersey, Chatterton and Kohler believed they might squeeze in another trip or two to the *U-Who*. Nagle, however, was of a different mind. Little more than a skeleton, he was no longer capable of captaining the *Seeker*.

His business had begun to fail. When prospective customers inquired about charters, Nagle would say, "Oh, that's a nice request, but how about this: Fuck you! I'm dying! I don't care about you or your sunny smiles or your bullshit artificial-reef wrecks! I never cared anything about you! Don't you get it? I'm gonna die! Good-bye!" As the season wore on, Chatterton found it painful to look at his old friend and mentor.

In October, Nagle was rushed by his girlfriend to the hospital, bleeding from the throat. Years of alcohol abuse had caused him to develop esophageal varices, varicose veins in his throat, which had then ruptured. Doctors hurried him to surgery and cauterized the damage. In the recovery room they told him, "You came within fifteen minutes of bleeding to death. If you continue to consume alcohol, even a single drink, we might not be able to save you next time."

Nagle's girlfriend broke up with him while he was still in the hospital. She could not bear to watch him kill himself. A few weeks later, Nagle checked himself out of the hospital. On the way home he stopped at the liquor store. That night, after consuming nearly a full bottle of vodka, he bled to death from the throat. Bill Nagle, one of the greatest shipwreck divers of all time, the man who had taken the bell off the *Andrea Doria*, was dead at forty-one.

Divers from across the Northeast made plans to attend Nagle's funeral in Pennsylvania. Chatterton, one of his dearest friends, did not. Kohler could not accept that decision.

"What do you mean you're not going to the funeral?" Kohler asked.

"The guy in that box is not Bill Nagle," Chatterton said. "The guy in that box killed my friend."

"You should go," Kohler said. "You need to say good-bye to your friend."

Chatterton could not bring himself to attend. At the funeral, Kohler and the other pallbearers lifted Nagle's coffin. As he walked Nagle to the grave, Kohler could not get over the lightness of the box. "It's like there's nothing inside," he thought to himself, and it was then that he wished most of all that Chatterton were beside him.

Three dive seasons had passed since the *U-Who*'s discovery. Though certain that the wreck was *U-857*, Chatterton and Kohler were no closer to proving it than they had been in 1991.

As winter claimed New Jersey, Chatterton noticed fraying around the edges of his marriage. While he had worked to master the *U-Who*, Kathy had become among the finest women pistol shooters in the world. Discordant schedules squeezed the couple's time together, and diverging interests made that time awkward. When Kathy asked about her husband's growing obsession with the U-boat, Chatterton told her, "I'm being tested. What I do with this U-boat is what I am as a person."

Neither Chatterton nor Kathy feared for the long-term future of the marriage; they still loved each other and allowed each other space for passions. But sometimes, when Chatterton looked up from his desk and realized that he and Kathy had not spoken for days, it reminded him of his time as a scallop fisherman. Every so often then, a shadow would creep up on the fishermen as they worked the dredges, sending the men scurrying to track the source of the shadow, which was always a great wave about to punish the boat. Now, at home, Chatterton was beginning to feel the shadow.

At Kohler's home five miles away, the wave had already hit the boat. For more than a year, he and his wife, Felicia, had argued over Kohler's availability to her, their two small children, and Felicia's ten-year-old daughter from a previous relationship. She understood the necessary evil that was Kohler's glass business—the company was growing and required near-constant attention as Kohler sought to expand it. She had less patience, however, for Kohler's use of his remaining free time. He spent nearly every day of the year working the *U-Who*—diving it, researching it, meeting with Chatterton, whisking off to Washington. He and Felicia seemed to fight every day. Felicia told him, "If you gave up diving our marriage would improve." That song was taps for Kohler. Around Christmas 1993, he and Felicia separated. She moved with the children to Long Island and he took a bachelor pad on the northeastern tip of the Jersey Shore. He insisted on having his kids every weekend.

For a month or two, Kohler reveled in his newfound freedom. He dated young lovelies, danced at nightclubs, and read his U-boat books with impunity. But he missed his son, Richie, daughter, Nikki, and stepdaughter, Jennyann. Weekend visits were not enough. He entertained notions of reconciliation with Felicia, but he believed she would not consider it unless he agreed to abandon diving, which would be the same as asking him to abandon food. As February 1994 froze the beaches near his apartment, he became convinced that something would have to change, that he was not in his natural state without his kids to chase off to school.

In late February, Chatterton and Kohler received a letter from Robert Coppock at the Ministry of Defence. Standing in his bathrobe and holding a cup of coffee, Chatterton began to read:

> *U-869* . . . was [originally] bound for the US East Coast [and] allocated a patrol area . . . about 110 miles south-east of New York. . . .

Chatterton went numb. *U-869* was Horenburg's boat. It was supposed to have been ordered to Gibraltar.

> *U-869* . . . may not have received a [new] signal ordering her to Gibraltar. . . .

Chatterton's heart pounded against his rib cage.

> In view of atmospheric conditions . . . it is certainly possible
> that Control's [new] signal ordering *U-869* to the Gibraltar
> area was not received by the boat. . . .

Now Chatterton was light-headed.

> In the light, therefore, of the absence of any tangible proof that
> *U-869* had received Control's signal ordering her to the Gibral-
> tar area, [along with] the evidence of the knife and the proxim-
> ity of the wreck's position to *U-869*'s original patrol area, I
> would concede that the possibility the wreck is *U-869* cannot
> be ignored.

Chatterton rushed to the phone and called Kohler.

"Richie, we just got an unbelievable letter from Coppock. He
dropped an atomic bomb. You won't believe it—"

"Slow down!" Kohler said. "What's it say?"

"It says this: *U-869*, Horenburg's boat, the one all the history
books say was sunk off Gibraltar, was originally ordered to New
York. And not just to New York, but just south of New York, right to
our wreck site! It says that headquarters later changed those orders
to Gibraltar. But get this, Richie, and I quote: 'It is certainly possible that Control's signal ordering *U-869* to the Gibraltar area was
not received by the boat.' "

"But what about all the reports that *U-869* was sunk off Gibraltar
by Allied escort ships?" Kohler asked.

"We've seen how accurate those reports can be, haven't we?"

"This is unbelievable. I'm stunned."

"Richie, can you conference-call Coppock from your office? We
have to ask him to explain where he got this information."

"I'm already dialing," Kohler said.

A moment later the phone rang at Great Scotland Yard. Coppock
had only a few minutes to talk. He told the divers that his information had been gleaned from reading intercepted radio messages between *U-869* and U-boat Control in Germany. The intercepted
messages and their interpretations by American code breakers, he
said, could be found in Washington, D.C.

Chatterton and Kohler sat flabbergasted. They had seen radio intercepts before but had never dreamed to inspect those relating to *U-869*, a boat conclusively recorded by history as having been sunk off Gibraltar. None of the experts to whom they had spoken—including Coppock—had thought to do so either.

"I'm going to D.C. tomorrow to investigate," Chatterton said. "The whole story is there."

Kohler wanted to join Chatterton in Washington, but he was still part of a two-man business and could not free up the time. Instead, Chatterton took Barb Lander, who had long been diving the *U-Who* and who had shown keen interest in its history. Chatterton promised he would call Kohler with details as they unfolded, and took along several rolls of quarters for pay phones to do so.

Chatterton and Lander landed first at the National Archives, where they requested Tenth Fleet U-boat intelligence summaries starting on December 8, 1944—the day *U-869* had departed for war. Archivists wheeled out cartloads of documents stamped ULTRA—TOP SECRET. Chatterton knew the word *Ultra,* the name for the Allied monitoring and decrypting of Enigma. For decades after the war, few had fathomed that the Allies had cracked Enigma and had been reading the German mail. Now Chatterton and Lander were about to read it too.

The divers scanned the U.S. Navy's intelligence summaries. They found a report dated January 3, 1945. Navy intelligence had intercepted radio messages between *U-869* and Control. The code breakers wrote:

> A U/Boat (*U-869*) now estimated in the central North Atlantic
> has been ordered to head for a point about 70 miles southeast
> of the New York approaches.

Chatterton could scarcely believe what he was reading—that would have put *U-869* directly on the wreck site. He pressed further. In a report dated January 17, 1945, navy intelligence wrote:

> The U/Boat heading for the New York approaches, *U-869*
> (Neuerburg), is presently estimated about 180 miles SSE of

Flemish Cap. . . . She is expected to arrive in the New York area at the beginning of February.

Chatterton checked his crew list. Neuerburg was *U-869*'s commander. He kept reading, his heart charging into his rib cage. In a January 25 report, navy eavesdroppers detected a communication problem between *U-869* and Control:

One U/Boat may be south of Newfoundland heading for New York approaches, although her location is uncertain due to a mix up in orders and Control assumes she is heading for Gibraltar. . . . [But] based on the signals she received it appears likely that *U-869* is continuing toward her original heading off New York.

"I can't believe it," Chatterton told Lander. "They were ordered right to our wreck site. Control changed the orders to send the U-boat to Gibraltar. But it looks like *U-869* never got those new orders. She just kept heading for New York."

"Oh, wow," Lander said, scanning the document. "Read the rest of what the navy says."

The *CORE* will begin sweeping for this U/Boat shortly prior to proceeding against the U/Boats reporting weather in the North Atlantic.

"The USS *Core* was an aircraft carrier attached to a hunter-killer group," Chatterton said. "The navy knew exactly where *U-869* was headed and was lying in wait for her."

Chatterton took his quarters and ran to the pay phone. He called Kohler and told him of his discoveries.

"Incredible," Kohler said. "The navy sent a hunter-killer group for *U-869* but they never got her, never even spotted her—we'd know it if they had. U-boats didn't get away from hunter-killer groups in 1945, John. This Neuerburg must have been some commander."

For a moment there was silence on the line.

"We didn't find *U-857* at all," Kohler finally said. "We found *U-869*."

"We found *U-869*," Chatterton said. "It was *U-869* all along."

Still unresolved, however, was the matter of *U-869*'s reported sinking off Gibraltar by two ships, the *L'Indiscret* and USS *Fowler*. Every history book had it recorded that way. Chatterton and Lander raced to the Naval Historical Center and requested attack reports for the sinking of *U-869*. Minutes later they were looking at butchered history.

On February 28, 1945, the American destroyer escort USS *Fowler* picked up a sonar contact in the area west of Rabat, southwest of Gibraltar. The *Fowler* fired a pattern of thirteen depth charges. Two explosions followed and debris of an "unknown identity" was spotted on the surface. The *Fowler* fired another pattern of depth charges. When the smoke cleared, crewmen dragged a towel through the debris, which "had the appearance of lumps and balls of heavy oil sludge but no samples were recovered." The destroyer searched the area for further evidence of damage. It found none.

Hours later, the French patrol craft *L'Indiscret* attacked a sonar contact in the same area, which "caused a large black object to break surface and immediately sink." The boat could not identify the object and spotted no debris.

Navy intelligence was unimpressed with the attacks and the flimsy evidence produced. They graded each of the attacks "G—No Damage."

But, Chatterton could see as he read the reports, postwar assessors soon changed the grade from "G" to "B—Probably Sunk."

"Why would they have done that?" Lander asked.

"I've seen this before," Chatterton said. "The postwar assessors were scrambling to account for lost U-boats. One of those U-boats was *U-869*. The assessors have no clue about intercepted radio messages—that was top secret—so they don't know *U-869* went to New York. They check the German records. The Germans believed *U-869* went to Gibraltar—they think she got the new orders to go to Gibraltar. When she doesn't come home, the Germans presume her lost off Gibraltar. Then the postwar assessors see these attacks by the *Fowler* and *L'Indiscret* near Gibraltar. They attach the attacks to *U-869*, change the grade from G to B, and that settles it for them."

Chatterton ran back to the pay phone. He told Kohler that the history books were wrong.

"We found *U-869*," Kohler said. "We found Horenburg, didn't we?"

"Horenburg was there the whole time," Chatterton said. "Think about it, Richie. If there were radio problems between *U-869* and Control, Horenburg would have been the guy front and center for it. He was the senior radioman. Listen, Richie, I'm out of quarters. But I'll tell you this: Horenburg must have been there for it all."

CHAPTER TWELVE

NONE OF US IS COMING BACK

**Deschimag Shipyard, Bremen, Germany,
January 1944**

IN THE CHILL MORNING of a new year, as ruins still smoldered in Berlin from fresh British bombings, hundreds of young German men from throughout the country made their way to the Deschimag shipyard in the seaport town of Bremen to begin naval training. Most brought just a simple suitcase of clothes and perhaps a cherished photograph or good-luck charm. Perhaps fifty of these men were told they would be the crew of a submarine temporarily titled *W1077*. In a few days that submarine would be commissioned as *U-869*.

Though only a handful of these men had previous U-boat experience, many either had volunteered for submarine service or had been chosen for it because of their technical skills and backgrounds. They were a young group—average age twenty-one, with twenty-two teenagers, including a seventeen-year-old—and were worlds away from the crews of 1939, when the U-bootwaffe selected only the most elite of the elite.

Among the most experienced men assigned to *U-869* was twenty-two-year-old Herbert Guschewski, a radio operator and veteran of three war patrols, all with *U-602*. Guschewski counted himself lucky to be alive. He had been ordered off *U-602* just before its most recent patrol; heavy U-boat casualties had created a shortage of radio operators, and his services were needed elsewhere. Guschewski was heartbroken—his crewmen were his brothers, his U-boat his home. *U-602* set sail for the Mediterranean. It never returned.

As Guschewski unpacked that evening in Bremen, he heard a knock at his door.

"Who is it?" Guschewski asked.

"A fellow crewman," came the reply.

Guschewski opened the door. A handsome man with wavy brown hair and jack-of-spades dark eyes asked if he might come inside. The man introduced himself as Martin Horenburg, the *Funkmeister* assigned to *U-869*. He told Guschewski that he was looking forward to working with him.

Guschewski shook Horenburg's hand, but his heart sank. He had expected to be the crew's most senior radio operator. But Horenburg ranked higher; he was a *Funkmeister*, or a radio master. The men spoke briefly before wishing each other a good night. "At least," Guschewski thought as he closed his door, "this fellow seems bright, capable, and friendly. At least Horenburg seems like a gentleman."

It would be a few days before the crew was officially assembled. In the meantime, several men assigned to *U-869*, including Guschewski and Horenburg, hopped a cable car to the Deschimag shipyard in hopes of glimpsing their U-boat. Inside the gates, diesel fumes collided with sea and fish, dusting the grounds with the perfume of maritime war. The men asked about *U-869*. A guard directed them to a dock.

And there she was. Lean and stealthy, her cigar-shaped hull grooved into the water at bow and stern, she appeared an eyebrow of the sea, raised for the moment to observe the curious. Everywhere she was painted overcast gray, the most impossible color to see when the world changed from light to dark or dark to light, the times when U-boats were deadliest. Affixed to *U-869*'s conning tower were the Olympic rings, the mark of a boat to be commanded by a graduate of the naval class of 1936, the year of the Berlin games. For a moment, Guschewski stood awestruck before the machine. In every way—weaponry, size, design—it seemed superior to the Type VII on which he had previously served. "There is no comparison," he thought to himself. "This is a great boat. This is something entirely different."

For the next two weeks, the men of *U-869* joined other crews for general instruction at the shipyard. They would not meet the submarine's top three officers—the commander, first officer, and chief engineer—until the U-boat's commissioning in late January. Until then, they could only speculate about the men who would lead them into war.

Commissioning was scheduled for January 26, 1944. On that day, those assigned to *U-869* dressed in formal navy uniforms and made their way to the submarine's dock. It was the first time the men had come together as a crew. An officer took attendance, calling out names: "Brizius, Dagg, Dietmayer, Dietz . . ." until each of the crewmen had confirmed himself present. All the while, the crew cast their eyes to the side, where a tall, deeply handsome man with black hair, broad shoulders, and penetrating dark eyes was observing the proceedings. They knew this man to be their commander—they could see a nobility in his posture, a certainty in the slowness of his breaths, a strength in his face's Teutonic angles. The men had grown up in a country wallpapered with images of the heroic and invincible U-boat commander, a man for whom anything was possible. Here, in the form of twenty-six-year-old commander Helmuth Neuerburg, that image had come to life.

The men climbed aboard the submarine and fell into rows of three on its stern deck, their hands at their sides, standing at attention. Commander Neuerburg looked over his men, over the water, and over Germany. By now, the men knew this to be Neuerburg's maiden command; some even whispered that he had been a Luftwaffe fighter pilot before volunteering for U-boat service. Neuerburg began to address his men from behind the winter garden's rail. His speech was short and in proper German, his voice military and exact. He spoke just a few words, all of them official and unemotional. But it took no more than these words for even a U-boat veteran like Guschewski to think, "There is great courage and competence in this man. You do not go against this voice. You do not go against this man."

After Neuerburg spoke, he gave the order to raise the ship's ensign. When the flag reached the top, Neuerburg saluted it not with the Nazi *heil* but rather in traditional military style.

"The boat is commissioned," Neuerburg announced.

And that was it. No one presented Neuerburg with a model of the U-boat, as had been done for Guschewski's previous commander on *U-602*. No brass band played songs of joy and country. The men simply left the boat and returned to shore.

"We are living in a different time," Guschewski thought.

That evening, the officers and crew of *U-869* gathered for a celebration dinner at a small guesthouse in Bremen. Seated with Neuerburg were his first officer, twenty-one-year-old Siegfried Brandt, and his chief engineer, thirty-year-old Ludwig Kessler. Guschewski surveyed the sparse room and saw the direction of Germany. Two years earlier, he had attended the commissioning dinner for *U-602*, a raucous feast of pork roast, dumplings, and wine, followed by a party for the crew—officers and enlisted men alike—at Hamburg's famed Reeperbahn. There, the men had watched a musical in specially reserved theater seats, then lit up the town. This night, there were no parties. Men ate herring and boiled potatoes at unadorned tables, and washed it down with beer. Conversation was reserved.

Still, Guschewski was excited. His brother Willi had traveled to Bremen to visit him. Earlier that evening, Guschewski had asked the cook if he might prepare a plate of food for Willi, one for which Guschewski gladly would pay. The cook obliged, and Willi joined his brother and the other crewmen for dinner. Neuerburg rose from his table and approached the brothers.

"What is this man doing here?" Neuerburg asked.

"He is my brother, sir," Guschewski answered. "He made a special trip from Bochum to say good-bye to me."

"He is not a member of the crew and is therefore not permitted in the same room as the crew," Neuerburg said. He turned to Willi. "You must leave immediately, sir. You may take your dinner to a different room in this guesthouse. Your brother may visit you after ten P.M. Go now."

Guschewski was stunned. He admired commanders who followed strict military protocol. But he had also prayed that *U-869* would be led by a man with a heart. As he watched his brother carry his plate of food from the room, he believed that part of Neuerburg's character still to be in question.

Onboard training began after *U-869*'s commissioning. As the men shimmied through the sub's three deck hatches, they found themselves in a technological wonderland. Swarms of instruments, gauges, dials, tubing, and wiring forested every centimeter of the boat. Everywhere, the boat smelled of fresh paint and oil and promise. The clocks, as the men had heard, had been set to Berlin time and would remain so no matter where in the world the U-boat traveled. Not a single photo—not of Hitler or of Dönitz—hung anywhere in the boat.

The men spent the next several days loading the submarine and becoming accustomed to U-boat protocol. No one was expected to salute officers aboard the vessel. Officers addressed one another by first name. In a matter of days, even as the U-boat still remained in port, a bond began to form between crewmen, each of whom likely sensed what Dönitz had written years before: that a U-boat crew was a *Schicksalsgemeinschaft*—a community bound by fate.

From the start, the crew studied Neuerburg. Whatever the task, he remained cool and restrained, the picture of military discipline. The men listened for him to make jokes as they walked through the officers' mess, but they heard him engaging only in serious conversation with Brandt and Kessler, and always in proper German. He used no slang for the U-boat's equipment and uttered no profanities. Even as news of Germany's worsening fate trickled into Bremen, Neuerburg betrayed no fear or hesitation. Instead, he spoke of duty, and when he did not speak of duty he acted and stood and moved as if it were his guiding principle. Though naval officers had to yield membership in a political party while on active duty—including the Nazi Party—the crewmen observed Neuerburg's intensity and wondered if his heart might not belong to the National Socialists. No one, however, wondered about his commitment. As he took them through the first weeks of training, they sensed that this was a man who would die before he disobeyed an order.

For all the crew believed about Neuerburg's character, they knew almost nothing about his life. He had flown as a navy pilot—that much he had told them—and had only recently transferred to the U-boat service. Some crewmen speculated that perhaps Neuerburg had joined the U-boats to treat a "sore throat"—slang for an officer's desire to win the Knight's Cross, which was worn around the neck—though Neuerburg did not discuss his motivations. Some had seen his wife, a strikingly beautiful woman, on the grounds one day, though Neuerburg never spoke of family. His privacy did not undermine the men's confidence in their commander. But if there was a mystery among the crew of *U-869* in the early days of training, that mystery was about the life of the man who had been chosen to lead them.

At age nineteen, Helmuth Neuerburg of Strasbourg decided to join the marines. The choice might have surprised those who knew him. As a young man, he had displayed a natural talent for the violin and a great facility for drawing caricatures, several of which lampooned the adults in his life. He had passed his *Abitur,* a prerequisite for higher study. Those closest to him expected that he might pursue a career in the arts. This was likely Helmuth's intention even as he joined the marines; he knew that if he committed to a few years of service, the military would pay him a lump sum upon discharge, money he could then invest in his higher education. He never considered joining the U-boat force. As boys, he and his older brother, Friedhelm, had talked about submarines, but neither of them had been awed by the legend. "There is a big price behind that stardom," they'd reminded each other. "You become a victim very fast in a U-boat."

And so Helmuth became a naval cadet, class of 1936. (The student's class was designated by year of enrollment, not year of graduation.) He scored high in most subjects, posting his best marks one year in machinery and English. He formed a band while in the service and, as graduation neared, composed a class song, for which he was given a special award by Erich Raeder, the head of the German navy. Upon graduation, he began pilot training as part of the naval air arm. By 1940, he was an officer flying North Sea reconnaissance missions near England, even strapping his beloved German shepherd into the cockpit for one mission. For the next three years, he continued to fly, to train other pilots, and to earn excellent reviews. But if Helmuth's military career looked to be the National Socialist ideal, his heart and mind told a different, more secret story.

While Helmuth did not dare speak against the Nazi regime publicly—an officer could be executed for such a crime—he had no such reservation when speaking to Friedhelm, a tanker in one of the army's panzer divisions. During visits, he told Friedhelm that he believed the Nazis to be authoring the downfall of Germany. Friedhelm recoiled at the public nature of his expression.

"Are you crazy, talking like that in the open?" he asked Helmuth whenever such conversations unfolded. "People are listening everywhere! What you are saying is very dangerous!"

Helmuth continued talking. On one occasion, after he spoke to a Nazi official near Nuremberg, Helmuth told Friedhelm that the man's anti-Semitic beliefs were "appalling" and "sickening." Friedhelm begged his brother to stay quiet.

"The walls have ears, Helmuth!" Friedhelm warned. "Everyone listens. Please, be very careful with what you say. Simply uttering such ideas aloud can be the end of you."

In 1941, Helmuth married twenty-two-year-old Erna Maas, the daughter of a brewery owner. Bright, beautiful, and energetic, Erna was also passionately antimilitary. The two loved each other deeply. At home, Helmuth collected American jazz records, a music form forbidden by the Nazis, and tuned to enemy BBC radio for news of the war—another wartime offense. One morning, while shaving in front of the mirror, he heard a BBC report of America's entry into the conflict.

"We have lost this war already," he told Erna.

He continued to see Friedhelm whenever possible. He continued talking. "After the war I will get rid of the skirt," he told his brother, referring to his uniform.

In 1943, Neuerburg and others were offered a choice: they could remain with the naval air arm or join the U-boats. Those who stayed with the air force would go into combat immediately; those who transferred to submarines might spend a year or more in training before going to battle. Neuerburg was father to a two-year-old son and a one-year-old daughter. He chose the U-boats, though he harbored no illusions about their safety. When informing Friedhelm of his decision, he said that he believed U-boat service to be a *Himmelfahrtskommando*—a command to report directly to heaven.

Neuerburg spent the next twenty-one months in U-boat training, using leaves to take his two-year-old son, Jürgen, for sailboat rides and bounce his infant daughter, Jutta, on his knee. Just before U-869's commissioning, he spoke to Friedhelm. This time, he mentioned nothing of the Nazis. He simply looked his brother in the eye and said, "I'm not coming back."

Classroom instruction complete, the U-boat loaded with food and supplies, the crew of U-869 pushed out of Bremen in late January 1944 and steered to the Baltic Sea for several months of training. From this point forward, there would be no true home base; instruction would be on board the boat, with stops at various Baltic ports.

By now, word of Black May—the month in 1943 when Allied forces destroyed forty-four U-boats—had trickled down even to the enlisted men. Dockworkers whispered about the scores of U-boats that never returned from patrol. Rumors of Allied technological superiority wafted through the naval barracks. Though few spoke of it, the crew of U-869 almost certainly knew that the world had shifted for U-boat men.

Early training on U-869 included testing of the sub's underwater noisiness, the repair of its periscope, and practice with its antiaircraft gun. (While U-869 had been built without a deck gun for engaging enemy warships, it retained its antiaircraft weapon.) They practiced "roll training," the complex art of turning and diving, until the men were so sick of it—and so good at it—that they believed they could maneuver the 250-foot U-boat through a creek. Some on board vomited until their innards acclimated to underwater life. Others took sick from diesel fumes and noise. Experienced men like Guschewski knew that the worst was still to come.

The men used February to get to know their jobs and one another. Torpedo operators generally socialized with torpedo operators, machinists with machinists. In the radio room, Guschewski and Horenburg groomed two *Oberfunkmaate,* or radiomen, one of whom was eighteen years old, the other nineteen. Though Guschewski still felt a bit wounded that Horenburg outranked him, he found him to be an excellent radioman and a personable fellow. Before long, the two had become synchronized in their teamwork, one coding Neuerburg's messages and the other transmitting them. They also became friends.

In addition to his other duties, the radioman played phonograph and radio music for the crew. One day while in port, Guschewski found a wonderful radio station playing Glenn Miller music, the kind he knew the crew loved. He turned up the volume. Feet began tapping and fingers snapping. Then, without warning, a radio announcer interrupted the music and said, "One of your U-boats recently left on patrol and two days later it went missing. We found body parts and pieces of the wreck. In a few days we will know the names of the commander and crew." Guschewski lunged for the radio dial—he knew this to be Radio Calais, a British-run propaganda station designed to wage psychological warfare on the Germans. As Guschewski cut the sound, Neuerburg stormed into the radio room from his quarters across the hall.

"Are you crazy?" Neuerburg exploded. "You are listening to an enemy radio station! The entire crew heard this! How can you possibly do this?"

"I tuned it in because the music was good," Guschewski answered. "By the time I realized what was happening, the message was out."

"I will tell you this," Neuerburg fumed. "You will not do this a second time."

Neuerburg turned and returned to his quarters. Horenburg drew close to Guschewski and rubbed his shoulder.

"Don't feel badly about this, Herbert," Horenburg said. "Radio Calais can move anywhere on the dial—you never know where it will be. They even play German music; they know the songs we love. Don't get gray over this, my friend. This could have happened to any radioman, even one as excellent as you."

If Neuerburg struck his men as strict and unyielding, few seemed to resent him for it. Each day in the Baltic added to the crew's appreciation for the dangers they would face in battle, and as their imminent war patrol drew nearer they found themselves watching Neuerburg—anticipating his moves, learning his instincts, studying his eyes for the kind of courage that could inoculate nearly sixty men as depth charges exploded around them and enemy airplanes attacked. Few could deny that in their commander they saw a sculpture of might, right, and duty, a man who demanded excellence not just that his crew might survive, but because he believed that this was the way a man should live.

While Neuerburg commanded respect and even a measure of fear, his first officer, twenty-one-year-old Siegfried Brandt, was growing beloved by the crew. In many ways, Brandt was Neuerburg's opposite. He was small of stature, perhaps five foot seven, with deeply warm and quiet eyes, and a measured voice flecked with humor. He nearly always seemed to be smiling. In a U-boat culture that shunned close personal relationships between officers and crewmen, Brandt seemed most in his element among the enlisted men, joking with them while on bridge watch, asking important questions about their families and girlfriends and hometowns, listening to fears and concerns they were officially not permitted to have. While Brandt was fully conversant in military protocol, he rarely insisted on it during downtime, preferring the meaningful conversation and sense of brotherhood that resulted when soldiers believed they could exhale beside superiors. Once, when Guschewski told a popular joke about a blowhard military officer, Brandt laughed so hard that Guschewski and the others present believed he might pass out. When he caught his breath, he begged, "Oh, please repeat that! I've never heard that one before!" Guschewski told it again, all the while thinking, "I would never dare tell this joke to Neuerburg."

While Brandt seemed at ease among the enlisted men, he undertook his duties with a palpable gravity. The first officer arranged the boat's bridge watches, kept the sub's torpedoes primed and ready, and directed all torpedo attacks made while surfaced. If the commander died or became incapacitated, the first officer would assume command of the submarine. A good first officer was often rewarded with command of his own U-boat. In his work, Brandt demanded an unrelenting excellence of himself, and by example rather than voice he asked the same of the crew. Perhaps more than anyone, Neuerburg appreciated such dedication and competence. In planning or conversation, the two officers seemed in sync and of a single mind. If Neuerburg had reservations about his first officer's closeness to the men, he betrayed them to no one, so that as the weeks passed, many of the crew came to feel close to Brandt, and many wondered about the life of a twenty-one-year-old man who seemed ready to bear the fears of so many. None could have imagined that Brandt, with his easy smile and ready comfort, considered himself to be training in an iron coffin.

Even before he joined the marines, young Siegfried Brandt of Zinten, East Prussia, was known in his town as an *"aufrechter Mensch"*—a genuinely good person. "Siggi," as he was called, had been raised an observant Protestant and a constant gentleman, the eldest of three brothers born to parents open to the world of new ideas and different people. The family believed strongly in their religion, which stood starkly opposed to the Nazi faith in the Thousand-Year Reich. When the Brandts walked to church the Nazis poked fun at their faith and reminded Siegfried's father, Otto, that on Sundays Siggi was also required to attend Hitler Youth leadership meetings. Otto told his son, "You may go to your leadership three times a month, but on the last Sunday, you go only to church." The instruction infuriated local Nazi Party members, who might have imprisoned Otto for such insolence had he not served Germany so nobly—and so obviously—in World War I. Otto had lost his left leg fighting for his country. He still had a wound in his chest.

During high school, Siggi and his two best friends had sworn an oath—an odd and even risky pact at a time of crescendoing Nazi power. From this point forward, they vowed, they would conduct themselves according to Prussian principles: discipline, order, honesty, tolerance, reliability, and loyalty. Those things, and not any other ideology, would guide the rest of their lives. As Siggi's high school graduation drew near and Germany prepared for war, the Nazis became even less patient with the Brandts. The family continued to worship at their church. Otto had refused party membership. And now, Siggi's mother, Elise, was telling the local Nazi Party members to back off about Norbert, her middle son. Norbert, unlike Siegfried, was a bit slow academically, perhaps the victim of a learning disability. To the Nazis, such a weakness in the Aryan gene pool could not be tolerated. They told Elise they planned to sterilize Norbert. She told them, in so many words, to go to hell. They threatened to send her to a concentration camp, even though she was married to a war hero, even though her eldest son, Siggi, was preparing to volunteer for the navy. She held firm. The tension between the Nazis and the Brandts grew hotter.

After high school, Siggi volunteered for the navy. In 1941, he began his naval officer training. During his visits home, Siggi's youngest brother, Hans-Georg, eavesdropped and heard Siggi making jokes about "Adolf"—sarcastic snips about how Hitler is "the greatest" and how Hitler "knows everything" and how Hitler "knows more about the navy than the admirals." Even at eleven, Hans-Georg knew that his brother neither liked nor trusted Hitler.

For a time, Siggi served aboard a minesweeper. Twice he saw battle action, the second occasion resulting in the sinking of the boat and requiring him to swim to safety. Later, when naval brass asked for volunteers for the U-boat service, the young Brandt raised his hand.

In February 1943, Brandt's submarine—*U-108*—was bombed by onrushing British airplanes and destroyers in the Atlantic west of Gibraltar, its conning tower severely damaged, its ability to dive erased. Crippled, the U-boat limped along the surface toward a base in Lorient, France, a sitting duck for enemy aircraft or ships that happened into the vicinity. The sub made it safely back to port, but the experience left a deep impression on Brandt. During the attack, he had begged the commander to dive, but the man had chosen to wait. As the enemy bore down, Brandt observed the commander looking at photographs of his children, an example of how U-boat combat could paralyze even the finest officer's nerves.

During home leaves, Brandt and his friend Fritz played their jazz and swing and talked about the hopelessness of the war. They continued to crack wise about Hitler and to question his leadership and decision-making abilities. If anything, since becoming an officer, Brandt had grown even more scornful of Hitler. Increasingly, however, he seemed resigned to the idea that he and so many others in the military were just cogs in a massive machine.

Brandt spent much of the rest of 1943 in U-boat training. Around this time, his brother Norbert—the one the Nazis had threatened to sterilize—joined the army. Zinten's Nazi Party members continued to harass Otto and Elise over their church worship and their refusal to join the party, despite the fact that Siggi was a U-boat officer. Always, the threat of deportation to a concentration camp loomed over the Brandt household.

Around October 1943, Brandt was made first officer of *U-869*, a brand-new Type IX being built at the Deschimag yard in Bremen. He met the boat's commander, Helmuth Neuerburg, and its chief engineer, a vaguely melancholy man named Ludwig Kessler. During training, Brandt was the consummate professional, duty-bound and willing to die for Germany. During his visits home, he referred to *U-869* as a "Nazi *Tauchboot*"—a Nazi diving boat—his emphasis on the word *Nazi* sarcastic and derogatory. Sometimes, thirteen-year-old Hans-Georg heard his brother call the U-boat an "iron coffin."

The *U-869* crew continued its training into spring 1944, anxious for the first of several tests by inspectors—called the "Agru-Front"— near the Polish fishing peninsula of Hela. At sea, First Officer Brandt took one of three watches, while Commander Neuerburg joined any of the watches that he pleased. The two men appeared strong and experienced to their men, though Neuerburg continued to struggle to squeeze his tall frame and broad shoulders through the narrow deck hatch that led to the control room.

U-869 would go through Agru-Front testing five times between late March and October. Each time Neuerburg performed excellently, controlling his boat and firing his torpedoes with a marksman's precision. Deadly aim with torpedoes inspired confidence in a U-boat crew, and as the men of *U-869* watched Neuerburg kill practice targets, their belief in him as a leader deepened. In alarm, or emergency, dive training, the crew was quick and nimble, a single organism of unified reflexes built from relentless training and a sober understanding of the odds they faced. In every phase of the Agru-Front, Neuerburg betrayed not a sliver of fear or apprehension. Like the famed U-boat aces who had become legend by casually perusing a novel as depth charges exploded around their subs, Neuerburg stayed cool no matter how threatening the moment. His crew grew to respect him even more.

Despite their growing proficiency and cohesion as a unit, the men of *U-869* remained realists. They knew that only a handful of them had previous U-boat experience. Most knew or suspected that the Allies owned antisubmarine technology for which the Kriegsmarine had no answer. While Guschewski and the *U-602* crew had laughed often in 1942, he found little levity aboard *U-869.* Monte Cassino had fallen. The Allies had landed at Normandy. Crewmen's hometowns were being bombed. Scores of U-boats went missing or killed in enemy waters. Germany, it was clear to many, was falling.

None, however, dared speak openly of his fears. A soldier who criticized Hitler or the war effort could be charged with *Wehrkraftzersetzung*—the undermining of military authority—and tried before a war tribunal. No one knew exactly whom to trust. If Guschewski witnessed no joking among the men of *U-869,* he also saw none of the quarreling of his earlier service aboard *U-602,* none of the screaming matches when men became frustrated or claustrophobic on that boat. Somber and sober, the men of *U-869* kept mostly to themselves. Sadly, to Guschewski's eyes, no one bickered with anyone.

Early in the summer of 1944, while docked in Gotenhafen, Neuerburg arranged an onboard celebration for his crew. Women were not invited. Brandt and Chief Engineer Kessler were sent ashore. Hard liquor, schnapps, and beer flowed freely aboard the submarine. Excellent foods were served. Popular music played on the boat's loudspeakers. Before long, many crewmen were drunk. All the while, Neuerburg took not so much as a sip. He just watched the men, studying their behavior, listening for their opinions. Though inebriated, the crew seemed to whiff the idea of the party: Neuerburg was testing them, feeling for each man's breaking point, waiting for any sign of disloyalty to him or, some likely thought, to the Nazi Party. Near his radio room, Guschewski drank slowly and thought, "This is unfair. This is not the way to test men." None of the crewmen said a derogatory word. None of them expressed doubts. As the party ended, Guschewski thought, "Brandt would not test his crew like this. The two men are opposites."

Neuerburg's celebration party caused some crewmen to further contemplate his Nazi Party allegiance. Though officers were forbidden to hold party membership, Neuerburg appeared so duty-bound and committed to formal procedure that it would have surprised few if it had turned out that he had Nazi sympathies.

One day, as Neuerburg boarded U-869, the crew gave him the *heil*—the Nazi salute—in place of their usual military salute. A recent assassination attempt on Hitler had resulted in a new governmental order: military officers were now to use the *heil* salute. Neuerburg tore into the crew, telling them that he expected the military salute and that the *heil* was not to be used aboard his boat. Some crewmen tried to explain about the new order. Neuerburg told them he did not care. The *heil* would never again be used aboard U-869.

If Neuerburg now seemed even more difficult to read, an incident in Hela only furthered the enigma. As the crew prepared to spend the night, Neuerburg announced that they would walk to a special barracks set in the thick woods of the peninsula. Inside, Neuerburg served Stark-Bier, a good and strong beer, and asked the men to gather their chairs in a circle. Inside the circle, he took a guitar, sat down, and began playing beautifully, an event that astounded the crew—no one had known of his musical talent. Neuerburg motioned for the men to join him in singing these lightly patriotic songs. Some sang along. Others only pretended. None questioned his motives. They could see by the way he sang and by the way he looked to no one in particular as he strummed the guitar that the music came from his heart. At eleven P.M., Neuerburg and the crew returned to their regular barracks.

One of the crewmen who had likely sung along that night was nineteen-year-old torpedoman Franz Nedel. Nedel nurtured two loyalties as he trained with U-869. The first was to Hitler and the Nazi Party. The second was to his fiancée, Gisela Engelmann, whose name he had written on one of the forward torpedo-tube hatches, and who despised Hitler and the Nazis as much as her beloved Franz admired them.

* * *

Nedel and Gisela had met in 1940 while she was attending a Hitler Youth program in the countryside and he was pursuing an apprenticeship as a butcher. He was fifteen, she fourteen. They loved each other straightaway. He delighted in her freethinking, fiery personality, and outgoing instinct. She adored his intellect—he seemed smart beyond his years, a thinker—and reveled in his compassion, his belly laugh, and even the way he spoke High German with the distinctive rolled r of his hometown region near Stettin. She was overwhelmed by Nedel's mastery of the butcher's craft; he oversaw the slaughter of animals with a confidence and equanimity she'd never seen in boys from her native Berlin. Inside a week they were boyfriend and girlfriend. He called her Gila. She called him Frenza. They knew they would spend their lives together.

The couple was inseparable. When he played accordion in the band he had formed with friends, she sang along and crowds would gather, and as they played their favorite song, a French tune with the lyrics "Come back home, Zurich, come back; / I'm waiting for you; / You are all my happiness," she believed that there was only one true love in a person's life, and that she had found that love in Nedel.

Nedel's gentle nature, however, seemed at odds with one of his passions. He was fascinated by U-boats. He spoke of them constantly, promising to enlist in the submarine service when the inevitable day came for him to join the military. Gila begged him to reconsider.

"These are swimming coffins," she told him. "Get on a battleship or a cruiser. Get on anything besides the U-boat."

"No, Gila," he replied time and again. "I want the U-boat."

Gila told him she understood. She had a shakier grasp, however, on Nedel's political beliefs. The Nazis had imprisoned his father, a butcher, for holding anti-Hitler beliefs. Nedel did not speak much about his father's ordeal, but his mother told Gila that her husband had been locked up for a considerable time before being released. Nedel loved his father. Still, he found himself sympathetic to Hitler and the rise of the Third Reich.

Gila's father also had been arrested by the Nazis. For months, he had delivered food and supplies to a Jewish family hiding in a nearby basement. In 1942, the Gestapo discovered the family. They hung the man by his feet from the ceiling, poured freezing water on him, and screamed, "Who is helping you?" When the man could take no more, he revealed that it was Gila's father who had hidden his family. The Gestapo took the man to Gila's house, where he pointed out her father and said, "I am so sorry. I could not take it any longer." Gila's father was arrested and sent to the Dachau concentration camp, where he remained even as Gila and Nedel were falling more deeply in love. When Gila asked her boyfriend how he could sympathize with the Nazis after such treatment of both their fathers, he could only say, "I am very sorry this has happened, Gila."

Still, Gila loved Nedel deeply. He was kind and gentle to her, and envisioned a lovely future for them. As Nedel entered naval training in 1943, the couple became engaged. "I will take care of anything we need," he promised. "When the war ends, we will have our life, I promise you."

That year, as Nedel left for home during leave from basic training, Gila waited for him at his mother's home. There, she saw a photograph of Hitler hanging on the wall. She exploded. "Good God, you have his picture up!" she exclaimed.

Before Nedel's mother could react, Gila took the photo from its frame and clawed out Hitler's eyes with her fingers. Then she placed the ruined photo in her fiancé's bed.

"Oh, my God, what is he going to do when he comes home and sees that?" Nedel's mother asked.

"I want him to see that! Leave it there!" Gila said.

When Nedel returned home, he discovered the mutilated photo.

"How can you do that?" he yelled at his fiancée. "How can you poke out Hitler's eyes?"

"Hitler is a *Schweinehund!*" she screamed.

They argued louder. Nedel defended Hitler and the Reich. Gila could not abide the opinion. The argument ended the same as the others. They still loved each other.

A few days later, after Nedel had returned to training, Berlin sustained a massive British bombing. When the explosions ended, Gila found a photo of Hitler and began to climb one of the large gas lanterns that lit the street. At the top, she hung the picture, a symbol of Hitler overseeing the devastation of Germany. She began cursing his name. A policeman arrived and warned her that the Gestapo was on its way.

"Go ahead and rage, Gisela," he said. "You have fifteen more minutes to curse up and down. Any more and they will pick you up."

"You pig!" Gila screamed. "You already picked up my father. Now you're going to have me picked up, too?"

"Fifteen minutes," he said.

Less than a year later, Nedel was aboard U-869. He told Gila that he admired Commander Neuerburg and trusted the sub's crew with his life. "When we're out at sea, all we have is each other," he said.

Baltic training continued into summer's dog days. At night, U-869's crew were permitted to leave the barracks and spend their free time about the town. In happier days, U-boat crews had enjoyed near-celebrity status during their off-duty hours, guests of honor at the liveliest nightclubs, desired dance partners for the area's prettiest ladies. Now U-869's crew found many of the bars and nightclubs shuttered. Few felt like dancing, anyway. Only beer was available to numb the men's worries. When the crew happened upon a band playing in a café, they sat quietly in their uniforms and listened.

That summer, First Officer Brandt took a short leave to visit his family in Zinten. He played with his thirteen-year-old brother, Hans-Georg, then enjoyed his mother's turkey and bacon and eggs. As the evening settled, he and his father went into the study and closed the door. Hans-Georg tiptoed to the room and pressed his ear against the keyhole.

"I am taking a pistol with me on U-869's patrol," Brandt told his father. "I will not wait until the end should something happen."

Hans-Georg's heart pounded. What did his brother mean by saying he would "not wait until the end"? Their religion prohibited the taking of one's own life. Still, Siggi had said he would not wait until the end. Hans-Georg strained to hear more.

"I can tell you this," Brandt continued. "I can fully count on each and every one of my men. From the youngest enlistee to Commander Neuerburg, every man aboard *U-869* is truly my comrade."

At the leave's end, Brandt dressed in his military uniform and kissed his brother and parents good-bye. Before walking out the door, he sat at the piano. He played his favorite song, "La Paloma," a longing sailor's lament with the words "Good-bye, my dove." His mother bit her lip and asked him to stop. The family members hugged one another. A moment later, Brandt disappeared down the street on his way back to *U-869*.

A short time later, Brandt invited Hans-Georg and his mother to visit the U-boat in Pillau, where it was stationed for training. Hans-Georg could barely contain himself during the train ride; soon he would see a real, battle-ready U-boat, and one on which his brother was an officer! At the harbor, Brandt picked up his mother and brother in a small boat and took them to a back port where the warships were docked. As the boat approached, Hans-Georg picked out *U-869* right away, a massive, miraculous sculpture of gray fighting technology, brand-new and proud and invincible, the Olympic rings standing sentinel on the U-boat's conning tower to protect his brother from everything.

Brandt invited Hans-Georg to board the U-boat, meanwhile apologizing to his mother; Commander Neuerburg did not permit women on his submarine, as he considered their presence aboard bad luck. If she would not mind waiting, he would give Hans-Georg a tour. She smiled and agreed. Hans-Georg's heart pounded. "This is the greatest moment in my life," he thought to himself. "None of my schoolmates has a brother like mine."

The Brandt brothers walked across a rickety wooden gangway to the U-boat. When they reached its deck, Hans-Georg saw a man dressed in shorts and with a scarf around his neck lying on his back, sunning himself. The man saw the Brandts and rose. Hans-Georg bowed, as was proper for a young man of the day. The man reached and shook Hans-Georg's hand.

"Ah, this is Brandt Junior!" he exclaimed.

"Commander Neuerburg, this is my brother Hans-Georg," Brandt said. "With your permission, I would like to show him the boat."

"Of course," Neuerburg said. "We are honored to have him as our guest."

Hans-Georg stood wide-eyed. All his life, he'd known that U-boat men were special, and that U-boat commanders were the most special of all. Now he had met a commander who was tall, handsome, and powerful, and as he walked with his brother across the deck, he knew he was living a truly amazing day, a day when he'd seen a U-boat commander standing on board his submarine in shorts.

The Brandts climbed through the conning tower down a smooth, freshly painted metal ladder. Inside, Hans-Georg stood mesmerized by the thickets of technology that grew from the walls and ceilings of the boat—could anyone possibly know the function of all these machines? Brandt began the tour. Hans-Georg knew not to touch anything. Brandt showed his brother the diesel engines, the electric motors, the radio room, the torpedoes. Everything smelled of oil. Brandt pointed Hans-Georg to his bunk. The boy looked at him as if to ask, "May I?" Brandt nodded. A moment later, Hans-Georg was sitting on his brother's bed.

At the base of the conning tower, Brandt showed his brother the periscope.

"You can look through it," he told Hans-Georg.

The younger Brandt white-knuckled the periscope's handles and pressed his face to the lens. Before him, he saw the harbor's warships, so close that he could read their names, and as he stared at these ships his brother told him exactly what he was looking at; he knew the name of every warship in the sea. Even though this was a U-boat destined for war, even though Hans-Georg knew his brother would be leaving soon, he felt safe with Siggi standing behind him.

"No one," he thought, "has a brother like mine."

On August 30, 1944, *U-869* was docked at the U-boat flotilla base at Stettin. Already, much of the town lay ruined from Allied bombing. That night, the crewmen were awakened in their barracks by the sound of air-raid sirens. Some dove into underground bunkers. Others, including Guschewski, remained in bed, presuming that the approaching airplanes would bypass Stettin. But when

Guschewski heard antiaircraft fire from German ships, he knew the attack was intended for them. He leaped from his bed and rushed toward the bunker. On his way, he noticed that a few men remained in the adjoining barracks. He flung open their door.

"People! Get out!" he yelled. "This attack is meant for us!"

Guschewski could hear the bombs falling. He ran for the underground bunker but found its door closed. He beat on it with all his might. A fellow crewman opened the door, and Guschewski jumped in. Bombs exploded. The crewmen waited inside the bunker. When it was safe to emerge, the men surveyed the area. Craters lay where their barracks had stood. One of *U-869*'s crewmen had been killed in the attack. At the bottom of one of the craters, Neuerburg and Horenburg sifted through charred corpses. As the men climbed out of the crater, the crewmen bowed their heads. Guschewski looked at his commander and at the crew. No one said anything, but he could read their thoughts. Each of them, he believed, was thinking, "The war is lost. Why isn't there peace?"

The fall season gave the crew a reprieve from the searing summer temperatures, which could reach 110 degrees inside the U-boat. It would now be just a matter of weeks before the boat was assigned a war patrol. In October, however, a scandal hit the submarine.

At night, while *U-869* was anchored and most men slept ashore, someone stole a large slice of ham from one of the several large hams stored onboard. When the cook discovered the theft, he alerted Neuerburg, who summoned the crew. Stealing from comrades—*Kameradendiebstahl*—was rare aboard a U-boat and was a grave offense in this community bound by fate. Neuerburg raged before the crew.

"I cannot assure you that I will not press charges for this theft," he yelled.

For a minute, no one moved. Then twenty-four-year-old machinist mate Fritz Dagg stepped forward. "I do not want anyone wrongly accused," he said. "I stole the ham."

Neuerburg motioned Dagg to his quarters. The crew dreaded the punishment Neuerburg was certain to impose on the well-liked Dagg. A few minutes later, Dagg emerged from Neuerburg's quarters. Neuerburg had not punished him. Instead, the commander told the crew to go about its business. The boat exhaled. Guschewski admired the decision. He believed Neuerburg appreciated that Dagg felt sick about the theft, and he also knew that Dagg—an excellent crewman—could not perform properly if further embarrassed. The men welcomed Dagg back to the fold. No one was angry with him. The war was growing more hopeless, but at least everyone had enough to eat.

By late October, U-869's crew knew that its maiden war patrol was just a week or two away. Brandt took a one-day leave to visit his family in Zinten. His father gathered the family in the living room and prayed. Siegfried was dressed in his full officer's uniform—he had not even brought along a change of clothes. Snow fell thick outside the window. Otto Brandt asked for peace and the safe return of his sons Siegfried and Norbert. He asked for a time like the one that now seemed from another life, a time when his family could eat and sing and wake up at ease together.

Brandt returned to U-869. He was entitled to several more days of home leave. Instead, he gave his remaining share to married crewmen so that they might spend more time with their families. While these men were away, he sat in his tiny bunk aboard the sub and wrote letters to his family.

"I learned yesterday," Brandt wrote in one such letter, "that Fritz C., the radioman with whom I always met, did not return from his first war patrol. It was his first deployment at the front. Just a few weeks ago we sat together in a restaurant. That's life—hard and inexorable."

In mid-November, he enclosed two small photos of himself along with a short note that asked his family, "Please think of me." In one photo, he was seated and asleep on the deck of U-869, his knees tucked into his chest, his back against the ship, his head bowed forward. Though his mother owned many photos of Siegfried, this was the only one that made her cry. When Hans-Georg asked why she wept at this picture, she told him that it was the way Siggi was sitting—it reminded her of a child, a baby, and even though Siggi was a proud warrior, she could still see her little boy in that picture.

In late November, Brandt sent another letter to his family. It read:

By the time you receive my letter I will already have started my journey. . . . I am so glad I heard from Norbert—this way I have certainty. I wish Hans-Georg a happy birthday. I hope to be back home for his confirmation. I also wish all of you a merry and blessed and healthy Christmas and New Year. Christmas is a family celebration; even if this time it is only in my thoughts. By thinking of each other we can remember how nice it used to be. Please don't forget me as you fold your hands, as we carry each other, let us look forward to our *"Wiedersehen."*

As Brandt wrote his letters and *U-869* prepared for its maiden war patrol, Neuerburg made a final visit home. He had joined the U-boats for just such opportunities and since 1943 had made the most of them. Upon returning home he always removed his uniform and changed into civilian clothes, in order to turn back into a *"Mensch"*—a human being. Often he took his three-year-old son, Jürgen, sailing with him, towing him behind the boat in a safety ring and allowing him to pretend to be captain of the ship. On other occasions—to his wife's horror and his son's delight—he placed Jürgen in a small wagon attached to his bicycle, then pedaled as fast as he could. He loved to photograph Jürgen and his year-old daughter, Jutta, and he sent one of Jürgen's shots to a baby-powder company for advertising consideration. At night, he and Erna, who had spent much of their marriage separated by his training, listened to music, talked, and fell more deeply in love. He never discussed training or the upcoming mission, except to say that *U-869* was manned by a fine and cohesive crew and that he admired First Officer Siegfried Brandt, not just for his professionalism but for the way in which he had become friend and comrade to the men. As he and Erna counted down the days until the U-boat's first patrol, they added entries to their "Baby Daybook," a diary they kept for Jürgen and Jutta. His final entry, written to Jürgen before *U-869* left on patrol, concluded this way:

A few days ago, mean "Tommy" [the English] dropped a lot of bombs and it was very loud. You were very quiet and you hid your little head under Mommy's coat. Jutta used to laugh during explosions but she too was very still. It was a terrible night and as you said, many houses were destroyed. In our house too there was a terrible mess. Since then you don't like to sleep alone and you want to go nighty-night with Mommy. Even you, my little rascal, are becoming aware of this terrible war.

Soon, Daddy will have to go out to sea with his U-boat, and our most ardent hope is that we will all see each other again soon, in good health and in peaceful times. Then hopefully you will again wait for me with Mommy and Jutta and cry out in a happy voice: "Mommy, there comes Daddy!"

May this time not be very far away. May a protecting hand keep you my dear ones from terrible things, protect and shield you till a sunny and carefree time reunites us again. Then the sun will shine again on you, my children, and especially on your parents who live only with and for you and indescribable happiness will make our life again worth living.

With much love,
Daddy

In mid-November, *U-869* stood just days away from her war patrol. As was customary, the crew created an insignia and motto as an emblem for the boat. Perhaps inspired by the movie *Snow White*, which the crewmen had recently seen together, they chose as their motto "Heigh-ho!," then wrote the words over a drawing of a horseshoe and the number 869. Beneath it, they inscribed a lyric from a popular song by the Swedish singer Zarah Leander. It read, "I know one day that a miracle will happen and a thousand dreams will come true."

U-869 was scheduled to depart for war around December 1, 1944. In the hours before the boat was to leave, one of Neuerburg's friends, a physician, made a quiet offer. He would write a note to the naval authorities stating that Neuerburg had taken sick and was too ill to command the U-boat. Erna urged her husband to accept the offer—she knew the U-boats were not returning from their patrols. Neuerburg thanked the doctor. He also knew that U-boats were not returning. He had a duty to Germany and to his men. He refused the note.

As Neuerburg said good-bye to his family, Erna noticed that he had left something behind.

"You have forgotten your gold pocket watch, Helmuth," she said. "Take it with you."

"No," Neuerburg said. "You keep it and count the minutes until I return home."

At around the same time, torpedoman Franz Nedel and a group of his *U-869* comrades traveled to his parents' house for a farewell party. His fiancée, Gila, threw her arms around Nedel. His mother went to the kitchen to serve food and drink. Ordinarily, Nedel and his friends already would have been talking and singing and enjoying their free time. Instead, they sat in the living room, still in uniform, and stared straight ahead, saying nothing. Gila's smile slowly faded away at the sight. She looked at the men. One of them began crying, then another, then all of them.

"What is wrong?" Gila asked, rushing to Nedel's side and taking his hand.

For a moment, the men could do nothing but cry. Nedel said nothing. Finally, one of the other men spoke.

"None of us is coming back," he said.

"What do you mean by that?" Gila asked. "Of course you're coming back."

"No, we're not coming back," said another.

The men could see Gila's face flush as she strained to contain her tears.

"Well, Franz will come back, but none of us will," said another.

"That makes no sense," she protested. "If Franz comes back, you will all come back."

The men shook their heads and kept crying. Nedel's mother was devastated by the sight. Still, she pulled herself together and stepped forward.

"Come on, boys, lie down and get a good night's sleep—you will stay here. Gila will stay here. You will feel better in the morning."

The next morning, the men dressed and rode the train with Engelmann and Nedel's mother back to *U-869*'s dock. Gila did not let go of Nedel's hand during the hours-long trip. No one mentioned the events of the previous night. No one said much of anything. At the gate, the women were given permission to accompany the men to the U-boat so that they might wave good-bye. *U-869* was to leave on its war patrol that day.

To reach the submarine, the women boarded a tiny boat that took them to a small island. There, Gila saw *U-869* for the first time—a magnificent and proud machine in which her future lay. Nedel took her hand.

"Gila, please wait for me," he said. "You won't be sorry. I will take good care of you."

"Of course I'll wait," she said.

"Pray for me when I leave."

"Of course I will."

Gila and Nedel's mother stood near the boat. They were joined by only two or three other family members. The men lined up in rows on the U-boat's deck, just as they had during its commissioning nearly a year ago. A four-man band made its way to the dock and played a melancholy German folk song. The U-boat began to move away from its dock. Nedel and the other crewmen stayed on the deck and waved, though most of them had no family or friends to wave to. A few minutes later, the U-boat disappeared into the overcast horizon.

CHAPTER THIRTEEN

THE U-BOAT IS OUR MOMENT

SINCE 1991, CHATTERTON AND KOHLER had believed in history. Every book, expert, and document listed *U-869* as sunk off Gibraltar. Now, two and a half years later, the intercepted radio messages between *U-869* and U-boat Control virtually proved that the New Jersey U-boat was *U-869*. The divers dug deep into their filing cabinets for *U-869*'s crew roster, one of several dozen such lists Chatterton had copied at the U-boat Archive in Germany. Kohler, who understood the German rank and position abbreviations, called Chatterton and read him the basics.

"There are fifty-six crewmen listed," Kohler said. "A guy named Neuerburg was the commander. He was born in 1917, which would have made him, what, twenty-seven years old? The first officer was, let's see . . . Brandt, Siegfried Brandt; Christ, he was only twenty-two. Here's our friend Horenburg, the *Funkmeister*, age twenty-five. There were four Willis aboard and three Wilhelms. Hey, there was even a Richard. And a Johann. That's like Richie and John."

"How young did they go?" Chatterton asked. Kohler did some computations.

"There are twenty-four teenagers," he said. "The youngest was Otto Brizius. When *U-869* left on war patrol, he was seventeen."

"We've been swimming past these guys and bumping into their

bones for three seasons and never had a clue who they were," Chatterton said. "Now we know their names."

Word of the radio intercepts flashed through the U-boat community. To many experts, the mystery of the New Jersey U-boat was now solved: originally ordered to New York, the submarine had missed her rerouting instructions to Gibraltar and had continued on to New Jersey, where she had sunk.

Chatterton and Kohler also believed the mystery to be solved. But they were not prepared to close the book on *U-869*. The wreck still had not surrendered evidence that conclusively proved her identity. The most ornery skeptics might still argue that the *U-Who* was, in fact, *U-857*, as the divers had earlier theorized; *U-857* had, after all, gone missing on the American East Coast and remained unaccounted for. They could argue that Horenburg's knife had been stolen or misplaced and had ended up on *U-857* as that submarine lay tied up near *U-869* in Norway before its battle patrols. However unlikely this scenario, it presented a sobering reality for Chatterton and Kohler. Until, say, a tag marked *U-869* or a builder's plaque engraved with a hull number was recovered from the U-boat, no one could conclude with absolute certainty that the wreck was *U-869*.

Chatterton and Kohler made a decision. They would return to the wreck.

Their fellow divers recoiled at the idea. Three men had died diving the U-boat. Others had come close. No accessible areas remained to be explored.

"You guys know it's *U-869*," their colleagues protested. "No one's disputing it. You rewrote history. Why risk your lives?"

Chatterton and Kohler responded identically: We need to know for ourselves.

To Chatterton, quitting the *U-Who* now would have been tantamount to quitting himself. For years, he had lived and dived according to a single set of principles, a belief that hard work, perseverance, thoroughness, preparation, creativity, and vision made the diver and the man. He had overlaid his life philosophy onto scuba and had become one of the world's great wreck divers. He had overlaid his diving ethos onto his daily existence and found himself leading an honorable and gratifying life. He could not walk away from the *U-Who* just short of certain.

To Kohler, the *U-Who* had evolved from an artifact site into a moral obligation. Alone among the divers he felt it his duty to give names to the fallen crewmen and closure to their families. Like Chatterton, he was now certain that the *U-Who* was *U-869*. But he could not announce to the Neuerburg or Brandt or Horenburg families that he was "pretty sure" their brothers and sons died off New Jersey, that *U-869* had "probably" sunk in American waters rather than off Africa. He, too, penciled in summer dates to dive the *U-Who*. He could not leave question marks hanging over these men any more than he'd been able to accept seeing dead bodies left behind in the water during his boyhood boating trips with his father. He would search for a tag or some other indisputable proof. He would give the dead their rest and the families their names.

A final motivation drove Chatterton and Kohler back to the *U-Who*, one upon which they agreed to the last detail. They were making history, and they intended to do it correctly. Time and again during their research, they had been astonished to discover that historians had been mistaken, books fallible, experts wrong. The *U-Who* was their chance to personally imprint history. They would not do it in a less than perfect way.

As spring signaled the start of the 1994 dive season, Chatterton set his mind to breaking new ground on the *U-Who*. The previous season had been the divers' most productive, yielding excellent artifacts and access to unexplored areas. But it had also left Chatterton at a loss. Every accessible compartment on the submarine had been combed over several times. Every idea about where to find an identifying tag or marking had been tested. He drew blueprints on coffee-shop napkins but found their lines identical to those he had sketched in 1991. He recommitted to seeing order in garbaged piles of randomness, but he could not envision fresh territory inside the sub in which to use this skill. April, traditionally a month of optimism and anticipation for Chatterton, began to darken for his inability to conceive a new plan. Every so often at night, while his wife slept beside him, Chatterton would lie on his back and stare at the ceiling and wonder why his art—this way of seeing a wreck in ways others could not fathom—was failing him when he needed it most.

Those were the times Kohler seemed divinely sent. Chatterton would hear the phone ring or receive a fax or see the Fox Glass truck in his driveway, and it would be Kohler—pushing, cajoling, stroking, insisting, wisps of disgust blended into his thickening Brooklyn accent as he cocked an eyebrow at Chatterton's lament.

"Look, John," Kohler would say. "I don't mean to be impolite or nothing, but I gotta ask: What the hell is wrong with you? What's happening to you? Nothing stops us! We're the guys! I'll go to the U-boat today. It's April. It's forty goddamned degrees and I'll go. And I'll drag your ass down there and we'll think of a plan while we're hanging on the anchor line if we have to. Someone's gonna pull a tag from that wreck. You wanna sit here and cry while one of Bielenda's boys does it? You wanna watch some greenhorn get it stuck to his fin and come out and be the guy? We're going to do it. *We're* the guys."

"Thanks, Richie," Chatterton would say. "You're exactly what I need right now." Then Chatterton would reach for a pen and a napkin and start another blueprint.

As the Atlantic warmed itself, Kohler's longing for his family deepened. He had never fully appreciated the depth of pleasure he took in full-time fatherhood, nor the undergirding importance of that role to his self-image. For years, he had considered himself a diver. Now, as his children began to know a new life and new adult figures in their new home, Kohler realized that he considered himself a father most of all. "I can't live without my kids," he told himself. "I love my kids more than diving. I love my kids more than anything. I'll do anything to get them back."

Kohler began to contemplate the impossible. He called Chatterton. They met at Scotty's. Kohler stared into his martini glass and told Chatterton that any reconciliation with Felicia would require him to give up diving. Chatterton glared.

"Ultimatums don't work," Chatterton said. "Marriages don't work when one person says, 'You and I will be fine together as long as you do what I say.' She wants you to give up diving? That alone shows that Felicia doesn't understand what you're made of. Diving is in your soul. How do you 'agree' to give up your soul?"

"It's for my family," Kohler said. "If I have to give up diving to save my family, I'll do it."

"That's great, Richie," Chatterton said, his face reddening. "You're on the verge of putting the final pieces of the U-boat puzzle together, and you're going to walk away."

"If I leave diving, I know it's going to affect you, too."

"Forget about me!" Chatterton exploded. "Being a diver is who you are."

For a minute, neither man spoke.

"This is a long road, John," Kohler said finally. "I love my kids. They're already learning to live without me. I gotta really think this through."

Chatterton began to hear from Kohler less often. In those moments of doubt when Chatterton could not contemplate where to go next on the U-boat, those moments when Kohler had always seemed to materialize and light a fire under him, now there was silence. At his office late one summer night, Kohler sat at his desk and pulled out a loaded nine-millimeter pistol. He was a diver; it was who he was. He needed his children and his family. He was a father; it was who he was. He put his finger on the trigger and drew the gun closer. A million images sped through his brain like a film that had come loose from the projector's sprockets. Should he shoot himself in the temple or the mouth? He was a diver; it was who he was. Would it hurt? A man needs his family. Children should know their father. He lifted the gun. He looked at a photo of his children on the corner of his desk. If he killed himself, they would grow up with only Felicia's account of who he was—a one-sided account. They would never really know him, and his bloody head would just be proof of what she inevitably would tell them, that Daddy was a loser who'd left his family. He looked deeper into the photo. *I want to smell my daughter's hair. I want to teach my son to ride a minibike. I miss them.* He put the gun back in the drawer.

A short time later Kohler called Felicia. He told her he wanted his family back. She gave him two ultimatums. First, he would have to join her for marriage counseling. Second, he would have to give up diving.

He told Chatterton the news that night at Scotty's. Kohler had never seen his friend so disgusted.

"I agreed to it, John," Kohler said. "I was getting so kooky that if she'd asked me to paint my ass pink and walk backwards I would have done that, too. I missed my family."

"You're walking away from diving?"

"I'm walking away from diving."

"It's not you, Richie. It's a big, goddamned, colossal mistake."

Kohler stared into his martini. Chatterton had become one of his best friends. But this night he thought, "John is not the gentlest person on these issues."

A month later, Kohler and his family reconciled and rented a house in suburban Middletown, New Jersey. At his office, across from the desk at which he had contemplated taking his life, he packed his U-boat work—the research, photos, documents, theories, artifacts, correspondence, translations—into a file cabinet and locked the drawer. He did not call Chatterton to tell him this part. That day, Kohler began his new life as an ex-diver.

Chatterton's first trip to the *U-Who* in 1994 was booked for the first weekend in July. He had spent months wrestling with a single question: Where do I go next on the wreck? On the eve of the dive, he still had no answer. Every accessible inch of the submarine had been searched. Some divers and observers had begun to whisper that no one would ever pull proof of the U-boat's identity from the wreck. Others insisted that a lucky greenhorn would find a tag stuck to the side of his face mask. Such talk was maddening to Chatterton, yet he found himself unable to make a convincing counterargument. He commanded himself to be creative. Nothing happened. He forced himself to write a list of ideas. Each was the same as in previous seasons. When friends saw the distress in his face and asked of his well-being, he could only reply, "I'm not myself. I'm out of ideas."

The July trip to the *U-Who* was as Chatterton expected. He rolled off the boat without a plan. He swam the wreck without priorities. He looked at the periscope for the builder's plaque—just as he had done three years earlier. Topside, he listened for Kohler to light the fire under his ass, to hear Kohler call him a pussy in just the right way, but Kohler was a hundred miles away with his family and a locked file cabinet and the boat sounded silent that day. He told Yurga, "Without a vision, I'm wasting my time."

As if to exact revenge against the *U-Who,* Chatterton turned his creative fury to the hunt for other shipwrecks. In July 1994 alone, he discovered and identified the tanker *Norness*—the first ship sunk by a U-boat on the American side of the Atlantic during World War II—and discovered the *Sebastian*—a World War I–era passenger liner sunk by fire and storm eight miles east of the *Andrea Doria.*

While Chatterton made these historic discoveries, Kohler undertook a dry-docked life in suburbia. He had resolved to repair his family so that he would never again face the prospect of losing his children. He tiptoed around Felicia, screwed up enthusiasm for family grocery trips, tried not to say "This is bullshit" during their marriage counseling. He bought his-and-her bicycles. Summoning facial muscles he'd never known he owned, he smiled as Felicia announced vacation plans to Disney World. Occasionally, he would slip. Pushing a baby stroller on a calm and sunny Sunday, he might remark, "I bet the ocean's like glass for those guys today."

"I don't want to hear that!" Felicia would say, stopping and glaring. "You're dreaming about diving? Don't you want to be with us?"

"Of course I do, honey," Kohler would say. Then he would keep walking and repeat his silent mantra. "I'm disgusted and I'm angry, but it's for the kids. It's for the kids. I love my family. It's for the kids . . ."

In the beginning, Chatterton called regularly.

"Richie, I'm going to the U-boat. You in?"

"Nah, I can't commit," Kohler would answer.

"What do you mean you can't commit? Richie, this is insane. You can't live like this."

Kohler's insides were shredding. But he would only say, "I'm sorry, John." When he got word that weather kept blowing out Chatterton's U-boat trips, he found himself feeling guilty for his sense of relief.

Kohler steeled his resolve and stayed out of diving. Between the cracks, he drip-fed his passions. He continued to hoard catalogs from the military book clubs, buying every volume that touched remotely on U-boats, cupping the phone receiver to surreptitiously check inventory with book dealers who knew his appetites. He bought a U-boat video game that contained a bonus wall map of the German naval grids, then compared that map to the handmade version he had fashioned from his research in Washington. Among his biggest thrills in 1994 was the closeness with which he found these maps to match.

Kohler expected the onset of fall to provide some respite from his longings. Instead, he found himself thinking about the *U-Who*'s crewmen. For years, he had envisioned the horror of their final moments—the explosion, singed bodies flung upside down, an ocean rushing in. Now that he knew their names, he began to imagine their lives. He pictured Germany as his father had when listening to Mr. Segal's stories—a land not of goose-stepping soldiers but of families and girlfriends, hometowns, regional delicacies, and plans. He read the crew list and wondered who among the men liked movies and who liked music, whether they rooted for local soccer clubs, if any had written his girlfriend's name on a torpedo-tube hatch. He could imagine their lives even to the final hours—a can of peaches awarded to the boat's checkers champion, the cook burning sausages, the radioman playing a phonograph record.

As winter crawled over New Jersey, these thoughts became an obligation to Kohler. More than ever he believed that he owed these men a duty, that they must not lie in an anonymous grave with their fate unknown to their loved ones. And it occurred to Kohler that he likely remained the last person in the world inclined to identify these men. Yet he was unable to move, bound by his own family obligations, and it struck him as strange that his commitment to his family was the very promise preventing him from doing right by the crewmen's families. Kohler watched the snow fall outside his rented home. For years, snow had meant that Kohler was just a few months from returning to the ocean. This year, he felt like he had never been further from himself, and the snow seemed as if it would keep falling forever.

In early 1995, Chatterton and Kohler met for dinner, but this time it was at a pizza joint, not Scotty's. In previous years, when the men were themselves, their dinners had lasted for hours. This night, it lasted a slice.

"You staying out this year, too?" Chatterton asked.

"Yeah," Kohler replied. "I gotta stick with this. Felicia's driving me crazy, but I gotta see this through for the kids."

"Uh-huh."

"Any trademark Chatterton breakthroughs on the *U-Who*?"

"It's all I think about. I have no ideas. I'm blind."

"What about the other divers? What's their direction?"

"Richie, no one wants to go there anymore."

At home, Kohler was white-knuckling his marriage just to keep it breathing. He had entered marriage counseling, rented a house, locked away his dive gear. Still, the fights grew worse. In the early spring of 1995, he wrote Felicia a twelve-page letter, took off his wedding band, then stuffed his clothes and belongings into a dozen Hefty Steel-Saks and moved onto his friend's floor in Levittown, Pennsylvania. He was nearly bankrupt from the spending that had been required to repair his family.

For a few months, Kohler took custody of his kids every weekend, summoning just enough strength to shave and get off the floor so that his five-year-old son and two-year-old daughter would believe Daddy was doing great. That lasted a few months. In July 1995, Kohler took over custody of the children. He was ecstatic. He called a real estate agent and requested a home in the best school district within a twenty-five-mile radius of his Trenton, New Jersey, shop. Two weeks later, he and his children moved to a town house in Yardley, Pennsylvania. He hired an au pair, registered his kids in school, scrounged up money for decorations for their rooms, and laid down family rules.

On the other side of New Jersey, bad weather limited Chatterton to just a single *U-Who* trip. As in 1994, he dove the submarine without a plan and came up empty. Stonewalled by the U-boat, he threw the entirety of his creative muscle into the quest he had started the previous year—nothing less than the discovery of several historic, undiscoverable shipwrecks.

He picked up his work on the SS *Carolina,* a passenger liner sunk by U-boat gunfire during World War I. To East Coast wreck divers, there was no greater prize than the *Carolina,* a beautiful vessel from which one hundred ninety-seven passengers and one hundred seventeen crew had been ordered into lifeboats sixty miles offshore before *U-151* sank the ship. Thirteen drowned when their lifeboat capsized overnight. Divers had spent decades searching for the *Carolina,* all to no avail—she remained the only undiscovered passenger liner in New York–New Jersey waters. Chatterton spent the off-season translating and studying German records, interviewing a shipyard archivist, poring over the captain's log, examining seventy-seven-year-old weather charts. He then assembled his research and put together a vision. He believed the *Carolina* lay in an area no diver had suspected.

On his first trip to the site, Chatterton found a wreck. He cleared sea anemones from the fantail, where his research indicated he would find the ship's name. There, he began to uncover brass letters—C-A-R-O-L-I-N-A. In a single day, he had found and identified the SS *Carolina,* for decades the most coveted prize among Northeast wreck divers.

A few weeks later, Chatterton made a trip to a wreck that some suspected was the freighter *Texel,* another ship sunk by a U-boat during World War I. Chatterton devised a plan based on his study of *Texel* photographs and deck plans: he would search the bow area for reference points like portholes that he knew to be positioned near the ship's name. Legendary diver Gary Gentile assured him that the bow was too busted up to yield the name. Chatterton went anyway. He found the brass letters. They spelled *Texel.* In the course of a year, Chatterton had discovered and/or identified four historic shipwrecks. Some began to call him the greatest wreck diver in the world. He sank further into despair.

Chatterton redoubled his efforts to crack the *U-Who.* He drew blanks. Ideas flowed into his head for other projects, mosaics of imagination, perseverance, and vision that promised discovery in whatever he fancied—except for the *U-Who.* At conferences at which he was asked to speak about diving the *Lusitania* or the *Carolina* or his other recent accomplishments, people invariably asked about the U-boat, a subject so depressing to Chatterton that he stopped attending these events.

For the first time in his career, Chatterton heard the clock tick. He was forty-three years old, already an elder statesman in a sport that wore down athletes half his age. Divers no longer wanted to explore the *U-Who*. If Chatterton got bent or broke bones in a car accident or developed cancer, the submarine likely never would be identified. Then the casual and the lazy would simply waltz in and proclaim it *U-869*. "We're virtually certain of it," they would announce—nightmare words to an artist.

Yet Chatterton was at a loss as to what to do next. Nightly, he lay awake in bed, telling the ceiling and the heavens that he would do anything to pull proof from the wreck, that he would help anyone who had an idea, that he would share his knowledge, that he would risk his life inside that U-boat if only he could conceive a vision. Friends like Yurga told him, "You've gotta cut yourself a break. You've done more in the last year than most great wreck divers do in a lifetime."

In his darkest moments, Chatterton brushed cheeks with the idea of quitting. He imagined a time when he could run out for pizza or take his car for a spin without seeing the *U-Who*'s crushed control room before him, a time when he no longer wondered if he was who he hoped he was. The fantasy always felt good for a minute, but it always ended with Chatterton thinking, "When things are easy a person doesn't really learn about himself. It's what a person does at the moment of his greatest struggle that shows him who he really is. Some people never get that moment. The *U-Who* is my moment. What I do now is what I am." When he thought that, Chatterton would snap out of his brush with quitting, sit down at his desk in front of Horenburg's knife, and start drawing sketches of the places on the *U-Who* he planned to go next.

Now separated from Felicia, Kohler began to receive invitations to go diving. The first came from Chatterton. Kohler told him what he would tell all his friends that season: "I can't dive. I physically and mentally can't do it. My head's not in it. I'll die."

As the 1995 dive season wound down, Kohler continued as a full-time father and businessman. He slept irregularly, running to midnight emergency business calls and making French toast for his kids when he returned. His children settled into a routine.

In September 1995, Kohler went to the Hudson City Savings Bank to do a glass job. There he met a very pretty, thirty-year-old blue-eyed blonde who complained of a problem door. When Kohler deduced that part of the problem was that the woman had been kicking the door with her high heels, he took a liking to her. The woman, Valentina Marks, looked a bit indignant at Kohler's bemusement. That made him like her more. He asked her to dinner. It went well. He asked her to dinner again. It was the real thing.

Kohler told her about the *U-Who,* and she leaned into his conversation and asked to know more, especially about the fallen crewmen. Tina was of German descent. She attended Oktoberfest in Germany every year with her father. Even before Kohler confessed it, she knew he felt an obligation to these men.

In Tina's house or in the park or even on the phone, she would lie on her back, close her eyes, and ask Kohler to describe the details of the things in life that moved him, a process she called "painting colors." Often, Kohler painted a trip to the *U-Who,* from the moment the *Seeker* pushed away from its dock to the feeling of gliding down the anchor line to moving respectfully past the crewmen's remains. Kohler told her of finding a skull and then replacing it so that the dead crewman might look out over his comrades, and Marks understood why he'd done it. She painted colors for him, scenes of Germany and the Black Forest and Neuschwanstein Castle, and of affection for her own German heritage and family. They watched *Das Boot* together and she remained on the edge of her seat for the entire movie. He told her about the intensity of his commitment to diving. She said she believed that everyone needed a room of one's own. As the months passed, Kohler began to paint colors of making a future together with Tina.

In late 1995, Kohler received the same phone call he had placed two years earlier. It was from Chatterton; his marriage was in trouble. They met at Scotty's. Chatterton's situation was different from Kohler's. Though he and Kathy were fighting, there had been no suggestion that Chatterton give up diving. The couple had simply grown apart. Each had a passion—Chatterton's was diving; Kathy's was pistol shooting—and each had become increasingly devoted to that passion. Over the years, the marriage had evolved into an arrangement of convenience. He understood currents, and the flow of the marriage was moving away from him.

"Maybe the worst part," he told Kohler, "is that the U-boat is hanging over me. It's with me at work and home. I take a step back and look at myself and I'm not who I used to be. I'm not as friendly. I'm not as happy."

"John, you have so much to be happy about," Kohler said. "You just had one of the greatest diving years in history. In two summers you conquered the world. In two summers you discovered the universe of shipwrecks while guys like Bielenda barked at the moon. How can you be unhappy at a time like this?"

"The U-boat is different," Chatterton said. "The U-boat is our moment."

For several minutes, neither man said anything. Finally, Chatterton spoke.

"You coming back, Richie?" he asked.

"I just don't know," Kohler said. "It's been a very long time."

Kohler spent the winter of 1995–96 contemplating a future with Tina. His life had stabilized, his kids were happy, and his business was growing. Some days, he did not dare consider a return to diving. Then spring began to dab warmth into the air and Marks said it would be a shame if a man turned his back on his passion. Kohler unlocked the storage shed at his shop. He picked up his dry suit. The trademark red by which other divers knew him from across the Horrible Inn's parking lot was as bright as it had been the day he and Chatterton first dove the *U-Who* together. He walked to the phone and dialed. Chatterton answered.

"John, it's Richie," he said. "I'm back."

The divers met at Scotty's. Chatterton had never seen Kohler so alive.

"You've done worlds of stuff over the last two years," Kohler said. "I, on the other hand, have done shit. But I've got one big advantage on you, John. I'm back with a vengeance. I'm a madman two years in the making. You're out of ideas? You don't know where to turn next? Let me tell you this: we're not stopping until we solve this thing. The proof is on that wreck, I know that in my heart."

Kohler reached into his briefcase and pulled out his long-entombed *U-Who* file. The divers began work on a plan. Their approach was primitive and ferocious. They would force their way into the electric motor room, the only unexplored compartment aboard the *U-Who*. That room and part of the adjoining diesel motor room remained blocked by a steel escape trunk, the vertical tunnel through which crewmen could escape a flooding or sinking boat. For years, the divers had figured the trunk to be unmovable, the electric motor room to contain nothing but machinery. Now they vowed to move the trunk at whatever risk and whatever cost. And it would no longer be good enough to presume that the electric motor room contained no identifying artifacts; they were going to bash their way in and see for themselves. The divers finished their dinners and shook hands. For two years, each of them had been removed from himself. Now reunited, the first draft of a plan secured on a napkin, they looked to be exactly where they were meant to be.

The plan took shape like this: Chatterton and Kohler would rig a three-ton chain fall to the escape trunk, which blocked the aft end of the diesel motor room. The chain fall, a heavy-duty, ratchet-driven hoist, was powerful enough to pull a car from a ditch. Divers almost never risked a move like this, even in shallow waters, as the dangers were myriad. The trunk could collapse on the divers, crushing or pinning them. The trunk could splinter, shooting shrapnel in all directions. The divers could become irreversibly winded by the physical exertion necessary to rig and move the trunk. The grated floor on which the divers would anchor themselves could cave in. The U-boat itself might collapse once the trunk was pulled free. The trunk could fall and block the divers' exit. Chatterton and Kohler discussed these possibilities. They considered each of them real. They decided to proceed.

Chatterton borrowed a chain fall from the commercial diving outfit for which he worked. The divers booked several trips. Time and again, however, inclement weather forced them to stay onshore. The entire 1996 season passed. If this audacious plan was to happen, it would have to wait until 1997.

The winter passed slowly for both men. The diving appetites Kohler had suppressed for two years now roared in his daily life, yet he was helpless to do anything but wait until the weather warmed. Chatterton's marriage continued to fossilize. His wife had taken a new job, further reducing their time together. They entered counseling. It didn't work. In May 1997, as the dive season began, they hired a divorce lawyer, though they agreed to continue living together until the fall, when each of their summer activities would subside.

The death knell of Chatterton's marriage broadsided him. One spring day, he called Kohler and said, "I've got to see you now." Kohler left work and met his friend at the Watchung Reservation, where they walked by a waterfall and through some woods. Chatterton needed to know how Kohler had dealt with his pain, how he had managed to show up to work every day as his family was disintegrating. He asked detailed questions about heartache. Kohler mostly listened. He told Chatterton that he believed that time healed nearly everything, but he said little else. He knew that Chatterton needed to talk and to be around someone who loved him and cared about him, and Kohler did.

As New Jersey's charter boat captains put their boats back in the water for the 1997 dive season, Chatterton and Kohler reviewed one of Henry Keatts's books on wreck diving. In one chapter, they came across photographs of several tags that had been recovered from U-853—a World War II U-boat of exactly the same type as the U-Who—located near Block Island, Rhode Island. Most of the tags were generic and contained no meaningful writing. One of them, however, stunned the divers. It read U-853. Chatterton and Kohler had recovered dozens of tags from the U-Who. None of them was marked with anything like this kind of identifying information.

Kohler rushed to the phone and called Keatts, whom the divers knew casually.

"Hank, in your book there's a photo of a bunch of tags from U-853. Where on the submarine did those tags come from?"

"I'm not sure," Keatts said.

"Where are the tags now? Who has the one that says U-853?"

"I think Billy Palmer pulled that tag."

"Thank you very much," Kohler said.

Billy Palmer was a hard-living, cigar-chomping, fiftyish captain who ran a small dive boat, *Thunderfish*, near Block Island. He was also a first-rate wreck diver. Chatterton and Kohler saw him every so often at the Boston Sea Rover show, and they had some friends in common. Kohler found Palmer's Connecticut home phone number and placed a call.

"You still have those tags from the 853?" Kohler asked.

"I got buckets of tags," Palmer said.

"Buckets?"

"Yeah, buckets."

"You happen to remember where you got the one that says *U-853*?"

"It's been a long time, Richie. My memory's a little cloudy."

Kohler asked if he and Chatterton might drive up for a visit. Palmer told them he'd be happy to see them.

A day later, the divers knocked on Palmer's door. He answered wearing an authentic Iron Cross award on a chain around his neck, one of the artifacts he had recovered from *U-853*. Chatterton and Kohler glanced at each other as if to say, "Is he serious with that Iron Cross?" but made no comment. Palmer gave them a guided tour of his house, much of which was filled with artifacts. The divers were itching to see the tags. Palmer took his time. Finally, he escorted them to his basement. There, dressed in a German sailor's uniform, complete with hat and coat, and standing beside a ship's helm, was a female mannequin Palmer introduced as "Eva." Palmer passed out beers.

"So you're interested in the tags?" Palmer asked.

"Yes, very much," Chatterton replied.

Palmer lifted the glass on a display case. Inside were at least fifty plastic tags. One of them was stamped *U-853*. The divers sat dumbstruck.

"Can you tell us where on the wreck you found this one?" Kohler asked.

Palmer turned away from the divers and toward the mannequin.

"Eva," he said calmly, "steer course zero-two-zero."

The divers studied Palmer's face. They could not tell if he was serious in addressing Eva. Palmer smiled pleasantly, the Iron Cross dangling against his shirt, and returned to the conversation.

"It was on a wooden spare-parts box, a little bigger than a shoe box," Palmer said.

"In what room?" Chatterton asked.

"It was in the electric motor room."

The divers nearly leaped from their chairs.

"The spare-parts boxes had to be labeled with the U-boat's number," Palmer explained. "That way, if a part was used during a mission, they could send the box to the warehouse, have it refilled, and know which U-boat to return it to."

Chatterton and Kohler sat frozen. Of all the places on the *U-Who*, the electric motor room was the only one that remained inaccessible, and the only one in which they had not imagined finding identifying tags. Now more than ever it was imperative that they move the massive steel escape trunk that blocked access to part of the diesel motor room and the adjoining electric motor room. They stood up and thanked Palmer.

"That all you fellows want?" he asked.

They told Palmer that he had been a great help. They glanced again at Eva. They told Palmer it had been a real experience, and bid the man good-bye.

The divers booked a trip to the *U-Who* for June 1, 1997. Chatterton brought the three-ton chain fall and an aluminum support beam. For the first time in nearly four years, they were attacking the *U-Who* with a plan. As the *Seeker* neared the dive site, Chatterton and Kohler paced the boat's rear deck.

"I'm so ready to go," Chatterton said.

"We're back," Kohler replied.

The plan would be executed in two stages. On the first dive, Kohler would take precise measurements of the escape trunk. He and Chatterton would study those figures between dives, then rig the chain fall to the trunk and pull it out on the second dive. If all went well, they would have unfettered access to both motor rooms—and hopefully spare-parts boxes marked by identifying tags.

The weather and current waved a gentle welcome to the divers. Chatterton glided down the anchor line and tied the anchor into the wreck. Kohler followed, swimming through the gaping wound in the control room and heading aft. Just inside the diesel motor room, he came face-to-face with the escape trunk, a massive steel tube that lay fallen at a thirty-degree angle between the two giant diesel engines built on either side of the room. Wire splayed like Einstein's hair from all parts of the trunk, some of it long enough to choke the life from a diver if he drifted too close. Kohler moved in slowly. Though he was supposed to measure the obstruction, he instead removed a crowbar strapped to his tank. When Kohler was a boy, his father had told him, "Give me a big enough lever and I can move the world," a lesson that suddenly took over his brain. Kohler nudged the tool between the trunk and the engine; perhaps the huge steel tube had a bit of give. He surveyed his surroundings, taking stock of how he might lunge to escape if the trunk began to fall. He pushed on the crowbar. The trunk rocked and groaned, billowing silt mushroom clouds into the compartment and causing wire to rattlesnake toward Kohler's face mask. Kohler went motionless and forced his breathing down. He was supposed to be measuring the obstruction. But now he was full of new ideas. He could muscle the trunk away. It could cost him his life, yes; there were a dozen ways he could die doing that. But he had been away from himself for too long. He owed the fallen crewmen a duty. He owed himself the attempt.

He moved the crowbar again. The trunk rocked in reply. The visibility was now less than a foot. He could lift this thing. Kohler looked behind him for an escape route, but that hardly mattered: if the trunk fell on him, it would pin him or strangle him or crush him through the rotting floor, and Chatterton—who was working forward in the sub to give Kohler space—would never hear him scream.

Kohler placed one hand under the lip of the trunk, the other on an engine block for purchase. He spread and planted his feet sumo wrestler–style on the steel beams that supported the engines, praying that he would not slip and plunge through the room's grated floor. Then he reached inside himself for every muscle he had ever used, arm and stomach and neck muscles he'd first summoned as an eight-year-old boy gaffing forty-pound stripers from his father's fishing boat. He lifted the trunk six inches off the ground. The metal ground against the steel engine blocks against which it had slept for a half century.

"Don't fall backward," Kohler told the trunk. "Don't bury me here."

He lifted harder. The trunk rose farther off the floor, and for a moment Kohler held it aloft, a lumberjack of the deep balancing a steel redwood. The floor creaked. His arms burned. He stepped backward. Now, able to glimpse himself clear of the front of the engines, he released the trunk, allowing it to plummet downward. As it fell, Kohler thrust the trunk away from him. It hit the floor and crashed to the left, raising storms of dark brown, oily silt and sounding thunder off the U-boat's steel walls. Kohler held his breath and looked down. He was not trapped. He was not dead. He could see nothing, but he knew he had made the biggest, most important move of his career. He had moved the unmovable. The obstruction to the electric motor room had been felled.

Kohler would have liked nothing more than to swim between the diesel engines and into the electric motor room. But he was winded, and the visibility had dropped to zero. He and Chatterton would have to wait until the day's second dive to move in. Kohler inched out of the submarine. On his way up the anchor line, he thought to himself, "This is the day."

Topside, Kohler told Chatterton the story. Chatterton squinted and cocked his head.

"You did what?"

"I muscled it. It's moved. We're in."

"We brought a three-ton chain fall to do that work. And you muscled it?"

"I felt it could be done. I had to make my move."

Chatterton shook his head.

"You've got a set of balls on you, Richie," Chatterton said. "Goddamn, that was dangerous. Goddamn, that's balls."

"Maybe it's better if we don't analyze exactly how dangerous it was," Kohler said, following Chatterton into the salon. "Here's the important thing: three hours from now and we're into the electric motor room."

Around noon, Chatterton and Kohler reentered the ocean carrying lift bags and goody bags for the spare-parts boxes they hoped to recover. A minute later they were inside the *U-Who*. The silt had cleared inside the diesel motor room, leaving a clear view aft. The divers could scarcely believe what they saw. Just a few feet past the escape trunk Kohler had moved lay another obstruction, this one a huge, crescent-shaped steel fuel tank that had once been bolted into the overhead pressure hull. Chatterton and Kohler stared at the tank, which had obviously fallen during the U-boat's demise. They swam closer and inspected it. The tank appeared to be about twelve feet long and very heavy. It lay wedged diagonally between the diesel engines, with just a whisper of space between its top and the room's ceiling, an even more severe obstruction than the escape trunk Kohler had just moved. The divers knew right away that even a three-ton chain fall could not move this mass. They looked at each other but did not have the energy to shake their heads. The net profit of Kohler's triumph had been an extra four feet of access into the diesel motor room. The electric motor room—the room they needed—was still a million miles away.

The divers turned around and swam back to the anchor line. Their heads hung during their decompression ascents. On board the dive boat, they undressed in silence. Every so often, one of them muttered an obscenity.

For an hour during the ride back to Brielle, neither man said a word. They just sat on a large cooler and watched the dive site disappear. Then, as the sun set over the horizon, Chatterton turned to Kohler.

"I have a plan," he said.

"I'm listening," Kohler answered.

For the next five minutes, Chatterton described a vision, a three-dimensional epiphany for moving past the fallen fuel tank and into the electric motor room. After he finished, Kohler looked him in the eye.

"You'll die," Kohler said.

"I'm going to do it," Chatterton said.

"You'll die for sure."

"I'm going to do it. But I can't do it without you."

"I won't be part of that. I won't watch you die."

"I'm going to do it," Chatterton said. "This is our last chance, Richie. More than I know anything, I know I'm going to do it. And I need you with me."

CHAPTER FOURTEEN

CIRCLE-RUNNER

Kristiansand, Norway, December 4, 1944

A WEEK AND A HALF after leaving Germany, Commander Neuerburg and *U-869* arrived in the southern Norwegian port town of Kristiansand, where they took on fuel and supplies. Brimming with provisions, the U-boat could now wage war anywhere in the Atlantic. Neuerburg's first assignment was to crawl northward along the Norwegian coast, then break into the open Atlantic via the Iceland-Faeroes gap. He would receive further orders—war orders—when the submarine reached the open seas. Radio traffic between the U-boat and Control would be kept to a minimum; by this time in the war, even the slightest chatter from a U-boat could be intercepted by the Allies.

On December 8, the U-boat's diesels belched to life and it pushed away from the Norwegian U-boat base. For three weeks, it crawled along Norway's coast and then onward into the Atlantic, submerged virtually nonstop to avoid Allied air patrols and ships. On December 29, Control radioed its next order. *U-869* was to head for naval grid CA 53, the center of which was about 110 miles southeast of New York. Neuerburg had been issued perhaps the most prestigious assignment a U-boat could receive: *U-869* had been sent to wage war against America.

The U-boat pushed westward. Protocol required Neuerburg to radio a brief passage report to Control once *U-869* broke into the open Atlantic. Control, which had been plotting *U-869*'s presumed progress, had expected such a report no later than December 29. None was received. On December 30, Control requested a passage report. Again, it received none. Control became "concerned," its officers reported in the diary, though they did not yet take the silence to mean that *U-869* had been lost. On January 1, 1945, Control requested a position report from *U-869*, this time in strong language. It received no reply. It repeated its requests. Still it heard nothing from the submarine. Now Control was worried.

Control did not know why it had not heard from *U-869*. Four possible explanations must have been considered. The first was that Neuerburg simply refused to use his radio for fear of Allied detection. That, however, must have seemed unlikely, as commanders would have been loath to ignore such urgent requests from Control. The second was that *U-869*'s radio equipment was malfunctioning, making reception and/or transmission impossible. The third was that atmospheric problems—known to be an issue in that area of the Atlantic—were wreaking havoc with the radios. The fourth was that the boat was no more.

For the next several days, and probably using increasingly urgent terms, Control demanded position reports from *U-869*. On January 3, Control noted its "considerable anxiety" at *U-869*'s silence. At around the same time, Allied intelligence studied its radio intercepts and made this assessment: "A U/Boat (*U-869*) now estimated in the central North Atlantic has been ordered to head for a point about 70 miles southeast of the New York approaches."

By January 6, Control was likely mourning for *U-869*. In almost every case in which a U-boat was five days late in reporting to Control, that U-boat was lost. Still, Control beseeched *U-869* to answer. That day, in a broadcast that must have seemed a miracle inside Control, *U-869* radioed her position. Even as Control officials celebrated they scratched their heads. *U-869* was in naval grid AK 63, about six hundred miles southwest of Iceland. The U-boat, they wrote in their diary, "should have been considerably further southwest." It was then that Control likely realized that Neuerburg had made a big and bold decision, one with which they probably were not pleased. Rather than use the Iceland-Faeroes gap—the most direct route from Norway into the open Atlantic—he had diverted much farther north, making a loop over Iceland before heading southwestward through the Denmark Strait. There could be no doubt as to why Neuerburg had spent the extra days and fuel going the long way: the Denmark Strait was less heavily patrolled by Allied airplanes and ships. Though a commander was allowed such discretion, Control never liked the move; every extra day spent in transit was an extra day spent away from the war. Neuerburg's crew, on the other hand, was likely grateful to their commanding officer. He had made his first major war move, and it had been in the name of protecting his men. What no one knew—not Neuerburg, his crew, or Control—was that Allied code breakers had intercepted their broadcast and knew where they were.

Neuerburg's decision to use the circuitous Denmark Strait sent Control strategists scrambling. They likely determined that he must have burned at least five extra days' fuel going the long way, meaning that it would cost the boat one hundred days to stay perhaps fourteen days off New York, an unacceptable ratio. Control requested a fuel-status report. Again, it received no reply from U-869 "in spite of continuous queries." As Neuerburg had shown himself willing to use the radio, and as the radios appeared at least sometimes to be working, Control probably blamed atmospheric conditions for the lack of communication from U-869. Unwilling to wait any longer for a fuel-status report, Control radioed a new order to Neuerburg: U-869 was to change course and head to Gibraltar, to patrol the African coast. By rerouting the submarine away from New York and to this closer operating area, Control could expect a longer patrol from U-869.

Control would not have expected U-869 to acknowledge receipt of this new order—it would have been too dangerous for Neuerburg to use his radio simply to confirm the directive. Control therefore presumed Neuerburg to have received the order and began plotting U-869 to Gibraltar, calculating that the submarine should arrive there around February 1. Had Neuerburg received the order, it is certain that he would have followed it—while a commander had discretion in choosing his routes, he had no such option when receiving a direct order. Whether because of equipment or atmospheric problems, it is virtually certain that U-869 never received the new order to Gibraltar. Neuerburg kept heading for New York.

The Allies, however, were intercepting almost everything. On January 17, their intelligence wrote, "The U/Boat heading for the New York approaches, U-869 (Neuerburg), is presently estimated about 180 miles SSE of Flemish Cap. . . . She is expected to arrive in the New York area at the beginning of February."

On January 25, American intelligence pegged the situation: "One U/Boat may be south of Newfoundland heading for New York approaches, although her location is uncertain due to a mix up in orders and Control assumes she is heading for Gibraltar."

Then, in the chillingly matter-of-fact language of war, American intelligence announced its plans for U-869: "The CORE will begin sweeping for this U/Boat shortly prior to proceeding against the U/Boats reporting weather in the North Atlantic."

The Americans would be sending a hunter-killer group to destroy U-869. They knew where the submarine was going.

All the while, Neuerburg and his crew continued their long push toward New York. U-boats went largely unmolested during travel in the open Atlantic—hunter-killer groups often waited for them to arrive in shallower waters closer to shore, where the U-boats could less easily run and hide. To pass the time, perhaps the crewmen organized a checkers tournament or a limerick contest or a lying competition, as had occurred on other U-boat patrols; a man could lose a day's rations for overconfidence in such matters. Or perhaps they adopted a mascot—one U-boat had selected a fly for this purpose, which they named Emma and whose daily routines they followed with keen interest.

U-869 likely approached American coastal waters in early February. From that point forward, Neuerburg certainly would have kept the submarine submerged full-time, using the snorkel for the fresh-air intake necessary to run the diesel engines underwater. By now, the American hunter-killer group had begun its search for U-869. Neuerburg, who knew well the Allies' ability to track and stalk a U-boat, must have navigated with extreme stealth—the hunter-killer group found only fathoms of empty sea.

Now U-869 was in American waters and bearing down on the

New York approaches. Neuerburg's targets would be whatever enemy vessels he could find. The crew's nerves must have been stretched taut against their knowledge of the odds against them. Perhaps a day passed, perhaps several days. Then, through the crosshairs of the U-boat's periscope, Neuerburg must have spotted an enemy ship. At that point, he would have ordered his men to their battle stations. The men would have remained silent. From this point forward, every order would have been whispered.

As U-869 crept forward at a speed of perhaps two knots, the crew likely heard the sound of water outside the submarine, the hum of the electric engines, and perhaps even the faint revolutions of the enemy target's propellers in the distance. All else would have been quiet. Now U-869 was ready to attack. At this moment, Neuerburg, Brandt, and the rest of the crew knew certain things. They knew that the war was being lost. They knew U-boats were not returning home. They knew that it was up to Neuerburg, not Control, to decide when U-869's patrol had concluded.

No one knows what Neuerburg thought then. He kept the periscope raised. The men remained at their battle stations. Seconds later, Neuerburg whispered this kind of order inside the steel, cigar-shaped hull of U-869:

"Tube one ready—fire."

CHAPTER FIFTEEN

AN AUDACIOUS PLAN

CHATTERTON'S FINAL PLAN for the *U-Who* was audacious and lethal. He would swim into the diesel motor room with just a single tank on his back, not the customary two. He would then remove that tank and hold it in front of him—much as a child holds a kickboard when learning to swim—and push it through the narrow opening between the fallen fuel tank and the U-boat's ceiling. Once on the other side of the diesel motor room, he would reattach the tank to his back and swim into the adjoining electric motor room, where he hoped to find identifying tags attached to boxes of spare parts. After recovering the bounty, he would swim back into the diesel motor room, pass it over the top to Kohler, again remove his single trimix tank, and slither back out the way he had come in. Only by carrying a single tank of trimix—and then taking it off—did Chatterton believe a diver could pass over the fuel tank that blocked nearly every inch of space between the electric motor room and the rest of the *U-Who*.

The plan's dangers were encyclopedic, a textbook on how to get killed inside a shipwreck. With just a single tank to breathe, Chatterton would have only twenty minutes on the other side of the obstruction.

"Forget it," Kohler said by phone on the evening Chatterton revealed the plan. "That is the single most insane plan I have ever heard in my life. I'm not watching you die. I'm not participating in your suicide."

312 • ROBERT KURSON

"This is vision," Chatterton said. "This can work."

"This is lunacy," Kohler said.

Kohler found a notebook and began scribbling a list of risks. Most of them ended with the phrase "then John runs out of gas and drowns." The list read like this:

— Chatterton could become entangled—in wire, pipes, fittings, fixtures, bent metal, anything.
— Chatterton could be pinned under falling debris.
— A piece of machinery could fall and block Chatterton's exit.
— Relying on a single gas supply eliminates the safety of redundancy—if a high-pressure hose or O-ring fails, Chatterton loses his sole breathing source.
— The dive's high risk will almost certainly cause Chatterton to breathe harder than usual, meaning he will burn through his already limited gas supply even faster.
— The electric motor room will be packed with cables, wires, and machinery no diver has seen before, meaning that Chatterton will not have his usual chance to mentally diagram the room's layout.
— There is no way out the other end of the electric motor room, as its aft end has been crushed downward.
— The water inside the electric motor room, undisturbed by divers or the ocean, has been stagnant for fifty years. Chatterton's activity inside the compartment will disturb the dusty brown silt and reduce the visibility to zero.
— Chatterton's bubbles could disturb fuel or lubrication oil floating on the compartment's ceiling, clouding his mask, blinding him, and seeping into his mouth.

"Any one of these can kill you," Kohler said. "But you'll be lucky if only one of them happens. More likely, a bunch of them will gang up on you and kill you even faster. And don't forget maybe the biggest danger, John."

"What's that?"

"You will be alone inside that compartment. Even if I agreed to this outrageous plan, even if I waited for you on the other side of that obstruction, I can't help you once you get into trouble. I can't take my tanks off. I've got kids. I have mouths to feed. The most I can do is peer over that fuel tank and watch you drown."

"We can't stop now," Chatterton said. "I have a plan. This is why I dive, Richie. This is the art."

"It's too goddamned dangerous."

"I need you with me."

"I'm bailing on this, John. I'm out."

The divers hung up. Word spread throughout the local diving community about Chatterton's plan. There were two schools of thought. Chatterton's friends, including John Yurga and Danny Crowell, pronounced Chatterton "out of his fucking mind." Those who knew him only in passing were more liberal: "If he wants to kill himself, let him," they said.

For three days, Chatterton and Kohler did not speak. Kohler envisioned the dive from a thousand angles and it always ended up the same—with Chatterton slumped over drowned or pinned under some piece of fallen steel, Kohler helpless to move through the crack to save him. But he also found himself remembering another scene, this one of his first dive to the *U-Who*. While hanging underwater, he had been overcome with joy at the sight of Chatterton's mesh bag filled with china, and had reached instinctively to take a closer look. Chatterton had snatched the bag away—the men did not like each other then, did not like what the other represented. For a moment there had been a standoff. Then Chatterton had seemed to look into Kohler's heart. A few seconds later he'd offered his bag to Kohler.

Kohler called Chatterton.

"John, I'm scared to death for you," Kohler said. "But we're partners. I'm not going to bail on you now."

"We are partners, Richie," Chatterton replied. "Let's do this."

The first attempt was scheduled for August 17, 1997. Chatterton spent the weeks leading up to the mission rehearsing his moves in his office, in his garage, in line at the grocery store, a combination mime and ballerina practicing for a recital in which a single misstep would mean death. By this time, his divorce was nearly final. In 1991, when he'd discovered the *U-Who,* he had believed his marriage would last forever. Now Kathy did not even know of this daring plan for the U-boat. Some nights, he mourned the marriage so deeply he found himself unable to move. At those times, he told himself, "I must put everything out of my mind for this dive. I must focus absolutely. If I don't, if I'm the slightest bit distracted, I won't come back."

On August 17, Chatterton, Kohler, and five other top wreck divers boarded the *Seeker* and set sail for the *U-Who.* No one said much during the trip. In the morning, Chatterton reviewed his plan with Kohler. He would use the first dive as a trial run to get a feel for taking off his tank, investigating the accessibility of the electric motor room, and learning the layout of the compartment. Kohler would hover near the top of the fallen fuel-tank obstruction, shining his flashlight as a beacon and waiting to take any artifacts Chatterton might pass through.

"Let's make a three-of-anything plan," Chatterton told Kohler as he pulled on his fins. "If I bang my hammer three times or flash my light three times or do anything three times, it means I'm in trouble."

"Okay, it means you're in trouble," Kohler replied. "I still can't squeeze through that crack in the top to help you. So three of anything basically means you're dead."

"Yeah, you're right. Forget it."

A few minutes later, Chatterton and Kohler were in the water. In total, Chatterton carried three gas tanks—the one he would breathe inside the electric motor room, plus two stage bottles for his trip down to the wreck and back. As the divers reached the *U-Who,* Chatterton placed his stage bottles on top of the wreck and began breathing from his primary tank.

The divers swam toward the fallen fuel tank that blocked much of the diesel motor room and the adjoining electric motor room. Chatterton removed the tank from his back and held it in front of him. Kohler ascended toward the gap between the fuel tank and the ceiling, through which Chatterton would pass. Chatterton kicked his fins and began gliding up and forward. He was now just a few feet away from pushing his tank through the gap and igniting this crazy plan, but he still had a moment to dip his shoulder and turn back, to U-turn on this mystery he had all but solved already. He never stopped kicking. A few seconds later, he pushed his tank through the gap—vigilant not to let it slip—and then sardined through himself. On the other side of the diesel motor room, he slung the tank onto his back. No diver had ever been in this part of the *U-Who*. He began to explore.

The path to the electric motor room was clear. Chatterton swam to the rectangular hatch that led into the compartment and passed through it. He was now floating inside the electric motor room, the place he and Kohler believed held proof of the wreck's identity. Chatterton felt six years of mystery pushing him farther inside. He talked that instinct down. He had done well enough on this trial run. He had ten minutes of gas remaining. He would use it to become accustomed to leaving these compartments. He swam back up to the fallen fuel tank in the diesel motor room and again removed his tank. A few seconds later, he pushed the tank and himself back through the opening near the ceiling and landed on the other side. From there, he reattached the tank, glided to where his stage bottles lay atop the wreck, and switched regulators. He now had plenty of gas with which to do his decompression. Kohler shook his head in amazement. Chatterton had made a near-perfect trial run.

Bad weather blew out the day's second dive. The next trip was scheduled for August 24, 1997. Kohler's nerves settled a bit in the intervening week. If Chatterton could replicate his trial dive, he thought, the S.O.B. might just be able to pull off this so-called vision.

The plan would be the same as on the first trip, with a single exception: Kohler would pass Chatterton a video camera once he got past the obstruction and reaffixed his tank. Chatterton would thus be able to videotape the compartments for future study, if necessary.

As before, Chatterton's tank maneuvering was seamless. The video camera he had taken from Kohler, however, would not work. Frustrated, he swam to the top of the compartment to hand it back through the gap to Kohler. By now, however, he had reaffixed the tank to his back, and he found that the equipment made him slightly too bulky to reach the gap. Chatterton spotted a massive steel beam near the ceiling, a piece he could use to pull himself closer to Kohler. He grabbed the beam and pulled. The steel shook for a moment, then gave way, crashing into Chatterton's lap and hurling him against one of the diesel engines. His heart pounded. He ordered himself to control his breathing. He looked at the beam—its ends had lodged in the surrounding machinery. Chatterton slowly reached to remove the steel from his lap. Its weight was enormous, at least two hundred pounds out of water. Still, he managed to begin lifting it. His breathing rate increased. His gas supply dropped. He lifted harder. The beam moved just an inch before stopping cold, the mirror image of an amusement-park roller coaster restraint. Chatterton pushed harder. The gauges on his tank moved lower. The beam would not budge. Chatterton pushed with his legs to get free. He could not move. He was trapped.

Chatterton began to talk to himself.

"Panic is how guys die," he thought. "Take thirty seconds. Take a little break. Collect yourself."

Kohler looked into the gap. Silt had billowed everywhere. He could see nothing. He presumed Chatterton was going about his dive.

"Deal with this problem," Chatterton told himself. "Guys die because they don't take care of the first problem. Don't let the snowball roll."

Chatterton's gas gauge crept downward.

"This thing got onto me," he thought. "It's just a matter of figuring the way it landed on me, then reversing the process. Stay calm. Don't make more problems. Just reverse the process."

Chatterton used his mind's eye to replay the collapse of the beam. For five minutes, he gently tried to push the steel in the opposite direction. The object would not move. He continued to concentrate, replaying the accident in his mind over and over. Another five minutes passed. The object would not budge. Primal instincts raged in Chatterton's head, begging him to thrash and flail and scream and lunge. He ordered his instincts to wait. He had five minutes of gas to breathe. He would watch more film.

With just a few minutes of gas remaining, Chatterton again reached to move the beam. There would be no more time for movies if this attempt failed. He pushed up and felt one end clank free. He pushed on the other end. The beam collapsed forward and pivoted away from his lap. Chatterton pushed himself off the diesel engine and swam swiftly but not wildly toward the gap near the ceiling. His gauge needle dipped farther into red. He removed his tank and pushed it through, then kicked his fins and wriggled out of the compartment. Kohler moved to join his partner, but he backed off when he saw Chatterton head directly for the tanks he had left on top of the wreck. A moment later, Chatterton had switched to one of his stage bottles. The gauge on his primary tank was near empty. He likely had exited the diesel motor room with less than a minute of air remaining.

Topside, Chatterton told the story. Danny Crowell, who had captained the boat that day, shook his head and turned to another diver.

"Any other diver in the world and we're calling the Coast Guard for a body recovery," he said.

Kohler turned white. He'd had no idea that Chatterton had experienced any trouble.

"Forget it," Kohler said. "This is too dangerous. This whole plan was a big mistake. John, you gotta reconsider. This is really bad."

"Let's get that video camera working," Chatterton said, reaching inside a cooler for a soda. "I'll want to shoot lots of film on my second dive today."

Kohler walked away.

"Crazy bastard," he muttered.

A few hours later, Chatterton was back inside the diesel motor room, Kohler hovering outside and waiting again to be helpless. This time, the camera worked. Chatterton moved through the rectangular hatch that led into the electric motor room. A half century of silt exploded in clouds around him. Chatterton pointed the camera to where his research indicated the spare-parts boxes and their identifying tags should be—the camera could always see better than the human eye underwater. When the visibility fell to zero, Chatterton exited the electric motor room and swam back up toward Kohler, then passed him the camera. He removed his tank—a move with which he was becoming comfortable—and made his way out of the diesel motor room. He had not recovered any artifacts. He had almost lost his life on the first dive. But now he had video. Topside, as the divers undressed and the boat headed back to shore, he thanked Kohler for his support.

"Next trip and I haul the boxes," Chatterton said. "I feel it. The next trip is the one."

The next charter to the *U-Who* was scheduled for a week later, on August 31, 1997. Chatterton spent the intervening days studying the videotape he had shot. In one of the spots he saw what appeared to be a stack of three or four boxes. Now he really knew the next dive would be the one.

At home, Kohler went to war with himself. His friend and partner had come within a minute of drowning. Worse, on Sunday Chatterton planned to go back in and recover the spare-parts boxes. Kohler knew that the electric motor room was jungled in the worst, most ravenous scream of wires, tubes, jagged metal, and silt. He also knew Chatterton's heart. His friend would breathe his tank dry on Sunday before he would exit without his answer. His friend would die inside that wreck on Sunday.

Kohler decided to quit. Whatever satisfaction he might derive from delivering an answer to the crewmen's families and to history would be smothered by his helpless proximity to a drowning friend.

Yet whenever he picked up the phone to deliver his resignation, he ended up putting the receiver back on its cradle. There might be, he thought, one scenario worse than watching his friend die in the wreck, and as Sunday drew near he knew that worst scenario to be allowing his friend to die while he stayed home and waited for the news.

On Saturday evening, August 30, 1997, the *Seeker* jockeyed away from her dock and pointed toward the *U-Who*. Chatterton and Kohler spoke little; each knew that today was the day.

The next morning's weather was perfect and calm. Over a bowl of cereal, Chatterton asked Kohler if he was ready to receive the spare-parts boxes he expected to recover and pass over the top of the fallen fuel tank. Kohler nodded. An hour later, they were on the wreck. Chatterton took off his tank, extended it in front of him, and, stretched horizontally like Superman, moved through the crack between the obstruction and the ceiling. Kohler turned on his flashlight and lifted it to the space, a beacon for Chatterton's return.

Visibility was good inside the diesel motor room. Chatterton reattached his tank and glided through the rectangular hatch that led into the electric motor room. The scene was just as his videotape had depicted it. He looked to the right. There, stacked in a freestanding pyramid, were four increasingly large boxes of spare parts, each fused to the next by decades of marine encrustation and rust. The smallest of them was slightly larger than a shoe box. They were exactly what Chatterton had come for.

Chatterton inched toward the boxes. Lying at a thirty-degree angle against the top box was what appeared to be a five-foot-tall section of pipe, one that had likely broken from the room's machinery and fallen atop the box. Chatterton pushed gently against the boxes. The pipe was wedged hard against them, and nothing moved. He thrust his palms, football lineman–style, into the stack. Nothing. The pipe, he could now see, had pinned the boxes in place. He reached for his knife and tried prying the pipe away. It did not budge. Silt billowed overhead, reducing the visibility to near zero. Chatterton turned back and exited the compartment. He now understood the final element of his plan. He would have to take drastic action.

Topside, Chatterton briefed Kohler.

"The boxes are fused together and pinned down by this huge pipe," Chatterton said. "But those are the boxes, Richie. If there are identifying tags on this wreck, they're on those boxes."

"That's great," Kohler said. "But if nothing's moving, what can you do?"

"A sledgehammer. I'm taking a short-handled sledgehammer down there. The boxes are mine."

Slinging a sledgehammer at 230 feet was perhaps the best way for a diver to blow through his gas supply. Kohler did not bother to object. Chatterton was on a mission being directed from somewhere deeper than good advice.

"I'll find you the sledgehammer," Kohler said.

Chatterton and Kohler splashed four hours later. Like pulling off a T-shirt, Chatterton removed his single tank and pushed it, the sledgehammer, and himself through the crack between the fallen fuel tank and the ceiling. Inside, he reattached his tank and swam for the electric motor room. Kohler noted the time on his watch. He grumbled a half prayer. Several of the words were *please*.

Chatterton moved swiftly into the electric motor room. The compartment remained brown and cloudy from his earlier dive, but he could still see the boxes and the pipe through the silt. His approach would be simple: he would use the sledgehammer to knock the pipe loose, then pry the boxes free from one another with a crowbar.

Chatterton crept to within two feet of the pipe. He spread his hands wide across the sledgehammer's handle—using the tool in the water required a different technique from on land, one in which the diver pushed from the chest rather than swung with the arms. He anchored his left knee on the ground in front of the boxes and his right foot across the aisle on solid machinery. Then, in a short, violent forward explosion, he thrust the sledgehammer's head into the section of pipe fused to the boxes. The compartment thundered with the impact as pieces of encrustation flew from the pipe and hailstormed the room in rust. Chatterton stayed motionless. When the pieces settled to the bottom, he stood, amazed at the sight. The pipe had not moved. And the pipe was not a pipe. Naked and shiny without its encrustation, the object flashed its true identity to Chatterton. This was a five-foot-tall pressurized oxygen tank. This was the colossal big brother to the miniature version that had destroyed Chatterton's garage. It was a miracle that the tank had not just exploded.

"I need to make a decision," Chatterton said to himself.

He flashed through his options; they numbered exactly two. He could turn and leave the compartment. Or he could take another swing at the giant oxygen tank, which he would have to strike on the cap—its most dangerous spot—in order to shake it loose.

"If the thing blows, I won't hear anything," Chatterton thought. "I'll be dead and in a billion pieces.

"If I leave now, I can leave in one piece."

He stepped forward and found purchase with his feet.

When things are easy a person doesn't really learn about himself.

He spread his hands across the sledgehammer's smooth, long handle.

It's what a person does at the moment of his greatest struggle that shows him who he really is.

He lifted the sledgehammer against his chest.

Some people never get that moment.

He breathed deeper than he had ever breathed.

The U-Who *is my moment.*

He thrust the head of the sledgehammer toward the cap of the oxygen tank.

What I do now is what I am . . .

The sledgehammer bashed into the tank. The room thundered. Silt flew everywhere. Chatterton waited for the sound of a million sticks of dynamite. He heard only the whoosh of his bubbles leaving his regulator and the clank of falling metal. He peered through the silt. The tank had dropped away from the boxes. He was alive.

"Oh, Christ," he said aloud.

Chatterton moved toward the boxes, pulled the smallest one free, and stuffed it into his mesh bag. He checked his watch—he had five minutes remaining. He swam out of the electric motor room and up toward Kohler's flashlight beam. Though the box was heavy, he managed to hoist it through the gap to Kohler, who passed it to another diver to take to the surface and inspect for tags. By all rights, Chatterton should have exited the diesel motor room then, while he still had three minutes of time remaining. He could not. It was possible that the first box did not contain a tag. There were other boxes inside the electric motor room. He needed to retrieve a second box. Kohler desperately flashed his light. Chatterton turned around.

A minute later, Chatterton found the second box. This one, however, was even heavier than the first and could not be picked up and swum to Kohler. Instead, Chatterton began to roll it end over end out of the electric motor room. The visibility dropped to zero. Chatterton shined his flashlight on his gauges but could see nothing—the room had gone entirely black. He pushed the box farther, huffing and puffing just to move it another foot closer to Kohler. He pressed his watch against his face mask. He could make out only the vague outline of his timer. He had already stayed longer than planned. He abandoned the box.

"I've gotta get my ass out of here," he thought.

Chatterton swam to the top of the electric motor room so that he could use the ceiling topography to feel his way out of the pitch-black compartment. His navigation was perfect, delivering him to the hatchway that led to the diesel motor room. He was now just a few kicks away from Kohler. He swam forward. Suddenly, his head jerked back. A wire noose had caught around his neck. Chatterton was being strangled.

He tried swimming backward gently. He could not move. In that small bit of motion, the equipment on his back had become tangled on dangling electrical cables. He was now fully sewn into the wreck. Chatterton knew he did not have time to relax and reverse the process, as was necessary in such a predicament. He knew he would have to fight. From his waiting post, Kohler checked his watch. Chatterton was not just late. He was crazy late.

Chatterton pulled at the wire noose around his throat and managed to muscle it off his neck. His breathing quickened even more. He reached up and clawed at the cables that had snared his equipment. Nothing gave. He could not move. He tore harder at the restraints. They hissed in protest and would not loosen. He pulled at them with all he had. Finally, they dropped away. Now free, he dug hard for Kohler, knowing that the slightest additional entanglement would kill him. A moment later he was there. All that remained was for Chatterton to remove his tank and swim through the gap. He took a breath as he reached for the tank. Only the tiniest trickle of gas came through the regulator. Chatterton knew this sensation. He was a breath from going empty.

Chatterton ripped off his tank and shoved it through the crack near the ceiling, then lunged through the space himself. As he reached the other side, he inhaled, but nothing came from his tank. He was entirely out of gas.

Chatterton spit the regulator from his mouth. His only remaining hope lay in reaching his stage bottles. But they were outside the compartment and on top of the wreck, a swim of at least fifty feet. He dared not risk buddy-breathing with Kohler, as even a slight delay or mix-up in communications could be deadly. Chatterton, his mouth now totally exposed to the ocean, kicked with force and equanimity. He had seen guys die flailing. He was near death. He would not flail.

Chatterton torpedoed out of the diesel motor room and up toward the top of the wreck. Kohler, stunned by the sight of his friend without a regulator, gave chase behind him. Chatterton's lungs screamed as his stage bottles came into sight. He kicked harder. Every cell in his body shrieked for oxygen and pulled at his jaws to breathe. He clenched his mouth shut. He reached the stage bottles. In a single motion, he grabbed a regulator from one of the bottles, stuck it in his mouth, and turned the valve. Fresh gas flooded into his lungs. Chatterton had come down to his final breath.

A few seconds later, Kohler arrived at his side. He looked Chatterton in the eye, then pointed to his chest, sign language for "You just gave me a heart attack—now I'm the one who's going to die instead of you." The divers began their long decompression hang. For nearly two hours, Chatterton thought only of the terrible risks he had taken during the dive. Often, he said aloud, "I can't ever let that happen again." He had long since forgotten the spare-parts box he had recovered, which Kohler had passed to another diver for tag inspection topside.

Near the end of their decompressions, Chatterton and Kohler saw another diver, Will McBeth, swim down the anchor line. McBeth handed Chatterton a slate just like the one on which Chatterton had written "SUB" during the discovery trip six years earlier. This time, however, the slate said something different. This time, it read:

The *U-Who* now has a name—it is *U-869*. Congratulations.

In his younger days, Kohler might have jumped for joy and slapped Chatterton on the back. Chatterton might have pumped his fists in triumph. Today, they looked into each other's eyes. Then, simultaneously, neither one before the other, each extended his hand. The divers shook. Today, they had found something important. Today, they had their answers.

CHATTERTON AND KOHLER identified *U-869* in 1997. To this day, mysteries remain. Why did *U-869* continue to New York after being rerouted to Gibraltar? How did *U-869* meet her end? How did the crew die?

The answers to these questions will probably never be known; the U-boat sank with all hands and without witnesses. It is possible, however, to construct a most-likely-case scenario. That scenario looks like this:

The cataclysmic damage to *U-869*'s control room was almost certainly caused by a strike from its own torpedo. U-boats such as *U-869* carried two types of torpedoes in 1945. Normal "pattern" torpedoes were programmed to run a specific course toward their targets and used a gyroscopic steering mechanism to get there. Acoustic torpedoes were more advanced, homing in on the sound of an enemy ship's propellers. Both types of torpedoes, however, occasionally turned back on their own U-boats. Those torpedoes became known as circle-runners. U-boats recorded several instances in which circle-runners passed beneath or above them. An acoustic circle-runner could be especially dangerous, as it chased the sounds of its own submarine's electric motors, pumps, and generators. To avoid being hit, U-boat commanders were ordered to crash-dive immediately after firing an acoustic torpedo.

Commanders often had advance warning of circle-runners. Torpedo propellers spun at several hundred revolutions per minute and produced a distinct, high-pitched whir-whine audible at great distances to the U-boat's radioman, and then to the entire crew as the weapon drew closer. When a commander got such a warning, he was often able to dive or otherwise change course to avoid the circle-runner. History will likely never know how many of the sixty-five still-missing U-boats met their ends by circle-runners. By its nature, a circle-runner gives little warning and bears no witness.

Under ideal conditions—calm seas, good underwater sound propagation, early detection, and fast reporting—Neuerburg might have had thirty seconds or more to respond to the circle-runner. In worse conditions or if the radioman hesitated (or both), he would have had less time.

The torpedo would not have blown up instantly upon striking *U-869*. Instead, there would have been perhaps a one-second delay between contact and detonation as the pistol on the weapon's nose clicked and triggered the explosion. That click—an unmistakable sound to submariners—could be heard even when a torpedo struck a distant target. It would have sounded just long enough before detonation to register in the awarenesses of the crewmen.

Most German torpedoes carried between 620 and 780 pounds of high explosives. Based on damage to the wreck, the circle-runner likely impacted just below the conning tower, in the center of the submarine. Men located in the boat's control-room area—including Neuerburg and Brandt—would have been blown apart and nearly vaporized by the explosion. Men in adjoining rooms likely also died immediately from the concussion or from being hurricaned into machinery. Rippling sheets of air pressure would have rampaged toward both ends of the 252-foot-long submarine, probably slingshotting some crewmen off ceilings and walls and one another, crumpling others like marionettes. Steel doors were blown open. So strong was the blast that it bowed the steel hatch leading into the diesel motor room and blew the steel hatch off the torpedo-loading tube in the forward torpedo room, the compartment farthest from the blast's epicenter. The force of the explosion was easily strong enough to blow open the overhead hatches—hatches Chatterton and Kohler once speculated had been opened by crewmen attempting to escape the sinking sub.

With the U-boat now open to the ocean, torrents of icy water would have rushed inside. A merciless process of replacing air with water in the sub would have begun, and it would have happened with great sound and violence. Bodies would have been rag-dolled off machinery and other structures. Rushing air would have sounded and impacted like a tornado to anyone still alive. Machinery and parts and clothes and tools would have flown at right angles in the furious columns of air rushing from the sub, some of which would have been expelled as ocean debris. No one could have held on. Corpses—some of them likely missing heads or limbs—would have begun a crooked float to the surface.

It probably took the U-boat less than thirty seconds to fill with water. The submarine would have sunk to the ocean bottom in less than a minute. If anyone had survived the explosion and somehow made it out of the boat and to the surface, he likely would not have lasted more than an hour in the icy waters. The enemy target ship, now as far as ten minutes away, its own engines running, wind and water lapping at its sides, would almost certainly have never heard or seen a thing.

The most likely explanation for the communications problems between *U-869* and Control involves atmospheric conditions, though it is possible that the boat also experienced mechanical problems with its radios. Though Neuerburg might have been hesitant to broadcast for fear of exposing his position to Allied eavesdroppers, the submarine placed itself in no danger by receiving messages from Control. That *U-869* continued to New York after Control ordered her to Gibraltar makes it virtually certain that Neuerburg never got the rerouting orders.

The fate of *U-857*—the submarine that had been hunting targets on the American East Coast in April 1945 and was believed for months by Chatterton and Kohler to be the *U-Who*—remains a mystery. It is still thought lost to unknown causes.

The Harbor Inn—a.k.a. the Horrible Inn—no longer exists. Standing in its place in the Brielle, New Jersey, parking lot adjacent to the *Seeker* is the upscale Shipwreck Grill, which serves its nattily dressed customers lobster bisque and honey-roasted salmon with Dijon lobster sauce. Older divers who drop in for a bite swear that if they stay long enough they can still hear Bill Nagle calling for another Jim Beam.

The *Seeker*, the dive boat conceived and built by Nagle and used to discover and dive the *U-Who*, continues to run charters. Its current owner, Danny Crowell goes to the *Stolt Dagali*, USS *Algol,* and many other popular wrecks. Crowell rarely runs to *U-869*. "I'd go if people were interested," he says. "There's just not that many of those kind of divers around these days."

A few dive boats, such as Howard Klein's *Eagle's Nest* and Joe Terzuoli's *John Jack,* continue to take customers to *U-869.* Since Chatterton pulled the identifying tag from the wreck in 1997, however, the U-boat has surrendered no important artifacts. Still, Chatterton and Kohler believe that there's a remote chance that Commander Neuerburg's diary survived and lies buried in silt and rubble. Were that diary to be recovered with its writing intact, history would have a first-person insight into the boat's doomed patrol.

The technology of deep scuba diving has evolved since Chatterton and Kohler identified *U-869.* Today, perhaps 95 percent of deep-wreck divers breathe trimix, the blended gas believed by many in the early 1990s to be voodoo. About half of deep-wreck divers have abandoned their open-circuit gear—the decades-old tank-and-regulator combination—in favor of the rebreather, a smaller, computer-controlled device that recycles exhaled air. Rebreathers make very deep dives possible by obviating the need to carry several tanks of decompression gas. They remain, however, more unreliable than open-circuit systems. It is thought that more than a dozen divers worldwide have died using rebreathers. Chatterton was one of the first to adopt the new technology. Kohler has stuck with his open-circuit gear.

In 1997, less than a month after he identified *U-869,* Chatterton and Kathy divorced. A year later, as a member of an elite expedition to Greece, Chatterton became the first person ever to dive HMHS *Britannic,* the sister ship to the *Titanic,* using a rebreather. As part of an October 2000 mission to the Black Sea sponsored by Yad Vashem, the Israeli Holocaust museum, and the U.S. Holocaust

Memorial Museum, he searched for the *Struma,* an overflowing refugee ship on which 768 people—mostly Romanian Jews—lost their lives fleeing persecution in 1942.

In November 2000, PBS's *Nova* series aired *Hitler's Lost Sub,* a documentary about the mystery U-boat. The program became one of *Nova*'s highest-rated episodes ever. The same month, Chatterton was diagnosed with metastasized squamous cell carcinoma of the tonsil, likely a result of his exposure to Agent Orange in Vietnam. He was back diving shipwrecks by May of the next year. On September 11, 2001, as terrorist-hijacked planes crashed into the World Trade Center towers, Chatterton was overseeing a commercial dive job under the World Financial Center, directly across the street from Tower One. He and his divers escaped the area without injury.

In January 2002, Chatterton married Carla Madrigal, his girlfriend of three years. The couple wed and honeymooned in Thailand, then moved to a beachfront home on the New Jersey shore. In September 2002, Chatterton quit commercial diving after a twenty-year career to pursue a history degree and teaching certificate at Kean University in Union, New Jersey. After graduation, he hopes to teach high school or college history. Chatterton and Kohler remain close friends and still dine together at Scotty's. By May 2003, Chatterton's cancer was in remission. In July 2003, he began hosting *Deepsea Detectives,* a program about shipwrecks, for the History Channel. Kohler even cohosted on several episodes.

Chatterton's involvement with *U-869* largely ended the day he identified the wreck. Unlike Kohler, he felt no pressing obligation to find the crewmen's families or to deliver news of their loved ones' fates. "I cared about those things," Chatterton says. "But they were in Richie's heart. There was no one in the world who should have done that besides Richie."

The first person Kohler called after he and Chatterton identified *U-869* was Tina Marks, his girlfriend. She had believed in him, understood his feelings of obligation to the crewmen and their families, and supported his diving. The couple grew closer. She became pregnant. Tina, however, was being harassed by a former boyfriend who begged her to return to him. She refused. One day in 1998, when Tina was eight months pregnant with Kohler's child, the man showed up at her door, shot her with a nine-millimeter pistol, then shot himself. The police found both of them lying dead inside the residence. In a moment, Kohler's love and future had disappeared.

As it had for years, diving served as his salvation. In 1999, he became co-head of a British-American expedition to identify previously discovered World War I and World War II U-boats sunk in the English Channel. Of twelve target boats, the team identified four. In the fall of that year, Kohler opened a second branch of Fox Glass, in Baltimore. His son, Richie, and daughter, Nikki, who continue to live with him, became honor-roll students.

Kohler remains a voracious reader of history, though he says he reads differently since his quest to identify U-869. "In the back of my mind I question a little of everything," Kohler says. "To me, that makes history even more interesting."

Kohler's involvement with U-869 entered a new phase after he and Chatterton identified the wreck. In 1997, he set out to find the crewmen's families and deliver them news of their loved ones' fates. With help from Kirk Wolfinger and Rush DeNooyer of Lone Wolf Pictures (who directed the Nova special), and from the German media giant Spiegel, which had begun work on a television documentary about the divers and U-869, he found contact information for Barbara Bowling, the half sister of Otto Brizius, at seventeen the youngest of U-869's crewmen. He also found Martin Horenburg's daughter.

Bowling, it turned out, had been living for nearly twenty years in Maryland. She and Otto shared the same father, a man who had spoken lovingly of Otto since Barbara had been a baby. All her life, Bowling had grown up admiring and loving this brother she had never known, always believing he lay at the ocean's bottom off Gibraltar. When Kohler visited Bowling at her home he could hardly believe his eyes. Her son, Mac, was the image of Otto, whose Kriegsmarine photos hung proudly in her house. Bowling, a fluent German speaker, agreed to help Kohler with his further search for family members.

Horenburg's daughter was less eager to speak to Kohler. Her mother had remarried after U-869's loss, and her stepfather had raised her as his own. Out of respect to this man, she preferred not to pursue contact with Kohler. Through an intermediary, she expressed gratitude to the divers and supplied them with several photos of her father. Chatterton took the knife off his desktop—a knife that had spoken to him for seven years—carefully packed the artifact, and drove it to the post office. A week later, the knife belonged to Martin Horenburg's daughter.

For a time, Kohler found himself frustrated in his efforts to locate more families. He focused on his personal life and began dating Carrie Bassetti, an executive for a New Jersey pharmaceutical company and the woman who would later become his wife. He had met Bassetti on a wreck-diving trip aboard the *Seeker*, and was moved not just by her passion for diving, but by her innate sense of adventure and old-school appetite for living. By 2001, he had secured excellent contacts with crewmen's families from his source at *Spiegel*. He booked a trip to Germany. He needed to see these relatives in person.

Just before departing for Europe, Kohler chartered a boat and took Bowling and her family to the wreck site. There, he read a short memorial he had written, then splashed into the ocean and affixed a wreath and ribbons to *U-869*. On New Year's Day 2002, accompanied by Bowling as his translator, Kohler landed in Hamburg. He had finally come to do what he had needed to do for years.

Kohler's first appointment was with Hans-Georg Brandt, First Officer Siegfried Brandt's younger brother. Now seventy-one years old and a retired auditor, Hans-Georg waited nervously at his son's home for Kohler's arrival, his son and grandchildren also eager to see the face of one of the divers who had risked his life to find Siggi. Kohler knocked. Hans-Georg, dressed for the occasion in fine tan slacks, a brown cardigan sweater, and a tie, opened the door. For a moment, the men just looked each other over. Then Hans-Georg stepped forward, took Kohler's hand, and spoke in halting English.

"I am deeply touched that you have come. And I am so sorry for what happened to the brave divers who lost their lives on the U-boat. Welcome."

For six hours, Hans-Georg remembered his brother Siggi, a brother he loved today as much as he had at thirteen when Siggi showed him the secrets of his U-boat and allowed him to look through its periscope out into the world. The conversation was emotional and painful for Hans-Georg at times. At the day's end, Hans-Georg thanked Kohler again and helped him find his coat.

"I brought you something," Kohler said. He reached into his briefcase. A moment later he produced a metal schematic he had recently recovered from U-869's electric motor room.

"You were probably in this room when you visited your brother," Kohler said.

Hans-Georg took the schematic and stared at the metal, at its writing and rust. For several minutes, he could not break his gaze from the artifact. Finally, he began tracing his fingers along its edges and over its crusty surface.

"I can't believe it," he said. "I will save this forever."

The next morning, Kohler and Bowling drove several miles outside Hamburg to meet with a sixty-year-old surgeon. The man, thin, tall, and handsome, welcomed the Americans into his home. He introduced himself as Jürgen Neuerburg, the son of U-869's commander, Helmuth Neuerburg.

Jürgen could produce no memories of his father, as he'd been just three years old when U-869 was lost. But he remembered well his mother's stories, and the fondness and love with which she'd told them. For hours, while his wife listened closely, he shared these stories with Kohler, showing dozens of photographs and diary entries in between.

"Since I was a child, I believed my father had been lost off Gibraltar," Jürgen said. "When I learned that divers had found the boat off the coast of New Jersey, I was very surprised. But in the end it did not change how I felt. I suspect it might have shocked my mother, such a revelation after so many years of believing the official version of events. For this reason, I'm happy she never found out about it. She loved him dearly. She never remarried."

Kohler asked Jürgen if his father had siblings. Indeed, his father had an older brother, Friedhelm. Kohler asked if Jürgen might provide a telephone number for Friedhelm. Jürgen gave him an old number.

"I don't even know if he's still alive," Jürgen said. "Sadly, we have fallen out of touch."

Jürgen and his wife thanked Kohler for his efforts and asked him to thank Chatterton when he returned to New Jersey. That night at the hotel, Kohler and Bowling dialed the number. An elderly woman answered. Bowling introduced herself as the sister of one of *U-869*'s crewmen. The woman said she would be happy to bring her husband to the phone.

For the next hour, eighty-six-year-old Friedhelm Neuerburg remembered his brother, Helmuth.

"When I close my eyes and picture my brother today," Friedhelm said, "I see him doing his duty. I think he had a premonition that he wasn't coming back. He did his duty."

In the morning, Kohler and Bowling drove from Hamburg to Berlin. That evening, Kohler met with forty-year-old Dr. Axel Niestlé, the head of a private engineering firm that works on waste-disposal projects. Niestlé's doctorate, earned in water-resources science, was based largely on work he did in North Africa. In his spare time, as a sort of hobby, Niestlé had made himself the world's foremost authority on the reassessment of U-boat losses. It was Niestlé who, in 1994, had thought to look at the intercepted radio messages between *U-869* and U-boat Control, an idea that had occurred to no one else in the world for history's certainty that *U-869* lay sunk off Gibraltar. He'd communicated his findings in a written report to Robert Coppock at the British Ministry of Defence, who'd then relayed the information to Chatterton and Kohler via letter. During their meeting, Kohler marveled not just at the depth of Niestlé's knowledge but at his passion for the subject. He asked Niestlé why he wasn't teaching at a university.

"U-boats are my avocation," he said. "Perhaps it would be boring if I were to earn money from it. It's the detective's way of treating these matters that moves me. Once you find out history is wrong, once you start investigating it and, with some luck, correcting it, that is satisfaction enough."

The next day, Kohler and Bowling took the Berlin subway to the quaint home of an elderly lady. On a mantelpiece in the living room's center were framed photos of her children and one of a young, handsome man from World War II who seemed to look forward into the ages. The woman introduced herself as Gisela Engelmann. The man in the photo, she said, was her fiancé, Franz Nedel, one of *U-869*'s torpedomen.

For hours, Engelmann told Kohler about tearing the eyes out of Hitler's picture, about climbing the gas lamp and displaying Hitler's photo for all Berlin to see, about the going-away party at which Franz and his fellow crewmen broke down in tears, about how she knows more than ever that there is only one true love in a person's life, and for her that love was Franz.

"My two husbands knew about Franz, of course," she said. "When I would speak of Franz to my children, they would roll their eyes and say, 'Mother, you've told us this story a hundred and fifty times already.'"

As with the Brandts, Engelmann was left to wonder about her loved one's fate long after the war's end. It was not until October 1947 that she received official word that U-869 had been declared a total loss.

"I missed him every day of my life," she told Kohler. "I have his photograph in my bedroom, and I have looked at it every day, through two marriages and four children, since I waved good-bye to him."

Kohler had one more appointment before flying back to New Jersey. He and Bowling flew to Munich, rented a car, and drove west through miles of breathtaking, snow-covered rural landscape. Kohler exited at the small town of Memmingen and followed his directions. A few minutes later, he found himself in the city center, a place of winding streets, centuries-old buildings, and church spires that reached into the heavens. Memmingen, he thought, was a painting, the storybook Germany that Mr. Segal, the circus strong man, had described to his father.

Kohler maneuvered down narrow side streets until he arrived at one of the town's most ancient homes. He rang the doorbell. A minute later, a handsome and dignified eighty-year-old gentleman opened the door. Dressed in a blue suit and red tie, his cotton-white hair combed perfectly, he looked as if he had been expecting his visitor for years.

"I am Herbert Guschewski," the man said. "I was the radioman aboard U-869. Please welcome to my home."

In his living room, surrounded by his family, Guschewski told Kohler the story of how he had survived U-869.

On a warm November morning in 1944, just days before U-869

was to leave for war, Guschewski found himself feeling ill. When he stepped outside for fresh air, he became dizzy and collapsed, unconscious. Onlookers rushed him to the hospital, where he remained in a coma with a high fever for three days. When he came to, the doctors told him he had contracted pneumonia and pleurisy. Though *U-869* was to depart in hours, he would be forced to remain in intensive care. He was also told he had visitors.

His hospital door opened. Standing before him, holding chocolate, cookies, and flowers, was Commander Neuerburg. Behind him were First Officer Brandt and Chief Engineer Kessler. And behind them were many of the U-boat's crew. Neuerburg approached Guschewski. He wiped the radioman's forehead and stroked his arm.

"You'll be all right, my friend," Neuerburg said.

Brandt stepped forward and took Guschewski's hand.

"Get well, friend," he said, smiling the same smile Guschewski had seen after he'd told Brandt his jokes. "You will pull through."

Kessler came forward, as did Horenburg and the other radiomen. Many had tears in their eyes. They wished Guschewski well.

"It finally came time to say good-bye," Guschewski told Kohler. "I had the feeling that we would not see each other again. When I looked into the eyes of some of my comrades, I could see they thought the same."

Like everyone else, Guschewski had believed that *U-869* had been sunk off Gibraltar. When he'd got word that divers had found the U-boat off New Jersey, he'd contacted *Spiegel*. It was through *Spiegel* that Kohler had come to know of Guschewski.

Kohler stayed for two days. Guschewski spoke for hours about Neuerburg, Brandt, Kessler, and the other men he knew from *U-869*. He recounted the bombing of the barracks in Stettin, singing along to Neuerburg's guitar playing, inadvertently dialing in Radio Calais, Fritz Dagg's ham theft, his friendship with Horenburg. He spoke at length about Brandt's kindness and ready laugh and his willingness, even at age twenty-two, to bear the fear and trembling of others. He told Kohler that he missed his friends.

"It is horrible for me to see the way the boat lies broken in the ocean," Guschewski said. "For more than fifty years I remembered it as new and strong, and I was part of it. Now I look at the film and pictures and see the remains of my comrades. . . . It is very difficult and sad for me to think of it this way.

"I believe in God and an afterlife. It would be wonderful to be reunited with my friends, to see them again, and to see them continue in peace, not in war, not in a time when so many young lives were lost for no reason. I would like to see them like that."

After a second day of conversation, Kohler and Guschewski rose and shook hands. Kohler's flight to New Jersey departed in just a few hours, and Guschewski, an esteemed town councillor, had a meeting that evening. Each had more questions for the other. Each promised another visit so that the questions would not go unanswered for long.

As Kohler reached for his coat, Guschewski made a request.

"Might it be possible to send me something from the boat?" Guschewski asked. "Anything would do. Anything I could touch."

"I would be happy to," Kohler said. "I will send you something the moment I return home." He already knew what he would send—a five-by-six-inch plaque from the emergency life raft canister explaining that item's operation.

"That would mean very much to me," Guschewski said. He waved good-bye to Kohler and closed the door.

As Kohler walked toward his car, he felt the bands of his obligation loosen. No one should lie anonymously at the bottom of the ocean. A person's family needs to know where their loved one lies.

It had grown colder outside since Kohler had arrived. He reached for his car keys. Guschewski pushed open his front door and walked into the winter. He was not wearing a coat. He moved toward Kohler and put his arms around the diver.

"Thank you for caring," Guschewski said. "Thank you for coming here."

	U 869	T	(56 + 1)

Kommandant: KptLt. Helmut Neuerburg

am 28.2.1945 im Mittelatlantik auf 34°30' N und 08°13' W versenkt

FkMt	Bienentreu	Mathias	04.12.21
MaschMt	Böhm	Otto	30.03.23
OLt	Brandt	Siegfried	19.06.22
MaschOGfr	Breit	Wilhelm	18.12.24
MaschOGfr	Brems	Ewald	25.03.24
MechGfr	Brizius	Otto	25.02.26
MaschMt	Dagg	Fritz	28.01.20
MaschOGfr	Dietmayer	Eduard	30.01.25
MaschGfr	Dietz	Hans	17.05.25
MaschMt	Dölcher	Karl	27.07.21
OBtsMt	Drabhoff	Walter	18.06.20
MaschOGfr	Dreyer	Karl-Heinz	13.09.24
MtrHGfr	Eder	Max	08.08.22
MaschMt	Eigenbrodt	Karl	27.12.21
MarSt Arzt Dr.	Esau	Ernst-Christian	28.12.13
FkOGfr	Gehlsen	Richard	20.10.24
MaschOGfr	Geißel	Otto	28.03.25
MaschOGfr	Geratzki	Gerhard	13.02.25
MechGfr	Gradl	Kurt	29.04.25
BtsMt	Grosser	Helmut	30.03.23
MechHGfr	Grunert	Hugo	01.10.19
MechOGfr	Häselbarth	Karl	06.02.22
MtrOGfr	Haun	Erwin	04.05.22
OMasch	Hentschel	Arthur	13.10.18
MaschOGfr	Hirsch	Horst	04.04.25
MtrGfr	Hitze	Heinz	04.02.25
FkMstr	Horenburg	Martin	01.10.19
OLt (Ing)	Keßler	Ludwig	10.06.13
MtrHGfr	Kischka	Rafael	25.09.19
OMasch	Koch	Robert	06.09.13
MaschOGfr	Kornweih	Helmut	29.01.24
MechMt	Kühnhold	Oskar	28.02.23
OStrm	Lenk	Heinz	08.02.17
Mtr	Mehlig	Paul	21.09.19
FkOGfr	Mehnert	Rolf	19.08.24
MtrOGfr	Meineke	Georg	14.04.25
MaschMt	Mocker	Erich	01.06.23
MtrOGfr	Moosmann	Fritz	15.06.25
MtrOGfr	Nedel	Franz	22.08.24
KptLt	Neuerburg	Helmut	25.08.17
MaschOGfr	Nolte	Willi	23.10.24
MtrGfr	Oßwald	Heinz	07.10.25
BtsMt	Plath	Leo	04.08.19
MtrOGfr	Reber	Hans-Georg	09.05.21
MaschOGfr	Rothsprak	Willi	26.01.21
MtrOGfr	Schnick	Willy	05.11.25
MtrOGfr	Seefeldt	Willi	18.04.19
OStrm	Stockhorst	Wilhelm	01.10.20
MaschOGfr	Tabel	Wilhelm	07.02.23
MaschOGfr	Tölke	Erich	06.10.10
FkOGfr	Uhlarsch	Johann	23.05.25
OMaschMt	Verhülsdonk	Heinrich	01.02.20
MaschOGfr	Voigt	Heinz	05.04.23
MtrOGfr	Volderauer	Vinzenz	13.04.24
MaschMt	Wernicke	Günter	18.10.22
MtrGfr	Zander	Peter	21.03.24

Einzelverlust

MechGfr(A)	Schmelzer	Richard	05.12.24

U-869 crew list.

Spare-parts box recovered by Chatterton from the electric motor room. Note the identifying number in the upper left corner of the box's tag—the number that finally identified the wreck and solved one of the last mysteries of World War II.

Martin Horenburg.

Martin Horenburg aboard *U-869*.

Herbert Guschewski, radioman, *U-869*.

Neuerburg (*far right*) saluting the ship's ensign after commissioning the boat on January 26, 1944.

Helmuth Neuerburg, commander, *U-869*.

Neuerburg used leaves to take his two-year-old son, Jürgen, for sail-boat rides and to bounce his infant daughter, Jutta, on his knee. Just before *U-869*'s commissioning, he spoke to his brother, Friedhelm. This time, he mentioned nothing of the Nazis. He simply looked Friedhelm in the eye and said, "I'm not coming back."

Siegfried Brandt, first officer, *U-869*.

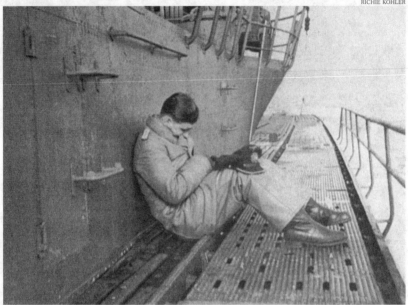

When Brandt's brother Hans-Georg asked their mother why she wept at this picture of Siegfried sleeping aboard *U-869*, she told him that it was the way Siggi was sitting—it reminded her of a child, a baby, and even though Siggi was a proud warrior, she could still see her little boy in that photograph.

Franz Nedel, torpedoman, *U-869*.

Gisela Engelmann, fiancée of Franz Nedel.

U-869 at sea during training. Note the Olympic rings on the conning tower, which indicates a submarine commanded by a graduate of the naval class of 1936, the year of the Berlin games.

Richie Kohler and
Gisela Engelmann,
Berlin, January
2002.

Crew of *U-869*, after commissioning, January 26, 1944. The three officers stand in
the bottom row on the right: Siegfried Brandt is on the far right, Helmuth
Neuerburg is to his right, and Ludwig Kessler is third from the end.

John Chatterton and Richie Kohler, the two divers around whom this story revolves, were my business partners in the writing of this book. They gave me full access to their files, photographs, videotapes, notes, and dive logs. I spent hundreds of hours interviewing Chatterton and Kohler: at their homes in New Jersey, by phone, by conference call, on the dive boat *Seeker*, while cruising the autobahn with Kohler in Germany, while crouching inside the captured German submarine *U-505* with Chatterton in Chicago. Their accounts of the quest to identify the mystery U-boat—both in the water and on land—were the foundation upon which this book was written. Each served as the first and most critical check on the other. Upon completing the book, I asked Chatterton and Kohler to review the manuscript for accuracy. Neither was allowed editorial control or input—a condition to which each had agreed before we became partners. Any manuscript changes they suggested were strictly of a technical nature.

For accounts of Chatterton's and Kohler's in-water exploration of the U-boat, I relied frequently on their recollection of events; deep-shipwreck diving is a solitary sport in which memory is often the only witness. I viewed videotapes of their dives on those occasions when videotape was shot. I studied photographs of the wreck, and consulted Chatterton's and Kohler's handwritten dive logs. I interviewed fourteen divers who accompanied them on overnight trips to the wreck, including nine of the original members of the team that had gone searching for the mystery set of numbers secured from the fishing boat captain by Bill Nagle.

The wreck came to life for me through a drawing, reproduced here in the frontispiece, made by Captain Dan Crowell, the current owner of the *Seeker* and a longtime diver of the U-boat. His rendering, an amazing work of memory and experience, remained taped to my desk throughout the writing of this book. It is considered by most who have dived the wreck to be a small masterpiece. Several divers, including Steve Gatto, Brian Skerry, Christina Young, and Kevin Brennan, shot excellent underwater photographs of the wreck, which helped me to envision the scenes described to me by Chatterton and Kohler. I also studied photos, diagrams, and plans of Type IX U-boats in various books, the most useful being *Vom Original zum Modell: Uboottyp IX C* by Fritz Kohl and Axel Niestlé. Equally valuable was the illustrated tour of *U-869* provided by PBS on their Web site for *Hitler's Lost Sub,* the *Nova* documentary on the mystery wreck (pbs.org/wgbh/nova/lostsub). On numerous occasions, I toured the captured *U-505* at Chicago's Museum of Science and Industry; each of those visits gave me a tangible feel for the Type IX U-boat, exactly the kind discovered by the divers in 1991.

I came to know the dive boat *Seeker* personally. Captain Dan Crowell showed me the vessel's corners and contours while it was dry-docked in Brielle, New Jersey, then invited me on an overnight trip—to also hunt mystery numbers—to a location about seventy miles offshore. The seas were constantly violent and I was tossed from my bunk several times; there is no more immediate way to understand a dive boat's character, foibles, and nobility than to spend twenty-four hours aboard it in the middle of an angry Atlantic.

Many of the stories about deep-wreck diving contained in this book were told to me by Chatterton and Kohler, as well as by other divers, boat captains, and witnesses. Because the sport is so dangerous and has so few participants (probably just a few hundred in the United States), many of its stories remain oral history. Whenever possible, these stories were checked with the principals involved. Occasionally, witnesses provided slightly different accounts of events, especially when their stories were of close calls or fatalities and they had been panicked, distracted, or distressed. Those inconsistencies were slight; when they occurred, I used the consensus version of events to conclude, say, that a diver had been underwater for ten minutes rather than twelve. For the deaths of the *Texas Tower* diver and of Joe Drozd, Chatterton was present and a witness to events. For the death of Steve Feldman, I interviewed nearly all of the divers present, including Feldman's dive partner Paul Skibinski, Doug Roberts and Kevin Brennan, who were in the water and witnessed much of the unfolding disaster, and John Hildemann and Mark McMahon, who did the dangerous sand sweeps searching for Feldman on the ocean's bottom. I also inspected the written accounts of the incident provided to the Coast Guard by each diver after returning to shore. For George Place's close call, I interviewed Place and Howard Klein, the captain of the *Eagle's Nest,* who set out to rescue his stricken diver. Kohler was present and a witness to that event as well. For Dr. Lewis Kohl's close call, I interviewed Kohl, his dive partner John Yurga, and Chatterton and Kohler; all were present and witnessed the event. For the deaths of Chris and Chrissy Rouse, I relied on interviews with Chatterton, Kohler, Yurga, and Crowell, all of whom were present and participated in the rescue attempt and subsequent recovery of equipment. I also read Bernie Chowdhury's book, *The Last Dive: A Father and Son's Fatal Descent into the Ocean's Depths,* from HarperCollins, which recounts the Rouse tragedy and is a very good account of the dangers of deep diving.

I gleaned insight into the culture of wreck diving in the American Northeast by spending time with and interviewing divers and boat captains. Bucky McMahon's story, "Everest at the Bottom of the Sea," published in the July 2000 issue of *Esquire,* was exceedingly useful to me and remains perhaps the best account ever written of *Andrea Doria* diving and the characters who challenge that legendary wreck. Kevin F. McMurray's book *Deep Descent: Adventure and Death Diving the* Andrea Doria, from Pocket Books, was also helpful to me in digesting the long and dangerous history of the *Doria* and the psyches of those who dive it.

The physiology of deep-water scuba diving was made understandable to me by several books, the most useful of which was Tim Ecott's *Neutral Buoyancy: Adventures in a Liquid World,* from Atlantic Monthly Press. Ecott writes beautifully, not just about diving physiology, but about the transcendent potential of scuba exploration. His work was inspiring. Physiologist R. W. Bill Hamilton was patient with me in explaining some technical aspects of deep scuba.

The life and times of Bill Nagle were described to me by Chatterton, Kohler, Yurga, Crowell, and Andrew Nagle. Nearly every diver and boat captain I interviewed had something to say about Nagle's legend. Captain Skeets Frink was very helpful to me in explaining how Nagle came to possess the numbers to the mystery wreck.

I learned about Atlantic Wreck Divers history and culture from Kohler, one of the group's original members, as well as from Pete Guglieri, John Lachenmeyer, and Pat Rooney. I talked to numerous sources about the age-old rivalries between dive boat captains; McMurray's *Deep Descent* and Gary Gentile's *The Lusitania Controversies—Book Two: Dangerous Descents into Shipwrecks and Law,* from Gary Gentile Productions, were also useful to me along those lines. For information on Steve Feldman, I interviewed his dive partner Paul Skibinski, as well as his friends Tommy Cross, Marty Dick, John Hopkins, Andrew Ross, and boat captain Paul Hepler. For the lives of Chris and Chrissy Rouse, Chowdhury's *The Last Dive* was quite interesting. For the lives of Chatterton and Kohler, I spoke to their ex-wives, current wives, friends, and family. For Chatterton's Vietnam experience, I interviewed John Lacko, with whom Chatterton saw combat, and Dr. Norman Sakai, a battalion surgeon who served with Chatterton. Charles Kinney, a former Vietnam medic and author, provided an enlightening overview of the medic's place in the Vietnam War.

I relied on several sources to confirm the process and substance of Chatterton's and Kohler's research. Their files contained copies of many of the original historical documents they used to pursue the identity of the mystery U-boat, including attack reports, analyses of antisubmarine action, radio-intercept intelligence summaries, translations of U-boat Control diary entries, and incident reports. In rare instances in which the divers gleaned information from historical documents they had not or could not have copied, I used books and consulted with experts to confirm the information. Invaluable to me in this endeavor (and many others) was Clay Blair's superbly researched and astonishingly complete two-volume set, *Hitler's U-boat War*, published by Random House. In these volumes, Blair includes information from both the German and Allied sides, which is not true of every book on the subject, while covering the operational, technical, and intelligence aspects of the U-boat war with rare readability and insight. The set was the single most useful written resource I used while writing *Shadow Divers*. On countless occasions, German naval researcher Axel Niestlé confirmed or refined the accuracy of Chatterton's and Kohler's research. I inspected dozens of letters between the divers and various sources with whom they corresponded about the mystery U-boat, many of which helped me understand the mood, evolution, and maturity of their research. At the Naval Historical Center in Washington, D.C., I interviewed Dean Allard, Bernard Cavalcante, William Dudley, and Kathleen Lloyd, all of whom spoke to me about the divers' methods, resources, approach, and character. Timothy Mulligan at the National Archives in Washington was similarly helpful. On the subject of the Civil Air Patrol and its possible role in the sinking of the mystery sub, I spoke to Lt. Col. Gregory Weidenfeld of that organization, and also read his monograph on the topic, *The Search for the Haggin-Farr Sub Kill*. On the subject of blimps and U-boats, I interviewed Gordon Vaeth, former intelligence officer for the Atlantic Fleet airships during World War II, and benefited greatly from his book, *Blimps & U-Boats: U.S. Navy Airships in the Battle of the Atlantic*, published by Naval Institute Press. The personal letters of U-boat ace Karl-Friedrich Merten, written to Chatterton in the early stages of the divers' research, helped me understand that officer's opinion about the mystery wreck. Most newspaper accounts cited in the book were saved by Chatterton and Kohler and kept in scrapbooks, and were easily checked. Finally, I studied the divers' extensive research notes, which chronicled not just their findings, but often their mind-sets. In very rare cases, where opinions in published sources or between experts conflicted, I relied on Blair's *Hitler's U-boat War*.

To learn the history of the U-boat war, no source was more valuable to me than Blair's books. I also relied regularly on a Web site—uboat.net—the best Internet resource for information on U-boat history, commanders, the fates of various submarines, and much more. It is virtually impossible to research U-boats without utilizing this excellent, thorough, and well-designed resource. The transcript to *Nova*'s program *Hitler's Lost Sub*, available at the aforementioned PBS Web site, was also useful for its interviews with various scholars and U-boat veterans. For the histories and fates of individual U-boats (other than *U-869*), Blair's books were a primary source, as was Niestlé's *German U-boat Losses During World War II: Details of Destruction*, from Naval Institute Press. When I needed information on U-boats that I could not find, I called or wrote to Niestlé, who was always helpful. Statistics on U-boats and U-boat losses vary widely among the many books and articles published on the subject; my figures were taken from the above-mentioned book by Niestlé. A German private researcher, Niestlé is among the most original minds writing about U-boats, and continues to work at the forefront of reexamining U-boat losses. His book, in addition to providing many of the most current U-boat statistics, also includes an excellent explanation of postwar assessment mistakes—the very kinds of mistakes that made the mystery at the core of this book so difficult to solve.

For information on the lives and times of U-boat crewmen, I constantly referred to Timothy Mulligan's excellent book *Neither Sharks nor Wolves: The Men of Nazi Germany's U-boat Arm, 1939–1945*, from Naval Institute Press. The book, set against the context of the larger war effort and the changing fate of Germany, is a classic overview of the men who fought the U-boat war. Mulligan, an archivist who specializes in captured German and World War II–era records, based much of his research on surveys of over a thousand U-boat veterans. I read several books by Jak P. Mallman Showell, many of which can be commended for painting incisive pictures of life aboard the U-boats, the command structure of the U-boat force, and the men who manned these vessels. The most useful to me among them was *U-boats Under the Swastika*, published by Naval Institute Press; at just 132 pages, it provided a fine and easily digestible primer. I spent invaluable time in Toronto with Werner Hirschmann, the former chief engineer of U-190. In a few days with Mr. Hirschmann, I learned more about U-boat life than I might have in years of reading.

In learning about the history, fate, and crew of U-869, I benefited greatly from the following sources:

For the life and career of commander Helmuth Neuerburg, I inspected his military records and interviewed his son, Jürgen, and brother, Friedhelm, in Germany. (Neuerburg's first name is spelled in various ways by various sources; I used "Helmuth," as that is how he appeared to sign his own name on his military records.)

For the life and career of First Officer Siegfried Brandt, I inspected his military records, interviewed his brother Hans-Georg Brandt, and his friends, Clemens Borkert and Heinz Schley, in Germany.

For the life and career of torpedoman Franz Nedel, I interviewed his fiancée, Gisela Engelmann, in Germany.

I devoted several days in Germany to interviewing Herbert Guschewski, the former radioman on U-869. It was through Guschewski that I gleaned insight into the sub's crew and officers, especially Neuerburg, Brandt, and Martin Horenburg, the U-boat's senior radioman. Many stories and details of U-869's training came from these interviews with Mr. Guschewski, as well as from the boat's training diary. General information about U-boat training, some of which informed the chapters on U-869's training, was taken from several books, most notably Mulligan's *Neither Sharks nor Wolves,* as well as from my interviews with Werner Hirschmann.

I was able to accurately envision the crew of U-869, as well as the submarine itself, thanks to dozens of photographs of the men and their boat, some of which were taken by the Kriegsmarine, others of which were given to Chatterton and Kohler by family members of the crewmen and by Mr. Guschewski.

I was able to reconstruct U-869's doomed patrol thanks in part to Niestlé's 1994 breakthrough monograph, *The Loss of U-869.* It was this written report that changed the thinking about the fate of U-869 and (indirectly) advanced the divers' efforts to identify the mystery wreck. Also invaluable was Blair's summary of the patrol in volume 2 of *Hitler's U-boat War*. Text from Allied intelligence analysis of radio intercepts between *U-869* and U-boat Control were taken from copies of those analyses. Over the course of a lengthy in-person interview in Germany, Niestlé helped me to envision the most likely scenario to explain and describe *U-869*'s final moments.

Finally, I accompanied Kohler to Germany in 2002; my account of his trip is taken from my own experience.

ACKNOWLEDGMENTS

The author is grateful for the kind help and support of the following people:

Heather Schroder at International Creative Management. A writer dreams of finding an agent like Heather. She is at once a fierce and tireless advocate, a lover of great story, an exceptional and eager reader, and a lovely person. I cannot imagine a journey without her. Thanks also to Chrissy Rikkers of ICM for reading my work and for her cheerful patience, and to Margot Meyers of ICM for her encouragement, good judgment, and confidence.

Jonathan Karp, my editor at Random House. In ways, Jon understood this book before I did. He distilled the essence of this story, and urged me to bet on it, and for that I will be forever grateful. To this day, I remain the lucky beneficiary of his storytelling instincts, and continue to admire his gracious and unhurried way and gentlemanly demeanor. While researching this book in Toronto, I had a short telephone conversation with Jon in which he outlined his conception of great narrative nonfiction. I have thought differently about writing ever since. Thanks also at Random House to: Jonathan Jao and Jillian Quint, assistants to Jonathan Karp, for reading and commenting on my work; Dennis Ambrose, my thoughtful production editor (and a scuba diver to boot); Bonnie Thompson, an extraordinary copyeditor and a true artist at her craft; Amelia Zalcman, for her fine review of my manuscript; and also to Gina Centrello, Elizabeth McGuire, Anthony Ziccardi, Carol Schneider, Thomas Perry, Sally Marvin, Ivan Held, Ann Godoff, Gene Mydlowski, Kate Kim-Centra, Claire Tisne, Nicole Bond, Rachel Bernstein, Susanne Gutermuth, Erich Schoeneweiss, Stacey Ornstein, Bridget Piekarz, Tom Nevins, Jaci Updike, Don Weisburg, Martin McGrath, Allyson Pearl, Sandy Pollack, Liz Willner, David Thompson, John Groton, Andrew Weber, David Underwood, Janet Cooke, Peter Olson, and Kelle Ruden.

John Chatterton and Richie Kohler. Once in his life, if he's lucky, a writer has the chance to work with a true pioneer. In Chatterton and Kohler, I got to work with two. Each is exceptionally bright, self-critical, and descriptive, a gift from the heavens for an author. And each was endlessly generous with his time, granting me hundreds of hours of interviews in person, over the phone, aboard the dive boat *Seeker*, on the autobahn in Germany, and even while crouching between compartments inside *U-505*, the captured German submarine on display in Chicago. I could phone either of them at midnight and each understood instinctively why I had to know right away rather than the following morning. In knowing these men, I feel closer to understanding what it means to be a seeker. Thanks also to Chatterton's wife, Carla Madrigal, and Kohler's wife, Carrie Bassetti, two wonderful people who indulged my demands on their husbands' time with kindness and hospitality.

Ron Bernstein at ICM, who intuitively understood the book and spoke so eloquently on its behalf. Elizabeth Gabler and Rodney Ferrell at Fox 2000 Pictures, who believed in *Shadow Divers* from the start and who connected with it in just the way I dreamed readers would.

Annette Kurson, among the finest writers I know, who tirelessly read and edited my manuscript, and who taught me years ago that good writing derives from good thinking.

Ken Kurson, my brother, my best friend, and the greatest champion a person could hope for in life, and also his family, Becky, Steve, and Karen. The Glovers—Jane, Larry, Mike, and Sam—for their encouragement, enthusiasm, and belief in me always. And the memory of Jack D. Kurson, the best storyteller I've ever known.

Axel Niestlé, an original scholar and thinker, and a true gentleman. Dr. Niestlé always was gracious and precise when I called upon his U-boat expertise. It is an honor to know such a person.

John Yurga, an extraordinary deep-wreck diver who was invaluable in the effort to discover the identity of the mystery U-boat. His insight, command of detail, dedication, and intellect—all in a soft-spoken and humble package—were inspiring.

Werner Hirschmann, chief engineer of U-190. No one speaks more insightfully and poetically about life aboard a U-boat than does Hirschmann. He received me at his home in Toronto, drove me in his vintage orange Karmann Ghia, and told beautiful and poignant stories about life as a U-boat officer. His account of the homesick crewmen adopting a fly aboard his submarine—and then nurturing and loving that fly—continues to linger with me.

In the United States, Captain Dan Crowell, Barbara Bowling, and Tim Requarth were exceedingly generous in lending their time, expertise, and reflection.

In Germany, these people opened their homes and memories to me: Hans-Georg Brandt and the Brandt family; Gisela Engelmann; Michael Foedrowitz; Friedhelm Neuerburg; and Jürgen Neuerburg. And special thanks to Herbert Guschewski, who devoted long days to recounting memories that have, for decades, been both painful and sacred.

The following people kindly granted me interviews, all of which made this book better and more complete:

Dean Allard, Bernard Cavalcante, William Dudley, R. W. Bill Hamilton, Hank Keatts, Kathleen Lloyd, Timothy Mulligan, Gordon Vaeth, and Lt. Col. Gregory Weidenfeld.

Captain Sal Arena, Steve Bielenda, Dr. Fred Bove, Kevin Brennan, Kip Cochran, Harry Cooper, Captain Skeets Frink, Lloyd Garrick, Steve Gatto, Pete Guglieri, John Hildemann, Jon Hulburt, Captain Howard Klein, Dr. Lewis Kohl, John Lachenmeyer, Mark McMahon, John Moyer, Ed Murphy, Andrew Nagle, Tom Packer, Captain Billy Palmer, George Place, Captain Paul Regula, Doug Roberts, Pat Rooney, Susan Rouse, Dick Shoe, Brian Skerry, and Paul Skibinski.

Patricia Arison, Felicia Becker, Lisa Biggins, Clemens Borkert,

Kathy Chatterton, Bernie Chowdhury, Tommy Cross, Don David-son, Bill Delmonico, Marty Dick, Captain Paul Hepler, Hank Hoke, John Hopkins, Charles Kinney, Fran Kohler, Frank Kohler, Frankie Kohler, John Kohler, Richard Kohler Sr., John Lacko, Ruby Miller, Paul Murphy, Inge Oberschelp, Andrew Ross, Dr. Norman Sakai, Heinz Schley, and the excellent filmmakers Rush DeNooyer and Kirk Wolfinger of Lone Wolf Pictures.

These men have believed in me and made me a better writer: David Granger, Peter Griffin, and Mark Warren of *Esquire*; Joseph Epstein of Northwestern University; and Richard Babcock of *Chicago* magazine. Without Babcock's generosity and patience, I could not have written this book.

I cannot adequately thank the Wisniewski family—Kazimiera, Eugeniusz, and Paula—for providing our family the love and care that allowed me the time and peace of mind to complete this work.

And, finally, thanks to my son, Nate, whose natural joy and sweetness inspires me every day, and to my wife, Amy Kurson, the smartest and kindest person I know. In the midst of raising a new baby and conducting her own demanding career, Amy talked for hours with me about the story and gave me endless space and sup-port, always with a smile. It is through her that I see good in the world I do not otherwise see.

INDEX

ROBERT KURSON

SHADOW DIVERS

A READER'S GUIDE

> To print out this or other
> Random House Reader's Guides,
> visit us at www.atrandom.com/rgg

BY ROBERT KURSON

Robert Kurson: Let's start with the topic of Bill Nagle. He was a very important figure in the early part of the book and, I know, a very important person to both of you. I wonder now, nearly ten years after his death, if you guys miss Bill Nagle.

Richie Kohler: I'd have to say absolutely, Rob. To me, Bill epitomized what I loved about wreck diving. He knew how to party, he had a good time on the boat. And not only that, he embraced the challenges of pushing beyond. He wasn't happy with the mediocre, with the day trips. He was always looking beyond the horizon. As a matter of fact, in the wheelhouse of his boat he actually had a plaque that said "Set course for the heart of the sun," and that pretty much wrapped up who he was. I miss him.

John Chatterton: I missed Bill Nagle while he was still alive. I mean, here's a guy who I knew as a diver and had a fantastic relationship with. The disease of alcoholism progressed to the point where the last couple of years he was alive I could hardly recognize him. Bill would have really appreciated the eventual identification of the U-boat, how difficult it was. This was exactly the kind of thing that Bill Nagle was all about. Richie, when you talk about Bill Nagle and the wheelhouse—he did have "Set course for the heart of the sun," which was a line from Pink Floyd, but he misspelled "course." It was "c-o-a-r-s-e."

Kohler: You touched on something earlier—that he so much wanted to identify this wreck. You recall how every dive he was just hoping that we were going to have the answer. He was literally hanging over the side of the boat, waiting for us to get up. And remember how angry he got whenever we headed back and we were empty-handed. . . .

Chatterton: Everything that Bill Nagle was about in diving is epitomized by what happened with the U-869.

Kurson: I still can't get over the amount of risk you guys took in pushing toward the solution to this mystery. In hindsight, do either of you regret any of the risks you took?

Chatterton: You know, risk is a huge part of diving. It's the challenge, and challenge somehow, some way, comes down to managing a certain amount of risk. And you definitely arrive at the point where you say, "Well, I learned something from that. Let me not do that again." But you also arrive at points where you say, "This is really the way to go." So it really is about experimenting, about trying new things out, developing new techniques. And you're going to find stuff that works really great, and then you're going to find stuff where you say, "I want to remember this as the textbook definition of what not to do."

Kohler: I would say that John was always more apt to take a chance and put his butt on the line, whereas I took a more pragmatic view. In hindsight, I'd have to say that my dives on air were probably the most dangerous thing that I did on that wreck. Although I would be nervous and my heart would be in my throat making penetrations, I always knew I could close my eyes and literally find my way out. And I held comfort in that belief. I never, ever felt that I would be lost. John has always applied himself to the new technology—How can I do this better? I've always said, "This is what's working, it's been working, I'm safe. I'm going to stay here. I'll let other people take the risks and pave new paths, and then I'll follow in their footsteps."

Chatterton: That's exactly the point. We all work within some sort of comfort zone. It's just that how we set the parameters for that comfort zone is what makes the difference.

Kurson: You know, John, I write about how you were an early adopter of breathing trimix, the so-called voodoo gas of the time, and how Richie was more conservative and waited awhile before he embraced it. Now today I find out that you're using a device called a rebreather to be even more productive in the water, while Richie is refraining from embracing the rebreather. Can you tell me what a rebreather is and why it has been so dangerous? There have been a lot of fatalities with the rebreather lately, haven't there?

Chatterton: Well, sure. A rebreather is a device that recycles your exhaust gases. In other words, instead of exhaling bubbles into the underwater environment, those gases go back through a closed-loop system. You breathe in and you breathe out, but there are no bubbles coming out of the diver. There are, of course, highly technical, automatic versions of rebreathers, and also very basic, manual ones. But typically, either the diver adds or the computer adds small amounts of oxygen to compensate for the oxygen your body is metabolizing, and somewhere else in the loop there is an absorbent that removes the carbon dioxide that your body's creating. You can consume very small amounts of gas as opposed to the really large amounts of gas in open circuit. So, from a logistical perspective, this gives you a huge advantage.

Kurson: But if a lot of guys are dying using it, why are you using it?

Chatterton: Well, a lot of guys die on trimix too. It's the change. It's the road to learning about new technology, so the challenge is definitely there. If you're careless with rebreather technology, it will kill you in a heartbeat.

Kohler: I don't want to interrupt here. You said that a lot of guys die diving trimix. They didn't die because of the trimix. They died because of diving accidents. A lot of the rebreather fatalities were because of an operator or a mechanical error. It's a very complicated piece of plumbing and the more complicated the plumbing, the easier it is to stop it up. When I dive open circuit—that is, basic scuba tanks—whatever I put into that tank is what I am going to breathe. That cannot be said about a rebreather. There are too many variables. There could be diver error. There could be an operator error in regard to what gas you're putting in. If anything stops up that plumbing, you don't know what you're breathing anymore. You could try to monitor it, but as the high rate of fatalities has shown, not all the bugs have been worked out. So I'm still shying away from that technology.

Chatterton: As are a lot of other people. And it reminds me of the villagers gathering in the square with torches, about to burn the heretic.

Kurson: One of the big surprises in the book is your discovery that written history had been wrong and that written history could be fallible. Do either of you view written history differently now because of this experience?

Kohler: Absolutely, especially in regard to U-boat warfare. At the end of the war the assessors really just wanted to go home, and for all those U-boats that were still missing at sea, they just as quickly as possible, willy-nilly, tried to attach a fate to them. And we're not just talking about World War II. We're talking about since the 1990s and prior. But I'm referring mostly to steamships and metal-hold vessels where there will be some remains on the sea floor. There are literally thousands of wreck sites that are just waiting to be discovered, that are unknown. Each discovery will in some way rewrite history.

Chatterton: I think the thing that was most enlightening for me about the entire project was that history is a work in progress. The thing I've come to realize since identifying the submarine is that there are people who really try to control and direct history. Certainly the assessors, as much as they might have wanted to complete their job and go home, didn't have all the cards. The governments that belonged to the Allied front didn't want them to have the information about the Enigma decrypts, so essentially the writing of history was being manipulated by the powers of the time. So now, more than half a century later, we're looking at certain aspects of history and seeing them for the first time.

Kurson: Do either one of you still dive the U-boat wreck? And if not, why not?

Chatterton: I was on the U-boat once since we identified it and that was to put a wreath on the wreck. I feel I've done everything. There's nothing there for me right now. While we were working on it, I wished we could identify it so I didn't have to go back there again. So now that we have identified it, I don't have to.

Kohler: I still make an annual pilgrimage to the wreck. It's like an old friend. I usually muck about in the debris field. I'm kind of hoping that one day I can find and photograph the torpedo. I still like to dive the wreck. It's still a challenging dive. As far as having fun on it and going inside, I don't go inside, I don't look to collect artifacts. I just appreciate aesthetically and appreciate searching around in the sand.

Kurson: John, we talked a lot about your experience in Vietnam as a young man, some of which, I think, was difficult for you to talk about. Was it tough for you to go over that ground, and is it still tough for you to think about those days?

Chatterton: Yeah. I don't wear Vietnam on my sleeve. There was a time when I thought about Vietnam every day, and then I passed that time. I'm glad that I don't have to address it every day. It is difficult for me to separate Vietnam from my personal philosophy on politics, and when I look at where America is today, I do reflect back, not just on my experience in Vietnam, but on our nation's experience in Vietnam. Being interviewed by you was the first time I really sat down and talked about it. Difficult? Yes. But I think that somehow, some way, I survived Vietnam and I came out of it much better than a lot of guys did. I'm sure a lot of guys would just kick me in the ass and say, "Move on, get on with it."

Kurson: Are there still rivalries between dive boats and dive boat captains? That's one of the things that amazed me the most, and I wonder if those feuds still survive to this day?

Kohler: Absolutely. Not only are the old ones still glowing brightly, but some new ones pop up. I think in a small community it's just bound to happen. There are petty rivalries. There are business issues that get challenged. Out with the old, in with the new. As soon as Bill Nagle was dead, I'm positive that Steve Bielenda found someone new to turn his ire against. There are definitely some very hot issues in the Northeast wreck community. When I speak to people from all over the world, I find that this is something that only seems to happen here. Although there are some issues in Europe—in England—and there are some issues in California, there is nothing that matches these blood feuds that are legendary in the wreck diving communities here in the Northeast.

Chatterton: I think it's more important that you are feuding, as opposed to what you're feuding over! That's secondary, really. Yeah, I think there's a lot of that that still goes on. I don't listen to it much anymore, but I'm sure it's still there. I hear about "This guy's mad at that guy" or "Billy put my pigtail in the inkwell," that kind of stuff.

Kurson: Was either one of you surprised by anything you read about the other in the book?

Chatterton: Reading the book, I got a lot of insight into Richie's heritage and how he perceived his link with other Germans. In his mind, no small thing.

Kohler: I came away from reading the book thinking to myself, *This guy's one heroic son of a bitch.* I've known John a long time and I knew he was in 'Nam. I watched him work futilely, trying to resuscitate Chris Rouse. I watched him with a stethoscope around his neck, monitoring the progress of Lew Kohl on the boat after his dirt-dart dive. I knew that he had been a medic in 'Nam. I knew that he had a medical background, and I could see a guy who could be goofy as heck one second turn dead serious about the well-being of another human being the next. But I had no idea until I read about his time in Vietnam—it's not something he ever talked about. And we're talking about a guy who, to my surprise, when he was in a dark part of his life, when his marriage was failing, reached out for me— I never thought he would have. You think that sometimes people don't have secrets. But that was something that I was—I won't say shocked—but I was surprised by, because that obviously had to have a great impact on his life.

Kurson: Richie, it's always been important to you to solve this mystery and identify these men, to give them their names and to give closure to these families in Germany. Are you still in touch with the families, or did you just wrap up your business once the diving was done?

Kohler: I'm going to start back at the beginning. I started diving the boat because I wanted a dish. I wanted an artifact. And what happened was a change that happened so gradually. You never see human remains in shipwrecks. But when you go into the inner compartments of the submarine, you cannot avoid them. They are everywhere. And this started to have an effect on me and somehow, like a shadow in the past, my German heritage started to come in and I felt like I owed these guys something. Once we identified the submarine, we located one person here in the United States—the sister of a crewman. Her name is Barbara Bowling, and her brother, Otto Brizius, was aboard the U-869. I met with her and that was the first time I could physically touch someone alive who had a connection to this boat. And with her we went to Germany and met other family members. To this day I'm still in contact with almost every one of them. I gave every one of them a photograph of the memorial wreath that we put on the wreck. And the survivor, Herbert Guschewski, I still maintain contact with him as well.

Kurson: Is there anything that is still a mystery to you about the U-boat?

Chatterton: Sure. I think you'd have a hard time disputing that it was a T-5 acoustic torpedo that sent it to the bottom. But if she fired a T-5 acoustic torpedo at a target, what was that target?

Kohler: There are a couple of things that haunt me, to which I don't think we'll ever have the answer. The first thing that comes to mind is that, on the upper deck, there was a life-raft canister that was partially opened. And if you looked at this thing you could see that it had butterfly nuts on it and it's not the sort of thing that could have been wrenched open. To me, it implied that there might possibly have been someone who tried to open it. There were other artifacts that were found by John Yurga that were outside on top of the wreck. All these things are mysteries. Was the boat on the surface? Did someone get out? Did someone try to launch a life raft?

Chatterton: Which is why history is a work in progress. You know, maybe some of these things there will be answers to. But the preponderance of them I doubt anyone in our lifetime will answer.

Kurson: What's going to become of this wreck? Will it last forever? Do wrecks deteriorate and how fast do they deteriorate?

Kohler: Everyone knows the story of *Titanic*, and have been amazed by the footage that came back from Dr. Ballard of this somewhat intact bow section sitting on the sea floor. People are amazed by that and think these wrecks will just remain forever like a tomb. But that's not the case. The U-boat is a lot shallower and subjected to storms and conditions and high salinity, and all of that adds up to the fact that the steel hull is rusting at an incredible pace. Not only that, fishing boats are still inadvertently getting their nets and cables on it and are ripping the boat to pieces and dragging off chunks of it. Eventually, it will be nothing more than a rust stain on the sea floor. All wrecks will be reclaimed—and I hate to get all biblical—but dust to dust. I would say in maybe a hundred to two hundred years, there will be nothing but glass and ceramics.

Chatterton: The wreck has changed significantly over the last decade since we first started diving it. The original drawing that Danny Crowell did of the wreck in 1991 is nothing like the way the wreck looks today.

Kurson: John, at one point in the book, at the height of your frustration at not being able to solve the mystery, you went out, and almost in an explosion of creative energy, discovered and/or identified four major shipwrecks. Are you still in pursuit of the missing, and if so, can you and Richie clue us in to the type of thing you might be looking for?

Chatterton: At that time, I was like the guy who was having trouble with his girlfriend and starts dating a whole bunch of other women. I was looking for distractions from diving the *U-869*. I think that whole experience has taught me how small the planet is, and there are projects that I have been involved with that weren't successful. One was looking for the wreck of the *Struma* in the Black Sea. But also, I kind of think that maybe the time wasn't right for it when I went there in 2000. I certainly haven't forgotten about that but I don't have the feeling for any shipwreck like I had with *U-869*.

Kohler: Once we identified the *U-869*, I was contacted by friends who had moved back to England and was invited to form an American contingent and dive on U-boat wrecks in the English Channel in an effort to try to identify them. Since that time, I've also applied my energies to finding some of the other boats that John and I thought the *U-869* could have been, namely the *U-857* and the *U-879*. They're out there somewhere; they say one might be in the Gulf of Maine. I've also invested some energy into trying to put together a trip to find the *U-215*, which would be quite a challenging technical dive. I've done some other work here close to home. Back in 2000, a dive-boat captain located the forward half of an American destroyer, and through some creative work, and with the help of a friend, Christina Young, I actually was able to nail the identification of that wreck as the USS *Murphy*. I'm quite proud of that effort. Other than that, I just keep on diving. I dive with my family. I dive with my wife. My son is going to start diving soon. And I'm looking to do a little of my own work and share my passion with my family.

Kurson: Did your experience on the U-boat change the way you dive now in any way?

Kohler: I'd say absolutely. The way that the Atlantic Wreck Divers took this Florida spearfishing kid and shook him around! The Atlantic Wreck Divers said, "You'll do this and you'll do this because of this reason." John, on the other hand, leads by example. He doesn't try to encourage anybody. Just like the rebreather. But if you rub shoulders with people and you see that they're doing something and it's working better, well, you'd be a fool not to change. During the course of our work on the U-boat I changed almost everything about the way I dive, short of the dry suit and the mask and fins. But basically, everything—from the way my tanks were strapped to my body, the regulators that I breathed out of, what I was breathing, the size of tanks that I was carrying—changed. At the time I was diving double aluminum 80s, which gave me a bottom-gas capacity of about 160 cubic feet of gas. When I changed to these larger-capacity gas tanks, it gave me 240 cubic feet of gas to have on the bottom. That's a major difference and a big safety factor. I would have to say that not only did I change equipment, but I changed breathing medium and I changed technique.

Chatterton: I think everything changes. The equipment changes, but that's like a snapshot. The thing that evolves is your philosophy, your approach. I think the U-boat was about being open to new ideas and new techniques, and understanding that time marches on. Understanding the concept of progress is what will

388 • A READER'S GUIDE

make you successful and productive in the water. My experience on the U-boat really reinforced my philosophy of being open to new ideas.

Kohler: I've got a personal motto that I'd like to share with you. During the course of our research I got to meet many German U-boat commanders in their homes, and one of them was an ace. His name is Erich Topp, and he was one of the most highly decorated U-boat commanders of the war. In getting to know him, I did some research on him and I had a translation of a comment that he made, a quote actually, from 1943 when he was in his heyday, when he was one of the most lauded U-boat commanders in Germany: "Life is a matter of luck and the odds in favor of success are in no way enhanced by extreme caution." That stayed with me throughout this entire time, and I still think that's a great way to live your life.

QUESTIONS FOR DISCUSSION

1. Is there something you would risk everything—your family, your sanity, your life—to discover?

2. Was it proper for Chatterton and Kohler to risk their lives, and the lives of others, by insisting that all divers allow the remains of the fallen U-boat sailors to remain undisturbed?

3. Chatterton and Kohler lost their marriages in their quest to identify the *U-Who*. Was it worth it?

4. Why weren't Chatterton and Kohler bothered more by the German sailors' mission—namely, to sink Allied ships and kill American sailors?

5. Do you think the *U-Who*'s crewmen would have appreciated the efforts of Chatterton and Kohler to identify their submarine and explain their story?

6. The German government told Chatterton that all requests by scuba divers to explore sunken German war graves had been denied. Chatterton politely explained his intentions, then dove the wreck of the *U-Who* anyway. Was this morally acceptable?

7. Gisela Engelmann dearly loved her fiancé, U-869 torpedoman Franz Nedel, despite Nedel's fervent commitment to Hitler and Nazi ideals—and despite the fact that the Nazis had imprisoned both Nedel's father and Engelmann's father. Could you love someone whose political beliefs were abhorrent to you?

8. Despite claustrophobic conditions, many Germans preferred submarine service to army ground service, where they might find themselves dug into trenches and dodging enemy bullets. Which would you opt for?

9. Given the grave danger of Chatterton's final plan to dive the wreck of the U-Who, should Kohler have stuck to his first instinct and refused to accompany Chatterton?

10. Chatterton did not attend the funeral of his dear friend, Bill Nagle. He never completely explains the decision. Why do you think he didn't attend Nagle's funeral?

11. Divers continue to debate the ethics of removing artifacts from shipwrecks. When is it proper to take artifacts from wrecks? Are there circumstances under which artifacts should never be disturbed? Does your answer change if there are human remains onboard?

12. Chatterton seemed emotionally ready for the Rouses to identify the U-Who. But he seemed incapable of accepting the possibility of a "greenhorn" diver doing the same. Why?

13. Kohler gave up diving for two years in an effort to keep his family together. Can a person ever surrender his true passion and hope to live a happy and fulfilled life?

14. Did the discovery of the U-Who hasten Bill Nagle's demise?

15. Given the intentions of the crewmen aboard U-869—to attack and kill Allied ships—do you think the book treated them too kindly?

Read on for a preview of Robert Kurson's new book, *Rocket Men: The Daring Odyssey of Apollo 8 and the Astronauts Who Made Man's First Journey to the Moon.*

PROLOGUE: COUNTDOWN

●

December 21, 1968—Four days before Christmas

THREE ASTRONAUTS ARE STRAPPED INTO A SMALL SPACE-craft thirty-six stories in the air, awaiting the final moments of count-down. They sit atop the most powerful machine ever built.

The Saturn V rocket is a jewel of the National Aeronautics and Space Administration, a vehicle that will generate the energy of a small atomic bomb. But it has never flown with men aboard, and it has had just two tests, the most recent of which failed catastrophically just eight months earlier. The three astronauts are going not merely into Earth orbit, or even beyond the world altitude record of 853 miles. They intend to go a quarter of a million miles away, to a place no man has ever gone. They intend to go to the Moon.

Beneath them, the United States is fracturing. The year 1968 has seen killing, war, protest, and political unrest unlike any in the coun-try's history, from the assassinations of Martin Luther King, Jr., and Robert Kennedy to the unraveling of Vietnam to the riots in Chicago. Already, *Time* magazine has named the dissenter its Man of the Year.

As the countdown begins, there are engineers and scientists at NASA who question whether the crew will ever return. Even the as-tronauts are realistic about their chances of surviving the flight, an operation riskier than anything the American space agency has ever attempted. One of them has recorded a final goodbye to his wife, to be played in the event he doesn't return.

In August, this mission did not exist. Nearly everything that has gone into its planning—the training, analysis, calculations, even the politics—has been rushed to the launchpad in a fraction of the time ordinarily required. If anything goes wrong, public opinion—and the will of the United States government—might turn against NASA. The fate of the entire space program hangs on the crew's safe return.

As the moment of launch draws near, one of the astronauts spots a mud dauber wasp building a nest on the outside of one of the spacecraft's tiny windows. Back and forth the insect moves, grabbing mud and adding to its new home. The astronaut thinks, "You are in for a surprise."

Vapors begin to spew from around the base of the giant rocket. Less than a minute remains before lift-off. When the five first-stage engines ignite, they will deliver a combined 160 million horsepower. In the final few seconds, a typhoon of flames unfurls to either side. Beneath the astronauts, it is not just the launchpad that begins to shake, but the entire world.

CHAPTER ONE

●

DO YOU WANT TO GO TO THE MOON?

August 3, 1968—Four months earlier

AS HE SAT ON A BEACH IN THE CARIBBEAN, A QUIET ENGI-
neer named George Low ran his fingers through the sand and wondered whether he should risk everything to win the Space Race and
help save the world.

At forty-one, Low was already a top manager and one of the most
important people at NASA, in charge of making sure the Apollo spacecraft was flightworthy.

Apollo had a single goal, perhaps the greatest and most audacious
ever conceived: to land a man on the Moon and return him safely to
Earth. In 1961, President John F. Kennedy had committed the United
States to achieving this goal by the end of the decade. Never had a
more inspiring promise been made to the American people—or one
that could be so easily verified.

Now, Kennedy's end-of-decade deadline was in jeopardy. Design
and engineering problems with the lunar module—the spidery landing
craft that would move astronauts from their orbiting ship to the lunar
surface and back again—threatened to stall the Apollo program and
put Kennedy's deadline, just sixteen months away, out of reach. And
that led to another problem. Every day that Apollo languished, the

Soviet Union moved closer to landing its own crew on the Moon. And that mattered. The nation that landed the first men on the Moon would score the ultimate victory in the years-long Space Race between the two superpowers, one from which the second-place finisher might never recover.

For months, NASA's best minds had worked around the clock to fix the issues with the lunar module, but the temperamental and complex landing craft only fell further and further behind schedule. By summer, many at the space agency had abandoned hope of making a manned lunar landing by the end of the decade.

And then Low had an idea.

It had come to him just a few weeks before he'd arrived at this beach, and it was wild, an epiphany, a dream. It was also dangerous, risky beyond anything NASA had ever attempted. But the more Low thought about it, the more he believed it could keep the Apollo program moving and save Kennedy's deadline—and maybe even beat the Soviets to the Moon.

Low inhaled the fresh, salty air and tried to push space travel out of his thoughts. At home, his mind burned nonstop with ideas, formulae, trajectories. Now he needed a break, and it should have been easy to find one in this tropical paradise. About the only reminder of America was the local newspaper, which told of the Newport Pop Festival in Costa Mesa, California, where more than a hundred thousand music fans were expected, and brought word of potential protests at the coming Democratic National Convention in Chicago. It had been an explosive year already, with assassinations, riots, and violence. A quiet beach was just where a man like Low needed to be.

But Low could not relax. He walked the beach, looking out over the ocean toward Moscow and the Moon, thinking, imagining, America and the world on fire behind him.

Five days after Low returned from vacation, a serious man with an oversized head went to work inside a giant assembly plant in Downey, California. His mission: to build a machine from the future that would help make the world safe for democracy.

Over and over, astronaut Frank Borman opened and closed the hatch on the Apollo command module, a cone-shaped capsule made to fly a three-man crew to the Moon. He'd already certified that the hatch worked, then certified it again, but he would not stop pushing on it, making sure it opened, no matter what.

Nearby, Borman's two crewmates, Jim Lovell and rookie Bill Anders, got ready to test the hundreds of dials, switches, levers, lights, and gauges that made the command module work. The spacecraft was small, measuring just eleven feet tall and thirteen feet wide at its base, but every inch of it had been designed by Borman and others to be impervious to a galaxy of deadly forces.

A nearby transistor radio played Top 40 music, which caught Borman's ear.

"That's a pretty slick song," Borman said. "Who's the fella singing it?"

"That's the Beatles, Frank," Lovell said, laughing.

Borman preferred the standards. As a kid, he'd memorized the lyrics to all the great Western songs played on the radio in Arizona. He could still sing "Cowboy Jack"—a ditty that dated to the nineteenth century—but didn't dare start, because he knew Lovell and Anders would insist that he sing it to the end.

Borman stuck to classic films, too. Alone among astronauts, it seemed, he hadn't bothered to see *2001: A Space Odyssey*, the new Stanley Kubrick film released in April that showed men flying to the Moon. That stuff was science fiction, Borman told his colleagues; America had real people to get to the Moon.

Borman and his crewmates knew that the lunar module was troubled and behind schedule. But until designers and engineers could make the fixes, these astronauts could do little more than make certain that the command module was perfect. So they climbed inside their spacecraft and began testing it, pushing the command module mercilessly, because that's what outer space would do to it, too.

And then the phone rang.

Smart people knew better than to bother Borman at work. But the man on the line went back a long way with Borman. And he said it was urgent.

Donald Kent "Deke" Slayton was in charge of managing astronaut training and choosing crews for manned space missions. If an astronaut flew on board a NASA spacecraft, it was because Slayton had chosen him to go.

When Borman heard who was calling, he wriggled out of the capsule and grabbed an extension.

"Deke, I'm in the middle of a big test here," he said.

"Frank, I need you back in Houston."

"Talk to me now."

"No, I can't talk over the phone. It's gotta be in person. Grab an airplane and get to Houston. On the double."

Borman grimaced—America did not have time for nonsense and delays—but Slayton was in charge, and NASA, no matter its official designation as a civilian organization, was a military operation to Borman, so he took his orders. Poking his head back inside the spacecraft, he told his partners, "You guys are stuck with the module. I've gotta go back to Houston."

Borman grabbed his rental car, drove to Los Angeles International Airport, and hopped into a T-38 Talon, a two-seat twin-engine supersonic jet used by astronauts for training, commuting, and even some fun, and pointed it toward Texas. At forty, he still looked every bit the West Point cadet: sandy blond near-crewcut, square jaw and chin set for combat, arched eyebrows that seemed a radar for anything askew. Even his head was military issue, all right angles and slightly larger than life, a feature that had earned him the childhood nickname Squarehead.

Borman couldn't imagine why he was needed in Houston, and so suddenly. He was commander of Apollo 9, the third of four manned test flights NASA planned before it would attempt to land on the Moon. Apollo 9 was to be a basic mission—orbit Earth, test the spacecraft, come home. It wasn't scheduled to launch for another six months. Still, Borman knew he hadn't been summoned for nothing. The last time he'd received a "drop everything" call had been the darkest day in NASA's history.

It had happened about a year and half earlier, on January 27, 1967, when a fire broke out in the spacecraft during a simulated countdown on the launchpad in Florida. The Apollo 1 rehearsal should have been safe and routine for the three astronauts inside, who were preparing for the actual flight about four weeks later. But a spark occurred in the electrical system and the men were trapped as the sudden fire spread in pure oxygen. Even Ed White, the strongest of all NASA's astronauts, couldn't muscle open the command module's hatch as flames spread through the space-craft.

Borman had been enjoying a rare break with his family at a lake-side cottage near Houston, where they lived, when Slayton's call came in that day.

"Frank, we've had a bad fire on Pad Thirty-four and we've got three astronauts dead—Gus Grissom, Ed White, and one of the new boys, Roger Chaffee. Get to the Cape as quick as you can; you've been appointed to the investigative committee."

The news stunned Borman, who considered Ed White the brother he'd never had. And it devastated Borman's wife, Susan, who counted Pat White among her best friends. Borman told Slay-ton he'd fly to Florida right away but first needed to stop at the Whites' home in Houston.

When he and Susan arrived, Pat was hysterical. She was the mother of two children, ages ten and thirteen, who suddenly had no father. Even in her raw grief, just hours after receiving the news, a Washington bureaucrat had informed her that despite Ed's wishes to be buried at West Point, the three fallen astronauts would all be laid to rest at Arlington National Cemetery.

"Give me the guy's name," Borman said.

He had the man on the phone a minute later.

"It's already been decided in Washington," the man insisted.

"I don't give a good goddamn what's been decided," Borman said. "Ed wanted to be buried at West Point and that's what's going to happen, and I'll go all the way to President Johnson to make sure it happens, so you better fucking well do it."

Four days later, White was buried at West Point. Borman and Lovell were among the pallbearers. Anders also attended.

After the funeral, Borman began his work on the investigative committee convened by NASA. He was the only astronaut on the panel, a sign that NASA considered him to be among its best. His first job was to help supervise the disassembly of the Apollo 1 spacecraft at Cape Kennedy in order to determine the cause of the fire. Days later, he became the first astronaut to enter the cabin. He found a burned-out nightmare. Rows of equipment and panels had been charred and covered in soot, debris was scattered everywhere. Hoses connecting the astronauts to their life support systems were melted. No matter where he looked, Borman could see no color, only grays and blacks.

That night, he joined Slayton and others at a restaurant in Cocoa Beach called The Mousetrap, a NASA haunt. Borman seldom drank to excess, but the smell of the scorched spacecraft needed bleaching, and he started in early. He raised toasts to his fallen brothers, then threw his glass into the fireplace. White was among the straightest arrows Borman had ever known—honest to a fault, a true patriot, and a man who didn't mess around with the sports cars or fast women so readily available to astronauts. For both men, family came first. The Bormans and Whites often shared a house on a lake near Houston for fishing trips. Borman couldn't remember missing someone as much as he missed Ed White that night.

Borman spent the next two months inside the burned spacecraft, studying the design, searching for flaws, making fixes in his mind. In April 1967, Congress held hearings into the cause of the fire, and Borman was called to testify.

Much of the questioning was aggressive and antagonistic, full of second-guesses and should-haves and pointed fingers, but Borman held firm, hiding nothing and acknowledging NASA's responsibility, but never allowing congressmen to kick the agency just because it was down. He still ached for the loss of his friend, Ed White, but never allowed those emotions to spill into his report. Near the end of the hearings, he offered some of its most memorable testimony.

"We are trying to tell you that we are confident in our management, and in our engineering, and in ourselves," Borman said. "I think the question is really: Are you confident in us?" A few days later, he told lawmakers, "Let's stop the witch hunt and get on with it." At NASA, it seemed there wasn't a person, from the administrator to the janitors, who didn't cheer him on. In the end, Congress took his advice and NASA continued on its mission to land men on the Moon.

Having survived the inquest, NASA approached Borman with an extraordinary offer: Take temporary leave from the astronaut program to head up the team tasked with implementing design changes to the command module. He accepted on the spot. He and others worked to make the new version of the capsule the most advanced, and safest, spacecraft ever built.

Borman could only hope there hadn't been another tragedy as he landed his jet at Ellington Air Force Base and made his way to Slayton's office. He suspected something unusual was afoot when he was asked to close the door behind him. Slayton addressed him without even sitting down:

"We just got word from the CIA that the Russians are planning a lunar fly-by before the end of the year. We want to change Apollo 8 from an Earth orbital to a lunar orbital flight. A lot has to come together. And Apollo 7 has to be perfect. But if it happens, Frank, do you want to go to the Moon?"

The idea startled Borman. Apollo 8 was meant to fly in December, just four months from now, but certainly not to the Moon. Apollo 8 was a conservative mission designed for low Earth orbit, perhaps at 125 miles altitude. It was one of several essential steps leading up to a manned lunar landing, hopefully before the end of 1969. Everything went in steps at NASA. Everything.

But Slayton meant exactly what he said. He wanted Borman to change missions and fly to the Moon. At a distance of 240,000 miles. In just sixteen weeks. Slayton didn't discuss the fact that the lunar module couldn't possibly be ready by then. He didn't discuss any of the other myriad reasons NASA couldn't be ready to fly men to the Moon by year's end. In fact, Slayton gave very few additional details. He didn't even ask if Borman cared to talk things over with his wife or crew.

Borman would have been justified in taking days, if not weeks, to consider such a proposition. And yet Slayton needed an answer, and he needed it now. Borman understood the urgency. If the Soviet Union sent men to the Moon first—even if those men didn't land—it would score a major victory in the Space Race and deal a devastating blow in the Cold War between the United States and Soviet Union. The mission Slayton was proposing would be exquisitely dangerous. But it also had the power to change history. Now, suddenly, it all depended on the decision of Frank Borman and his crew.

PHOTO: © MATT FERGUSON

ROBERT KURSON earned a bachelor's degree in philosophy from the University of Wisconsin and a law degree from Harvard Law School. His award-winning stories have appeared in *Rolling Stone*, *The New York Times Magazine*, and *Esquire*, where he was a contributing editor. He is the author of three *New York Times* bestsellers: *Shadow Divers*, the 2005 American Booksellers Association's nonfiction Book Sense Book of the Year; *Crashing Through*, based on Kurson's 2006 National Magazine Award–winning profile of the blind speed skier, CIA agent, inventor, and entrepreneur Mike May in *Esquire*; and *Pirate Hunters*. His latest book, *Rocket Men*, tells the story of the historic Apollo 8 mission to the Moon. He lives in Chicago.

RobertKurson.com
Twitter: @robertkurson